Streamline ENGLISH

BERNARD HARTLEY & PETER VINEY

DESTINATIONS

An intensive English course for
intermediate students

Oxford University Press

Oxford University Press
Walton Street, Oxford OX2 6DP

Oxford
Delhi Bombay Calcutta Madras Karachi
Petaling Jaya Singapore Hong Kong Tokyo
New York Toronto Melbourne Auckland
Nairobi Dar es Salaam Cape Town

and associated companies in
Beirut Berlin Ibadan Nicosia

OXFORD is a trade mark of Oxford University Press

ISBN 0 19 432241 6 (student's edition)
ISBN 0 19 432242 4 (teacher's edition)
ISBN 0 19 432243 2 (set of 3 cassettes)
© Bernard Hartley and Peter Viney 1982
First published 1982
Seventh impression 1987

Illustrations by:
David Brown   Bill Prosser
Ken Cox   Susanna Ray
Peter Dennis   Paul Sample
Richard Draper   David Scutt
Ron Jobson   Mike Saunders
Stephen Johnson   Turnround Studio
Paddy Mounter   Mike Vaughan
Ellis Nadler

Photographs by:
Photographs and All That, Terry Williams

Recording produced by:
Terry O'Neill

*The publishers would like to thank the
following for their time and assistance:*
British Rail, Budgen Supermarkets, Elliott
Brown Agency, Holland and Barrett Health Foods,
The Knowledge of London Driving School,
Oxford United Football Club.

*The publishers would like to thank the
following for permission to reproduce
photographs and maps:*
BBC Hulton Picture Library, Camera Press,
Colorific, Elizabeth Photo Library, Fiat,
Gordon Fraser Gallery, Richard and Sally Greenhill,
Hallmark Cards Inc., John Hillelson Agency Ltd.,
Alan Hutchinson Library Ltd., The Image Bank,
P and PF James, Jean Photographs, Keystone
Press Agency Ltd., The Kobal Collection,
London Art Technical Drawings Ltd., London
Transport (Underground Map Registered User No. 83/010),
N.A.S.A., Network, Press Association, Rex Features,
Chris Schwarz, Space Frontiers Ltd., Sunday Times,
Syndication International, Talking Pictures,
John Topham Picture Library,
Trustees of the British Museum,
Western Americana Picture Library,
Elizabeth Whiting and Associates.

Composition in Sabon by
Filmtype Services Limited, Scarborough
Printed in Hong Kong

CONTENTS

Streamline English Destinations consists of

1 a student's book, divided into 80 units,
2 a teacher's book, containing all the pages from the student's book interleaved with a full teaching manual for each unit,
3 tape-recordings on three cassettes which contain the dialogues, the listening passages and, where appropriate, the texts from the student's book,
4 workbooks. Workbook A covers units 1–40 in the student's book, Workbook B covers units 41–80.

Streamline English Destinations is an integrated, intensive course in English for adult and young adult students at an intermediate level. It is designed for use with students who have already completed *Streamline English Departures/Connections* or other elementary/pre-intermediate courses.

Streamline English Destinations aims to revise, consolidate and extend the student's linguistic and communicative competence. Previously learned language is re-cycled and new and more advanced language is introduced.

Streamline · English Destinations adopts a practical approach to language teaching and learning, and aims to lead the student towards competence in English by

1 presenting the target language in interesting contexts,
2 providing manipulative practice of the language,
3 extending the language into real communicative functions insofar as the classroom will allow,
4 encouraging creative application of the newly acquired language.

Selection and grading

At the intermediate level, the students have a number of conflicting needs. They often realize that much of what has been learned has been imperfectly learned and that there is a constant need for revision and further practice. At the same time the students want to feel that they are making progress by acquiring new elements of the language. We have tried to balance these two needs by ensuring that there is a blend of old and new in each unit. Previously learned language is re-cycled in new settings which demand more extensive vocabulary and deeper insight into language function. New language items are always introduced in the context of previously learned language. The new elements of the language have been selected and graded in terms of

1 complexity,
2 frequency,
3 general usefulness,
4 immediate usefulness.

Assumed knowledge of the language

At the intermediate level it is difficult to state in a concrete way what knowledge of the language is assumed. Clearly students who have completed *Streamline English Departures* and *Streamline English Connections* will be in a position to start work on *Destinations*. The book will also be suitable for a range of students with different experiences of English language learning. Broadly speaking, they will have met all or most of the language items listed in the Council of Europe's 'Threshold Level' documents, (*The Threshold Level for Modern Language Learning in Schools*, J.A. van Ek, Longman 1977), although some of these may have been learnt imperfectly.

In structural terms they should be familiar with at least those items which appear in Parts I and II of *English Grammatical Structure*, L.G. Alexander, W.˙Stannard Allen, R.A. Close, R.J. O'Neill, Longman 1975. Students who have completed *Connections* will also be familiar with much of Part III. The indices to *Departures* and *Connections* will show what has been covered in the earlier parts of the *Streamline* course. The re-cycling, clear presentation and revision in *Destinations* of major structural areas, such as conditionals types 1 and 2, passives and reported speech, which have appeared in *Connections*, mean that students who have not previously met these areas should be able to cope with *Destinations*.

PACING AND INTEGRATION

THE FOUR SKILLS

Streamline English Destinations is an intensive course and, as a general rule, each unit should be considered as a lesson. Obviously different groups of students have different learning rates and each unit can be adapted to suit their varying needs. With a very fast class, an imaginative teacher could easily expand the transfer stage of the lesson. Some of the role-plays suggested could be extended into whole lessons. In some situations, the teacher may wish to proceed more slowly and the workbooks could be used in the classroom to provide additional consolidation.

There are, however, great advantages in completing one unit per lesson. Each unit has been carefully phased to provide variety of stimuli and activities. Unlike many courses, we have not planned the lessons according to a single formula. No matter how good a single formula is, the constant employment of it is often counter-productive in terms of student interest.

In *Streamline English Destinations* there is a great variety of lesson types and the structure of the course ensures that successive lessons are of a different nature.

Streamline English Destinations is a fully integrated course, providing all the material necessary for an intermediate course.

Streamline English adopts as its first principle the maxim that people learn to do something by doing it.

People learn to listen by listening.
People learn to speak by speaking.
People learn to read by reading.
People learn to write by writing.

Listening

In *Streamline English Destinations* the listening activities for the student include:

1 Listening to the teacher. The teacher from the outset will provide the most important model on which the student will base his/her own language behaviour.

The teacher should speak English at a speed consistent with normal stress, rhythm and intonation patterns. 'Teacher-speak' should be avoided, however great the temptations. It may help the students to understand the teacher, but not to understand authentic English.

2 Listening to recorded voices. The obvious advantage of exposing the student to a variety of voices is that in any authentic situation the student will have to cope with such variety. The talented teacher can often role-play a variety of voices, but it is always second-best.

3 Listening to fellow students. There are certainly risks in such activities as pair-work and role-playing in that the students may be exposed to imperfect language models. We feel that the advantages far outweigh the disadvantages.

4 Listening to himself/herself. This activity is a much underrated one. The student should be constantly encouraged to compare his/her own speech with that of accurate models. This can be done by constant monitoring by the teacher in the classroom and in the laboratory, or by the student himself/herself in the laboratory.

5 Listening to more extensive passages of recorded material where the student is expected to listen either for specific information or for general gist. These listening passages are not printed in the main body of the student's book, but appear in full in the Appendix.

Speaking

In *Streamline English Destinations* the speaking activities for the student include:

1 Selective repetition of model utterances. These model utterances are first presented by the teacher or by voices on tape and the student is encouraged to approximate as closely as possible to the model.

2 Manipulative Drills. These drills are designed to give the student practice in the accurate formation of language patterns. Such practice is an essential step towards the ultimate goal of creative speaking. The student must be able to say what he wants when he wants to say it.

3 Controlled Practice. These activities are designed to enable the student to use the newly-acquired language in situations which minimize the possibility of error. Response Drills, Question and Answer work, Reproduction, Invention, Oral Completion Exercises, and Pair Work are all used to provide this kind of language activity.

4 Transfer. Whenever possible the student is encouraged to use the newly-acquired language in some way meaningful to him/her. The degree of real communication that takes place is of course limited by the nature of the classroom environment. However, by setting up simulated situations and discussions, we hope to give the student practice in generating the language necessary to cope with real communicative situations.

Reading

In *Streamline English Destinations* the reading activities for the student include:

1 Reading from the board. The teacher will often feel it useful and necessary to write up language models, vocabulary items, grammar summaries, etc.

2 Reading everything that appears in the student's book. This will include dialogues, texts, letters, forms, charts, signs, instructions, and exercises. *Streamline English Destinations* also includes units which are specifically designed to improve the student's ability to read for gist and to skim for specific information.

The student's book does not include linguistic descriptions either of the traditional grammatical kind (the present perfect progressive, the passive, etc.) or of the functional type (inquiring about intention, expressing gratitude, etc.). Such descriptions can be of value to the teacher and are confined to the teacher's book. They may be confusing to the students and we would not recommend exposing the students to them.

Reading silently (or aloud) does not help the student to speak, but nevertheless serves a useful purpose in the learning sequence even when the major aim is oral ability. Reading can help to reinforce and fix in the memory what has already been heard and practised orally.

Moreover, the student gets a sense of satisfaction and achievement from reading. Silent reading also serves the practical purpose of providing oases of calm in the general hurly-burly of an active language lesson. These give both the students and the teacher time to reflect and to gather their thoughts.

Writing

In *Streamline English Destinations* the writing activities for the student include:

1 Copying from the board. The student may be asked to copy language models, vocabulary items, grammar summaries, etc.

2 Exercises. These appear in the student's book and fulfil a number of purposes. They reinforce and consolidate what has been heard, said, and seen. They also give the teacher useful feedback. The exercises are so designed that they form a summary of the focal points of the lesson. They can be done orally at first and then written either in class, or for homework. In the case of fill-in exercises students should write out the complete sentences.

3 Compositions. Subjects for compositions are suggested in both teacher's and student's books.

4 Comprehension Questions. The questions which appear in the student's book should always be used orally but, at the discretion of the teacher, can be used to provide written reinforcement.

5 Dictation. Formal dictation phases are not suggested in the teacher's book. Individual teachers, however, may occasionally feel the need to include a short dictation phase.

USING STREAMLINE ENGLISH DESTINATIONS IN THE CLASSROOM

The teacher's book provides detailed lesson plans for each unit. The precise numbering system enables exact reference to be made to specific lesson phases. This will prove useful where the course is shared between two or more teachers. Throughout the notes speeches by the *teacher*, the class in *chorus* and individual *students* are introduced by the letters T, C and S respectively.

Because of space available, instructions to the teacher may often seem rather terse or abrupt. We say 'Do this!' rather than 'This is a possible method of exploitation which may be found useful'. Obviously, many teachers will wish to exploit the material in their own teaching styles, and will add to or subtract from our notes. Various standard instructions are given in the teacher's notes on each unit, and there follows an explanation of each of these.

1 Classroom set

The target language is always introduced in context. This context may take the form of an illustrated dialogue or text, a listening passage or a reading passage. Occasionally, however, the classroom situation itself seems to provide a more appropriate context in which to present a new structure for the first time, before going on to the material in the student's book.

2 Set the situation

Before presenting a dialogue, text or listening passage for the first time, it should be placed in some kind of setting, rather than just presented 'cold'. The teacher should establish the place, time and characters involved.

3 Masking the text

In many units it will be necessary to refer students to an illustration, chart or diagram while they are listening, doing repetition work, manipulative practice or question and answer. We have always given the instruction 'Ensure the text is masked' when we feel that the students should not be able to refer to the text while doing this.

4 Listening

A full text of the listening passages (Units 1, 13, 15, 44, 52, 65, 72, 75 and 78) appears in the Appendix to the student's book. In the index (p.10), ■ indicates a unit with a listening passage and □ indicates a unit where all or part of the printed material is recorded. When material has been placed in the Appendix there should be no need for students to refer to it any time during the lesson. They may wish to check through it after the lesson, but again this will not be essential.

The dialogues and texts which are printed in the student's book are often presented with the text masked and therefore also provide listening practice. The passages in the Appendix, however, require the students to perform some kind of listening task, by completing a chart or answering questions. Students should be shown how to perform the task before the cassette is played. As a general rule it would seem best to listen to the passage once before attempting to perform the task, but this will depend on the level and ability of the class.

If cassettes are not available, the teacher can use the Appendix to read, or act out, the listening passages.

5 Pre-questions

Apart from the listening exercises which appear in the student's book, pre-questions are sometimes suggested in the teacher's notes before listening to some recordings and before reading passages. These questions should be written on the board.

Where an overhead projector is available, transparencies may be prepared with the pre-questions on. This will save time during the lesson.

6 Playing the cassette

Great care has been taken in preparing the recordings of *Streamline English Destinations* so that students will be able to familiarize themselves with speakers of various ages and nationalities, using a range of regional accents. Background noise and background music have been used to give authenticity and to create atmosphere, and we would recommend using the recordings with the course. Sometimes this will not be possible because the necessary equipment is lacking or broken. The teacher will still be able to use the material, and by changing voice, tone, stance and position, will be able to bring it to life. However, while the teacher acting out the material may prove more entertaining to the class than the use of the cassette, it can also distract from the listening task.

7 Repetition

The repetition phase is an important part of the learning process. When new items of vocabulary or structure appear, it is just as valid at the intermediate level as at the lower levels. Great care must be taken, however, to avoid student boredom. Students should not be asked to repeat things which they are already capable of handling fluently.

Sometimes 'Listen and repeat' is given as an instruction, and this would mean repeating all or most of the utterances on the recording. More often 'Selective repetition' is suggested. The teacher should, in these cases, concentrate on new items of structure and vocabulary and important points of phonology. Careful attention should be paid to accurate stress, rhythm and intonation. The recordings provide speakers using a variety of accents in a variety of roles and settings.

Repetition will be more challenging if the recording is used as an initial model. The class should repeat a phrase in chorus first, then individuals should be selected at random for further repetition. Choral repetition gives all the students oral practice. Individual repetition enables the teacher to check for accuracy. If no problems occur with repetition of the recording, the teacher should move on. Where problems become apparent, the teacher may provide a model and can add gesture and expression to the spoken word. Longer utterances can be broken into more manageable pieces by 'chaining', either from the beginning of the utterance ('front chaining') or from the end ('back chaining'), depending on where the problems lie in the sentence. Back chaining is usually preferable as it more easily retains the intonation pattern of the target sentence.

7.1 Back chaining
Target sentence:
Could you tell me the way to the nearest bank?
Repetition stages:
the nearest bank?/the way to the nearest bank?/tell me the way to the nearest bank?/Could you tell me the way to the nearest bank?

7.2 Front chaining
Target sentence:
I'd've been very surprised.
Repetition stages:
I/I'd/I'd've/I'd've been/I'd've been very surprised.

8 Oral drills

Oral drills help the student to internalize the forms of the language so that he/she can produce the required utterance fluently when he/she needs to. Constant practice leads to fluent production.

There is a great variety of drills in *Streamline English Destinations* and each is set out in a clear fashion for ease of classroom reference by the teacher. The teacher can use all or some of the drills at his/her discretion. We would also hope that the teacher would improvise drills, when they were needed.

8.1 The model sentence. The model sentence for the drill is always contextualized and wherever possible an element of contextualization is sustained throughout the drill.

8.2 The prompts. The prompts are always familiar to the student. Only previously learned lexical items are used.

8.3 The set. Drills should be carefully set up by the teacher so that students know exactly what they have to do. The teacher should give two or three examples to show how the drill works.

8.4 At speed. The drills themselves should be done at speed for the students to reap maximum benefit. It also introduces an element of challenge to the activity.

8.5 In chorus. Choral drilling maximizes the amount of language practice and gives confidence to the learners.

8.6 Individually. This would normally follow the choral phase to enable the teacher to check accuracy. The teacher gives the prompt but does not indicate who is to respond until all the students have had time to think of the response. In this way, every student is encouraged to formulate mentally each response.

9 Silent reading

In this phase students read the text silently, at their own speed. Silent reading can:

9.1 Encourage students to deduce meaning.

9.2 Train students to read rapidly for general gist.

9.3 Train students to scan a text for specific information.

9.4 Reinforce material which has already been heard and practised.

9.5 Prepare the way for further practice, such as question work and reproduction.

Students should be encouraged to mark difficult words and to keep any queries until the end of the phase.

10 Check vocabulary

There are many techniques which can be used for vocabulary explanation, such as definition, the use of a monolingual dictionary, question and answer, deduction from context, synonyms and antonyms, translation or the use of visual aids. Wherever possible, students should be encouraged to use the new vocabulary items in sentences of their own.

11 Play the cassette again

This confirms and reinforces what the student has read. The students can follow the text in the book.

12 Questions

Questions are used to check comprehension, elicit information or simply to give language practice. The teacher should use as great a variety of questions as possible.

12.1 Short, closed questions.
Did you go to London?
to elicit: *Yes, I did/No, I didn't.*

12.2 Long, closed questions.
Did you to to London, or did you go to Paris?
to elicit: *I went to Paris.*

12.3 Open questions, where there is no guide to the expected response.
Where did you go?

12.4 Question generators, to set up student interactions.
Ask him/her/them/me/us/each other.

For example:
T: *Maria, have you ever been to London?*
S1: *No, I haven't.*
T: *Ask Pierre.*
S2: *Have you ever been to London?*
S3: *Yes, I have.*
T: *Ask 'When?'*
S4: *When did you go to London?*
S3: *Last year.*
T: *Ask 'How?'*
S5: *How did you go there?*
S3: *I went by plane.*
T: *Hans, have you ever been to London?*
S6: *No, I haven't.*
T: *Ask Gina ... 'Amsterdam'.*
S7: *Gina, have you ever been to Amsterdam?*

12.5 Indirect question. These are also question generators, except that the prompt is always full.
Ask him if he's been to London.
Ask him when he went there.

12.6 Tag questions.
You went to London, didn't you?
You didn't go by boat, did you?

13 Reproduction

At the intermediate level, reproduction is generally much freer than at the lower levels. However, if difficulty is encountered in free reproduction, the teacher can assist by giving prompts, asking questions or by making blatantly false statements about the passage which the students are invited to correct.

14 Pair work

In this activity students practise a dialogue, go through an exercise, work from a chart or ask and answer questions in pairs. The teacher should circulate, helping where necessary. It is advisable to get students to change partners at regular intervals.

15 Role-play

Role-plays are sometimes suggested at the end of lessons. In role-plays the students are asked to act characters and to speak as they think the character would speak in a given situation. It is important to set up the situation clearly and to define the roles which students are expected to play. Sometimes role-plays will parallel situations in the student's book fairly closely. On other occasions students will need to improvise a situation, working out the details of the conversation as the role-play develops. Subjects for role-play have been sketched out only briefly in the teacher's notes. Teachers may wish to develop them at some length. Teachers who are not happy with role-plays can easily miss out this section of the lesson.

There are several positive advantages in role-play. When students are acting a character, they are able to distance themselves from the subject matter and to take up positions and give opinions which they might feel embarrassed or hesitant to make if they were speaking for themselves. As a result subjects and situations can be practised in the classroom which would not otherwise naturally occur in the course of normal transfer. Conflict situations can be set up, and students who are too polite or nervous to enter into the full flow of a discussion can take part. Shy students will often perform better in role-play 'discussion' than when asked to express their own feelings. Student talking time is increased and students usually enjoy the activity.

The flow of a role-play, whether in groups or in pairs, should not be interrupted for correction. We would suggest that the teacher simply tries to remember repeated errors and corrects them quietly at the end of the session. Role-play sessions help to develop fluency and enable students to use the language actively. Students are forced to find ways of expressing themselves under the pressure of the situation, even if this means rather tortuous paraphrase and errors.

The key to successful role-play is careful preparation, a clear setting, clear roles and a clear starting point. Sometimes role-plays will fail to 'take off', but when they do 'take off' they should provide an enjoyable climax to the lesson.

Role-plays do not depend on acting ability. It will not always be necessary or useful to get groups to present their role-play to the rest of the class. The aim is not a polished performance, but the creation of an opportunity for students to test their ability in unpredictable situations.

16 Transfer

This phase aims to encourage the student to use the newly-acquired language in some way meaningful to him/her. The classroom situation obviously limits the amount of real communication possible. Transfer strategies are suggested throughout the course, but their application will vary according to the teaching situation, as, by definition, transfer must be related to particular students, their backgrounds and needs. Transfer might include question and answer related directly to the students, simulated situations and role-plays, language games, songs, projects, discussion and writing tasks.

17 Written phase

In this phase the teacher can write up or dictate key sentences and language summaries. The students copy. Actually writing down the information tends to fix it more firmly in the memory. It also provides a change of activity.

18 Exercises

Exploitation techniques are usually described in the teacher's notes. The exercises may be done by the teacher asking individuals, by the students in pairs, and in writing either in class or for homework. More creative writing tasks are suggested in both the teacher's book and the student's book.

19 Extension

Various optional extension activities are suggested, for example:

Unit 2 Students could be encouraged to keep a personal diary in English throughout the course.

Unit 33 Students are asked to write out the lyrics of an English language pop song of their choice.

Unit 48 Students cut out and assemble authentic English language newspaper articles to create a front page.

20 Visual aids

Extra visual aids are not essential. However, a collection of flashcards can be easily built up by sticking pictures from magazines on to plain cards. These could be grouped in sets to cover 'Describing people'/'Describing things'/'Famous places'/'Famous people'/'Occupations'/'Actions'/'Comparisons' etc. Sets can be related to specific units.

21 Workbooks

Workbook A covering units 1–40, and *Workbook B*, covering units 41–80 are optional elements of the course, which provide language summaries, vocabulary building exercises, reading comprehension passages and a variety of written exercises to provide reinforcement of the language which has appeared in the student's book. Many of these exercises are also suitable for paired practice and oral exploitation.

INDEX OF TEACHING POINTS IN UNITS 1-80

□ = *all or most of printed material is recorded.*
■ = *listening passage: text in Appendix.*

1 Arrivals □ ■	▷ Greetings ▷ Introductions ▷ Polite enquiries and responses ▷ Thanking and accepting thanks ▷ Apologies ▷ Listening for specific information	*How do you do? Hello, how are you?* *etc.* *I'd like you to meet ...* *How's work?* *Thanks. That's all right.* *Sorry.*
2 Is everything ready? □	▷ Future arrangements ▷ Future tenses: simple and progressive	*I'll do it.* *I'll be doing it.*
3 This is your life! □	▷ Personal identification ▷ Form filling	
4 The Monte Carlo Rally □	▷ Future perfect tense ▷ Revision of adjectives and adverbs ▷ Revision of comparison of adjectives ▷ Revision of present perfect tenses: simple and progressive ▷ Revision of future progressive tense	*I'll have done it.* *how old/fast?*
5 Out of work □	▷ Verb + -ing form (1)	*I enjoy doing it.* *I'm afraid of doing it.*
6 Getting a job	▷ Talking about yourself ▷ Interviews ▷ Formal letters ▷ Verb + -ing form (2) ▷ Revision of verb + infinitive ▷ Revision of imperatives	 *like doing* *need/want to do* *Do this, don't do that.*
7 Battle of Trafalgar Street □	▷ Verb + infinitive	*hope to do*, etc.
8 Sending a card	▷ Congratulating/expressing sympathy ▷ Informal letter endings ▷ Adjective + infinitive (1) ▷ *Enough/too* + infinitive	 *I'm delighted to do it.* *I was too ill to come.*
9 Marriage Guidance Council □	▷ Verb + object + infinitive ▷ Adjective + infinitive ▷ *Here/there* + infinitive ▷ *Seem* + infinitive	*Someone advised me to do it.* *He's too young to do it.* *I'm not here to listen.* *We seem to have rows all the time.*
10 A funny thing happend to me ... □	▷ Revision of *do* in contrast with *make*	*He went to London to do the shopping.* *I'd made some arrangements.*

10

11 **Polite requests** □	▷ Polite requests, including use of -ing and infinitive	*Would you mind doing . . .?* *Would you be kind enough to do . . .?*
12 **A trip to Spain** □	▷ Noun + infinitive ▷ Pronoun/adverb plus infinitive ▷ *remember/forget to do* ▷ *I hope so./I hope not.*	*The label to put on the suitcase.* *Nothing to worry about.* *Somewhere to stay.*
13 **Flying to Spain** □ ■	▷ Listening for specific information ▷ Verb + infinitive ▷ Revision of polite requests	*expect to do, recommend you to do* *Would you mind doing . . .?* *Would you like something to drink?*
14 **Money**	▷ Reading comprehension from a formal text ▷ Vocabulary expansion, deducing meaning ▷ *It is used for doing something.* ▷ Compound nouns with -ing ▷ Revision of active and passive	*filling station, cooking oil*
15 **Money, money, money** ■	▷ Listening for specific information ▷ Guided discussion ▷ Revision of questions using simple present, present perfect and simple past	
16 **Inside story** □	▷ Infinitive patterns with and without *to* ▷ -ing form structure	*force/allow somebody to do* *make/let somebody do* *He was seen driving a Land Rover.*
17 **Preferences** □	▷ Stating preferences	*I like it. I'd like to do it.* *Which do you like best?* *I'd rather do it,* etc.
18 **Where have all the fans gone?** □	▷ Advisability and desirability ▷ *to spend time doing something* ▷ *We've got a lot to learn.* ▷ *Winning has become the most important thing.*	*They ought to do it.* *We'd better do it.*
19 **Night flight** □	▷ Revision of infinitive and -ing form patterns	*try to do,* etc. *keep doing,* etc.
20 **The junk shop** □	▷ Speculating about the present (1)	*must be, could be, may be, might be, can't be*
21 **Noisy neighbours** □	▷ Speculating about the present (2)	*must be doing, may be doing, might be doing, can't be doing, probably/possibly doing*

22 You're in the army now □	▷ Obligations, duties, and preferences	*should (not) be doing, ought (not) to be doing, supposed (not) to be, would rather (not) be doing*
23 Migration □	▷ Reading comprehension from a formal text ▷ Listening for specific information ▷ *They navigate by using the sun.*	
24 Murder at Gurney Manor (1) □	▷ Revision of past tenses ▷ Revision of reported speech ▷ Revision of question tags	
25 Murder at Gurney Manor (2) □	▷ Speculating about the past (1)	*must have done, could (not) have done, may (not) have done, might (not) have done, can't have done*
26 Know your rights	▷ Complaining (1) ▷ Reading comprehension ▷ Revision	
27 Making a complaint □	▷ Complaining: letters of complaint	*should (not) have done, ought (not) to have done*
28 The 'Mary Celeste' (1) □	▷ Revision of nationalities ▷ Revision of past tenses ▷ Revision of past passives	*They were given money for doing it.*
29 The 'Mary Celeste' (2) □	▷ Speculating about the past (2)	*must have been doing, could (not) have been doing, may/might have been doing, can't have been doing, should (not) have been doing*
	▷ Revision of *must/can't/could have done*, etc. ▷ Infinitive of purpose ▷ Revision of pattern *after* + -ing form	*He jumped in to save the others.* *He killed himself after doing it.*
30 Speculation	▷ Revision of speculating about the past and present	
31 Apologies □	▷ Apologies and accepting apologies	*Sorry./Don't worry about it./I didn't mean to do it./etc.*
	▷ Revision of *must/should (not)/could do/have done/have been doing*	
32 They didn't stop to tell me. □	▷ Verb + -ing form compared with verb + infinitive ▷ Revision of verb + infinitive ▷ Revision of *might/could/must have done*	*stop/remember doing, stop/remember/forget to do try/manage/decide to do*

ARRIVALS

1

n HP computer

HEWLETT PACKARD

Business succeeds our way.
Cwmbran
Development Corporation Tel: (06333) 67777

1

← 2 to 9
← Area Manager
← Taxis
← Underground

Left luggage ↑
Lost Property ↑
Travel Centre ↘
Information ↘

Hall Drive
car rental

Left luggage ↘
Lost property ↘

Ladies
waiting room

Reservations

Teaching points

▶ Greetings

A: *How do you do?*
B: *How do you do?* (formal)

A: *Hello, how are you?*
B: *Very well, thanks, and you?*
A: *I'm fine, thanks.* (polite, friendly)

A: *Hi!*
B: *Hi!*
A: *How's things?/How are you getting on?*
(very familiar, casual)

Good morning/afternoon/evening. (neutral)

▶ Introductions

I'd like you to meet .../May I introduce .. ?/I'm ...

▶ Polite enquiries and responses
A: *How's work?/How's the family?*
B: *All right./O.K./Fine.*
Did you have a good trip/journey?

▶ Thanking and accepting thanks

A: *Thanks./Thank you./Thank you for coming to meet me.*
B: *That's all right./Not at all.*

▶ Apologies

Sorry./I'm terribly sorry./I'm afraid not.

Expressions

Excuse me!   *Shall I take one of your bags?*
There you are.   *I haven't seen you for ages!*
Here you are.
I beg your pardon?
A: *Do you fancy a coffee?* B: *Yes, I'd love one.*

Key vocabulary

ages (a long time ago)	cheap day return	return
	financial director	single
announcement	platform	– – – – –
bags	rail fares	someone else

Note: On the cassette there are the five dialogues with station announcements preceding each one. Until Exercise 3 is done in class, the announcements should be used only to create a station atmosphere, and neither explained nor exploited. In Exercise 3 the whole recording is played and the students have a specific listening task. The rest of the information in the announcements is redundant and should not be explained. A complete text of the five announcements appears in 1.15 for teachers who are not using the cassette.

1 Classroom set. Introduce yourself to the class, and get them to introduce themselves to you and each other. Focus attention on the picture. Ensure the text is masked. Exploit the picture with question and answer to set the situation.

Where is it?   *Who can you see?*
What time is it?   *What are they doing?* etc.
What can you see?

2 Dialogue 1 (A and B). Set the situation. Play the cassette.

3 Listen and repeat.

4 Silent reading.

5 Pair work.

6 Transfer. Pair work. Get students to circulate around the class introducing themselves in a similar way.

7 Exercise 1. Get students to go through this orally in pairs, and to complete it in writing, either in class or for homework.

8 Dialogue 2 (C and D). Follow the procedure 1.2–1.6, but include this drill.

9 Drill: Continue:
T: *ages*   *ages*
T: *I haven't seen you for ages.*   *Monday*
T: *Monday*   *a long time*
T: *I haven't seen you since Monday.*   *January*
T: *ages*   *months*
C: *I haven't seen you for ages.*   *last month*

10 Dialogue 3 (E and F). Follow the procedure 1.2–1.6.

11 Dialogue 4 (G and H). Follow the procedure 1.2–1.6.

12 Exercise 2. Get students to go through orally in pairs. Get one or two pairs to role-play in front of the class. Students could be asked to write out one or both of the conversations, either in class or for homework.

13 Dialogue 5 (I and J). Follow the procedure 1.2–1.6.

14 Get one or two pairs to role-play Dialogue 5 in front of the class. First take the part of 'I' yourself. Use the names of famous people, e.g. *Aren't you John McEnroe?/Mrs Thatcher?*

15 Exercise 3. (A map of England might be a useful visual aid.) Focus attention on the chart. Play (or read) the first announcement and show students how to complete it. Suggest using abbreviations i.e. 'Lon' or 'L' is quite sufficient to note 'London'. Make it clear that they do not need to understand every word of the announcement, but just the information which is asked for. Play the whole tape, including the dialogues, and get students to note the information silently. Play the cassette again if necessary. Check the answers. A complete text of the announcements follows:

Announcements:

1) *The train now standing at Platform 5 will be the 10.25 to Exeter St David's calling at Reading, Pewsey, Westbury and Taunton.*
2) *The train now standing at Platform 3 is the 10.20 Inter-City service to Bristol.*
3) *The train now arriving at Platform 2 is the 9.12 from Oxford.*
4) *The next train leaving from Platform 9 will be the 10.25 Inter-City service to Plymouth and Penzance. The train will be divided at Plymouth. Passengers for stations to Penzance should take the front six carriages.*
5) *The train now arriving at Platform 12 is the 7.10 from Swansea. Trains from Swansea are running approximately 15 minutes late due to maintenance work between Swansea and Cardiff.*

The completed chart should look like this:

Number	Train Time	Platform	From	To
1	10.25	5	Lon.	Exeter
2	10.20	3	Lon.	Bristol
3	9.12	2	Oxford	Lon.
4	10.25	9	Lon.	Penzance
5	7.10	12	Swansea	Lon.

16 Exercise 4. Get students to do it in pairs. Check a few responses round the class by giving prompts. Set it in class or for homework as a written exercise.

17 If there is time, refer back to the illustration and run through some of the vocabulary associated with railways and stations.

18 Extension. A collection of authentic train/bus timetables could be used to provide further practice. Students in pairs could role-play a railway enquiry office.

Unit 1

A Excuse me ... Mr Ward?
B Yes?
A I'm Charles Archer, from Continental Computers. How do you do?
B How do you do? Thank you for coming to meet us.
A Not at all. Did you have a good trip?
B Yes, thank you. Oh, I'd like you to meet Philip Mason. He's our sales manager.
A How do you do?

Exercise 1

A Mrs Bond?
B ....
A I'm Steven Robson, from Anglo Exports. How do you do?
B ....
A That's all right. Did you have a nice journey?
B ....
A Oh, may I introduce John Benson? He's our financial director.
B ....

C Sarah!
D Hi.
C Hi. I haven't seen you for ages. How's things?
D All right. And you?
C Fine. How's work?
D OK. Do you fancy a coffee?
C Oh, yes, I'd love one.

E Hello, Dorothy.
F Hello, Margaret. How are you?
E Very well, thanks, and you?
F Oh, I'm fine. How's the family?
E They're all fine. My car's just outside the station. Shall I take one of your bags?
F Oh, yes ... thank you.

G Good morning.
H Good morning.
G Single to Exeter, please.
H £14.70, please.
G There you are. Thank you ... er ... what time's the next train?
H 10.25.
G Thank you.

Exercise 2

Look at the conversation between G and H, and practise two similar conversations, one for Exeter St David's, and one for Penzance.

Rail Fares	Exeter St David's	Penzance
Single	£14.70	£25.80
Return	£23.40	£47.90
Cheap day return*	£17.40	£28.10

*You must return on the same day.

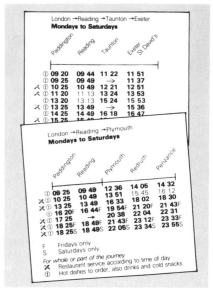

I Hello, there!
J I beg your pardon?
I Hello! How are you getting on?
J Fine, thank you ... sorry ... do I know you?
I Yes, it's me, Nick Fowler!
J Sorry, I don't think I know you.
I Aren't you Harry Shiner?
J Er, no ... I'm afraid not.
I Oh, I'm terribly sorry, I thought you were someone else!

Exercise 3

Listen to the announcements at London–Paddington. Look at the example and complete the chart in the same way.

Number	Train Time	Platform Number	From	To
1	10.25	5	Lon. (London)	Ex. (Exeter St David's)
2				
3				
4				
5				

Exercise 4

How are you?
Very well thanks, and you?
1 Hi!
2 Good afternoon.
3 I'm very sorry.
4 Thank you very much for helping me.
5 How do you do?
6 Aren't you Elton John?
7 How are you getting on?
8 Excuse me.
9 Here you are.
10 Goodbye!

Unit 1

IS EVERYTHING READY?

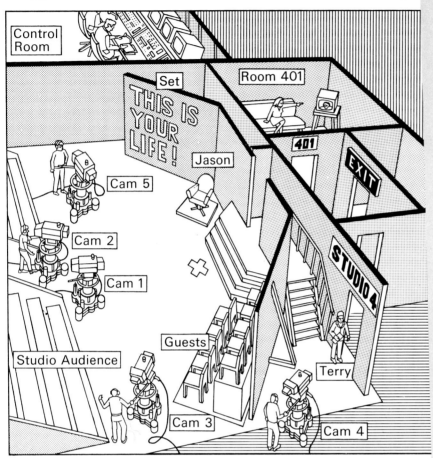

Control Room

Set

THIS IS YOUR LIFE!

Room 401

401

EXIT

Jason

STUDIO 4

Cam 5

Cam 2

Cam 1

Studio Audience

Guests

Terry

Cam 3

Cam 4

Northern T.V.

Programme	This is Your Life
Date	3rd Nov.
Studio	4
Subject	Jason Douglas
Compère	Terry Donovan
Director	Chris Price

Running order

Pre-show

7.00 Admit studio audience.

7.30 'Warm-up' (Comedian tells jokes to studio audience.)

7.55 Studio car arrives. (7 minute walk to studio.)

Show

8.00 Start videotape, titles & music.

8.01 Terry introduces show.

8.02 Jason arrives. Terry greets him.

Guests

8.03 Jason's sister from Australia.

8.05 His schoolteacher.

8.08 Maria Montrose, actress.

8.10 Father

8.13 Mother

8.15 Charles Orson, film director.

8.18 His first girlfriend.

8.20 Steve Newman, actor (his best friend).

8.22 Norma Phillips, film critic.

8.25-8.28 Show videotape extract from Jason's latest film.

8.29 His brothers and sisters.

8.30 Show ends. Start videotape, credits and music.

Post-show

8.30-8.45 Studio audience leaves.

8.45 Champagne party for Jason and guests.

'This is Your Life' is one of the most popular programmes on British and American television. Every week a famous person is invited to a television studio, without knowing that he or she will be the subject of the programme. The compère meets the person outside the studio and says 'This is your life!'. The person then meets friends and relatives from his or her past and present. Studio 4 is where the programme is recorded. The programme begins at eight o'clock. It's 6.45 now and the director is checking the preparations with his new production assistant. The subject of tonight's show will be an actor, Jason Douglas. The compère, as usual, will be Terry Donovan.

Director Let's just check the arrangements. We're bringing Jason Douglas here in a studio car – he thinks he's coming to a discussion programme! The driver has been told to arrive at exactly 7.55. Now, the programme begins at eight o'clock. At that time Jason will be walking to the studio. Terry Donovan will start his introduction at 8.01, and Jason will arrive at 8.02. Terry will meet him at the studio entrance ... Camera 4 will be there. Then he'll take him to that seat. It'll be on Camera 3. Jason will be sitting there during the whole programme. For most of the show Terry will be standing in the middle, and he'll be on Camera 2. The guests will come through that door, talk to Terry and Jason ... and then sit over there.

Director Now, is that all clear?
Production Assistant Yes ... there's just one thing.
Director Well, what is it?
PA Who's going to look after the guests during the show?
Director Pauline is.
PA And where will they be waiting during the show?
Director In Room 401, as usual. Pauline will be waiting with them, and she'll be watching the show on the monitor. She'll tell them two minutes before they enter.
PA I think that's everything.

Exercise 1
Each of the guests will say a few words about Jason.
A *Who'll be speaking at 8.06?*
B *His schoolteacher will.*
Ask and answer about: 8.04, 8.10, 8.16, 8.19, 8.23.

Exercise 2
A *What'll be happening at 7.45?*
B *A comedian will be telling jokes to the audience.*
Ask and answer about: 7.57, 8.35 and 9.00.

Exercise 3
The guests will be waiting in Room 401 from 7.50 until they enter.
A *How long will his sister be waiting?*
B *She'll be waiting for thirteen minutes.*
Ask and answer about the other guests.

Unit 2

Teaching points

▶ Future progressive in contrast with simple future

I'll be doing it.
I'll do it.

Expressions

Is that all clear?
There's just one thing . . .
Is everything ready?
I think that's everything.

Key vocabulary

arrangements	production assistant	greet
audience	relative	– – – – –
comedian	running order	whole
compère	set	– – – – –
credits	subject	as usual
entrance	titles	during
extract	warm-up	– – – – –
monitors	– – – – –	post- . . .
preparations	admit	pre- . . .

1 Set the situation. Ask students to read the introductory text silently.

2 Ask students to tell you what the programme is about.
Who's the compère?
Who's the subject?
What time does it begin?
What time is it now?
Have you ever seen a programme like this?
(Ask him/her/each other.)
What are some of the popular programmes in your country?
What are they about?
Ask each other.

3 Play the cassette of the introductory text.

4 Director's speech. Focus attention on the studio plan. Ensure the text is masked. Play the cassette twice.

5 Silent reading.

6 Question and answer:
Is Jason coming to the studio by bus? Ask 'How?'
Does he know the programme is 'This is Your Life'?
What does he think?
What's the driver been told?
What time does the programme begin?
Will Jason be in the studio then?
What will he be doing?
When will he arrive?
Who'll meet him?
Where will he meet him?
Where will he take him?
During the programme, will Jason be sitting in the audience?
Ask 'Where?'
Will Terry be standing outside the studio? Ask 'Where?'
What will the guests do?

7 Drill. (Pay attention to contracted *'ll*.) Continue:
T: *He*   *I*
T: *He'll be sitting there.*   *They*
T: *I*   *She*
T: *I'll be sitting there.*   *We*
T: *He*   *You*
C: *He'll be sitting there.*   *Jason*

8 Dialogue. Focus attention on the studio plan. Ensure the text is masked. Play the cassette.

9 Listen and repeat.

10 Silent reading.

11 Question and answer:
Where will the guests be waiting?
When will they be waiting there?
Who'll be waiting with them?
How will she be watching the show?
When will she tell them to enter?

12 Pair work.

13 'Running Order'. Focus attention on the running order. Silent reading.

14 Question and answer:
What's the date of the programme?
What's the date today?
When's your birthday?
Ask him/her/each other.
Who's the programme directed by?

15 Exercise 1. Set the situation. Students do the exercise in pairs. Check through the answers orally in class. Set for written homework.

16 Exercises 2 and 3. Follow the same procedure as in 2.15.

17 Written phase.

He'll	be doing it	at 7.30.
She won't		for 10 minutes.
		during the show.

Will you be doing it?	Yes, I will.
	No, I won't.

18 Transfer. Get students to note down some of their activities over the next week. Give examples on the board:
Thursday 7–8 p.m. Playing tennis.
Set up pair work along these lines:
A: *What are you doing on Thursday evening?*
B: *I'm playing tennis.*
A: *When'll you begin?*
B: *I'll begin at 7.*
A: *And when'll you finish?*
B: *I'll finish at 8.*
A: *Oh, so you'll be playing tennis at 7.30.*
After the pair work, ask one member of each pair to tell you what the other will be doing at fixed times later in the week.
e.g. *Maria will be playing tennis at 7.30 on Thursday.*

19 Extension. Students could be encouraged to keep a personal diary in English throughout the course. This could provide source material for further language practice in later lessons.

Teaching points

▶ Personal identification: name, date and place of birth, nationality, education, address, marital status and profession

Expressions

I don't believe it!
It's great to be here.
all the way from
even in those days

Key vocabulary

marital status	fall off	brilliant
movie (Am.E.)	initiate	furious
profession	move to	leading (actor)
stage name	scream	– – – – – –
voice	take part	specially
– – – – – –	– – – – – –	

1 Set the situation. (Refer back to Unit 2.) Ensure the text is masked. Play the first part of the dialogue.

2 Set pre-questions:
What's the compère's name?
What's the subject's name?
What was the subject's name?
When was he born?
Which city was he born in?
Play the first part again. Check the answers orally.

3 Silent reading.

4 Question and answer:
Who's waiting?
Who's he waiting for?
Who's Jason Douglas?
Why is he coming to the studio?
He's surprised, isn't he?
When was he born?
Ask 'Where?' Where's Balaclava Street?
How many brothers and sisters did he have?
What did his father do?

5 T: *Jason Douglas is one of the world's leading actors.* Use currently popular figures to elicit similar sentences e.g. *Maradona – He's one of the world's leading footballers.* Use a singer, an actress, a boxer, a writer, a conductor, a composer, a swimmer, a racing driver, etc.

6 Give sentences to elicit *I don't believe it!* e.g. *I'm a millionaire/a friend of Queen Elizabeth/one of the world's leading chess players/singers/composers.* or *England beat Brazil 6–0 at football.* or *A spaceship has just landed on Venus.* etc.

7 Part Two. Follow the procedure 3.1–3.3, but include these pre-questions:
Who is she?
Where's she from?
When did he start school?
When did he move to another school?

8 Question and answer:
What did Jason use to do?
How old was he then?
Why did she come to England?
Is she married?
How do you know?
When did they last see each other?
What did he do in 1952?
What did he do in 1958?
When did you start school?
Ask him/her/each other.

9 Part Three. Follow the procedure 3.1–3.3. Include these pre-questions:
What was the teacher's name?
When did he start drama school?
When did he go to Hollywood?

10 Question and answer:
Did Mr Hooper teach history?
Ask 'What?'
Was Jason a good student?
Was he a good actor?
What could he do?
Can you imitate your teachers?
How long was he at Drama School?
Did he leave in 1973? Ask 'When?'
Did he go to Hollywood in 1972? Ask 'When?'
Have you ever been to Hollywood?
Would you like to go? Why/Why not?

11 Part Four. Follow the procedure 3.1–3.3. There are no pre-questions.

12 Question and answer:
Who is she?
Why has she come from Hollywood?
When were they in a movie together?

13 Ask students to relate the anecdote. Prompt if necessary.

14 Play the complete recording.

15 Focus attention on the notes. Silent reading.

16 Ask questions with tags to check the information, e.g.
His name's Smith, isn't it?
He was born in 1947, wasn't he?
He was born on July 2nd, wasn't he?
He's British, isn't he? etc.

17 Transfer. Put questions to individuals.
What's your name?
Can you spell it?
When were you born?
Where were you born?
What nationality are you?
Where did you go to primary school?
When did you go to primary school?
What's your address?
Are you married?
What do you do?
What do you want to do?

18 Pair work. Students ask similar questions about Jason Douglas.

19 Transfer/Pair work. Students ask questions as in 2.17 and complete the form for their partners.

20 Ask students questions about their partners' lives.

21 Get students to ask you questions about your life in the same way.

22 Role-play. Students work in groups to prepare a 'This is your Life' role-play, and then present it. They should refer to Unit 2 for additional characters.

Unit 3

THIS IS YOUR LIFE!

Terry Good evening and welcome to 'This is Your Life'. This is Terry Donovan speaking. We're waiting for the subject of tonight's programme. He's one of the world's leading actors, and he thinks he's coming here to take part in a discussion programme ... I can hear him now ... yes, here he is! Jason Douglas ... This is your life!

Jason Oh, no ... I don't believe it! Not me ...

Terry Yes, you! Now come over here and sit down. Jason, you were born at number 28 Balaclava Street in East Ham, London on July 2nd 1947. You were one of six children, and your father was a taxi driver. Of course, your name was then Graham Smith.

Terry Now, do you know this voice? 'I remember Jason when he was two. He used to scream and shout all day.'

Jason Susan!

Terry Yes ... all the way from Sydney, Australia ... she flew here specially for this programme. It's your sister, Susan Fraser!

Jason Susan ... why didn't you tell me ... oh, this is wonderful!

Terry Yes, you haven't seen each other for 13 years ... take a seat next to him, Susan. You started school at the age of five, in 1952, and in 1958 you moved to Lane End Secondary School.

Terry Do you remember this voice? 'Smith! Stop looking out of the window!'

Jason Oh, no! It's Mr Hooper!

Terry Your English teacher, Mr Stanley Hooper. Was Jason a good student, Mr Hooper?

Mr Hooper Eh? No, he was the worst in the class ... but he was a brilliant actor, even in those days. He could imitate all the teachers!

Terry Thank you, Mr Hooper. You can speak to Jason, later. Well, you went to the London School of Drama in 1966, and left in 1969. In 1973 you went to Hollywood.

Terry Do you know this voice?. 'Hi Jason ... Can you ride a horse yet?'

Jason Maria!

Terry Maria Montrose ... who's come from Hollywood to be with you tonight.

Maria Hello, Jason ... it's great to be here. Hello, Terry. Jason and I were in a movie together in 1974. Jason had to learn to ride a horse ... well, Jason doesn't like horses very much.

Jason Like them! I'm terrified of them!

Maria Anyway, he practised for two weeks. Then he went to the director

... it was Charles Orson ... and said, 'What do you want me to do?' Charles said, 'I want you to fall off the horse'. Jason was furious. He said, 'What? Fall off! I've been practising for two weeks ... I could fall off the first day ... without any practice!'

Look at this

Northern T.V.	
Programme:	This is your life
Date:	3rd November
Studio:	4
Subject:	Jason Douglas
Compère:	Terry Donovan
Director:	Chris Price
Surname:	Smith
First name(s):	Graham Anthony
(stage name:	Jason Douglas)
Date of birth:	2/7/47
Nationality:	British
Place of birth:	London, England
Education:	
	Lane End Secondary 1958-65
	London School of Drama 1966-69
Address:	3280 Sunshine Boulevard,
	Hollywood, California.
Marital status:	Single
Profession:	Actor

Northern T.V.	
Programme:	
Date:	
Studio:	
Subject:	
Compère:	
Director:	
Surname:	
First name(s):	
Date of birth:	
Nationality:	
Place of birth:	
Education:	
Address:	
Marital status:	
Profession:	

Ask questions, and complete the form for another student.

HELSINKI

STOCKHOLM

1 278km

2 657km

COPENHAGEN

GLASGOW

1 475km

YORK

2 730km

3 798km

DOVER

FRANKFURT

4 631km

3 640km

GENEVA

4 438km

4 632km

BELGRAD

CLERMONT-FERRAND

5 521km

3 648km

4 753km

CORUNA

BARCELONA

TRIESTE

1 623km

2 724km

MONTE CARLO

LISBON

3 705km

MADRID

Driver Russell Cook
Nationality British   *Age* 28
Starting point Glasgow
Car Talbot Sunbeam Lotus
Engine capacity 2172 cc
Maximum speed 196 km/h
Petrol consumption:
urban cycle 15.59 litres/100 km
constant 90 km/h 13.1 litres/100 km
Length 3.82 m
Width 1.60 m
Height 1.39 m

Driver Hannu Larsen
Nationality Finnish   *Age* 32
Starting point Helsinki
Car Audi Quattro
Engine capacity 2144 cc
Maximum speed 220 km/h
Petrol consumption:
urban cycle 15.69 litres/100 km
constant 90 km/h 7.91 litres/100 km
Length 4.40 m
Width 1.72 m
Height 1.34 m

Driver Danielle Bernard
Nationality French   *Age* 31
Starting point Lisbon
Car Renault 5 Gordini
Engine capacity 1397 cc
Maximum speed 176 km/h
Petrol consumption·
urban cycle 11.2 litres/100 km
constant 90 km/h 6.1 litres/100 km
Length 3.50 m
Width 1.52 m
Height 1.39 m

Teaching points

▶ Future perfect

How far | *'ll* | *she have driven?*
         | *will* |

She'll have driven 600 km.

Revision points

▶ Adjectives and Adverbs

How old?/fast?/long?/wide?/high?/far?/much?/many?

▶ Comparison of adjectives with -er/-est, more/most, as/as

▶ Present perfect progressive in contrast with present perfect simple

▶ Future progressive

Key vocabulary

competition	*medium wave*	*urban cycle*
competitor	*petrol consumption*	(a special
conditions	(number of litres	test route in city
constant 90 km/h	used for 100 km)	to measure petrol
(standard	*point* (place)	consumption)
measurement	*points* (scores)	– – – – – –
on test track for	*points system*	*be unable*
petrol	(scores)	*consist*
consumption)	*production car*	*continue*
control point (place)	(i.e. standard	*lead*
engine capacity	model)	*withdraw*
event	*rallying point*	– – – – –
km/h (kilometres per	*stage* (a post	*average*
hour)	or step in a	*daily*
length/width/height	continuous	*equal*
maximum speed	process)	*motoring*
		single
		unhurt

1 Set the situation (books closed). Ask questions (including *Ask him/her/me/each other.*):
Can you drive?

Are you a | *good* | *driver?*
       | *careful* |
       | *fast* |
       | *slow* |

Do you drive | *well?*
         | *carefully?*
         | *fast?*
         | *slowly?*

How long have you been able to drive?
Have you got a car?
Would you like a car?
Have your parents got a car?
What kind is it?
Do you like it?
Why?
If you had a lot of money, which car would you buy?
Why would you choose that one? (size? speed? economy?)
Have you ever seen a race?
What about a rally?
Do you know anything about the Monte Carlo Rally?

2 Focus attention on the map. Point out that there are more starting points than those shown on the map, and that many cars leave from each one. Just four drivers are shown, and their routes. The routes are not the shortest ones between towns. Allow students to study it. Ensure the text is masked. Play the cassette (or read) 'The Monte Carlo Rally'.

3 Silent reading.

4 Get the students to explain how the Monte Carlo Rally works. Prompt if necessary. Check the difference between the two meanings of 'points' (= 'scores' or 'places').

5 Ask the students to study the information about the drivers and their cars silently. Point out that the statistics relate to ordinary production cars (standard models). Check through the vocabulary and the abbreviations. Pay special attention to '15.59' litres (fifteen point five nine) and the placing of the decimal point in English.

continued

6 Focus attention on Exercise 1. Get students to do it in pairs. Check orally with questions to the class.

7 Follow the same procedure for Exercises 2 and 3.

8 If necessary briefly revise comparative and superlative forms using objects in the classroom, and students' possessions. This could be followed by pair work.

9 'Motoring news'. Ensure the text is masked. Set the situation – a radio report on Monday evening. (The rally began on Sunday morning.)

10 Set these pre-questions:
Write down the time and the date.
Who's leading?
What car is he driving?
Where did a car crash?
How many cars have withdrawn?
What's the weather like in Wales?

11 Play the cassette (or read) twice.

12 Check through the answers to the pre-questions by playing the tape with pauses.

13 Silent reading.

14 Question and answer:
What's the reporter's name?
Where is he?
Who's just arrived in Dover?
What happened to Tony Bond?
Is he in hospital?
Why not?
He won't be able to continue, will he?
Why did the other cars withdraw?
(Check: *withdraw/withdrew/withdrawn*.)
What will the cars be doing tonight?

15 Focus attention on Exercise 4. Get students to do it in pairs. Check orally with questions to the class.

16 Follow the same procedure for Exercise 5.

17 Check through Exercise 6 with questions about Russell Cook before getting them to do it in pairs. Check orally with questions to the class.

18 Written phase.
On Tuesday he'll be driving from Dover to Clermont-Ferrand.
He'll arrive in Clermont-Ferrand on Tuesday night.
He'll have driven a long way.

19 Transfer questions.
What will you have done by the end of today? this week? this month?
Ask each other.
What will we have done by the year 2050 (two thousand and fifty)?

Give examples:
Maybe we'll have built cities under the sea.
Maybe we'll have travelled to Mars.
Maybe we'll have used all the oil.
Get students to work in pairs to draw up a list. Each pair then reports back to the class.

Unit 4

Start

Sunday

Monday

Tuesday

Wednesday

Thursday

2   703km

<< THESSALONIKI

1   543km

<< ATHENS

Driver Sandro Rossi
Nationality Italian   *Age* 30
Starting point Athens
Car Fiat 131
Engine capacity 1585 cc
Maximum speed 168 km/h
Petrol consumption:
urban cycle 11.92 litres/100 km
constant 90 km/h 6.99 litres/100 km
Length 4.26 m
Width 1.65 m
Height 1.39 m

THE MONTE CARLO RALLY

The Monte Carlo Rally, which started in 1911, is Europe's most famous motoring event. Competitors leave from several points around Europe and follow routes of approximately equal length to a rallying point which will be Geneva this year. They then follow a single route to the finish. The rally consists of five daily stages, beginning on Sunday morning, and each competitor will have driven about 3000 kilometres by Thursday night. It is not a race. The winner is decided on a points system. Drivers have to maintain an average speed between control points, and there are also special tests of driving skill in different conditions on the way.

Motoring news

This is Radio Wessex on 203 metres, medium wave. It's nine o'clock on Monday 25th January and this is Barry King reporting from Dover. The British competitors in the Monte Carlo Rally have just arrived here at the end of the second stage in this year's competition. Russell Cook, who's driving a Sunbeam Lotus, is leading. The Triumph driven by Tony Bond, who won last year's rally, crashed in Yorkshire this morning. Tony was unhurt but will be unable to continue. Seven other cars have withdrawn due to bad weather conditions. Tonight the cars, which left from Glasgow on Sunday morning, will be crossing the English Channel.

Exercise 1
Look at the first driver.
What's his name?
His name's Russell Cook.
Where does he come from?
He comes from Britain
How old is he? He's 28.
Ask and answer about the other drivers.

Exercise 2
Look at the first car. (All statistics are for production cars.)
What make is it? It's a Sunbeam Lotus.

How fast can it go? The top speed is 196 km/h.
How much petrol does it use? 15.59 litres per 100 km around town, and 13.1 litres at a constant 90 km/h.
How long is it? 3.82 m.
How wide is it? 1.60 m.
How high is it? 1.39 m.
Ask and answer about the other cars.

Exercise 3
Look at the drivers and the cars.
Danielle Bernard's older than Sandro Rossi.
Russell Cook isn't as old as Danielle Bernard.
Hannu Larsen's the oldest.
Make comparisons about the cars using: fast/long/wide/high/economical.

Exercise 4
Look at the first driver. All the cars started on Sunday morning.
Where is he now? He's in Dover.
Where did he start? He started from Glasgow.
How long has he been driving? He's been driving for two days.
How many kilometres has he driven? 1205 km.
Ask and answer about the other drivers.

Exercise 5
Look at the first driver. It's Monday night.
Where will he be tomorrow night? He'll be in Clermont-Ferrand.
What will he be doing tomorrow? He'll be driving from Dover to Clermont-Ferrand.
Ask and answer about Wednesday and Thursday.
Do the same for the other drivers.

Exercise 6
Look at the first driver.
On Tuesday night he'll be in Clermont-Ferrand.
How far will he have driven on Tuesday? He'll have driven 640 km.
Ask and answer about Wednesday and Thursday.
Do the same for the other drivers.

Unit 4

OUT OF WORK

In Britain a lot of people are out of work. Tracey Chapman is 18, and she left school a year ago. She lives in the North East, an area of high youth unemployment. She hasn't been able to find a job yet.

'My dad just doesn't understand. He started working in a steel mill when he was 15. Things are different now, but he thinks I should start bringing home some money. Oh, I get my unemployment benefit, but that isn't much and I'm fed up with queuing for it every Thursday. I hate having to ask my mum and dad for money. Oh, my mum gives me a couple of pounds for tights now and then, but she can't stand seeing me at home all day. I've almost given up looking for a job. I buy the local paper every day but I'm really tired of looking through the "Situations Vacant" column. There are 50 applicants for every job. I was interested in being a dentist's receptionist because I like meeting people, but now I'd take any job at all. People ask me why I don't move to London, but I don't want to leave my family and friends. Anyway, I'm scared of living on my own in a big city.'

Tracey Chapman went to the Careers Advisory Service. She had to complete this questionnaire.

QUESTIONNAIRE

1 Are you seeking

a full-time employment? ☐

b part-time employment? ☐

2 Which of these is most important for you? (Please number 1 – 5 in order of importance.)

money ☐ people ☐ security ☐

job satisfaction ☐ an interesting job ☐

3 Do you like	yes	no
a meeting people?	☐	☐
b working alone?	☐	☐
c working with other people?	☐	☐
d working with your hands?	☐	☐
e travelling?	☐	☐

4 What do you like doing in your free time?

George Morley is 54. Until last year he was a production manager in the textile industry. He had worked for the same company since he left school. He had a good job, a four-bedroomed house and a company car. When his company had to close because of economic difficulties, he became redundant.

'It's funny really ... I don't feel old, but it isn't easy to start looking for a job at my age. I've had so many refusals. Now I'm frightened of applying for a job. All the interviewers are twenty years younger than me. You see, I'm interested in learning a new skill, but nobody wants to train me. I can see their point of view. I'll have to retire in ten years. It's just ... well, I'm tired of sitting around the house. I've worked hard for nearly forty years and now I'm terrified of having nothing to do. When I was still with Lancastrian Textiles I was bored with doing the same thing day after day, but now I'd really enjoy doing a job again ... any job really. It's not the money ... I got good redundancy pay, and the house is paid for ... and I've given up smoking ... no, it's not just money. I just need to feel ... well, useful ... that's all.'

Exercise 1
I like meeting people.
Make sentences about yourself with: love/enjoy/don't like/dislike/hate/can't stand.

Exercise 2
I'm scared of living on my own.
Make sentences about yourself with: afraid of/frightened of/terrified of.

Exercise 3
I'm bored with doing the same thing.
Make sentences about yourself with: fed up with/tired of/interested in.

Exercise 4
I gave up smoking.
Make sentences about yourself with: start/begin/stop/give up.

Teaching points

▶ Verb + -ing form (1)

| I | enjoy
love
like
don't like
dislike
can't stand
hate | doing it. |

| I'm | afraid of
terrified of
frightened of
scared of
tired of
bored with
fed up with
interested in | doing it. |

| I | began
started
stopped
gave up | doing it. |

Expressions

now and then	out of work (=unemployed)
It's funny . . .	on my own
You see, . . .	at my age
day after day	in order of importance
That's all.	

Key vocabulary

applicant	point of view	unemployment
Careers Advisory	production manager	benefit
Service	redundancy pay	youth
column	refusal	– – – – – –
couple (two)	security	seek
dental receptionist	'Situations Vacant'	sit around
economic difficulty	skill	– – – – – –
employment	steel mill	full-time
free time	textile industry	part-time
job satisfaction	tights	redundant
the North East	unemployment	useful

1 Set the situation. Ensure the text is masked. Play the cassette of the introduction about Tracey Chapman.

2 Question and answer:

What's her name?	*Where does she live?*
How old is she?	*Does she work?*
She isn't a student, is she?	*Why not?*

3 Briefly check through the points of the compass (N, S, E, W, NE, NW, SE, SW) using a board diagram.

4 What Tracey Chapman says. Ensure the text is masked. Play the cassette twice.

5 Silent reading.

6 Play the cassette. After each sentence with an -ing form pause to ask questions, for example:
Cassette: *He thinks I should start bringing home some money.*
(Pause)
T: *What does he think?*
C: *He thinks she should start bringing home some money.* etc.

Questions:

Where did he start working?	*What has she almost given up?*
What does he think?	*What's she tired of?*
What's she fed up with?	*What was she interested in?*
What does she hate?	*What does she like?*
What can't her mother stand?	*What's she scared of?*

7 Play the cassette again. Ask students to go through the text underlining all the -ing forms while they're listening.

8 Ask students to read through the text and find words or phrases which mean:
a) £2
b) a place where a lot of young people haven't got jobs
c) a place where steel is made
d) a section of a newspaper where jobs are advertised
e) money paid to people who are out of work

9 Set the situation for George Morley. Ensure the text is masked. Play the cassette of the introduction about George Morley.

10 Question and answer:
What's his name?
How old is he?
What was his job?
How long had he worked there?
Why did his company have to close?
What happened to him?

11 What George Morley says. Ensure the text is masked. Play the cassette.

12 Silent reading.

13 Play the cassette, pausing as in 5.6.
Questions:

What isn't easy?	*What's he terrified of?*
What's he frightened of?	*What would he enjoy?*
What's he interested in?	*What's he given up?*
What's he tired of?	

14 Play the cassette again. Students underline the -ing forms (see 5.7).

15 Ask students to read through the text and find words or phrases which mean:
a) I've stopped smoking.
b) not needed any more
c) negative replies
d) money paid to workers who are not needed any more
e) I understand why they don't want me.

16 Focus attention on the 'Questionnaire'. Ask students to read it silently. Check vocabulary.

17 Pair work. Students complete the questionnaire for a partner.

18 Ask a few students about their partners' answers.

19 Exercise 1. Get students to make sentences in pairs. Question them about their partners' likes and dislikes. Set the exercise for written homework.

20 Follow the same procedure for Exercises 2–4.

Unit 5

Teaching points

▶ Talking about yourself

▶ Interviews

▶ Format for formal letters

Revision points

▶ verb + -ing form
like doing

▶ verb + infinitive
need/want to do

▶ Imperatives

Key vocabulary

ability	prospects	put in some thought
accounts dept.	spare time	require
activities	spelling mistake	show interest
clerk	techniques	slouch
details	Trade Union	think about
experience	trainee	– – – – –
extract	vacancy	detailed
firm	– – – – –	further
good points	be bothered	junior
impressions	be faced by	lively
interests	be held up	previous
leaflet	chew	tidy
National Insurance	do well	unlined
personnel	find out	– – – – –
department	involve	neatly
personnel officer	make sure	

1 Set the situation. (Refer back to Unit 5.) Read the introduction. Get students to read it silently.

2 Ask these questions:
Have you ever had an interview for a job?
Is there a Careers Advisory Service in your country/school?
How do people find jobs?
How would you find a job?/How did you find your first job?
Where can you find job advertisements?

3 Focus attention on the extract from the leaflet about interviews. Silent reading. Check vocabulary.

4 Ask students to re-read the 'Before the interview' section. Ask questions.
What would you want to find out about the firm? (Discuss in pairs, make up a list and report back – size, location, business, etc.)
What would you wear?
Would you wear jeans?/a suit?/a tie?/a dress?
Say, 'The job is in the next town.'
How would you get there? (Check *by bus/ car/train/underground/bicycle, on foot,* etc.)
How long would it take you to get there?

5 'At the interview.' Ask students to re-read this section. *Do you agree with the advice? Why?/Why not?* (Discuss in pairs and report back.)

6 'The interview.' Ask individuals questions.
(Ask him/her/me/each other.)
What are your spare-time interests? (Suggest some vocabulary.)
What's your family like? Have you got any brothers or sisters? How many? How old are they? What do they do? Do they like their jobs?
What do you like doing? Why?
What don't you like doing? Why?
What subjects have you studied at school? Did you study . . . ?
Do/Did you enjoy studying history/geography/mathematics/etc?
Do/Did you enjoy learning English/French/etc?
What do you do well? What do you do badly?
What are your good points? (*I'm friendly, honest, sensible, practical,* etc.)
What school activities do/did you do? (*sports, clubs,* etc.)
Have you worked before?
Have you done a part-time job? (In the English leaflet, note it is a 'Saturday job'.)

7 Focus attention on the job advertisements. Silent reading. Check vocabulary. Ask:
Which would you apply for?
Why would you like this job?

8 Interview one or two students using the information in 6.6. Ask the class to decide whether they would get the job.

9 Pair work (using the questions in 6.6).

10 Focus attention on the rest of 'The interview' (the questions to ask). Ask students to suggest questions using the prompts (a) in pairs (b) to the class. Draw up a list of possible questions, and ask a few individuals.
What does the job involve?
What are the working hours?
What are the holidays?
Is there a restaurant?
Is there any training? What is it?
Will I get any qualifications?
Can I see where I would be working?
What's the salary?
What are the prospects for promotion?
Is there a pension?

11 Ask students to re-read 'At the interview' in preparation for a role-play.

12 Pair work. Students role-play an interview, using 6.6 and 6.10, and the job advertisement (select one job only for each pair). The interviewer and interviewee might like to draw up a list of answers to the questions in 6.10 first.

13 Possible extended role-play. An interview board. In this case set the attitudes of the members of the board to the interviewee, e.g. one hostile, one friendly, and one neutral. Try and get them to bring out these attitudes in the interview.

14 Focus attention on 'Applying by letter'. Silent reading. Check vocabulary.
Do you agree with the advice? Why/Why not?

15 Focus attention on the letter. Silent reading. Check letter format. Set a letter applying for one of the three jobs in class or for homework. Note that the 'junior clerk' and 'shop assistant' letters will require the student to give more personal information. This information could be discussed in class.

Unit 6

GETTING A JOB

In Britain there is a special service for school leavers, The Careers Advisory Service, which helps young people who are looking for their first jobs. Careers Officers give practical advice on interview techniques, application forms, letters, pay, National Insurance and Trade Unions. This is an extract from a leaflet which is given to young people by Dorset Careers Service.

THE INTERVIEW

You've got an interview for a job – good! So now for the hard work. To do well at an interview you need to put in some thought first.

The employer wants to know if you are the person he wants, so you'll be asked about yourself. Think about it now:

What do I do well?   School activities?
What are my good points?   School subjects?
Why would I like this job? Previous work?
Spare-time interests?   Saturday job?
What is my family like?

What do I like doing and why?
What do I not like doing and why?

You will want to ask questions too.

The job itself?   Can I see where I
Training?   would be working?
Prospects?   Hours?
Further Education?   £ £ £ £ ?
Conditions?

Write your questions down and take them with you.

BEFORE THE INTERVIEW

1 Find out what you can about the firm.
2 Find out the interviewer's name and telephone number.
3 Find out where the interview is.
4 Find out how long it will take to get there.
5 Make sure you know what the job involves.
6 Dress to look clean and tidy.

AT THE INTERVIEW

1 Do arrive early. Phone if you're held up.
2 Do try to smile.
3 Do show interest in the job and ask questions.
4 Do be polite.
5 Don't panic, even if faced by more than one person.
6 Don't slouch around and look bored.
7 Don't smoke or chew.
8 Don't give one word answers or say you don't care what you do.

Look at these job advertisements.

Trainee computer programmer
Good opportunity for a start in computers. Ability at maths is essential. Application forms from: Personnel Department, Continental Computers, Honeywell Rd., Bournemouth.

Fernside Engineering
Require a junior clerk for the accounts department.
Apply in writing to: The Personnel Officer, Fernside Engineering, Western Rd., Poole.

Shop assistant
A vacancy for a smart, lively young person. Good prospects. Please write to:
Mrs J.. Frost, 'Cool Boutique', 39 High St., Dorchester.

Applying by letter
1 Remember that first impressions are important.
2 Write clearly and neatly on good notepaper, unlined if possible.
3 Check for spelling mistakes. Use a dictionary if you are not sure of a word.
4 Describe yourself, your qualifications and your experience clearly.
5 If the advertisement asks you to write for an application form you will not need to give detailed information in your letter.
6 Address the letter and the envelope clearly.

44 Deepdale Road,
Boscombe,
Bournemouth,
BH92 7JX

4th April, 1982

The Personnel Department,
Continental Computers,
Honeywell Road,
Bournemouth

Dear Sir or Madam,
I read your advertisement in yesterday's 'Evening Echo'. I am interested in training as a computer programmer. Could you please send me an application form, and any further details.

Yours faithfully,

Joanne Evans

BATTLE OF TRAFALGAR STREET

Last night, for the third time this week, police and County Council officials had to turn and run when they were showered with boiling water from the upstairs window of No 10 Trafalgar Street. They were hoping to speak to Mrs Florence Hamilton, an 83-year-old widow, who is still refusing to leave her home. Every other house in the street has been demolished. The Council are planning to build four 20-storey blocks of flats in the area. All the other residents agreed to move when the Council offered to provide them with new flats nearby. On Tuesday evening a social worker who wanted to speak to Mrs Hamilton was attacked and badly bitten by one of her dogs.

Radio report 1

This is Pennine Radio News, Alan Nelson reporting from Trafalgar Street. Mr Hardy, the Tadworth Housing Officer, has agreed to speak to us.

Alan Now, Mr Hardy, has the situation changed since last night?

Hardy No, it hasn't. Mrs Hamilton is still there, and she's still refusing to talk to us.

Alan Well, what are you going to do?

Hardy It's a very difficult situation. We'd like her to come out peacefully. The police don't intend to prosecute her ... but she's a very stubborn lady!

Alan Stubborn? Yes, well, it is her home.

Hardy I agree, and it's been her home for a long time, I know. But nobody else refused to move. You see, a lot of people in this area are living in sub-standard accommodation and we are going to build over 300 flats on this site. Families are expecting to move into them next year! It's all being delayed because of one person!

Alan But Mrs Hamilton was born in that house.

Hardy Of course, of course. But we have promised to give her a modern flat immediately, a very nice flat which is ideal for an elderly person living alone.

Alan So, what happens next?

Hardy I don't know. I really don't ... but we can't wait forever. The police will have to do something soon. It won't be easy. She's got two very big dogs, and they don't like strangers!

Radio report 2

We have also managed to arrange an interview with Mrs Hamilton. She has decided to speak to us but she has demanded to see me alone.
Mrs Hamilton!

Mrs H. Who are you?

Alan I'm Alan Nelson ... Pennine Radio News.

Mrs H. Well ... don't come any closer, or I'll let the dogs out. Down Caesar! Sit, boy!

Alan I'm sure our listeners would like to hear your side of the story.

Mrs H. There's not much to say. I'm not moving! I was born here, I had my children here, and I intend to die here.

Alan But the Council really need to have this land, and they have arranged to provide a new flat for you ...

Mrs H. Oh, yes. I know, but I can't take my dogs with me ... and I need to have company. My dogs are all I've got. Down boy!

Alan How long can you stay here?

Mrs H. Oh, I've got plenty of food. The Council have threatened to cut off the water and electricity, but I'll be all right.

Alan Well, thank you, Mrs Hamilton ... and good luck!

Mrs H. And you can tell the Council from me ... I want another house where I can keep my dogs, not a little flat in a bloody high-rise block!

Exercise

'... a Social Worker who **wanted to speak** to Mrs Hamilton ...' 'wanted to speak' is 'verb + to (do)'.
Go through the page and underline the other examples of verbs with 'to (do)'.

Teaching points

► Verb + infinitive

hope to (do)
refuse to (do)
plan to (do)
offer to (do)
agree to (do)
want to (do)
would like to (do)
arrange to (do)
threaten to (do)
intend to (do)
expect to (do)
promise to (do)
manage to (do)
decide to (do)
demand to (do)
need to (do)
had to do ...
have to do ...
going to do ...

Expressions

There's not much to say.
What happens next?
Good luck!

Key vocabulary

battle	bite	elderly
block of flats	cut off	forever
county council	delay	ideal
housing officer	demolish	(20) storey
officials	let out	stubborn
resident	prosecute	sub-standard
site	provide	– – – – – – .
situation	shower with	nearby
social work	– – – – –	peacefully
– – – – – –	bloody (taboo)	

1 Focus attention on the picture. Set the situation. Refer students to the newspaper article. Ask them to read it silently.

2 Question and answer.
What's the name of the newspaper?
What's the date?
Who was showered with boiling water?
What did they have to do?
Where did the water come from?
Have the police been before?
How many times have they been before?
What were they hoping to do?
How old is Mrs Hamilton?
Is she married? Was she married? How do you know?
What is she refusing to do?
What's happened to the other houses?
What are the Council planning to do?
What have the other residents agreed to do?
What has the Council offered to do?
What did the social worker want to do?
He was attacked, wasn't he?
He wasn't attacked by Mrs Hamilton, was he?
She didn't bite him, did she?
What happened?

3 Let the students tell you about the 'Battle of Trafalgar Street'. Prompt where necessary.

4 'Radio report I'. Ensure the text is masked. Play the cassette.

5 Play the cassette again, pausing after each example of verb and infinitive to ask questions, e.g.
Cassette: *She's still refusing to talk to us.*
T: *What's she refusing to do?*
C: *She's refusing to talk to them.*

6 Silent reading.

7 Pair work.

8 'Radio report 2'. Follow the procedure 7.4–7.7.

9 Question and answer:
What's the housing officer's problem?
What's Mrs Hamilton's problem?
What's the problem for the police?
What would you do if you were the Housing Officer?/
Mrs Hamilton?/a police inspector?

10 Pair work. Discuss possible solutions to the problems in 7.9. Draw up a list.

11 Get each pair to report back its list of possible solutions. Discuss them in class.

12 Role-play. A discussion between Mr Hardy and Mrs Hamilton
a) in pairs,
b) one or two pairs in front of the class.

13 Set the exercise in class. Check through the answers. There are 25 examples in the text.

14 Transfer. Ask questions. *(Ask him/her/me/each other.)*
What would you like to do after school today?/next summer
holiday?/on Saturday? Do you think you'll do it?
Have you arranged to do anything at the weekend?
Ask 'What?/When?'
Have you planned/agreed/promised/offered/decided to do anything
this evening? Ask 'What?'
Have you refused to do anything this week? Ask 'What?'
Have you demanded/threatened to do anything recently?
Ask 'What?'
Is there anything you need to do tonight?
Is there anything you have to do? etc.

15 Extra transfer.
Do you like dogs? Why/Why not?
Are you afraid of dogs? Why/Why not?
Have you got a dog? Describe it.
Have you ever been bitten/chased by a dog?
Ask 'Where?/When?/What happened?'
How would you solve the problem of Mrs Hamilton's dogs?

Teaching points

▶ Congratulating/expressing sympathy

▶ Informal letter endings

▶ Adjective + infinitive (1)

I'm delighted/willing/sorry/happy/sad/ready/surprised/upset to do it.
It's lovely/nice/difficult/great/interesting to do.

▶ *Enough/too + infinitive*

You don't look old enough to be ...
I was too ill to come ...

Expressions

With deepest sympathy.   *at the same time*
Congratulations on ...   *St. (Saint)*
lose a daughter and gain a son   *née (refers to a woman's*
As you know ...   *surname before marriage)*

Key vocabulary

cancer research	illness	enclose
donation	promotion	gain
engagement	retirement	miss
funeral	St. Valentine's Day	– – – – – –
gift	(Feb 14th)	double
greetings card	suitcase	eldest
happiness	– – – – – –	willing
holidaymaker		

1 Introductory text. Silent reading.

2 Question and answer:
Do you send cards?
Ask 'How often?/When?/Why?/Who ... to?'
Ask each other.
Can you buy cards for these occasions in your country?
Can you buy any other cards?
Have you sent many cards this year?
Do you like sending cards?
Do you like receiving cards? etc.

3 Focus attention on the newspaper extract. Students read 'Births' silently. 'Née' indicates the woman's surname before marriage.

4 Question and answer:
What are the parents' names?
What are the children's names?
When were they born?
Where were they born?
What was Linda's name before she was married?
Would you like to have twins?
Do you know any twins?
Are they the same?
How many children would you like to have?
Were you born at home or in hospital?
What was your mother's maiden name? (i.e. before she was married)
If you had twin daughters what would you call them?
What about sons?

5 First card. Focus attention on the picture. Silent reading.

6 Point out 'We were delighted to hear ...'. Can you think of any other words to replace 'delighted'? (*pleased/happy/*etc.)

7 Point out 'It's lovely to have ...'. Ask for words to replace 'lovely' (*nice/great/*etc.)

8 Focus attention on 'Marriages'. Silent reading.

9 Question and answer:
Who got married? Ask 'When?/Where?'
Is Michael an only son? How do you know?
Has Christine got any brothers and sisters? How do you know?
Have you been to any weddings recently? Ask 'Whose?/When?/Where?'
Did you give a present? Ask 'What?'
Note: In England you can get married in a church or in a registry office, you don't go to both. Ask *What about your country?*

10 Second card. Follow the procedure 8.5–8.8. Ask students to find appropriate adjectives in pairs for these sentences.
It was nice to read about ...
I expect you're sorry to lose a daughter.
You're happy to gain a son.

11 Focus attention on 'Deaths'. Silent reading.

12 Question and answer:
Who has died?
Did he die in an accident? Ask 'How?/Where?/When?'
How old was he?
Does his wife want any flowers? Ask 'Why not?'
Have you ever been to a funeral? Ask 'Whose?/What was it like?'

13 Third card. Follow the procedure 8.5–8.8. Ask students to find appropriate adjectives in pairs for these sentences.
I was very sorry to learn about Albert's death.
It's difficult to know what to say.
He was always ready to help everyone.
I was too ill to come to the funeral.

14 Focus attention on 'Best Wishes for your 21st Birthday'. Silent reading.

15 Question and answer:
Note: In England the legal age of majority is 18, but the traditional one is 21. A key is a traditional symbol of the responsibilities of the adult householder. Ask *What about your country?*

16 Fourth card. Follow the procedure 8.5–8.8. Ask students to find substitutions for 'It's really great to be 21'.

17 Focus attention on 'Silver wedding'. Silent reading.

18 Question and answer:
When did they get married?
How long have they been married?
Where were they married?

19 Fifth card. Follow the procedure 8.5–8.8. Ask for substitutions for 'I was really surprised to hear it'.

20 Point out 'You don't look old enough to have a diamond wedding'.
T: *He/rich/Rolls Royce.*
S: *He isn't rich enough to have a Rolls Royce.*
1 *She/old/driving licence.*
2 *He/strong/lift it.*
3 *She/fast/catch it.*
4 *She/tall/touch it.*

21 Sixth card. Follow the procedure 8.5–8.8 Ask for substitutions for 'I was very upset to hear about ...', and 'You'll need something interesting to look at ...'.

22 Exercise. Go through this orally. Get students to make suggestions in pairs, and to report back to the class.

23 Transfer. If students know of anyone who has been born, married, etc., get them to compose a newspaper insert. Get others to write letters related to it.

SENDING A CARD

Greetings cards are big business in Britain. Millions of cards are sent every year, and you can buy cards for nearly every special occasion. There are cards for Christmas, New Year, Easter, birthdays, engagements, funerals, St Valentine's day, Mother's Day, Father's Day, retirement, illness, passing examinations and driving tests, promotions, and the picture postcards sent by holidaymakers.

TWINS! How Wonderful!

To Linda & David,
We were delighted to hear about the twins! It's lovely to have two at the same time... double the happiness (and double the work!) We're willing to help at any time. Don't hesitate to ask.
Lots of love,
Alison & Kevin

Best Wishes for Your 21st Birthday

You've never been 21 before,
Now you've got the key of the door,
It's really great to be 21.
Now you are a man, my son.

Love, Dad

Christine

Best Wishes on your Wedding

It was very nice to read about your wedding. I expect your parents are sorry to lose a daughter but happy to gain a son! My best wishes to you and your new husband.
Sarah Roberts

To Harold and Enid,

Congratulations on your Silver Wedding

Twenty five years together! I was really surprised to hear it. You don't look old enough to have a silver wedding! Very best wishes,
Gladys.

With Sincere Sympathy

I was very sad to learn about Albert's death. It is difficult to know what to say. As you know, I worked with him for thirty years. He was a wonderful person... He was always ready to help everyone. He will be sadly missed. I am sorry, but I was too ill to come to the funeral. Yours sincerely,
Walter Brown

Get Well Soon

I was very upset to hear about your accident. I enclose some magazines. You'll need something interesting to look at! I hope the nurses are nice.
All the best,
Freddie

Wedding anniversaries
The traditional gifts to give for each one:

1st paper	13th lace
2nd cotton	14th ivory
3rd leather	15th glass
4th linen	20th china
5th wood	**25th silver**
6th iron	30th pearl
7th wool	35th jade
8th bronze	40th ruby
9th pottery	45th sapphire
10th tin	**50th gold**
11th steel	55th emerald
12th silk	**60th diamond**

Exercise
Can you suggest a suitable gift for each anniversary?
2nd anniversary
A cotton table-cloth or some cotton towels

Unit 8

MARRIAGE GUIDANCE COUNCIL

Malcolm and Barbara Harris have been married for nearly fifteen years. They've got two children, Gary aged thirteen, and Andrea, who is eleven. During the last couple of years Malcolm and Barbara haven't been very happy. They argue all the time. Barbara's sister advised them to go to the Marriage Guidance Council. There is one in most British towns. It's an organization which allows people to talk with a third person about their problems. This is their third visit, and Mrs Murray, the counsellor, always sees them.

Barbara's interview

Mrs Murray Ah, come in Barbara. Take a seat. Is your husband here?

Barbara Yes, he's waiting outside. He didn't want to come here this week, but ... well, I persuaded him to come.

Mrs Murray I see. How have things been?

Barbara Oh, much the same. We still seem to have rows all the time.

Mrs Murray What do you quarrel about?

Barbara What don't we quarrel about, you mean! Oh, everything. You see, he's so inconsiderate ...

Mrs Murray Go on.

Barbara Well, I'll give you an example. You know, when the children started school, I wanted to go back to work again, too. So I got a job. Well, anyway, by the time I've collected Gary and Andrea from school, I only get home about half an hour before Malcom...

Mrs Murray Yes?

Barbara Well, when he gets home, he expects me to run around and get his tea. He never does anything in the house!

Mrs Murray Mmm.

Barbara And last Friday! He invited three of his friends to come round for a drink. He didn't tell me to expect them, and I'd had a long and difficult day. I don't think that's right, do you?

Mrs Murray Barbara, I'm not here to pass judgement. I'm here to listen.

Barbara Sorry. And he's so untidy. He's worse than the kids. I always have to remind him to pick up his clothes. He just throws them on the floor. After all, I'm not his servant. I've got my own career. Actually, I think that's part of the trouble. You see, I earn as much money as he does.

Malcolm's interview

Mrs Murray Malcolm! I'm so glad you could come.

Malcolm Hello, Mrs Murray. Well, I'll be honest. Barbara had to force me to come, really.

Mrs Murray Does it embarrass you to talk about your problems?

Malcolm Yes, it does. But I suppose we need to talk to somebody.

Mrs Murray Barbara feels that you ... well, you resent her job.

Malcolm I don't know. I would prefer her to stay at home, but she's very well qualified... and I encouraged her to go back to work. Now the kids are at school, she needs an interest ... and I suppose we need the money.

Mrs Murray How do you share the housework?

Malcom I try to help. I always help her to wash up, and I help Gary and Andrea to do their homework while she does the dinner. But she doesn't think that's enough. What do you think?

Mrs Murray I'm not here to give an opinion, Malcolm.

Malcolm I think we're both too tired, that's all. In the evenings we're both too tired to talk. And Barbara ... she never allows me to suggest anything about the house or about the kids. We always have the same arguments. She's got her own opinions and that's it. Last night we had another row. She's forbidden the kids to ride their bikes to school.

Mrs Murray Why?

Malcolm She thinks they're too young to ride in the traffic. But I think they should. She always complains about collecting them from school. But you can't wrap children in cotton-wool, can you?

Exercise 1

'Barbara's sister advised *them* to go ...'
There are fifteen sentences like this. Underline them or write them out.

Exercise 2

They're very tired. They can't talk.
They're too tired to talk.
Continue.

1 They're very young. They shouldn't ride to school.
2 He's very old. He can't go to work.
3 We were very surprised. We couldn't say anything.
4 She's very ill. She shouldn't go out.

Teaching points

▶ verb + object + infinitive

Someone	advised allowed encouraged expected forbade forced helped invited persuaded preferred reminded told wanted	me you him her us them Malcolm the children	to do	something.
It	embarrassed			

▶ Adjective + infinitive (2)

He's too	young tired	to do it.

▶ Here/There + infinitive

I'm not	here there	to	pass judgement. listen. give an opinion.

▶ Seem + infinitive

We seem to have rows all the time.

Expressions

How have things been?   I'm so glad you could come.
much the same   I'll be honest . . .
After all . . .

Key vocabulary

cotton wool	collect	honest
counsellor	pass judgement	inconsiderate
Marriage Guidance	quarrel	qualified
Council	resent	untidy
organization	run around	– – – – –
– – – – –	share	individually
argue	wrap	
	– – – – –	

1 Introductory text. Set the situation. Ensure the text is masked. Play the cassette.

2 Silent reading.

3 Question and answer:
Have they been married for 20 years?
Ask how long?
How old are their children?
They aren't happy, are they?
How often do they argue?
What did Barbara's sister advise them to do?
What is a Marriage Guidance Council?
How many times have they been before?
Does Mrs Murray see them together, or individually?
Are there 'Marriage Guidance Councils' in your town/country?

4 'Barbara's interview'. Ensure the text is masked. Play the cassette.

5 Selective repetition. (Play the cassette with pauses. Focus particularly on the teaching points.)

6 Drill: Continue:
T: *I persuaded him to come.*   *she*
T: *she*   *me*
T: *She persuaded him to come.*   *told*
T: *me*   *them*
T: *She persuaded me to come.*   *we*
T: *told*   *advised*
T: *She told me to come.*   *he*
T: *I persuaded him to come. Repeat!* *wanted*
C: *I persuaded him to come.*   *us*
                                                        go

7 Silent reading.

8 Question and answer:
What didn't her husband want them to do?
What did she persuade him to do?
When the children started school, what did she want to do?
What did Malcolm want her to do?
When he gets home from work, what does he expect her to do?
What did he do last Friday?
What didn't he tell her?
What does she have to remind him to do?

9 Pair work. (Students read the dialogue in pairs.)

10 'Malcolm's interview'. Ensure the text is masked. Play the cassette.

11 Selective repetition.

12 Drill: Continue:
T: *She's forbidden the kids to ride to school.*   *them*
T: *them*   *I*
T: *She's forbidden them to ride to school.*   *Have you?*
T: *I*   *Why?*
T: *I've forbidden them to ride to school.*   *smoke*
T: *Have you?*   *him*
T: *Have you forbidden them to ride to school?*   *she*
T: *She's forbidden the kids to ride to school. Repeat!* *us*
C: *She's forbidden the kids to ride to school.*

13 Question and answer:
She had to force him to come. Ask 'Why?'
It embarrasses him to talk about his problems. Ask 'Why'?
He would prefer her to stay at home. Ask 'Why?'
He encouraged her to go back to work. Ask 'Why?'
He helps her to wash up. Ask 'How often?'
She doesn't allow him to suggest anything. Ask 'Why?'
She's forbidden them to ride to school. Ask 'Why?'

14 Pair work.

15 Go through exercises 1 and 2 in class (or set for homework).

16 Discuss Malcolm and Barbara's problems. Ask for the students' opinions.
What would you advise him/her to do?
Who do you think is right? etc.

17 Role-play. Set up groups of three. Malcolm and Barbara confront each other, with Mrs Murray as 'referee'. Point out things Mrs Murray should use to avoid entering the argument.
I'm not here to pass judgement/give an opinion.
I'm here to listen.
Each group role-plays the interview. Get one or two groups to act out the conversation in front of the class.

Revision points

▶ Do in contrast with *make*

He went to London to do the shopping.
I'd made some arrangements.

Expressions

A funny thing happened to me.
I couldn't believe my eyes!
in fact

Key vocabulary

buffet	fold	wander
course	get stuck	– – – – –
crossword puzzle	glance	funny
traffic jam	ignore	typical
– – – – –	look like	
afford	make a fuss	casually
avoid	pop	except
be relieved	pretend	nervously
be shocked	reach across	– – – – –
carry on	stare	by/by the time
dip	take a taxi	

1 Set the situation. Ensure the text is masked. Play the cassette of the whole story.

2 Paragraph 1. Play the cassette again.

3 Silent reading.

4 Question and answer:
When did it happen?
Where had he gone? Ask 'Why'
What did he want to get?
What did he need to find?
What does he do?
How did he travel to London?
He got everything he wanted, didn't he?
Does he like London? Why not?
Why did he want to go home early?
Did he walk to the station? Ask 'How did he get there?'
Does he usually travel by taxi? Why not?
Which train did he want to get?
He missed it, didn't he? Ask 'Why?'
Did he have to wait? Ask 'How long?'
Which newspaper did he buy?
Was the buffet busy?
What did he buy?
He likes chocolate biscuits, doesn't he?
Did he sit with other people? Ask 'Where?'
What did he begin doing? Ask 'Why?'

5 Reproduction. Get the students to tell you the story so far. Prompt if necessary.

6 Invention exercise.
He/London/shopping.
He went to London to do some shopping.

Give prompts:
He/station/train. (He went to the station to get/catch the train.)
He/taxi/station early. (He took a taxi to get to the station early.)
He/kiosk/newspaper. (He went to the kiosk to buy/get a newspaper.)
He/newspaper/crossword. (He bought/got a newspaper to do the crossword.)
He/buffet/coffee. (He went/wandered over to the buffet to buy/get a coffee.)
He/table/coffee. (He sat down at a table to drink/have his coffee.)

7 Paragraph 2. Play the cassette again.

8 Silent reading.

9 Reproduction. *(Correct my statement.)*
T: *After fifteen minutes.*
C: *After a couple of minutes!*

Continue:
A woman sat down next to me/There was something special about her/Except that she was very small/In fact he looked like a typical pop singer/You know, white suit and guitar/I said something/I carried on with my dinner/Suddenly he fell across the table/opened my newspaper/took three/and threw it into my coffee/and slipped it into his pocket/I couldn't believe my eyes/I was too happy to say anything/Anyway I didn't want to catch a bus/so I decided to hit him/I always make trouble if I can/I just took a cigarette myself/and went back to the buffet.

10 Paragraph 3. Play the cassette again.

11 Silent reading.

12 Question and answer:
What did he do when the man took a second biscuit?
What did he pretend to be interested in?
What did he do after a couple of minutes?
How was the man staring?
What did he decide to do?
What did the man suddenly do?
How did the student feel?
How long did he decide to wait?
What did he do before he stood up?
What did he see?
How do you think he felt?

13 Reproduction. Get the students to tell the story in paragraph 3. Prompt if necessary.

14 Play the whole cassette again.

15 Drill:
T: *He looked interested, but he wasn't really.*
C: *He pretended to be interested.*

Continue:
She seemed calm, but she wasn't really.
They looked angry, but they weren't really.
He seemed tired, but he wasn't really.
They looked furious, but they weren't really.
He looked dead, but he wasn't really.

16 Focus attention on 'Look at this'. Go through it.

17 Go through the exercise orally. Get students to do it in pairs. Set in class or for homework.

18 Get students to write an anecdote beginning with 'A funny thing happened to me . . .'.

Unit 10

A FUNNY THING HAPPENED TO ME...

A funny thing happened to me last Friday. I'd gone to London to do some shopping. I wanted to get some Christmas presents, and I needed to find some books for my course at college (you see, I'm a student). I caught an early train to London, so by early afternoon I'd bought everything that I wanted. Anyway, I'm not very fond of London, all the noise and traffic, and I'd made some arrangements for that evening. So, I took a taxi to Waterloo station. I can't really afford taxis, but I wanted to get the 3.30 train. Unfortunately the taxi got stuck in a traffic jam, and by the time I got to Waterloo, the train had just gone. I had to wait an hour for the next one. I bought an evening newspaper, the 'Standard', and wandered over to the station buffet. At that time of day it's nearly empty, so I bought a coffee and a packet of biscuits ... chocolate biscuits. I'm very fond of chocolate biscuits. There were plenty of empty tables and I found one near the window. I sat down and began doing the crossword. I always enjoy doing crossword puzzles.

After a couple of minutes a man sat down opposite me. There was nothing special about him, except that he was very tall. In fact he looked like a typical city businessman ... you know, dark suit and briefcase. I didn't say anything and I carried on with my crossword. Suddenly he reached across the table, opened my packet of biscuits, took one, dipped it into his coffee and popped it into his mouth. I couldn't believe my eyes! I was too shocked to say anything. Anyway, I didn't want to make a fuss, so I decided to ignore it. I always avoid trouble if I can. I just took a biscuit myself and went back to my crossword.

When the man took a second biscuit, I didn't look up and I didn't make a sound. I pretended to be very interested in the puzzle. After a couple of minutes, I casually put out my hand, took the last biscuit and glanced at the man. He was staring at me furiously. I nervously put the biscuit in my mouth, and decided to leave. I was ready to get up and go when the man suddenly pushed back his chair, stood up and hurried out of the buffet. I felt very relieved and decided to wait two or three minutes before going myself. I finished my coffee, folded my newspaper and stood up. And there, on the table, where my newspaper had been, was my packet of biscuits.

Exercise

I always do my homework.
We have to do military service in my country.
I never make a fuss.
I made my bed this morning.
Write ten sentences, five with 'do' and five with 'make'.

Look at this:

'I'd gone to London to *do* some shopping.'
'I always enjoy *doing* crossword puzzles.'
'I'd *made* some arrangements.'
'I didn't want to *make* a fuss.'
'I didn't *make* a sound.'

Do	Make
shopping	arrangements
work	an offer
homework	a suggestion
housework	a decision
cleaning	an attempt
washing up	an effort
gardening	an excuse
military service	a mistake
mathematics,	a noise
history,	a phonecall
literature, etc.	a date
(at school)	a profit
something	a bed
interesting	a cake
a (boring) job	a speech
	trouble

POLITE REQUESTS

Max Millwall used to be a popular comedian on British radio. He's nearly 70 now, but he still performs in clubs in the Midlands and North of England. He's on stage now at the All-Star Variety Club in Wigan.

Well, good evening, ladies and gentlemen ... and others! It's nice to be back in Wigan again. Well, I have to say that, I say it every night. I said it last night. The only trouble was that I was in Birmingham. I thought the audience looked confused! Actually, I remember Wigan very well indeed. Really! You know, the first time I came here was in the 1930s. I was very young and very shy ... thank you, mother. No, you can't believe that, can you? Well, it's true. I was very young and very shy. Anyway, the first Saturday night I was in Wigan, I decided to go to the local dance-hall. Do you remember the old 'Majestic Ballroom' in Wythenshawe Street? There's a multi-storey car park there now. It was a lovely place ... always full of beautiful girls, (the ballroom, not the car park). Of course, most of them are grandmothers now! Oh, you were there too, were you, love? I was much too shy to ask anyone for a dance. So I sat down at a table, and I thought I'd watch for a while. You know, see how the other lads did it. At the next table there was a lovely girl in a blue dress. She'd arrived with a friend, but her friend was dancing with someone. This bloke came over to her, he was very posh, wearing a dinner-jacket and a bow tie! Well, he walked up to her and said, 'Excuse me, may I have the pleasure of the next dance?' She looked up at him (she had lovely big blue eyes) and said 'Eh? What did you say?' So he said, 'I wonder if you would be kind enough to dance with me ... er ... if you don't mind.' 'Eee ... no, thank you very much,' she replied.

A few minutes later, this other chap arrived. He had a blue suit, a nice tie, and a little moustache. He gave her this big smile, and said, 'Would you be so kind as to have the next dance with me?' 'Pardon?' she said. I thought to myself 'She's a bit deaf ... or maybe she hasn't washed her ears recently.'

'Would you mind having the next dance with me?' he said, a bit nervously this time. 'Eee, no thanks, love. I'm finishing my lemonade,' she replied. 'Blimey! I thought. This looks a bit difficult.'

Then this third fellow came over. He was very good-looking, you know, black teeth, white hair ... sorry, I mean white teeth, black hair! 'May I ask you something?' he said, ever so politely. 'If you like,' she answered. 'Can I ... I mean ... could I ... no, might I have the next dance with you?' 'Oooh, sorry,' she said. 'My feet are aching. I've been standing up all day at the shop.'

By now, I was terrified. I mean, she'd said 'no' to all of them! Then this fourth character thought he'd try.

'Would you like to dance?' he said. 'What?' she replied. She was a lovely girl, but I didn't think much of her voice! 'Do you want to dance?' he said. She looked straight at him. 'No', she said. That's all. 'No.' Well, I decided to go home. I was wearing an old jacket and trousers, and nobody would say that I was good-looking! Just as I was walking past her table, she smiled. 'Er ... dance?' I said. 'Thank you very much,' she replied. And that was that! It's our fortieth wedding anniversary next week.

Exercise 1
Go through and underline all the 'requests'. How many are there?

Exercise 2
There are six words that mean 'man'. What are they?

Exercise 3
Find expressions that mean:
1 smart and upper class
2 with several floors
3 unable to hear well
4 handsome
5 a short time

Teaching points

► Polite requests

(see Expressions below)

► Use of -ing form

Would you mind doing...?

► Use of infinitive

Would you be kind enough to do...?
Would you be so kind as to do...?

Expressions

Lend me 20p.
Shut the door, will you?

| Do you want | a coffee? |
| Would you like | |

Can I	ask you something?
Could I	
May I	
Might I	
I wonder if I could	
Do you mind if I	

Would you mind if I (asked) you (something)?

The only trouble was...
Good evening, ladies and gentlemen.
You know...

Would you mind doing something?
I wonder if you would mind...
Would you be kind enough to do...?
Would you be so kind as to do...?

| I wonder if you | can | help me? |
| | could | |

Not at all.
I don't mind at all.
Thank you so much.
No, thanks. I'm just looking.

Key vocabulary

ballroom	scarf	good-looking
bloke	stage	multi-storey
bow tie	– – – – –	posh
clap	ache	shy
character	perform	stuffy
dance hall	– – – – –	terrified
dinner jacket	close	– – – – –
lemonade	confused	actually
rack	deaf	

Note: In making polite requests it is often the way that you say something which is important rather than the choice of a particular formula. For example, it is possible to say 'I wonder if you would mind helping me?' in a very terse and rude way, and equally possible to say 'Give me a cup of tea, please' in a polite and friendly manner. Notice that in the first two mini-dialogues, where close acquaintances are speaking, there is no need to use elaborate formulas.

1 First page. Focus attention on the picture. Ensure the text is masked. Ask a few questions about the picture to set the situation. Play the cassette of the introductory text.

2 Silent reading.

3 Question and answer:
What's his name?
How old is he?
What does he do?
Where did he use to work?
Where does he generally work now?
Where is he at this moment?

4 Max Millwall's monologue. Ensure the text is masked. Play the cassette.

5 Selective repetition. Play the cassette, getting students to repeat all the polite requests.

6 Get the students to do Exercises 1, 2 and 3.

continued

Unit 11

7 Second page. Dialogue 1 (A and B). Focus attention on the picture. Ensure the text is masked. Set the situation – the two men share an office and are close acquaintances. Play the cassette.

8 Listen and repeat.

9 Silent reading. Note that 'will you?' is used with imperatives.

10 Pair work. The students should also substitute the other vocabulary items given, and any others they can think of. Select a student and act out the dialogue.

11 Dialogue 2 (C and D). Follow the same procedure (11.7–11.10). Note again that the women are close friends, and work together.

12 Dialogue 3 (E and F). Follow the same procedure (11.7–11.10) but note that the speakers are either strangers or do not know each other very well.

13 Dialogue 4 (G and H). Follow the same procedure (11.7–11.10). Note that the speakers are strangers on a railway train and are therefore using a more polite register.

14 Dialogue 5 (I and J). Follow the same procedure (11.7–11.10). Note that these are the same speakers as in Dialogue 4. Point out that the affirmative reply to 'Do you mind . . .?' is 'No' (i.e. No, I don't mind . . .).

15 Dialogue 6 (K and L). Follow the same procedure (11.7–11.10). Point out that this is a manager/junior employee situation.

16 Dialogue 7 (M and N). Follow the same procedure (11.7–11.10). Note the shop situation and the usefulness of 'No, thank you. I'm just looking'.

17 Dialogue 8 (O and P). Follow the same procedure (11.7–11.10). Note the very formal and hesitant 'Might I suggest . . .?'.

18 Dialogue 9 (Q and R). Follow the same procedure (11.7–11.10).

A Mike ...
B Yes?
A Shut the door will you? It's freez-
   ing in here!
B Right ... sorry.

close window/cold
open door/very hot

C Karen ...
D Yes?
C Lend me 20p. I've left my purse in
   the office.
D Oh, OK. Here you are.
C Thanks.

£1/wallet   50p/handbag

E Excuse me, could you pass me the
   sugar?
F Oh, yes. Of course. There you are.
E Thank you very much.

vinegar   salt   pepper

G Can I help you?
H Oh, thank you. Would you mind
   putting my case on the rack?
G Not at all. There you are.
H Oh, thank you so much. You're
   very kind.

luggage/up there   bags/rack

I Excuse me. It's a bit stuffy in here.
   Do you mind if I open the window?
J No, no. I don't mind at all. I feel
   like some fresh air too.

cold/close/cold too
feels hot/stuffy too

K Excuse me, Mrs Howe. May I ask
   you something?
L Yes, Wendy, What is it?
K May I have the day off next
   Friday?
L Well, we're very busy. Is it impor-
   tant?
K Er, yes, it is, really. It's my cousin's
   wedding.
L Oh, well! Of course you can.

Tuesday Wednesday Thursday
cousin brother nephew niece

M Can I help you, sir?
N I beg your pardon?
M Can I help you, sir?
N Oh, no ... no, thank you. I'm just
   looking.

madam miss
pardon? sorry?

O Good morning.
P Good morning. I wonder if you
   can help me. I'm trying to find a
   Christmas present, for my father.
O Might I suggest a tie?
P Hmm ... perhaps. Could you
   show me some ties?

wedding/cousin/some towels
birthday/sister/scarf

Q Excuse me ...
R Yes?
Q I wonder if you'd be kind enough
   to get me one of those tins ... on
   the top shelf. I can't reach it.
R Certainly. There you are.
Q Thank you very much indeed.

packet jar box bottle

A TRIP TO SPAIN

Norman Garrard is a trainee sales representative. He's 22, and he works for a company that sells toys. He's going to Spain on business. It's his first business trip abroad, and he's packing his suitcase. He lives with his parents, and his mother is helping him, and fussing.

Mrs Garrard Norman ... haven't you finished packing yet?

Norman No, Mum. But it's all right. There isn't much to do.

Mrs Garrard Well, I'll give you a hand. Oh, there isn't much room left. Is there anywhere to put your toilet bag?

Norman Yes, yes ... it'll go in here. Now, I've got three more shirts to pack ... they'll go on top ... but there's another pair of shoes to get in. I don't know where to put them.

Mrs Garrard Put them down the side. Right. I think we can close it now.

Norman Right. Where's the label?

Mrs Garrard Which label, dear?

Norman The airline label to put on the suitcase. Ah, here it is.

Mrs Garrard Now, have you got the key?

Norman Which key?

Mrs Garrard The key to lock the case, of course.

Norman It's in the lock, Mum. Don't fuss. There's nothing to worry about. There's plenty of time.

Mrs Garrard Have you forgotten anything?

Norman I hope not.

Mrs Garrard And you've got a safe pocket to keep your passport in?

Norman Yes, it's in my inside jacket pocket.

Mrs Garrard Have you got a book to read on the plane?

Norman Yes, it's in my briefcase.

Mrs Garrard And has everything been arranged?

Norman What do you mean?

Mrs Garrard Well, is there someone to meet you at the other end?

Norman Oh yes. The Spanish representative's meeting me at the airport.

Mrs Garrard And you've got somewhere to stay tonight?

Norman I hope so! Now, everything's ready. I'll just have to get some pesetas at the airport. I'll need some small change to tip the porter, but that's all.

Mrs Garrard Well, have a good trip, dear ... and look after yourself.

Norman Thanks, Mum.

Mrs Garrard Oh! I nearly forgot! Here are some sweets to suck on the plane, you know, when it's coming down.

Norman Oh. Mum ... don't worry. I'll be all right, really! I'll see you next week.

Exercise 1

Norman lives in Southampton. He went by taxi to the station, then by train to Woking, then by bus to Heathrow and finally by plane to Madrid. How can you get to your nearest international airport? Which is the best way for you?

Exercise 2

Norman made a list. Look at it.
He remembered to pack his shirts.
He forgot to pack his raincoat.
Write seven sentences.

Exercise 3

Imagine that you have just been on a plane. The airline has lost your suitcase. Think about the clothes you would pack for a one week holiday in London, in Spring. Make a list of the clothes you had in your suitcase.
One dark blue woollen pullover.
One brown leather belt.

Teaching points

▶ Noun + infinitive

▶ Pronoun/adverb + infinitive

Is there anywhere to put it?
There's nothing to worry about.
You've got somewhere to stay tonight ...
There isn't much to do.

▶ *Remember/forget to do ...*

▶ *I hope so/I hope not.*

Expressions

I'll give you a hand.   *Have a good trip!*
Don't fuss!   *Look after yourself!*
There's nothing to worry about!   *by train/taxi/bus/plane*
There's plenty of time.

Key vocabulary

abroad	underclothes	at the other end
label	– – – – –	down the side
sales representative	pack	inside
small change	suck	on top
sweets	tip	
toilet bag	– – – – –	

1 Set the situation. (Books closed.) Ask these questions:
Have you ever been abroad? Ask him/her/me/each other. Ask
'Where?/When?/Why?'
Have you been on holiday recently? Ask 'Where? When?'
Did you take a lot of luggage? Ask 'How much?'
Do you like packing? Ask him/her/me/each other.
Do you usually forget something? Ask 'What?' etc.

2 Introductory text. Ensure the text is masked. Play the cassette.

3 Silent reading.

4 Question and answer.
What's his name?   *What's he doing?*
How old is he?   *Where does he live?*
What does he do?   *Who's helping him?*
Where's he going?

5 Dialogue – Section 1. Ensure the text is masked. Play the cassette.

6 Selective repetition.

7 Drill:
T: *There's another pair of shoes. You must get them in.*
C: *There's another pair of shoes to get in.*

Continue:
There are three more shirts. You must pack them.
There are five pairs of socks. You must put them in.
There's another suit. You must get it in.
There's a toilet bag. You must pack it.
There are two pullovers. You must put them in.

8 Silent reading.

9 Question and answer:
He hasn't finished packing yet, has he?
There isn't much to do, is there?
She offers to help, doesn't she?
What does she say?
There isn't much room left, is there?
How many shirts are there to pack?
Can he get the shoes in? Ask 'Where?'

10 Pair work. (Students read the first part in pairs.)

11 Dialogue – Section 2. Ensure the text is masked. Play the cassette.

12 Selective repetition.

13 Drill:
T: *He's got a key. He can lock the case.*
C: *He's got a key to lock the case.*

Continue:
He's got a label. He can put it on his suitcase.
He's got a safe pocket. He can keep his passport in it.
He's got a book. He can read it on the plane.
He's got a briefcase. He can keep his important papers in it.
He's got a suitcase. He can carry his clothes in it.

14 Silent reading.

15 Question and answer:
Which label is he looking for?
Which key does she ask about?
Where is the key?
Should he worry? Why not?
Has he got a safe pocket to keep his passport in? Where is it?
Has he got anything to read on the plane? Ask 'What?' Where is it?

16 Pair work.

17 Dialogue – Section 3. Ensure the text is masked. Play the cassette.

18 Selective repetition.

19 Drill:
T: *Here are some sweets. You can suck them on the plane.*
C: *Here are some sweets to suck on the plane.*

Continue:
Here's some small change. You can tip the porter.
Here's an umbrella. You can use it if it rains.
Here are some traveller's cheques. You can change them in Spain.
Here's a credit card. You can pay the hotel bill.
Here's a phrase book. You can use it in Spain.

20 Drill:
T: *Is there anyone who can meet you?*
C: *Yes, there's someone to meet me.*

Continue:
Is there anywhere you can stay?
Is there anywhere you can put your toilet bag?
Is there anyone who can translate for you?
Is there anywhere you can change money?
Is there anything you can read on the plane?

21 Silent reading.

22 Question and answer:
There's someone to meet him, isn't there? Ask 'Who?/Where?'
He'll have to change some money, won't he? Ask 'Why?'
Where will he get the pesetas?

23 Pair work.

24 Play the complete cassette.

25 Go through Exercises 1–3 orally. Get students to do them in pairs, and set them for written homework.

Unit 12

Teaching points

▶ Listening for specific information

▶ verb + infinitive

expect	to do
recommend you	
would like	
hope	

Revision points

▶ Polite requests

Would you mind	opening the window?
	completing this card?

Would you like (something) to (drink)?

Key vocabulary

agent	tray	remind
Air Traffic Control	turbulence	– – – – –
belt	– – – – –	complete
clearance	board	enjoyable
Departure Lounge	cruise	fortified
descent	expect	non-
destination	extinguish	pleasant
gate	fasten	rather
landing-card	make sure	slight
miniature	pass	soft
pleasure	permit	sparkling
purpose	proceed	– – – – –
smoking materials	regret	at once
spirits	remain	without delay
tariff		

Note: 'At the airport' and 'In flight' are listening exercises. A complete text of the material in these sections appears in 13.2/.4/.7 for teachers who are not using the cassette.

1 At the airport. Focus attention on the 'Flight departures information'. Set the situation. Silent reading of the introductory text. Ask *Where is he? What's he just done?*

2 Focus attention on the example. Play the first announcement. Text:
1) *'This is the last call for the twelve o'clock British Airways Flight BA 412 to Amsterdam. Would passengers for this flight please proceed without delay to Gate 17.'*

3 Play the other five announcements. On the first listening students should write in the time and destination. (This could be two separate activities with a slower class.) On the second listening, the destination should be added. Teach the idea of noting in abbreviations when listening, e.g. 'Am' for Amsterdam. On the third listening students should try and fill the information column. For complete text see 13.4.

4
2) *'Scandinavian Airlines announce the departure of the 12.05 flight SK 526 to Stockholm. This flight is now boarding at Gate 8.'*
3) *'Would passengers for the 12.10 Iberia flight IB 341 to Madrid please go at once to Gate 16 where this flight is now boarding.'*
4) *'Alitalia regret to announce that their 12.15 flight AZ 281 to Rome will be delayed for approximately 30 minutes.'*
5) *'Olympic Airways announce the departure of the 12.30 flight OA 260 to Athens. Would passengers on this flight please proceed to Gate 19.'*
6) *'This is a call for Mr Gaston Meyer. Would Mr Gaston Meyer travelling on the 12.45 Sabena flight SN 604 to Brussels report to the airport information desk, please.'*

5 Check through by playing the cassette again, pausing to elicit the information to fill the columns. Note 'Now Boarding' and 'Delay' as the authentic way to fill the column. Point out that they have been listening for specific information and that other items are irrelevant.

6 In-flight announcements. Play each one separately, again limiting the listening task in each playing. (This will depend on the performance in the previous exercise.) A full text follows in 13.7.

7
1) *'Good afternoon, ladies and gentlemen. Captain Perez and his crew welcome you aboard Iberia flight IB 341 to Madrid. I am sorry to announce a slight delay. We are still waiting for clearance from Air Traffic Control. The delay won't be too long and we hope to arrive in Madrid on time.'*
2) *'This is your captain speaking. We are now passing over the English coast. Our Boeing 727 is cruising at a height of 30,000 feet and our speed is approximately 560 miles per hour. The temperature in Madrid is 18°C and it is a clear and sunny day. We expect to pass through some slight turbulence and would recommend passengers to remain in their seats and keep their belts fastened.'*
3) *'We are now beginning our descent to Madrid. Would passengers please make sure that their seat belts are fastened and extinguish all smoking materials. We would like to remind passengers that smoking is not permitted until you are in the airport building.'*
4) *'We hope you have had a pleasant and enjoyable flight. We would like to thank you for travelling on Iberia, and we hope to see you again soon. Would passengers please remain seated until the plane has come to a complete stop and the doors have been opened.'*

8 'Lunch on the plane'. Focus attention on the picture. Ensure the text is masked. Play the cassette.

9 Listen and repeat.

10 Silent reading.

11 Pair work. Students use the 'In Flight Tariff' to make up other conversations.

12 'Landing-cards'. Follow the same procedure, 13.8 – 13.11.

13 Focus attention on the 'Landing-card'. Students ask questions in pairs to complete a landing card for each other. Check through the questions with one student.

14 'Passport control'. Follow the same procedure 13.8 – 13.11.

15 Transfer: (*Ask me/him/her/each other.*)
Do you like flying?
Have you ever flown? Ask 'When?/Where to?/Why?/Which airline?'
Are you afraid of flying?
Did you have a meal? What was it like?
Did you have to complete a landing-card?
Could you understand the announcements?
What's the national airline of your country?
Did you buy anything on the plane?' Ask 'What?'
Explain Duty Free Goods and Allowances. *What are the allowances for your country?*

FLYING TO SPAIN

At the airport

Norman is at Heathrow Airport. He's checked in. He's been through Passport Control and he's in the Departure Lounge. Listen to the announcements. Look at the chart, look at the example, and complete the chart in the same way.

FLIGHT DEPARTURES INFORMATION TIME NOW 11.45				
Carrier	Flight	Time	Destination	Information
British Airways	BA 412	12.00	Amsterdam	Last call Gate 17
S.A.S.				
Iberia				
Alitalia				
Olympic Airways				
Sabena				

In flight

Norman is now on the plane. Listen to the four announcements, and answer these questions.

1 What's the pilot's name?
  How long will the delay be?
  When will they arrive in Madrid?
  What are they waiting for?
2 Where is the plane?
  What kind is it?
  How high is it?
  How fast is it going?
  How hot is it in Madrid?
  What's the weather like?
  Why should the passengers remain in their seats?
3 What's the plane beginning to do?
  What two things should the passengers do?
  When can they start smoking again?
4 What should the passengers do?
  When can they stand up?

EXCUSE ME, YOUNG MAN... WOULD YOU MIND OPENING THE WINDOW? IT'S RATHER HOT IN HERE.

Lunch on the plane

Steward Here's your tray, sir.
Norman Oh, thank you.
Steward Would you like something to drink?
Norman Er ... yes, please. Some red wine.
Steward That's 100 pesetas.
Norman Thanks. Can I pay in British money?
Steward Of course. You needn't pay now, I'll collect it later.

Landing-cards

Steward Spanish national or non-Spanish, sir?
Norman Er ... I'm British.
Steward Would you mind completing this landing card, sir?
Norman Right. Thank you.

Landing-card

Family name...... GARRARD
Forename(s) ...... NORMAN IAN
Father's name ... DUNCAN ALISTAIR
Place of birth... WINCHESTER
Nationality ...... BRITISH
Passport no N1054372
Permanent address... 37 CUNARD AVENUE, SOUTHAMPTON, ENGLAND.
Point of departure... LONDON (HEATHROW)
Destination ...... MADRID
Date 14. 4. 83 Signature N. I. Garrard

Passport control

Official Passport, please. Thank you. Where have you come from, sir?
Norman London.
Official And what's the purpose of your visit ... business or pleasure?
Norman Business.
Official Fine ... and how long will you be staying here?
Norman Just for five days.
Official Thank you, Mr Garrard. I hope you enjoy your visit.

MONEY

Money is used for buying or selling goods, for measuring value and for storing wealth. Almost every society now has a money economy based on coins and paper notes of one kind or another. However, this has not always been true. In primitive societies a system of barter was used. Barter was a system of direct exchange of goods. Somebody could exchange a sheep, for example, for anything in the market-place that they considered to be of equal value. Barter, however, was a very unsatisfactory system because people's precise needs seldom coincided. People needed a more practical system of exchange, and various money systems developed based on goods which the members of a society recognized as having value. Cattle, grain, teeth, shells, feathers, skulls, salt, elephant tusks and tobacco have all been used. Precious metals gradually took over because, when made into coins, they were portable, durable, recognizable and divisible into larger and smaller units of value.

A coin is a piece of metal, usually disc-shaped, which bears lettering, designs or numbers showing its value. Until the eighteenth and nineteenth centuries coins were given monetary worth based on the exact amount of metal contained in them, but most modern coins are based on face value, the value that governments choose to give them, irrespective of the actual metal content. Coins have been made of gold (Au), silver (Ag), copper (Cu), aluminium (Al), nickel (Ni), lead (Pb), zinc (Zn), plastic, and in China even from pressed tea leaves. Most governments now issue paper money in the form of notes, which are really 'promises to pay'. Paper money is obviously easier to handle and much more convenient in the modern world. Cheques, bankers' cards, and credit cards are being used increasingly and it is possible to imagine a world where 'money' in the form of coins and paper currency will no longer be used. Even today, in the United States, many places – especially filling stations – will not accept cash at night for security reasons.

Exercise 1
Find expressions which mean:
1 A place to buy petrol.
2 A place where goods are bought and sold.
3 The period between 1801 and 1900.
4 The bony structure of the head.
5 Round and flat in shape.
6 An exchange of goods for other goods.

Exercise 2
Find words which mean:
1 Can be divided.
2 Lasts a long time.
3 Can be carried.
4 Can be recognized.

Exercise 3
Put these words in the correct places in the sentences below:
coins/cash/currency/money.
1 The ... of Japan is the yen.
2 She has got a lot of ... in her bank account.
3 It costs £10 if you're paying .... It'll be more if you pay by cheque.
4 Can you change this pound note into ... for the coffee machine?

Exercise 4
Money is used for buying goods means: You can buy goods with it. Write similar sentences which mean:
1 You can measure value with it.
2 You can store wealth with it.
3 You can sell things for it.

Exercise 5
Money is used for buying and selling goods.
People use money for buying and selling goods.
Change these sentences in the same way.
1 A system of barter was used.
2 Cattle, grain and tobacco have all been used.
3 Paper currency will no longer be used.
4 Cheques, bankers' cards and credit cards are being used.

Exercise 6
Somebody could exchange a sheep.
A sheep could be exchanged.
Change these sentences in the same way.
1 People needed a more practical system.
2 Most governments now issue paper money in the form of notes.
3 Filling stations will not accept cash at night.

Exercise 7
Money *is used for buying things.*
Shampoo *is used for washing your hair.*
Make sentences with: knife/pen/key/camera/suitcase/saucepan/toothpaste/detergent/wallet/hair-dryer.

Exercise 8
A place where you can fill your petrol tank is a *filling station.*
Complete these sentences.
1 A special room where you can wait is a ....
2 A pill which helps you to sleep is a ....
3 A licence which allows you to drive is a ....
4 A glove which boxers wear is a ....
5 Oil you can cook with is ....
6 A pool where you can swim is a ....
7 Special liquid you can wash up with is ....
8 A boat with sails is a ....

Teaching points

▶ Reading comprehension from a formal text

▶ Vocabulary expansion, and deducing meaning

▶ It | is | used for (doing) (something).
They | are | [juzd]

▶ filling station, cooking oil, waiting room, sleeping pill

▶ Revision of active/passive transformations

Key vocabulary

aluminium	sailing boat	bony
amount	skull	convenient
banker's card	society	direct
barter	structure	disc shaped
boxing-glove	system	divisible
cattle	tea leaves	durable
coin	tusk	exact
contempt	value	flat
copper	washing-up liquid	gradually
credit card	wealth	increasingly
currency	zinc	irrespective
design	– – – – –	monetary
economy	base on	obviously
face value	bear	portable
feather	coincide	practical
filling stations	consider	precious
goods	contain	precise
grain	develop	pressed
lead	divide	primitive
lettering	handle	recognizable
market-place	imagine	security
member	issue	seldom
nickel	recognize	unsatisfactory
note	stare	various
period	take over	
reason	– – – – –	
shell	actual	

1 Set the situation. Silent reading. Students should be told to read it for at least five minutes, and to read to the end before marking difficult words. Do not answer questions on vocabulary at this stage.

2 Exercise 1. Students do this silently. This will make them skim the text several times to find the words. They should mark them. Check through the answers, and explain any difficulties with these items.

3 Exercise 2. Follow the same procedure.

4 Exercise 3. Follow the same procedure.

5 Exercise 4. Follow the same procedure.

6 Exercise 5. Follow the same procedure.

7 Exercise 6. Follow the same procedure.

8 The six exercises should have answered several of the vocabulary problems. Students should now read the first paragraph again.

9 Question and answer:
What is money used for?
What is a money economy usually based on?
What is a barter system?
Why was the barter system unsatisfactory?
What kinds of things did people use before they used coins and notes?
Why did people begin to use coins?

10 Silent reading. The second paragraph.

11 Question and answer:
What is a coin?
What have coins been made from?
What is the difference between modern coins and the coins of two hundred years ago?
(Note: A British gold half-sovereign has a face value of 50p. A sovereign is a pound but was sold by the Royal Mint (a government department) for £65.00 in 1980.)
Why do governments issue paper money?
What do people often use in place of notes and coins?
Why don't filling stations in the United States accept cash at night?
Can you imagine a world without money?

12 Check through any remaining vocabulary problems, but stress that the aim is comprehension rather than detailed word study.

13 Go through Exercise 7 and Exercise 8. Ask students to think of any other examples (like 'filling station' and 'cooking oil').

14 Transfer (*Ask him/her/me/each other.*):
Have you ever bartered with somebody for something?
(Note: Children and people in agricultural communities often barter with each other.)
What's the currency in your country? What about Britain/The United States?/France?/Germany? etc. (Note: British currency is 'the pound sterling'.)
What are the coins made of in your country?
Have you got any gold coins/silver coins?
Do you collect coins? Why?
Have you got a bank account?/cheque book?/banker's card?/credit card? Why? When do you use them?

Teaching points

▶ Listening for specific information

Revision points

▶ Guided discussion on topics associated with money

▶ Simple present, present perfect and simple past questions

Expressions

See the six 'sayings' in the student's book.
In the listening passage:
How much do you want for this plate?
I'm only asking £15 for it.
It's worth every penny!
It's a real bargain!
You must be joking!

Key vocabulary

antique	*love* (friendly	*stallholder*
borrower	expression)	– – – – –
budget	*mattress*	*owe*
debt	*misery*	*pick* (a pocket)
deposit	*money-box*	– – – – –
discount	*offer*	*annual*
expenditure	*overdraft*	*brass*
expenses	*pillow*	*final*
gambling	*quid*	*illegal*
hire purchase	*rate*	*legal*
income	*record*	*second-hand*
interest	*receipt*	*Victorian*
lender	*safe*	
lottery	*stall*	

1 Listening: 'Bargaining'. Focus attention on the picture. Set the situation. Silent reading of introductory passage.

2 Play the cassette once.

3 Focus attention on the questions. Play the cassette again. Students note the answers. (Play again if necessary.)

4 Check through the answers, by playing the cassette with pauses. A full text appears in the Appendix, and below (15.5).

5 'Bargaining' – text of listening passage:
Lucy *Excuse me.*
Stallholder *Yes, miss?*
Lucy *How much do you want for this plate?*
Stallholder *Let me see. Oh, yes ... that's a lovely example of Victorian brass. It's worth twenty quid.*
Lucy *Twenty pounds! Oh, that's too much for me. It's a pity. It's really nice.*
Stallholder *Ah, I said it's worth twenty quid. I'm only asking fifteen for it.*
Lucy *Fifteen pounds?*
Stallholder *Yes. It's a real bargain.*
Lucy *Oh, I'm sure it is ... but I can't afford that!*
Stallholder *Well, look ... just for you I'll make it fourteen quid. I can't go any lower than that.*
Lucy *I'll give you ten.*
Stallholder *Ten! Come on, love. You must be joking! I paid more than that for it myself. Fourteen. It's worth every penny.*
Lucy *Well, perhaps I could give you eleven.*
Stallholder *Thirteen. That's my final offer.*
Lucy *Twelve.*
Stallholder *Twelve fifty.*
Lucy *All right, twelve fifty.*
Stallholder *There you are, love. You've got a real bargain there.*
Lucy *Yes, thank you very much.*

6 'Neither a borrower ...'. (Polonius' advice to his son in *Hamlet*.) Ask students what they think it means. Ask the questions in the student's book (plus *Ask him/her/me.*) to individuals. Students ask each other the questions in pairs.

7 'Look after the pennies ...'. Follow the same procedure.

8 'Live now ...'. Follow the same procedure.

9 'Annual income ...'. Follow the same procedure.
Note: 'Nineteen nineteen six' means '19 pounds 19 shillings and sixpence' (£19.19s.6d); 'Twenty pounds ought and six' means '20 pounds no shillings and sixpence' (£20.0s.6d). 'Ought' is a slang form for expressing 'nought', though we would say 'no shillings' in modern English. Until 1971 the pound was divided into 20 shillings and each shilling into 12 old pence. A shilling became '5p' in decimal money, and 2.4 old pennies became '1p' or 'one new penny'.

10 'A fool ...'. Follow the same procedure.

11 'The customer ...'. Follow the same procedure.

MONEY, MONEY, MONEY

Bargaining

Lucy is in the Portobello Road street market in London. She's looking at an antique stall, and she's just seen a brass plate. She collects brass ornaments and she's interested in buying it. Listen to her conversation with the stall-holder, and answer these questions.

1 How much does he say it's worth?
2 How much is he asking for it?
3 What does 'quid' mean?
4 He suggests four different prices. Write them down.
5 She makes four offers. Write them down.

Some English sayings about money:

Neither a borrower nor a lender be.

From 'Hamlet' by William Shakespeare.

Have you ever borrowed money from anyone?
Who from? How much?

Have you ever lent money to anyone? Who to? How much?

Are you in debt at the moment? (i.e. Do you owe anyone any money?)

Does anyone owe you any money? Who? How much?

Look after the pennies, and the pounds will look after themselves.

Do you save money? Are you saving for anything at the moment? What?

Do you keep your money a in the bank? b in a safe? c in a money-box? d under the bed?

Have you got a bank account? Do you get any interest? What's the rate of interest? If you had a bank overdraft, how much interest would you have to pay?

Live now – pay later.

Have you bought anything on hire purchase? What? Did you pay a deposit? Do you think it's a good idea?

Have you got a credit card? Which one? (Visa? American Express? Diner's Club? Access?)

When you pay cash, do you ask for a discount? Do you usually get it?

Annual income twenty pounds, annual expenditure nineteen nineteen and six, result happiness. Annual income twenty pounds, annual expenditure twenty pounds ought and six, result misery.

Mr Micawber from 'David Copperfield' by Charles Dickens.

Do you spend more than you earn, or less than you earn?

Do you have a budget for your money?

Do you keep a record of your expenses?

A fool and his money are soon parted.

Where do you keep your money?
a in a purse b in a wallet c in a handbag d in a pocket

If you keep it in a pocket, which pocket do you keep it in?
a inside jacket-pocket
b back trouser-pocket
c side trouser-pocket
d top front jacket-pocket

Have you ever had your pocket picked?

When you stay in a hotel, do you hide your money? Where?
a in your suitcase b under the mattress c in the pillow d in a book e somewhere else

Is gambling legal or illegal in your country? Do people bet? What do they bet on?
a cards b horses c dogs d football e boxing f national lottery e something else

The customer is always right.

Have you bought anything this week? What?

What did it cost? Was it worth it?

Was it new or second-hand?

Was it a bargain? Did you get a receipt?

INSIDE STORY

"NEWS" REPORTER MISSING IN MANDANGA

Julian Snow, the 'Daily News' war correspondent, who is covering the civil war in Mandanga, has been reported missing.

He was last seen yesterday morning driving his Land Rover near the front line. The vehicle was found yesterday evening, but there was no sign of him. It is possible that he was ambushed and captured by guerilla forces. Snow has been a war correspondent for many years and has covered a number of conflicts, including Vietnam, Kampuchea, Zimbabwe and the Middle East.

STOP PRESS

JULIAN SNOW FREE War correspondent alive and well. Julian Snow walked into a government forces camp this morning, after spending two weeks with MLF (Mandanga Liberation Front) guerrillas. His exclusive story will appear in tomorrow's 'Daily News'.

IBC NEWS

This is IBC News. Julian Snow, the missing 'Daily News' reporter, was interviewed this morning by Dominic Beale of IBC News in Mandanga.

Beale Julian, can you tell us how you were captured in the first place?

Snow Well, I was on my way to visit a village near the front line. I came round a bend in the road and there was a tree lying across the road. I only just managed to stop in time! Suddenly, armed men appeared on all sides!

Beale What did you do?

Snow What would you do? I just sat there with my hands in the air! Anyway, they made me get out of the Land Rover, and made me lie on the ground ... I thought 'This is it! They're going to shoot me!' I started saying my prayers!

Beale What happened next?

Snow Well, they searched me. Of course, I didn't have any weapons, just a camera. It's funny, they let me keep it. Then they tied my hands together and blindfolded me. Then they made me get in the back of a truck and lie under some sacks. I've no idea where they took me, except that it was quite a large training camp. I was there for ten days.

Beale Were you treated well?

Snow Yes, I suppose I was. They let me walk about the camp and they let me take photographs, but they wouldn't let me photograph any faces. I was able to interview some of the leaders.

Beale How did you escape?

Snow I didn't! They put me back in the truck, blindfolded me again, drove for a few hours, then made me get out, pointed me in the direction of town and let me go!

Beale And what exactly did the guerrilla leaders say about the situation?

Snow Ah! Well, if you want to know that, you'll have to buy tomorrow's 'Daily News' ...

Exclusive!

JULIAN SNOW's inside story! In today's issue, Julian Snow tells his exclusive story. He was captured by Mandangan guerrillas two weeks ago. They forced him to go with them to their camp. However they allowed him to keep his camera, and to interview guerrilla leaders. Turn to page two for the story of his captivity!

Exercise
When I was younger, my parents made me go to bed early.
When I was younger, my parents didn't let me go out in the evenings.
Write true sentences about when you were younger.

Teaching points

▶ Infinitive structures with and without *to*

force	
allow	*someone to do something*

make	
let	*someone do something*

▶ -ing form

He was seen. He was driving his Land Rover.
He was seen driving his Land Rover.

Expressions

on my way
no sign of him
in the first place

Key vocabulary

bend	guerrilla	force
camp	prayers	point
captivity	sack	treat
civil war	vehicle	– – – – – –
conflict	weapon	alive
(war) correspondent	– – – – –	armed
forces	ambush	exclusive
front line (line	blindfold	missing
between two	capture	
armies)	cover	

1 'News reporter missing . . .'. Set the situation. Students read silently.

2 Question and answer:
What does Julian Snow do? Where is he?
Where's Mandanga? (to elicit: *I don't know where it is!*)
Is he missing? How do we know?
When was he last seen?
What was he doing?
Where was he?
The vehicle's been found, hasn't it? Ask 'When?'
Did he leave anything behind?
What has happened to him, perhaps?
How long has he been a war correspondent?
He's travelled a lot, hasn't he?
Ask 'Which countries?'

3 Drill:
T: *He was seen. He was driving his Land Rover.*
C: *He was seen driving his Land Rover.*

Continue:
He was in Mandanga. He was covering the civil war.
He left yesterday. He was wearing a safari suit.
They saw him. He was carrying a camera.
The vehicle was found. It was standing in the road.

4 'Julian Snow free . . .'. Students read silently.

5 Question and answer:
When did he come back?
How long had he been missing?
Where had he been?
Will you be able to find the story in other papers?
Why not? (to elicit *Because it's an exclusive story.*)

6 'IBC News' (dialogue). Focus attention on the picture. Ensure the text is masked. Play the cassette.

7 Selective repetition. (Play the cassette, pausing to repeat expressions with 'make someone do' and 'let someone do'.)

8 Drill:
T: *They/him/Land Rover.*
C: *They made him get out of the Land Rover.*

Continue:
The guerrillas/Julian/on the ground.
They/him/back of the truck.
They/Julian/under some sacks.
The guerrillas/him/not to photograph any faces.

9 Drill: Continue:
T: *they*   *him*
T: *They let me go.*   *we*
T: *him*   *her*
T: *They let him go.* *he*
T: *They let me go. Repeat!* *us*
C: *They let me go.*   *she*

10 Silent reading.

11 Pair work. (Students read the dialogue in pairs.)

12 Question and answer:
How was he captured?
What did they make him do?
What did they let him do in the camp?
What wouldn't they let him do?
Where did they let him go?
Why wouldn't he be able to find his way back to the camp?

13 'Exclusive! Julian Snow's inside story!' Students read silently.

14 Question and answer:
When was Julian captured?
What did the guerrillas force him to do?
What did they allow him to do?
Who did he interview?

15 Drill:
T: *They made him go with them.*
C: *They forced him to go with them.*
T: *They let him keep his camera.*
C: *They allowed him to keep his camera.*

Continue:
They made him get out of the Land Rover.
They made him lie on the ground.
They made him lie under some sacks.
They let him walk about the camp.
They let him take photographs.
They let him go.

16 Exercise. Go through in class. Set for homework.

17 Transfer:
T: *Robert Gibbs is in prison.*
What do you think they make him do every day? Ask each other.
What won't they let him do? Ask each other.
Tommy Biggs is a soldier. He's doing military service.
What do you think they make him do every day?
What won't they let him do? Ask each other.
If you were the Prime Minister, what would you make people do?
What wouldn't you let them do?

Teaching points

▶ Stating preferences

I like it ... I'd like to do it.
Which do you like best?

I prefer it ...   *I'd prefer to do it.*
Which do you prefer?   *Which would you prefer to do?*

I'd rather do it ... I'd rather not do it.
I'd much rather do it.
Which would you rather do?

I like both.

I don't | *like* | *either* | *of them.*
        | *fancy* | *any* |

There isn't much choice.
I can't make up my mind.

Expressions

See above, plus:
What are you doing tomorrow night?
It's not worth it.

Key vocabulary

bust	preference	beige
choice	reggae	full
collar	review	huge
cords	selection	maroon
custard	steak and kidney pie	navy blue
Levi and Wrangler	subtitle	pale
(famous makers of	– – – – –	pure
jeans and cord	cut out	unbeatable
trousers)	state	– – – – –
Lunchtime special	– – – – –	in stock
plaice	alternative	
post and packaging	available	

1 Dialogue 1 (A and B). Focus attention on the picture and 'What's on in London'. Ensure the text is masked. Set the situation. Play the cassette.

2 Listen and repeat.

3 Silent reading.

4 Pair work. (Substituting other items from 'What's on in London' first, then free substitution of other items.)

5 Act out the conversation with one or two individuals, playing both parts and substituting items.

6 Transfer (+ *Ask him/her/me/each other.*):
Revise likes and dislikes.
Do you like jazz/pop/rock/classical music/opera/reggae/folk?
Which is your favourite group/singer/musician/composer?
Have you ever seen him/her/them? Have you been to a concert?
What was it like? If you haven't, would you like to?

7 Pair work. Students draw up a list in pairs of their favourite singer/pop group/classical piece/composer (pop or classical) by asking *Which group do you like best?* etc. Ask students about their partners' choices by alternately asking *What's his favourite group?/Which singer does she like best?* Then ask *Would you like to see that group/that singer?*

8 Dialogue 2 (C and D). Follow the procedure 17.1–17.5.

9 Transfer (+ *Ask him/her/me/each other.*):
Look at the list of colours. Which do you prefer? Do you prefer dark colours or light colours? Which colour do you like best? (N.B. This question doesn't relate to the list.)
Have you got any cords? What colour are they?
Which do you prefer: cords or jeans? skirts or trousers?
Do you like shopping for clothes?
Do you like shopping with a friend? Why?
Which do you prefer: tea or coffee? cassettes or records? wine or beer? beef or lamb? digital watches or ordinary watches? Ask each other. (Encourage them to add other preferences.)
What would you prefer to do: listen to a record or go to a concert? visit England or visit the USA? watch a film on TV or at the cinema? meet a pop star or meet a politician? eat at home or in a restaurant? etc.
Ask each other. (Encourage them to add other preferences.)

10 Dialogue 3 (E and F). Follow the procedure 17.1–17.5.

11 Transfer (+ *Ask him/her/me/each other.*):
Look at the cinema programmes. Which film would you rather see? Would you rather see 'War in Space' or 'A Moment of Peace'? etc.
Would you rather see (a current film) or (another current film)?
Would you rather live in the town or in the country?
Would you rather have a holiday on the beach or in the mountains?
Would you rather be a student or a teacher? Ask 'Why?'

12 Pair work.
You both have to go and live in another country. Which would you rather live in: a hot, wet country? a hot, dry country? a cold, wet country? a cold, dry country? Why?

13 Request the students to do fairly undesirable things, to elicit *I'd rather not*. (*Can you lend me £20? Would you go and clean my car?* etc.)

14 Dialogue 4 (G and H). Follow the procedure 17.1–17.5.

15 Transfer. Refer to the menu. Ask *What do you fancy?* to elicit *I can't make up my mind/There isn't much choice.* Keep substituting new pairs of foods, e.g. *What do you want: spaghetti bolognese or pizza? Quickly!* etc. Encourage students to use *I don't want either of them at the moment.* Then list 3 food items to elicit *I don't want any of them at the moment.* (e.g. *What do you want: steak, chicken or lamb?*)

16 'Mail order advertisement'. Silent reading. Check through vocabulary, then ask students to complete the form in pairs by asking questions. Demonstrate:
What's your name/address?
Do you want shirts or blouses?
How many do you want?
How much are you going to send?
What size are you?
Which colour do you prefer?
What's your second choice?
What's your third choice?

Unit 17

PREFERENCES

A What are you doing tomorrow night?
B Nothing. Why?
A Well, do you like jazz?
B Yes, I do, very much.
A Which do you like best? Modern or traditional?
B I like both, really.
A There's a 'Weather Report' concert at the Hammersmith Odeon. Would you like to come?
B Oh, yes! They're my favourite group.

C Lisa, look over here. They've got a very good selection of Levi cords.
D Oh, yes! And they've got my size, too.
C But only in navy blue and black. Which do you prefer?
D Hmm. I don't like either of them very much. I really wanted green.
C They haven't got green in your size. Go on, try a pair on.
D No, no. I'd prefer to look somewhere else.

E Have you decided yet? What do you want to see?
F 'A Moment of Peace' is on at the Continental. I'd like to see that.
E Would you really? Oh, I'd rather see 'War in Space'.
F Oh, no! The reviews were terrible.
E I know, but it sounds fun. 'A Moment of Peace' is in French, and I'd rather not have to read subtitles.
F Then how about 'California Sunset'?
E I'd rather not ... I can't stand Steve Newman.
F Well, you choose.
E I don't fancy any of them. I'd much rather stay in and watch TV!

G What do you fancy?
H I don't know. There isn't much choice, is there?
G No, there isn't, really. What would you rather have? Steak and kidney or plaice?
H I can't make up my mind. I'd rather have a hamburger.
G We can ask for the full menu, if you like.
H No, it's not worth it. I'll have the plaice.

What's on in London

Jazz

Modern Jazz
★ **Weather Report** Hammersmith Odeon £2.50–£4

Traditional Jazz
★ **New Orleans Jazz Band** 'The Bull' Barnes 75p

Pop

Rock
★ **Ian Dury and the Blockheads** Rainbow Theatre £3–£6

Reggae
★ **Burning Spear** Strand Lyceum £2.50–£4.50

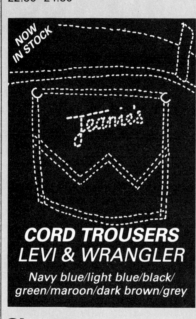

CORD TROUSERS LEVI & WRANGLER
Navy blue/light blue/black/ green/maroon/dark brown/grey

Cinema

ⒶⒷⒸ ①&②
❶ WAR IN SPACE (A) 2.00/5.15/8.15
❷ CIRCUS OF HORROR (X) 1.00/4.30/8.00

★ **Gaumont**
'California Sunset' (X) Starring Steve Newman 3.10, 5.50, 8.30

★ **Continental**
'A Moment of Peace' (U) (Jean le Brun) 1.10, 3.30, 6.00, 8.35

★ **Classic**
Humphrey Bogart in 'Casablanca' (A) 2.15, 4.15, 6.15, 8.15

★ **Odeon**
'Juke Box – 1958' (AA) Separate programmes 2.45, 5.30, 8.20

37

Unit 17

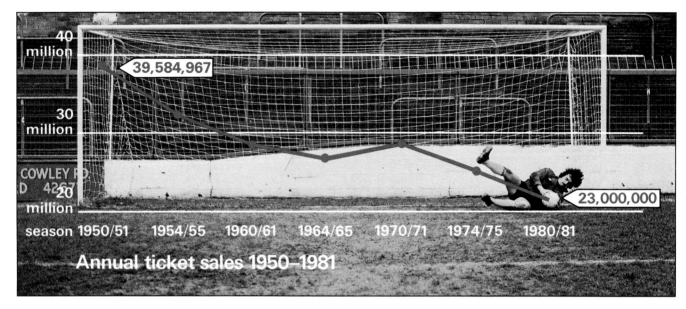

Annual ticket sales 1950–1981

40 million	39,584,967					
30 million						
20 million						23,000,000
season 1950/51	1954/55	1960/61	1964/65	1970/71	1974/75	1980/81

WHERE HAVE ALL THE FANS GONE?

'Good evening and welcome to the 'Michael Parkhurst Talkabout'. In tonight's 'Talkabout' we're looking at the problem of soccer's missing millions. Since 1950 attendance at football matches has fallen by nearly fifty per cent. Many clubs are in financial trouble, and tonight we hope to identify the major causes and discuss some possible solutions.

First of all, we'll hear from one of soccer's lost millions, Mr Bert Woods from London, who used to be a regular Chelsea supporter.'

'I stopped going five or six years ago. I'd rather stay at home and watch it on telly. You get a better view and I like the action replays. I'm too afraid to go now, really! All this violence, you know. When I was a lad there was the occasional fight on the terraces, but nothing like you see these days – whole gangs of teenagers who aren't interested in football. Somebody ought to do something about it! These kids aren't real fans, they just come looking for trouble. The police ought to sort out the real fans from the troublemakers. You know, I always used to go with my dad, but I wouldn't take my kids. There's too much foul language. And I don't only blame the kids. There ought to be more discipline at home and in schools.'

'Thank you, Mr Woods. Let's go over to Brian Huff, the manager of Eastfield United, one of our most successful clubs. Brian.'

'I sympathize with Mr Woods, and there are plenty of people like him. Anyway, we'd better do something about it, or we'll all go broke! The clubs and players must share the blame. Football's big business, and it's very competitive. Winning has become the most important thing. There's too much violence on the field. Referees have to get tougher with players. They should send off players for deliberate fouls. The other problem is television. There's too much football on TV, and they only show the most exciting parts, goals, fouls and violence. People are bored when they see the real game. Anyway the clubs started talking about these problems ten years ago, and nothing's been done. We'd better not spend another ten years talking. We'd better do something, and do it soon!'

'Our next guest is a young fan. Kevin Dolan, a Manchester United supporter, who is sixteen years old. What do you think, Kevin?'

'Well I'm not one of soccer's missing millions. I never miss a match. I've travelled all over the country with United and I've never been in trouble. I blame the media for most of this violence. They only show young people when they're doing something wrong. They ought not to give so much publicity to trouble-makers. It only encourages the others, doesn't it? The violence always starts when there's a TV camera near. If they banned alcohol from football grounds, there'd be much less trouble.'

'Thank you, Kevin. Our last speaker is Jimmy MacTavish, the ex-Scotland striker who has just returned from the United States after spending two years with Miami Galaxy. Well, Jimmy. What ought we to do?'

'I agree with a lot of what's been said, Michael, but hadn't we better look at some solutions? I've been playing in the States for the last two seasons and I haven't seen any violence over there. A football match is a day out for the family. More than half the supporters are women and children, and there are much better facilities. Everybody gets a comfortable seat. There are good restaurants and there's entertainment before and after the game, and at half-time. Football stadiums are old, cold and dirty over here. We'd better take a good look at American soccer. I think we've got a lot to learn! Entertainment is what football is all about and we'd better not forget it!'

Exercise
Find words which mean:
1 television or TV
2 forbidden
3 not accidental
4 stadium
5 boy
6 young person or child
7 disgusting
8 without money
9 an action against the rules
10 share the same feelings

Unit 18

Teaching points

▶ Advisability and desirability

They ought to do it. / They ought not to do it.
What ought they to do?

$$We \left| \begin{array}{l} 'd \\ had \end{array} \right| \begin{array}{l} better \\ better\ not \end{array} \right| do\ it.\ Hadn't\ we\ better\ do\ it?$$

▶ *to spend time doing something*

▶ *We've got a lot to learn.*

▶ *Winning has become the most important thing.*

Key vocabulary

action replay	gang	encourage
attendance	a good look	go broke
cause	publicity	identify
discipline	referee	send off
a day out	soccer	share
facilities	solution	sort out
fan	striker	sympathize
field	telly (TV)	– – – – –
football ground	terrace	competitive
football league	view	deliberate
football season	violence	ex-
foul (in football)	– – – – –	financial
foul language (foul	ban	major
= obscene)	blame	regular

1 Focus on the graph. Ask *What do you learn from it? Ask each other.*

2 Introductory text. Ensure it is masked. Play the cassette.

3 Silent reading.

4 Question and answer:
What's the name of the programme?
What's it about?
How much has attendance fallen?
What do they hope to do?
What are they going to discuss?

5 Bert Woods. Ensure the text is masked. Set this listening task:
Note three reasons why he doesn't go to football matches.
Play the cassette (twice if necessary).

6 Silent reading.

7 Question and answer:
Which club did he use to support?
When did he stop supporting them?
What would he rather do? Ask 'Why?'
Why is he afraid to go now?
Was there any football violence when he was young?
Is it worse now, or is it better? Ask 'Why?'
Somebody ought to do something about it, oughtn't they?
Why aren't the gangs of teenagers real fans?
What ought the police to do?
Who did he use to go with?
Would he take his children now? Why not? Who does he blame?
Where does he think there ought to be more discipline?

8 Free reproduction.

9 Transfer:
Would you rather watch football on television? Why/Why not?
Would you rather not watch football at all?
Have you been to a football match? Was there any violence?
Is it a problem in your country?
Why does it happen?
Did you hear any foul language?
Does foul language annoy you?
What ought they to do about football violence?

10 Brian Huff. Ensure the text is masked. Listening task:
Television programmes focus on three exciting parts of football. What are they?
Play the cassette.

11 Silent reading.

12 Question and answer:
Who must share the blame?
What's become the most important thing in football?
What ought referees to do?
Why are people bored when they see the real game?
How long have the clubs been discussing the problems?
What had they better not do? What had they better do?
When had they better do it?

13 Free reproduction.

14 Transfer:
Do you think there's too much football/sport on TV?
Do you think football/sport has become too competitive?
What's the most important thing for you about a sport?
Is it playing? winning? taking exercise? meeting people? something else?
Ask each other.
Do you think referees are too weak or too tough?
Do you like seeing fouls and violence?
Does it make you want to be violent?
Do you think referees ought to send players off for deliberate fouls?

15 Kevin Dolan. Ensure the text is masked. Listening tasks:
He blames three things. What are they?
Play the cassette.

16 Silent reading.

17 Question and answer/transfer:
What ought newspapers and television not to do? Why?
Why ought they to ban alcohol from football grounds?
What do you think?
Is it true in your country?
Are newspapers and TV unfair to young people?
Do they concentrate on the bad things about young people?
Give examples.

18 Jimmy MacTavish. Ensure the text is masked. Listening tasks:
Write down three good things about football in the USA.
Play the cassette.

19 Silent reading.

20 Question and answer/transfer:
Is football in your country more like Britain or the USA?
Where would you rather watch football?
Do women go to football matches in your country?
Would you take children to a game in your country?
Is attendance falling in your country? Ask 'Why/Why not?'
What would you do to improve attendance?

21 Set the exercise in class or for homework.

22 Written phase. (See Teaching points.)

23 Possible role-play.
a) Students role-play the four guests with a chairman and discuss the issues.
b) Set up a panel of four, plus a chairman. The rest of the class forms the studio audience and questions the panel.

Teaching points

▶ Revision and consolidation of infinitive and -ing form patterns

try to do

keep doing

get used to doing

tell | *someone to do*
ask |
help |

Expressions

How the hell are we going to do it?
Any chance of a job?
Well done!
estimated time of arrival (ETA)
doubled up with pain

Key vocabulary

aisle	unconscious	general
blackness	– – – – –	jammed
bump	be sick	perfect
buzzer	circle	routine
care	collapse	severe
chance	contact	slumped
descent	flash	smooth
desert	groan	tremendous
fighter plane	land	unusual
food poisoning	lead	vast
fuel gauge	lower	– – – – –
galley	moan	brightly
ground control	overhear	dramatically
halt	realize	nervously
horizon	register	shortly
landing	revive	– – – – –
radio operator	screech	ahead
runway	shake	below
tarmac	sob	on board
thump	spread	
	– – – – –	

1 Announcement/first paragraph. Ensure the text is masked. Play the cassette.

2 Silent reading.

3 Question and answer:
What did the hostess start doing at the beginning of the flight?
What were most of the passengers doing?
What were a few trying to do?
Why weren't they looking out of the windows?
Why do you think the plane was nearly full?
Where were the hostesses when the first buzzers sounded?
What were they doing?
What had they finished doing?
When the buzzers sounded, what did one of the hostesses do?
Why was she surprised?

4 Free reproduction.

5 Second paragraph. Follow the procedure 19.1–19.4, but ask these questions:
What was happening twenty minutes later?
What was the doctor doing?
Why did he want to speak to the captain?
What had caused the food poisoning?
Where did the hostesses lead him?
Was it easy to open the door? Why not?
Who helped her to open it?
Where was the captain?
Where was the co-pilot?
What was the radio operator trying to do?

6 Pair work. What would you do in that situation? Discuss.

7 Third paragraph. Follow the procedure 19.1–19.4.
Ask these questions:
What did the doctor do first?
What did the radio operator think they ought to do?
What did the doctor think they ought to do?
Did the hostess want to make an announcement? Ask 'Why not?'

8 Pair work. Should they make the announcement or not?
Discuss.

9 Fourth paragraph. Follow the procedure 19.1–19.4.
Ask these questions:
What had she overheard the man saying?
What did she ask the man to do?
What did he use to be?
What kind of plane did he use to fly?
Why is he worried about flying this plane?

10 Pair work. What should they do next? Discuss.

11 Fifth paragraph. Follow the procedure 19.1–19.4.
Ask these questions:
Where did the man sit?
What did the radio operator do?
What did they tell him to do?
How long did it take to reach Brisbane?
Where was the airport?
Did he land immediately? Ask 'Why not?'
What did Air Traffic Control tell him to do? Ask 'How long?'
What was happening as he approached the runway?
Describe the landing.

12 Play the complete cassette.

13 Transfer. *(Ask him/her/each other.)*
Have you ever had food poisoning? Were you very ill?
Did you call a doctor?
What usually causes it?
What had you eaten?
Do you think this story is possible? Why?/Why not?
(Note: On modern flights it is normal to serve different food to the two pilots because of the danger of food poisoning.)
Have there been any air disasters recently?
What causes them?
Are you afraid of flying? Why/Why not?

Unit 19

NIGHT FLIGHT

'This is Captain Cook speaking. Our estimated time of arrival in Brisbane will be one a.m., so we've got a long flight ahead of us. I hope you enjoy it. Our hostesses will be serving dinner shortly. Thank you.'

It was Christmas Eve 1959, and the beginning of another routine flight. The hostesses started preparing the food trays. A few of the passengers were trying to get some sleep, but most of them were reading. There was nothing to see from the windows except the vast blackness of the Australian desert below. There was nothing unusual about the flight, except perhaps that the plane was nearly full. A lot of the passengers were travelling home to spend Christmas with their families. The hostesses started serving dinner.

It was a smooth and quiet flight. The hostesses had finished collecting the trays, and they were in the galley putting things away when the first buzzers sounded. One of the hostesses went along the aisle to check. When she came back she looked surprised. 'It's amazing,' she said. 'Even on a smooth flight like this two people have been sick.'

Twenty minutes later nearly half the passengers were ill – dramatically ill. Several were moaning and groaning, some were doubled up in pain, and two were unconscious. Fortunately there was a doctor on board, and he was helping the hostesses. He came to the galley and said, 'I'd better speak to the captain. This is a severe case of food poisoning. I think we'd better land as soon as possible.' 'What caused it?' asked one of the hostesses. 'Well,' replied the doctor, 'I had the beef for dinner, and I'm fine. The passengers who chose the fish are ill.' The hostess led him to the flight deck. She tried to open the door. 'I think it's jammed,' she said. The doctor helped her to push it open. The captain was lying behind the door. He was unconscious. The co-pilot was slumped across the controls, and the radio operator was trying to revive him.

The doctor quickly examined the two pilots. 'They just collapsed,' said the radio operator. 'I don't feel too good myself.' 'Can you land the plane?' said the doctor. 'Me? No, I'm not a pilot. We've got to revive them!' he replied. 'The plane's on automatic pilot. We're OK for a couple of hours.' 'I don't know,' said the doctor. 'They could be out for a long time.' 'I'd better contact ground control,' said the radio operator. The doctor turned to the hostess. 'Perhaps you should make an announcement, try to find out if there's a pilot on board.' 'We can't do that!' she said, 'It'll cause a general panic.' 'Well how the hell are we going to get this thing down?' said the doctor.

Suddenly the hostess remembered something. 'One of the passengers ... I overheard him saying that he'd been a pilot in the war. I'll get him.' She found the man and asked him to come to the galley. 'Didn't you say you used to be a pilot?' she asked. 'Yes ... why? The pilot's all right, isn't he?' She led him to the flight deck. They explained the situation to him. 'You mean, you want me to fly the plane?' he said. 'You must be joking. I was a pilot, but I flew single-engined fighter planes, and that was fifteen years ago. This thing's got four engines!'

'Isn't there anybody else?' he asked. 'I'm afraid not,' said the hostess. The man sat down at the controls. His hands were shaking slightly. The radio operator connected him to Air Traffic Control. They told him to keep flying on automatic pilot towards Brisbane, and to wait for further instructions from an experienced pilot. An hour later the lights of Brisbane appeared on the horizon. He could see the lights of the runway shining brightly beyond the city. Air Traffic Control told him to keep circling until the fuel gauge registered almost empty. This gave him a chance to get used to handling the controls. In the cabin the hostesses and the doctor were busy attending to the sick. Several people were unconscious. The plane circled for over half an hour. The passengers had begun to realize that something was wrong. 'What's going on? Why don't we land?' shouted a middle-aged man. 'My wife's ill. We've got to get her to hospital!' A woman began sobbing quietly. At last the plane started its descent. Suddenly there was a bump which shook the plane. 'We're all going to die!' screamed a man. Even the hostesses looked worried as panic began to spread through the plane. 'It's all right!' someone said, 'The pilot's just lowered the wheels, that's all.' As the plane approached the runway they could see fire trucks and ambulances speeding along beside the runway with their lights flashing. There was a tremendous thump as the wheels hit the tarmac, bounced twice, raced along the runway and screeched to a halt. The first airport truck was there in seconds. 'That was nearly a perfect landing. Well done!' shouted the control tower. 'Thanks,' said the man. 'Any chance of a job?'

THE JUNK-SHOP

Justin Wedgewood and Lenny Smith are antique-dealers. They've got a very successful business. They travel around the country buying antique furniture and paintings from junk-shops and from elderly people, and then they sell them from their shop in Kensington, a fashionable part of London. Today they're in a small Welsh town. Justin's just come out of a little junk-shop, and he seems very excited.

Justin Lenny, we're in luck! There's a painting in there, a landscape, it's a good one. I thought it might be valuable, so I had a good look at the signature. It isn't very clear. I think it may be a Constable.

Lenny A Constable? It can't be! They're all in art galleries. They're worth a fortune!

Justin Well, someone found one two years ago. This might be another. It's dirty and it isn't in very good condition.

Lenny How much do you think it's worth?

Justin I don't know. It may be worth a hundred thousand, it might even be worth more!

Lenny Be careful, Justin. We'd better use the old trick.

Justin Right. There's a chair in the window. It must be worth about five pounds. I'll offer the old lady fifty quid for it. She'll be so pleased that she won't think about the painting.

Lenny Don't say you want the painting, say you want the frame. OK?

Justin Fine, you'd better wait in the van. I'd rather do this on my own.

Lenny Er ... Justin, check the signature before you give her fifty quid for the chair.

Justin Don't worry, Lenny. I know what I'm doing.

Mrs Griffiths I'll be with you in a minute.

Justin Hello. I'm interested in that chair in the window.

Mrs Griffiths What? That old thing? It's been there for years!

Justin Has it? Er ... it's very nice. I think it could be Victorian.

Mrs Griffiths Really?

Justin Yes, I think I'm right. I've seen one or two other chairs like it. I think I could get a good price for that in London. I'll offer you fifty pounds.

Mrs Griffiths Fifty! You must be mad, man!

Justin No, no. It's a fair price.

Mrs Griffiths Well, then, it's yours.

Justin There you are then, fifty pounds. Goodbye. Oh, by the way, that painting's in a nice frame.

Mrs Griffiths It's a nice picture, dear. Early nineteenth century, I've heard.

Justin Oh, no ... no, it can't be. I've seen lots like it. It must be twentieth century. There's no market for them. Still, I could use the frame.

Mrs Griffiths All right. How much will you give me for it?

Justin Er ... how about twenty pounds?

Mrs Griffiths Oh, no, dear. It must be worth more than that. It came from the big house on the hill.

Justin Did it? Let me have another look at it. Yes, the frame is really nice. I'll give you a hundred.

Mrs Griffiths Oh, dear, I don't know what to do. You see, I like that painting myself.

Justin All right, a hundred and twenty. That's my final offer.

Mrs Griffiths Shall we say ... a hundred and fifty?

Justin OK. It's a deal.

Mrs Griffiths Shall I wrap it for you?

Justin No, no. I've got the van outside. It was nice doing business with you. Goodbye!

Mrs Griffiths Bye-bye, dear. Thank you.

Mrs Griffiths Owen?

Mr Griffiths Yes, my love?

Mrs Griffiths I've sold another of your imitation Constables. You'd better bring another one downstairs, if the paint's dry. The gentleman who bought it seemed very pleased with it.

Look at this

I'm certain ...	It must be ...
I'm almost certain ...	

I think it's possible ...	It could be ...
	It may be ...

I think it's possible ... (but a little less possible than 'may')	It might be ...

I think it's nearly impossible ...	It can't be ...
I think it's impossible ...	

Teaching points

▶ Speculating about the present (1)

I'm (almost) certain . . .	*It must be . . .*
I think it's possible . . .	*It could be . . .*
	It may be . . .
I think it's possible but unlikely . . .	*It might be . . .*
I think it's nearly impossible . . .	*It can't be . . .*

Expressions

We're in luck!	*By the way . . .*
They're worth a fortune.	*How much will you give me for it?*
I know what I'm doing.	*Shall we say £150?*
There's no market for them.	*It was nice doing business with you.*
You must be mad!	

Key vocabulary

art gallery	*landscape*	*imitation*
dealer	*trick*	*superb*
fortune	– – – – – –	– – – – – –
frame	*fair*	*still*
junk-shop	*fashionable*	

1 Classroom set. Take in an object concealed in a bag, or paper (a lipstick, a compact, a pocket knife, a lighter, a tin opener, etc.).
Ask *Do you know what it is?* to elicit

I don't know	*what it is.*
I've got no idea	

Get one or two students to feel it.
Say, for example, *Is it a watch?*
Then say, *No, it can't be . . . it's too small.*
Give other suggestions to elicit
No, it can't be, it's too big/small/long/light/heavy/ etc.
T: *What do you think it is?*
S1: *A knife?*
T: *Yes, it may be a knife. What do you think it is?*
S2: *A pen?*
T: *Well, it might be a pen.*
Then describe the object, without stating what it is.
Say *It must be a lighter. Do you agree?*
This could be done with a number of different objects. Students could supply objects, or even do the same in pairs.

2 Introductory text. Ensure the text is masked. Play the cassette.

3 Silent reading.

4 Question and answer:
What are their names?
What do they do?
Do they make a lot of money? How do you know?
How do they make money?
Where are they today?
Where has Justin just been?

5 First dialogue (Justin/Lenny). Ensure the text is masked. Play the cassette.

6 Selective repetition. (Focus particularly on the target structure.)

7 Silent reading.

8 Question and answer:
What was Justin excited about?
What kind of painting is it?
What did he look at?
Why did he look at the signature?
What does he think it may be?
Have you heard of Constable?
(John Constable 1776–1837, perhaps the most famous English landscape artist.)
Constable's paintings are worth a lot of money, aren't they?
Ask *How much?* to elicit *It may be worth £100,000 . . . it might even be worth more.*
Do they want to pay so much money for it?
What are they planning to do?

9 Pair work.

10 Second dialogue (Justin/Mrs Griffiths). Ensure the text is masked. Play the cassette. Set this listening task:
He suggests three prices for the painting. Note them.
Check the answers with the cassette.

11 Selective repetition.

12 Silent reading.

13 Question and answer:
What does he say he's interested in buying?
He isn't really interested in the chair, is he?
She thinks he must be mad, doesn't she? Why?
Does he pay by cheque? Ask 'How'
What does he say about the painting?
He isn't really interested in the frame, is he?
She bargains very well, doesn't she?
How much does he pay in the end?
Why are they both pleased?

14 Pair work.

15 Third dialogue (Mrs Griffiths/Mr Griffiths). Ensure the text is masked. Play the cassette.

16 Silent reading.

17 Question and answer:
It wasn't a Constable, was it?
Her husband painted it, didn't he?
They've done this before, haven't they?
They'll do it again, won't they?

18 Focus attention on 'Look at this'. Silent reading.

19 Ask them to go back and mark all the examples in the text.

20 Play the complete cassette.

21 Discuss with the students using the following:
The man was a forger. The painting was a forgery. What other things can be forged? (signatures, money, documents, furniture, stamps, etc.) *A lot of people buy antiques. How do they know they are genuine? How would you check?*

Teaching points

▶ Speculating about the present (2)

They	must may might can't	be doing it.

She's	probably possibly	doing it.

▶ *Have* + nouns

to have	a row a good time a party a look

Expressions

Thank goodness for that!
Go back to sleep!
What's the matter?

Key vocabulary

bang	row	plant
body	spade	sleep through
farewell	tank	(something)
milkman	– – – – –	– – – – –
neighbour	bury	nosey
pans	clear up	– – – – –
pots	hammer	pretty (noisy)

1 Section 1. Focus attention on the picture. Set the situation. Ensure the text is masked. Play the cassette.

2 Selective repetition, focusing particularly on the target structures.

3 Silent reading.

4 Question and answer:
Where are they?
What time do they usually wake up? How do you know?
What time is it?
Why has she woken him up?
Who's making a noise?
What does he think is happening next door?
What exactly does he say?
Is it very, very noisy? How do you know?
How many children have their neighbours got?
Why does Sybil think the noise is disgusting?
Does Sydney think the neighbours are enjoying themselves?
What exactly does he say?

5 Pair work. (Students read the dialogue in pairs.)

6 Section 2. Ensure the text is masked. Play the cassette. Pause after each of the four sound effects.
Say *What was that noise?* to elicit

It must be	a car door.
It could be	a front door.
It may be	a garden gate.

Ask *What do you think is happening?* to elicit
They must be saying goodbye.
The guests must be going.
The party must be finishing. etc.

7 Selective repetition.

8 Silent reading.

9 Pair work.

10 Section 3. Ensure the text is masked. Play the cassette. Pause after the sound effect. Ask *What is that noise? What do you think is happening?*
Play the rest of the cassette.

11 Selective repetition.

12 Silent reading.

13 Question and answer:
Does Sybil know exactly what they are doing? to elicit
No, she doesn't.
What does she say?
What time is it?
What exactly does she ask?
Ask *What can they be doing? What do you think?* to elicit

They	may might could	be repairing something. be hitting each other. be making some shelves.

Get students to ask each other for ideas in pairs. Encourage wild guesses – but note that the wilder ones will use *might be doing* e.g. *He might be making a coffin.* Give this example to the class.

14 Pair work.

15 Section 4. Ensure the text is masked. Play the cassette. Pause after the sound effect as in 21.10.

16 Selective repetition.

17 Silent reading.

18 Question and answer:
There's someone in next door's garden, isn't there?
Do you know who it is?
What does Sydney suggest?
Does Sybil agree?
What does she say?
Who is it?
What's he carrying? Why?
(Invite speculation with *may be doing* and *might be doing*.)
Say *What can he be doing at this time of night?*
Ask each other.
Say *Try and tell me some things that he can't be doing.*
Why does Sydney want to phone the police?

19 Pair work.

20 Section 5. Ensure the text is masked. Play the cassette.

21 Silent reading.

22 Pair work.

23 Play the complete cassette.

24 Focus attention on the exercise. Go through it, putting questions to individuals. Students then do the exercise in pairs (and possibly as a written homework).

Unit 21

NOISY NEIGHBOURS

Sybil Sidney! Sidney! Wake up!

Sidney Eh! What? What's the matter? It can't be eight o'clock already!

Sybil No, it's half past one. It's those people next door again. Listen!

Sidney Oh, yes. They must be having another party.

Sybil Listen to that! They must be waking up the whole street. And they've got three young children. They can't be sleeping through that noise. It's disgusting! Somebody should call the police! Sidney, wake up!

Sidney Eh? I wasn't asleep, dear. They're all laughing. They must be having a good time! They never invite us, do they?

Sybil Sidney!

Sidney Yes, dear. What is it now?

Sybil Listen! They must be leaving.

Sidney Thank goodness for that! Maybe we'll get some sleep.

Sybil I hope so. It's nearly three o'clock. Goodnight, dear.

Sidney Oh, hell! They're having a row, now.

Sybil I'm not surprised. They always have rows after parties.

Sybil Oh! They must be throwing the pots and pans again.

Sidney No, I think that was a plate, dear, or maybe the television. They'll be sorry in the morning.

Sybil Sidney! Wake up!

Sidney Eh! Oh, what's that?

Sybil He can't be hammering at this time of night.

Sybil What time is it?

Sybil Four o'clock. What can they be doing at four o'clock in the morning?

Sidney I can't hear any voices. Go back to sleep, Sybil.

Sybil Sidney! Listen. There's someone in the garden next door.

Sidney Eh? It must be the milkman.

Sybil No, it can't be. It's too early. It's only quarter to five. Who could it be? You'd better have a look.

Sidney All right. Ooh! It's Mr Sykes, and he's carrying a spade.

Sybil Oh, no! You don't think he's killed her, do you?

Sidney Well, we haven't heard her voice for a while. No, she's probably sleeping.

Sybil But what can he be doing at this time of night?

Sydney If he has killed her, he might be burying the body!

Sybil What! You don't think so, do you?

Sidney Well, he can't be planting potatoes, can he? I suppose you want me to phone the police?

Sybil No. Ask him what he's doing first!

Sidney Hello, there, Mr Sykes. You're up early this morning.

Mr Sykes I haven't been to bed yet. We had a party last night. I hope we didn't keep you awake.

Sidney Oh, no. We didn't hear anything, nothing at all.

Mr Sykes Well, it was a pretty noisy party. My wife knocked over the goldfish tank while we were clearing up. The poor fish died. I'm just burying them before the children wake up.

Exercise

What do you think your parents/brothers/sisters/friends are doing at this moment?

If you think you know what they are doing answer with:

They must be doing this.
They can't be doing that.
They're probably doing this.

If you don't know, use:
They could/may/might be doing this.
or:
They're possibly doing this.

What about the President of the USA/the Queen of England/the students in the class next door/the director of the school/a famous pop star/a famous sports personality?

YOU'RE IN THE ARMY NOW!

It's Saturday afternoon at Botherington Army Camp. The new recruits are supposed to be working, but they aren't. The Colonel's away today and they're lazing around in the barracks. The Sergeant-Major has just opened the door. He's brought the duty roster with him, so he knows exactly what each of them should be doing.

Sergeant-Major 'Hello, hello ... what's going on here?'

Exercise 1

Look at Smith in the picture. Ask and answer about the other soldiers.

1 *What's he doing?*
He's sitting on the bed.
He's drinking.
He's listening to the radio.
2 *Should he be drinking?*
No he shouldn't.
Should he be mowing the grass?
Yes, he should.
3 *What should he be doing?*
He should be mowing the grass.
What shouldn't he be doing?
He shouldn't be sitting on the bed.
He shouldn't be drinking.
He shouldn't be listening to the radio.

Exercise 2

Smith ought to be mowing the grass, he ought not to be drinking.
Write similar sentences about the other soldiers.

Sergeant-Major Smith! What are you doing?
Smith I'm listening to the radio, sir.
Sergeant-Major And what are you supposed to be doing, Smith?
Smith I'm not sure, sir.
Sergeant-Major Well, let me tell you, Smith. You are supposed to be mowing the lawn!
Smith Yes, sir. I'm sorry sir. It won't happen again, sir.
Sergeant-Major It'd better not, Smith. And when I come back, Smith, you'd better be mowing that grass! Do you understand?
Smith Yes, sir.
Sergeant-Major This isn't a holiday camp. You're in the army now!

Exercise 3

Make similar conversations between the Sergeant-Major and the other soldiers.

Look at this.

SMITH

JONES

MURPHY

McCOY

KILROY

Exercise 4

Smith's mowing the grass.
He'd rather not be mowing the grass.
He'd rather be lying on the beach.
Make sentences about the other soldiers.

Exercise 5

What are you doing?
What would you rather be doing?
Make five sentences.

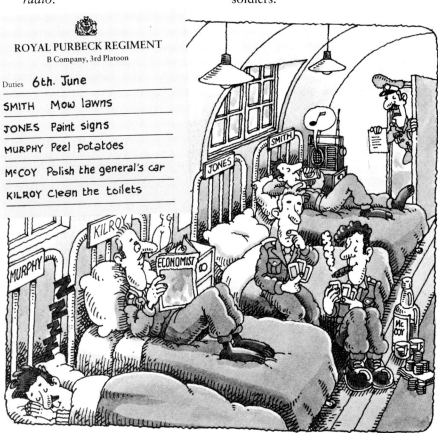

ROYAL PURBECK REGIMENT
B Company, 3rd Platoon

Duties 6th. June

SMITH	Mow lawns
JONES	Paint signs
MURPHY	Peel potatoes
McCOY	Polish the general's car
KILROY	Clean the toilets

Teaching points

▶ Obligations. Duties. Preferences.

He	should shouldn't	be doing it.
	ought to *ought not to* *are supposed to* *are not supposed to*	
They	*would rather* *would rather not* *had better (not)*	

Key vocabulary

barracks	*platoon*	*mow*
colonel	*recruit*	*peel*
company	*regiment*	*polish*
duty roster	*sergeant-major*	
holiday camp	– – – – – –	
lawn	*laze around*	

1 Focus attention on the picture and duty roster. Ask students to study it.

2 Introductory text. Ensure the text is masked. Play the cassette.

3 Silent reading.

4 Question and answer:
What are the recruits doing?
Where's the colonel?
Where do you think he is?
What do you think he's doing?
Who's just come in?
What's he holding?

5 Exercise 1. Go through the three sections orally, asking individuals.

6 Pair work. Students do Exercise 1 in pairs.

7 Exercise 2. Go through orally, asking individuals.

8 Ask students to write the sentences. Check the answers.

9 Dialogue. Ensure the text is masked. Play the cassette.

10 Listen and repeat.

11 Silent reading.

12 Question and answer:
What's Smith doing?
Does Smith know what he is supposed to be doing?
What is he supposed to be doing?
What had he better be doing when the Sergeant-Major comes back?

13 Pair work. Students read the dialogue in pairs.

14 Ask questions about the other soldiers, as in 22.12.
What's Jones doing?
What is he supposed to be doing?
What had he better be doing when the Sergeant-Major comes back?

15 Exercise 3. Students practise conversations in pairs between the Sergeant-Major, Jones, Murphy, McCoy and Kilroy. Get one or two pairs to demonstrate in front of the class.

16 Set one conversation as a written homework.

17 Look at this (picture strip). Ask students to study the pictures. Go through Exercise 4 orally, asking individuals.

18 Pair work. Students ask and answer, e.g. *What's Smith doing? What would he rather be doing?*

19 Exercise 5. Go through orally. Students do it in pairs.

20 Written phase. See Teaching points above. Write it on the board, ask students to copy it.

21 Revision. Focus attention on the picture and duty roster. Ask about the Sergeant-Major.
What's he going to make Smith do?
What isn't he going to let Smith do?
Do the same with Jones, Murphy, McCoy and Kilroy.

22 Pair work. Students ask and answer as in 22.21.

23 Transfer:
Is there conscription in your country? (Do young people have to do military service in your country?)
How long is it?
What age does it begin?
Have you had to do it?
Will you have to do it?
Do you know anyone who has done it?
Did they like it? Why/Why not?
What do they make you do in the army?
What don't they let you do?
Would you rather be an officer or an ordinary soldier? Why?

24 Get students to ask and answer about friends and relations, on this pattern:
Where's your brother at the moment?
What's he supposed to be doing?
Do you think he's doing it?

Unit 22

Teaching points

▶ Reading comprehension from a formal text

▶ Listening for specific information

▶ *They navigate by using the sun.*

Key vocabulary

arctic tern	lemming	turtle
bar magnet	magnetic field	valley
bat	mammal	whale
breeding ground	method	– – – – –
butterfly	migration	approach
chick	mystery	attach
circuit	nature	breed
clifftop	nest	detect
coastline	overland	drift
compulsion	pigeon	exist
creature	pond	experience
cycle	region	feed
the East	reindeer	glide
estuary	reptile	migrate
exhaustion	round trip	navigate
experiment	salmon	plunge
explanation	seabird	release
feature	seal	remain
flock	sea-level	ring
eel	sonar	set off
frog	stream	succeed
hectare	suicide	– – – – –
insect	theory	presumably
instinct	tip	
larvae	tunny	

Note: A map of the world or a globe would be a useful visual aid.

1 Set the situation. Ensure the text is masked. Play the complete cassette.

2 Introduction. Silent reading. Students should be told to read it two or three times, and to read to the end of the introduction before marking difficult words. Do not answer questions on vocabulary at this stage.

3 Run through and check difficult words.

4 Question and answer:
A lot of animals migrate, don't they? Ask 'Why?'
It's a mystery, isn't it?
Do they learn how to, or is it an instinct?
Tell me some of the creatures that migrate. Can you think of any more?
Can you tell me some other reptiles/insects/fish/mammals?
We don't know exactly how they navigate, do we?
Say
1 *They may navigate by using the sun.*
2 (Select an individual to answer.) *They may navigate by using the stars.*
Go through the list in this way. Describe the experiment with the young seabird.

5 Play the cassette of the introduction; students follow the text.

6 'The Arctic Tern'. Set these listening tasks by writing them on the board:
1 *When do they begin the journey?*
2 *How long is the journey south?*
3 *How far do they travel in 90 days?*
4 *How long is the round trip?*
5 *How long does it take?*
6 *How many kilometres a day do they fly?*
Play the cassette once; students don't make notes. Play again; students make notes.

7 Check through the answers, by playing the cassette with pauses.

8 Silent reading. (See 23.2.)

9 Run through and check difficult words.

10 Reproduction:
Describe the Arctic Tern's journey.
Tell me about the Norwegian chick.

11 'The European Freshwater Eel'. Silent reading. (See 23.2.)

12 Play the cassette; students follow the text.

13 Run through and check difficult words.

14 Question and answer:
It isn't a reptile, is it?
It's a fish, isn't it?
Why do some people think it's a reptile?
Where do they begin their lives? Where's that?
How do they reach Europe? What happens on the way?
Where do they spend most of their lives?
How long do they live?
When and why do they return to the Sargasso Sea?
Which is bigger, a pond or a lake? a stream or a river?
How do they travel overland?
How does the eel navigate in local waters? to elicit
It navigates by using its sense of smell.
How do they find their way to the Sargasso?

15 'The Lemming'. Ensure the text is masked. Play the cassette.

16 Silent reading. (See 23.2.)

17 Run through and check difficult words.

18 Question and answer:
When do they usually migrate?
Why do they migrate?
What occasionally happens in Norway?
Why do lemmings jump over cliffs?
Is it really 'suicide'?
What are the two theories?

19 Play the complete cassette. Students follow the text.

20 Extension. Find out about another migration. Write about it for homework. (Set a maximum length of 150 words.)

One of the greatest mysteries of nature is the instinct to migrate. Every year millions of creatures feel the need to move for one reason or another. Most of us have seen the arrival or departure of migrating flocks of birds. Migration, however, is not confined to birds, but can be seen in reptiles (for example turtles, frogs), insects (butterflies, locusts), fish (eels, salmon, tunny) and mammals (reindeer, seals, lemmings, whales, bats). Many of these creatures succeed in navigating over long distances. How exactly they manage to do this still remains a mystery. There are several possibilities. They may navigate by using one or more of the following:

1 The sun.
2 The stars.
3 The Earth's magnetic field. (When a small bar magnet is attached to a pigeon, it is unable to navigate.)
4 A sense of smell.
5 Geographical features. (Birds flying from North Africa to France seem to follow coastlines and valleys.)
6 Changes in temperature. (Salmon can detect a change in water temperature as small as 0.03°C.)
7 Sound. (Whales and bats seem to use sonar.)

Experiments suggest that these navigational abilities are partly instinctive. In one famous experiment a young seabird from the island of Skokholm, off the Welsh coast, was taken across the Atlantic by plane to Boston, 5100 km away. It was released, and was back in its nest twelve and a half days later.

MIGRATION

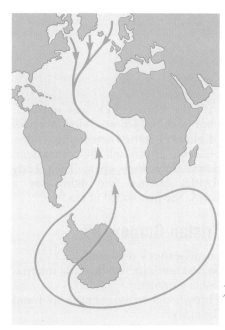

Ocean and down to Antarctica, where they spend the Antarctic summer. On the way back they sometimes make a complete circuit of Antarctica before returning to their breeding-grounds. The round trip is over 35,000 km in eight months (240 km a day when they are flying.) The Arctic Tern sees more hours of daylight than any other creature, because it experiences two summers a year, one in the Arctic region, and one in the Antarctic. These regions have almost constant daylight in summer. One tern, which was ringed in Norway as a chick, died in exactly the same place, twenty-seven years later. Presumably, it had made the journey twenty-seven times.

The Arctic Tern

This seabird holds the record for long-distance migration. Arctic Tern breed in Northern Canada, Greenland, Northern Europe, Siberia and Alaska. In late August they set off on a 17,500 km journey which takes them south, past the West coasts of Europe and Africa to the tip of Southern Africa (14,000 km in 90 days). They then fly round to the Indian

The European Freshwater Eel

European Freshwater Eels, which look like snakes but are really fish, begin and end their lives in the Sargasso Sea, southeast of Bermuda. As eggs and larvae they drift for three years towards Europe, changing both shape and colour as they reach the fresh-water estuaries of European rivers. They spend the next nine to nineteen years in rivers, streams, lakes and ponds. As they approach old age they seem to have an unexplained compulsion to return to the Sargasso Sea to breed. Many eels which have found their way into ponds and lakes come out of the water and travel overland, gliding through damp grass. When they reach the sea, they make their way to the Sargasso, where they breed and die. No eels make the journey twice. The eel has an acute sense of smell, which is used for navigation in local waters, but inherited memory seems the only explanation for their migration to the Sargasso.

The Lemming

The Brown Lemming is a small mammal (10–18cm long) found all over Northern Canada, Scandinavia and Northern Russia. Lemmings usually make short, annual migrations in spring, travelling by night and feeding and sleeping by day. Every three or four years, however, they make much longer migrations in large numbers. The lemming population seems to change over a three or four year cycle, from one lemming per four hectares to between 400 and 700 lemmings per four hectares. Migration seems to be a method of population control, and is most spectacular in the well-known 'mass suicides', where thousands of lemmings plunge over cliff tops into the sea, and swim till they die of exhaustion. These 'mass suicides' only occur infrequently, and then only in Norway where mountains touch the sea. Nobody knows what makes them do it, but there are two theories. One is that migrating lemmings cross rivers and lakes and can't tell the difference between a river and the sea. The other, more interesting theory is that they are migrating towards ancient breeding-grounds which existed beneath the North Sea millions of years ago, when the sea-level was lower.

MURDER AT GURNEY

Part 1

Lord Gurney was found dead on the library floor of his country house in Norfolk. He had been shot five times. The police have been called. There are six people in the house and they all heard the shots at about nine o'clock. The police have taken statements and made the following notes about each of the six people.

Lady Agatha Gurney, 62

Married to Lord Gurney for thirty-five years.
Disabled – has been in a wheel-chair since a riding accident, twelve years ago.
Very jealous woman.
Had a row with Celia Smart in the afternoon.
Told Lord Gurney to sack her.
After long argument, Lord Gurney refused to sack her.

Lady Agatha's statement.

I was in my room. My bedroom's on the ground floor because I can't walk. I was reading. I heard the shots; there were four or five. I wheeled myself into the hall. The door of the library was open. Miss Smart was standing in the doorway, screaming. Gillespie was standing at the French windows. The gun was on the floor by the body.

Celia Smart, 24

Secretary to Lord Gurney.
Young, beautiful, intelligent – works to support her sick mother.
Employed by Lord Gurney for a year.
Report in gossip column in today's 'Daily News' that she had been seen last Saturday with Tristan Gurney at a new disco, 'The Charteris Club' in London's Mayfair.
Lord Gurney very angry about it.
Threatened to sack her, but didn't.

Celia Smart's statement.

I was in the drawing-room, writing some letters, job applications actually. I heard the shots, ran across the hall, the library door was open ... poor dear Horace was lying in a pool of blood. I started screaming. Gillespie came in through the French windows, they were open. Then Lady Agatha arrived. She didn't say a word. She just stared at me.

Tristan Gurney, 33

Lord Gurney's only son.
Reputation as a playboy and international gambler.
Thrown out of boarding-school and the army.
Has large gambling debts.
Arrested last year for possessing drugs.
Is heir to the Gurney estate – will inherit £2 million.
Lord Gurney had refused to give him any more money.

Tristan's statement.

I was in the billiard room. I was practising. Suddenly there were five shots. I thought it was Chivers shooting birds in the garden again, Then I heard a scream. It sounded like Celia, so I opened the connecting door to the library and saw father lying there, Gillespie at the window, and Celia and mother together in the main doorway. I couldn't believe my eyes.

Major Chivers, 60

At school and in the army with Lord Gurney.
Was army pistol-shooting champion.
Drinks heavily.
Drives a Bentley.
Doesn't work – spends time shooting and fishing.
Was Managing-Director of Gurney Property Ltd.
Went to prison for two years when the company collapsed with debts of £½ million after a big property scandal.
Has lived at Gurney Manor since leaving prison.

Major Chivers' statement.

I was by the lake, fishing in my usual place. When I heard the shots, I hurried through the trees towards the house. I saw Gillespie running across the lawn towards the library. When I got there, everybody was in the room, except Tom Giles, the gardener. Poor old Gurney was dead. I was absolutely sure he was dead. After all, I was in the army for twenty years.

Gillespie, 65

Butler. Has worked for the Gurneys for nearly fifty years.
Retires in two months.
Likes good wine and good food.
Takes Lady Agatha out every day in her wheelchair.
Knows everything about the family.
Had long argument with Lord Gurney in the morning.
Knows Celia Smart's father very well – introduced her to Lord Gurney.

Gillespie's statement.

I was taking my evening walk. I had just come out of the kitchen door, I was walking round the corner of the house when I heard shooting. I ran across the lawn to the French windows. I saw Lord Gurney's body, and Miss Smart in the doorway.

Tom Giles, 29

Gardener.
Often goes fishing with the Major.
Proposed marriage to Celia Smart, but was rejected.
Been in trouble with the police several times, for fighting in the village pub.
Has a violent temper.
Had argument about a pay rise earlier in the day.

Tom Giles' statement.

I was working in the kitchen garden. I heard shots, but that's not unusual around here. Lord Gurney and the Major are very fond of shooting. Then I heard lots of screaming and shouting, so I went into the house through the kitchen door to see what was happening. They were all there. I wasn't sorry. He deserved it. Everybody hated him.

Revision points

▶ Past tenses

▶ Reported speech

▶ Question tags

Key vocabulary

Bentley (similar to a Rolls-Royce)	manor	propose
	murder	reject
billiard room	pay-rise	sack
blood	pistol	support
butler	pool	throw-out
debt	property	– – – – – –
doorway	reputation	connecting
drawing-room	scandal	disabled
drugs	shot	following
estate	temper	jealous
French windows	wheelchair	violent
gambler	– – – – –	– – – – – –
gossip column	collapse	after all
heir	deserve	
lawn	possess	

1 Introductory text. Focus attention on the picture. Ensure the text is masked. Ask students to describe the picture. Play the cassette.

2 Silent reading.

3 Question and answer:
Where's Gurney Manor?
Why have the police been there?
How had he been killed?
How many people are in the house?
When was he killed?
What have they done?

4 Lady Agatha – Notes. Silent reading.

5 *Tell me what you know about her.* (The students should make complete sentences, i.e. '62' ... *She's 62.* 'Married to Lord Gurney for 35 years' ... *She was/has been married to Lord Gurney for 35 years.* 'Disabled' ... *She's disabled.* etc.) Follow this procedure for the other five characters. Note: for the next sections, students may wish to refer to the map at the top of 'Part Two' (Unit 25) on the facing page.

6 'Lady Agatha's statement'. Ensure the text is masked. Play the cassette.

7 Silent reading.

8 Play the cassette, pausing after each sentence.
e.g. 'I was in my room'.
T: *What did she say?*
S: *She said she had been in her room.*

9 Follow the same procedure for Celia Smart, Tristan, Major Chivers, Gillespie and Tom Giles.

10 Say:
We don't know if they are all telling the truth. Ask each other in pairs about each person.
Where was she?
What was she doing?
What did she do?
What/Who did she see?

11 Check the information by asking individuals the same questions.

12 Pair work. Students role-play each of the people being interviewed by a policeman. The policeman is checking the information given in the statement by repeating sentences with a tag question.
S1: (Policeman) *You were in your room, weren't you?*
S2: (Lady Agatha) *Yes, I was.*
S1: *Your bedroom's on the ground floor, isn't it?*
S2: *Yes, it is.*
S1: *You can't walk, can you?*
S2: *No, I can't.*
The policeman can try to trick each person by making deliberate errors.
S1: *There were two shots, weren't there?*
S2: *No, there were four or five.*
Demonstrate this with an individual.

Teaching points

▶ Speculating about the past (1)

Could	it have been	him? her? them?

It	must could may (not) might (not) can't couldn't	have been	him. her. them.

Could	he she they	have	done it? killed him? shot him?

He She They	must could may (not) might (not) can't couldn't	have	done it. killed him. shot him.

Expressions

a skeleton in the cupboard (unpleasant or shameful secret)

Key vocabulary

alibi
care
evidence
fingerprint
motive
outsider
skeleton
suspect
------
in charge

1 Refer back to Unit 24. Ask students to read it through briefly.

2 First dialogue. Set the situation. Ensure the text is masked. Play the cassette.

3 Selective repetition. (Focus on the Teaching points.)

4 Silent reading

5 Pair work (students read the dialogue in pairs).

6 Explain that they are going to hear Marples and Watts discussing only two of the suspects, Lady Agatha and Major Chivers. For both dialogues follow the procedure 25.2–25.5.

7 Focus attention on 'Look at this'. Ask students to study it silently.

8 Pair work. Students make a list of sentences about each of the six suspects. Before discussion draw up a list of possible points about each. For example:

Celia Smart
She was the first into the room. She could have been there all the time.
She could have been in love with Lord Gurney, Tristan, Giles, or even Major Chivers or Gillespie.
There may have been some family connection with Gillespie.
She didn't have any money. She could have planned it alone, or with any of the other characters.
She'd had an argument that day.
She may have hoped to marry Tristan and he would inherit the money.

Tristan
He could have done it for the money. He was in debt.
He said he heard five shots. Did he count them?
He might have used the connecting door.
He might have needed money for drugs/gambling debts.
His father had refused to give him any more money.
He might have been in love with Celia.
His father might have objected either because of Tristan's bad reputation, because he had no money or he might have been in love with her himself.

Gillespie
He has expensive tastes, and he is going to retire soon.
He must have expected to inherit something in Lord Gurney's will.
He may have been in love with Lady Agatha.
He might have been angry about a relationship between Lord Gurney and Celia.
He knew everything about the family.
He might have tried to blackmail Lord Gurney about the property scandals and failed.
There might have been a secret family relationship between him and Celia.
He could have shot Lord Gurney, gone out and come back in.

Tom Giles
He proposed marriage, so he must have been in love with Celia.
She might have rejected him because of Lord Gurney.
He must have been jealous.
He was a violent man. He could have lost his temper.
One of the others might have paid him to do it.
He might not have been in the kitchen garden.
He was the last to appear, he could have been in the kitchen or in the hall.

9 Discuss (either as a class or in groups) who they think did it, why and how.

10 Discuss the possible combinations of two or three characters.

11 Ask students to vote on who they think is guilty.

12 Students will probably ask for the truth. You could use this theory:
It was Lord Gurney. He shot himself once. Lady Agatha was in the room, and was terrified of the scandal of suicide. She also wanted to make the police suspect Celia, who she hated. She picked up the gun and fired four more bullets into the body. The door to her room was already open, and she wasn't really disabled.
Encourage students to dispute it.

MANOR

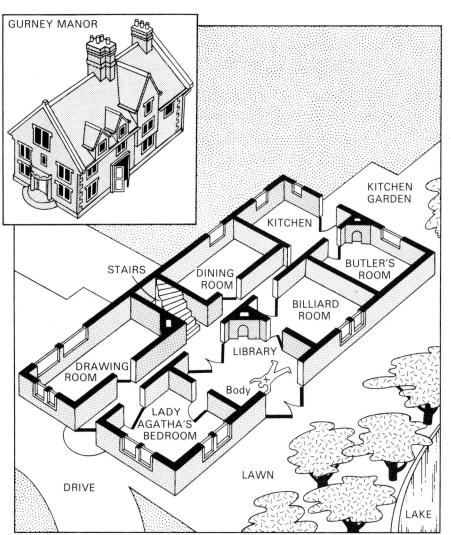

GURNEY MANOR

KITCHEN GARDEN

KITCHEN

BUTLER'S ROOM

STAIRS

DINING ROOM

BILLIARD ROOM

LIBRARY

DRAWING ROOM

Body

LADY AGATHA'S BEDROOM

DRIVE

LAWN

LAKE

Part 2

Inspector Marples is in charge of the case. Sergeant Watts is his assistant. They're in the library.

Marples Where is everybody, Sergeant?

Watts They're all in the drawing-room, sir. Constable Dickson's with them. What do you think, sir?

Marples It could have been any one of them, couldn't it? We don't know what skeletons are in the cupboard! It may have been two of them together. It might even have been all of them. Nobody seems very sad!

Watts No, sir. Lord Gurney was a very unpopular man in the village. Nobody liked him. It could have been an outsider.

Marples No, no, Watts. It must have been one of them. Let's look at the evidence.

Watts It seems to me that everybody has got a motive, sir, and nobody's got an alibi. They all say they were alone when it happened.

Marples Yes, and there are no finger-prints on the gun.

Lady Agatha?

Watts It couldn't have been her, sir.

Marples Why not, Watts?

Watts Well, she's in a wheelchair. She can't move very fast. Anyway, they've been married for thirty-five years. It can't have been her.

Marples Most murders are inside the family, Watts, and there is a door between her room and the library.

Watts Ah, yes, sir. But it was locked!

Marples Doors have keys, Watts!

Watts But why would she want to kill him?

Marples Miss Smart's a very attractive young woman. We don't know what was going on. She could have been jealous.

Watts But, sir, he was over sixty! He was old enough to be her father!

Marples Ah, well, Watts, he was a good-looking man, and very rich!

Major Chivers?

Marples What about the Major, Watts? He's a strange fellow.

Watts I've been thinking about that. It can't have been him, sir!

Marples Really! Why not?

Watts Why would he need to fire five times? He was an army pistol champion. He could have killed him with one shot.

Marples Maybe he did, Watts. Maybe he did.

Watts I don't understand, sir.

Marples There are a lot of things you don't understand, Watts. Perhaps he's more clever than he looks.

Watts But there's no motive, sir.

Marples There may have been. I mean there was that scandal with the property company.

Watts But he was at the lake, sir.

Marples He might not have been, Watts. He's a pistol champion. He could have shot him from the trees and thrown the gun into the room.

Watts Oh. Do you really think so, sir?

Marples I don't know, Watts. It's just a theory.

Look at this

Can Could	it have been	him? her? them?

It	must could may (not) might (not) can't couldn't	have been	him. her. them.

Can Could	he she they	have	done it? killed him? shot him?

He She They	must could may (not) might (not) can't couldn't	have	done it. killed him. shot him.

Exercise

Discuss each character. Make a list of sentences about all six suspects. Who do you think did it? How? Why?

KNOW YOUR RIGHTS

Complaining about faulty goods or bad service is never easy. Most people dislike making a fuss. However, when you are shopping, it is important to know your rights. The following extract is taken from a leaflet produced by the British 'Office of Fair Trading', and it gives advice to consumers.

Your rights when buying goods

When you buy something from a shop, you are making a contract. This contract means that it's up to the shop – not the manufacturer – to deal with your complaints if the goods are not satisfactory. What do we mean by satisfactory?

The goods must not be broken or damaged and must work properly. This is known as 'merchantable quality'. A sheet, say, which had a tear in it, or a clock that didn't go when you wound it would not pass this test.

The goods must be as described – whether on the pack or by the salesman. A hairdryer which the box says is blue should not turn out to be pink; a pair of shoes the salesman says is leather should not be plastic.

The goods should be fit for their purpose. This means the purpose for which most people buy those particular goods. If you wanted something for a special purpose, you must have said exactly what for. If, for instance, the shop assures you that a certain glue will mend broken china, and it doesn't you have a right to return it.

If the shop sells you faulty goods, it has broken its side of the bargain.

If things go wrong

If goods are faulty when you first inspect or use them, go back to the shop, say that you cancel the purchase and ask for a complete refund. If you prefer, you can accept a repair or a replacement.

If the goods break down through no fault of yours, after you have used them for a time, you may still be entitled to some compensation. In some cases it would be reasonable to expect a complete refund – if, for instance, without misuse your shoes came apart after only one day's wear, or your washing machine irreparably broke down after only three wash days. But if your washing machine worked perfectly for a while and then broke, you could only expect some of the purchase price back. You and the supplier must negotiate a reasonable settlement.

You need never accept a credit note for faulty goods. If you do so, then later find you do not want anything else in the shop or store, you may not get your money back.

If you have to spend money as a direct result of goods being faulty, you can also claim this from the shop. You could, for example, claim the cost of using a laundry while the washing machine wasn't working. But you must keep such expenses down to a minimum.

There are four golden rules:

1 Examine the goods you buy at once. If they are faulty, tell the seller quickly.

2 Keep any receipts you are given. If you have to return something, the receipt will help to prove where and when you bought it.

3 Don't be afraid to complain. You are not asking a favour to have faulty goods put right. The law is on your side.

4 Be persistent (but not aggressive). If your complaint is justified, it is somebody's responsibility to put things right.

Remember

● You can't complain about defects that were pointed out to you, or that you could reasonably have been expected to notice.

● Stop using the item as soon as you discover a fault.

● You are not entitled to compensation if you simply change your mind about wanting the goods.

Unit 26

Teaching points

► Complaining (1)

► Revision

Expressions

It's up to the shop. (= It's the responsibility of the shop.)
a golden rule
The law is on your side.

Key vocabulary

china	settlement	prove
compensation	sheet	put (something
consumer	tear	right)
contract	washday	wind
credit note	wear	– – – – –
defect	– – – – –	aggressive
extract	assure	complete
favour	cancel	direct
fuss	change (your mind)	faulty
glue	claim	fit
hair dryer	come apart	justified
item	complain	merchantable
laundry	damage	(quality)
law	deal	particular
minimum	discover	persistent
misuse	entitle	pink
refund	examine	reasonable
replacement	inspect	– – – – –
responsibility	negotiate	irreparably
rights	point out	

1 Introductory text. Silent reading. Check vocabulary.

2 Question and answer (+ *Ask him/her/me/each other.*)
What goods have you bought recently?
What are services?
Have you bought any faulty goods recently?
What was wrong?
Did you complain? What did you do? Who did you speak to?
Do you dislike making a fuss? Why/Why not?
Have you ever taken anything back to a shop?
Did they exchange it?
Did they refund your money?
Did they ask to see a receipt?

3 'Your rights when buying goods.' Pre-questions:
Find out what the following mean: 'merchantable quality', 'as described', and 'fit for their purpose'.
Silent reading of 'Your rights when buying goods' (including the three sections beginning 'The goods . . . '). Check vocabulary.

4 Ask students to give examples of 'merchantable quality', 'as described', and 'fit for their purpose'.
Ask them to add other examples to those in the text.

5 Question and answer:
Who is responsible for dealing with complaints about unsatisfactory goods?
For goods purchased to be satisfactory, three conditions must be met: what are they? Write them down.

6 'If things go wrong.' Ask students to read it silently two or three times. Encourage them to read to the end, marking difficult words and expressions.

7 Question and answer:
If new goods are faulty, there are three things you can do.
What are they?
(You can ask for a refund, a repair, or a replacement.)
What happens if the goods break down after you have used them for some time?
When would it be reasonable to expect a complete refund?
When would you have to negotiate a reasonable settlement?
(Ask for examples, apart from those in the text.)
What do you think a credit note is?
Must you accept one?
Why shouldn't you accept one?
What kinds of expenses can you claim from a shop? Give examples.

8 'Remember.' Silent reading. (See 26.6.)

9 *What three things is it important to remember? Why?*

10 'Four golden rules.' Silent reading. (See 26.6.)

11 Question and answer:
1 *Why should you examine the goods at once?*
  What should you do if they are faulty?
2 *Why should you keep any receipts you are given?*
3 *Why shouldn't you be afraid to complain?*
4 *Why should you be persistent?*
  Why shouldn't you be aggressive?

Unit 26

Teaching points

▶ Complaining (2)
  Letters of complaint

He	should	have done it.
	shouldn't	
	ought to	
	ought not to	

Expressions

Come on!
Please find enclosed...
in working order
on battery
on mains

Key vocabulary

branch	*pocket*	*obtain*
cheque-stub	*postage*	*refund*
customer	*product*	*state*
date	*proof*	*subtract*
digital alarm clock	*– – – – – –*	*– – – – – –*
guarantee	*add*	*together with*
manufacturer	*multiply*	

1 Focus attention on the picture. Set the situation. Ensure the text is masked. Play the cassette.

2 Selective repetition.

3 Drill:
T: *He didn't obtain a receipt.*
C: *He should have obtained a receipt.*

Continue:
He didn't keep the guarantee.
He didn't check the radio.
He didn't read the instructions.
He didn't switch it on to 'battery'.

4 Drill:
T: *He threw the receipt away.*
C: *He shouldn't have thrown the receipt away.*

Continue:
He left the guarantee in the box.
He expected the radio to work.
He got aggressive.
He left the switch on 'mains'.
He shouted at the manager.

5 Repeat Drill 27.3 to elicit *He ought to have obtained a receipt.*

6 Repeat Drill 27.4 to elicit *He ought not to have thrown the receipt away.*

7 Drill:
T: *He didn't read the instructions.*
C: *He should have read the instructions.*
T: *He got aggressive.*
C: *He shouldn't have got aggressive.*

Continue:
He left the guarantee in the box.
He didn't obtain a receipt.
He didn't check the radio.
He shouted at the manager.
He left the switch on 'mains'.
He didn't switch it on to battery.

8 Repeat Drill 27.7, substituting *ought to* and *ought not to* for the responses.

9 Silent reading.

10 Pair work. Students read it in pairs.

11 Role-play. Students role-play parallel situations using different objects, in pairs. Get one or two pairs to demonstrate.

12 Focus attention on the letter. Silent reading.

13 Questions and answer:
What did he buy? Ask 'When?'/Where?/Did it work in the shop?'
He found that it was faulty, didn't he? Ask 'When?'
What could it do? What couldn't it do?
Where did he take it first? What happened?
What did they say he would have to do? Can he do that?
Ask 'Why not?'
What did he enclose with his letter?

14 Exercise. Ask students to read the guarantee silently.
Set the exercise in class or for homework.

15 Written phase. Write up the Teaching points above on the board. Ask students to copy them.

Unit 27

MAKING A COMPLAINT

Customer Good morning, miss. I'd like to speak to the manager.

Manager I am the manager, sir. How can I help you?

Customer Oh, really? It's this radio. It doesn't work.

Manager Mm ... did you buy it here?

Customer Pardon? Of course I bought it here. Look, you switch it on and nothing happens.

Manager Could I see your receipt?

Customer Receipt? I haven't got one.

Manager Oh, you should have obtained a receipt when you bought it.

Customer I probably did. I must have thrown it away.

Manager Ah, well, have you got any other proof of purchase, the guarantee, for example?

Customer No. It must have been in the box. I threw that away too.

Manager Oh, dear. You really ought to have kept it. We need to know the exact date of purchase.

Customer What? I only bought it yesterday! That young man over there served me. Oh, I paid by cheque. I've got the cheque stub.

Manager That's all right then. Did you check the radio before you left the shop?

Customer Check it? No, it was in the box. I expected it to work. It wasn't a cheap radio, it's a good make.

Manager You should have checked it.

Customer Come on! Stop telling me what I should have done, and do something! Either give me my money back or give me another radio.

Manager There's no need to get aggressive, sir. Let me look at it ... mm ... you see this little switch on the back?

Customer Yes?

Manager It's on 'mains', and it should be on 'battery'. You really should have read the instructions.

Customer Oh!

97 Cuckoo Lane,
Tunbridge Wells,
Kent

22nd May, 1982

Customer Service Dept.,
Dicken's Electrical Ltd.,
Harlow,
Essex

Dear Sir or Madam,

Last week I bought a pocket calculator at your branch in Cheltenham. It seemed to work in the shop. When I got home, I found that it was faulty. It adds and subtracts perfectly well, but it does not divide or multiply. I took it back to your branch in Tunbridge Wells, but they refused to exchange it, saying that I would have to return it to the branch where I bought it. This is impossible because I do not live in Cheltenham. Please find enclosed the calculator, together with the receipt, showing price and date of purchase, and the manufacturer's guarantee.

Yours faithfully,

C. R. S. Sketchley

Exercise

DIGITAL ALARM CLOCK

This product should reach you in perfect working order. If it does not, please return it to Electric Clocks Ltd., Hounslow, Middlesex, stating where and when it was bought. We will be glad to exchange it and refund the postage.

Write a letter of complaint. You bought the clock at a branch of W. H. Samson in Oxford Street, London, last week. It said 'blue' on the box, but it was pink. The alarm doesn't seem to work. You paid cash, and you didn't keep the receipt.

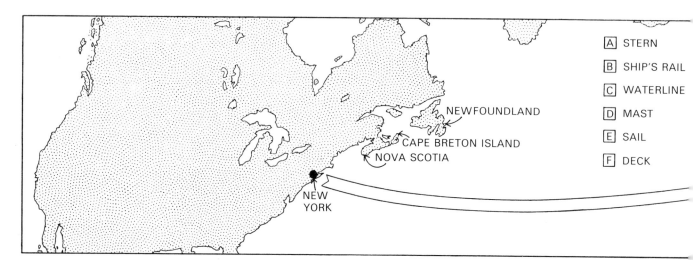

A	STERN
B	SHIP'S RAIL
C	WATERLINE
D	MAST
E	SAIL
F	DECK

THE 'MARY CELESTE'

The 'Mary Celeste' was built in 1861 in Nova Scotia, Canada, as a cargo-carrying sailing-ship. When it was launched, it was given the name 'The Amazon'. It was not a lucky ship. The first captain died a few days after it was registered, and on its first voyage in 1862 it was badly damaged in a collision. While it was being repaired in port, it caught fire. In 1863 it crossed the Atlantic for the first time, and in the English Channel it collided with another ship which sank. 'The Amazon' was badly damaged itself. Four years later, in 1867, it ran aground on Cape Breton Island, off the Canadian coast. The ship was almost completely wrecked and had to be rebuilt. It was then sold and the name was changed to the 'Mary Celeste'. Sailors are very superstitious and dislike sailing on ships which have been unlucky or which have changed their names. Many sailors refused to sail on the 'Mary Celeste'.

On November 5th 1872, the 'Mary Celeste' left New York, carrying a cargo of commercial alcohol to Genoa in Italy. There were eleven people on board, Captain Briggs, his wife and two-year-old daughter, and a crew of eight. Briggs was an experienced captain, and a very religious man. In his cabin there was a harmonium, which was used for playing hymns. A month later the 'Mary Celeste' was seen by another ship, the 'Dei Gratia', about halfway between the Azores and the Portuguese coast.

Captain Moorhouse of the 'Dei Gratia', a friend of Captain Briggs, noticed that the ship was sailing strangely. When the 'Mary Celeste' did not answer his signal, he decided to investigate. He sent a small boat to find out what was wrong.

The 'Mary Celeste' was completely deserted.
☞ The only lifeboat was missing.
☞ All the sails were up, and in good condition.
☞ All the cargo was there.
☞ The ship had obviously been through storms. The glass on the compass was broken.
☞ The windows of the deck cabins had been covered with wooden planks.
☞ There was a metre of water in the cargo hold, which was not enough to be dangerous.
☞ The water pumps were working perfectly.
☞ There was enough food for six months, and plenty of fresh water.
☞ All the crew's personal possessions (clothes, boots, pipes and tobacco etc.) were on board.
☞ There were toys on the captain's bed.
☞ There was food and drink on the cabin table.
☞ Only the navigation instruments and ship's papers were missing.
☞ The last entry in the ship's log-book had been made eleven days earlier, 1000 km west, but the ship had continued in a straight line.

☞ The fore-hatch was found open.
☞ There were two deep marks on the bows, near the water-line.
☞ There was a deep cut on the ship's rail, made by an axe.
☞ There were old brown bloodstains on the deck, and on the captain's sword, which was in the cabin.

Captain Moorhouse put some sailors on the 'Mary Celeste', who sailed it to Portugal. There was a long official investigation, but the story of what had happened on the ship, and what had happened to the crew, still remains a mystery. Captain Moorhouse and his crew were given the salvage money for bringing the ship to port. Many explanations have been suggested, but none of them have ever been proved.

Exercise
Find words which mean:
1 All the people working on a ship.
2 The official, daily, written record of a ship's voyage.
3 A religious song.
4 Put a boat into the water.
5 An instrument that shows the position of 'north'.
6 A musical instrument, like a small organ.
7 A long, thin, narrow, flat piece of wood.
8 Payment given to those who save others' property at sea.
9 Goods carried on a ship.
10 A machine for forcing water into or out of something.

Unit 28

Revision points

▶ Nationalities

▶ Past tenses + past passives

They were given money for doing it.

Key vocabulary

axe	plank	launch
bloodstain	port	notice
bow	salvage money	rebuild
cargo	ship's rail	register
collision	signal	run aground
compass	stern	sink
crew	storm	wreck
entry	sword	– – – – –
fore-hatch	voyage	commercial
halfway	water-line	experienced
harmonium	water pump	personal
hold	– – – – –	religious
hymn	catch fire	superstitious
lifeboat	collide	wooden
log-book	damage	– – – – –
mast	desert	strangely

1 Focus attention on the diagram of a sailing ship. Silent study for vocabulary.

2 Check vocabulary. Ask these questions:
Have you seen an old sailing ship? Ask him/her.
Ask 'Where?/When?'
Have you ever been on one?
Are they used nowadays? Will they be used again in the future?

3 Paragraph 1. Ensure the text is masked. Focus attention on the map. Play the cassette.

4 Silent reading.

5 Question and answer:
Where was it built? Ask 'When?'
It carried cargo, didn't it?
It was a sailing ship, wasn't it?
It was a cargo-carrying sailing ship . . . What was it?
What was its first name?
It was an unlucky ship, wasn't it?
When did the first captain die?
What happened on its first voyage?
It caught fire, didn't it? Ask 'When?'
When did it first cross the Atlantic?
It hit another ship, didn't it? Ask 'Where?/What happened to the other ship?'
The Amazon ran aground, didn't it? Ask 'When?/Where?'
It was rebuilt, wasn't it? Ask 'Why?'
The name was changed, wasn't it? Ask 'When?'
What did many sailors refuse to do? Ask 'Why?'
Are you superstitious? Ask him/her/me/each other.
What are your superstitions? Ask him/her/me/each other.

6 Drill:
T: *Someone launched it.*
C: *It was launched.*

Continue:
They gave it the name 'The Amazon'.
They registered it.
Something damaged it.
They were repairing it.
The collision wrecked it.
They sold it.
They changed the name.

7 Paragraph 2. Follow the procedure 28.3–28.4. Ask these questions:
What and who was on the 'Mary Celeste' when it left New York?
Where was it sailing from?
Where was it sailing to?
When was it seen by Captain Moorhouse? What happened?

8 Drill:
This could be done as an oral drill, or as a dictation.
T: *Portugal*   C: *Portuguese*
T: *Canada*   C: *Canadian*
T: *England*   C: *English*

Continue:

Portugal	Canada	Russia	Spain
China	Brazil	India	Scotland
Japan	Argentina	England	Ireland
Burma	Algeria	Finland	Poland
Vietnam			

9 Paragraph 3. Follow the procedure 28.3–28.4.

10 Question and answer:
Where was the lifeboat?
Where were the sails?
Where was the cargo?
Had the ship been through storms? What was broken? What had they done to the windows? How much water was in the hold? Was that dangerous? Were the water pumps broken?
How much food was there? How much water was there?
Where were the crew's possessions?
What was on the Captain's bed? What was on the table?
What was missing?
When had the last logbook entry been made? Where had the ship been?
Was the fore-hatch open or closed?
Where were the deep marks? Where was the deep cut? What had made the cut?
Where were the bloodstains? Where was the sword? Spell 'sword'.

11 Pair work. Students ask each other questions about the facts as above (one student covers the text).

12 Drill:
T: *They used the harmonium for playing hymns.*
C: *The harmonium was used for playing hymns.*

Continue:
The 'Dei Gratia' saw it.
They covered the windows with planks.
They made the last entry eleven days earlier.
They found the fore-hatch open.
An axe made the cut.

13 Paragraph 4. Follow the procedure 28.3–28.4.

14 Question and answer:
How did the 'Mary Celeste' get to Portugal?
What was Captain Moorhouse given? Ask 'Why?'

15 Drill:
T: *They brought the ship to port. They were given money.*
They were given money for sailing the ship to port.

Continue:
He came first in the race. He was given a gold medal.
She passed the exam. She received a certificate.
He carried the luggage. He got a big tip.
She worked very hard. She was given a higher salary.
They robbed the bank. They received a long prison sentence.

16 Written phase. Write up two or three of the answers to 28.15, underlining 'for doing'. Ask students to copy them. Set the exercise in class, or for homework.

17 Ask the students to read through Unit 28 at home, and to try and find some possible solutions. They could write out a list of possibilities and bring them to the next lesson.

Unit 28

Teaching points

▶ Speculating about the past (2)

They	must	have been doing it.
	could	
	may	
	might	
	might even	
	couldn't	
	can't	
	should	
	shouldn't	

▶ Revision of *must/can't/could have done*/etc.

▶ Infinitive of purpose

He jumped in to save the others.
They launched a boat to rescue them.

▶ *He killed himself after throwing the bodies into the sea.*

Key vocabulary

Atlantis (mythical city below the sea)	*religious mania*	*overturn*
barrel	*rope*	*row*
disease	*rye*	*run down*
emergency drill	*sea serpent*	*steer*
ergot	*site*	*tow*
fungus	*tornado*	– – – – – –
gust	*wave*	*abandoned*
monster	*whale*	*giant*
mutiny	– – – – –	*infectious*
octopus	*abandon*	*mad*
pirate	*drift*	*medieval*
	interrupt	

1 Set the situation. Refer back to Unit 28. Ask students to re-read the third paragraph silently.

2 Pair work. Students make questions about Unit 28, paragraph 3, using 'Why'? e.g. *Why was the lifeboat missing? Why were the windows covered with planks?* etc.

3 Dialogue. Two people are discussing the mystery of the 'Mary Celeste'. Ensure the text is masked. Play the cassette.

4 Selective repetition. Focus on the target structure.

5 Drill:
T: *must*
C: *He must have been doing it.*

Continue:
should	*shouldn't*
might	*couldn't*
can't	*may*
could	*might even*

6 Silent reading.

7 Pair work.

8 Written phase. Write up the paradigm on 'must have been doing', etc. from the teaching points above. Students copy it.

9 Some possible explanations. For each possibility read the idea aloud, tell students to read it silently. Get students to speculate after each one. e.g. *Do you think this is possible?*
They could have panicked because of water in the hold. It might have been coming in very quickly. They could have thought the ship was going to sink, so they could have left in the lifeboat.
But . . . the captain was very experienced. He must have known it wasn't dangerous. He shouldn't have panicked. They can't have expected to reach land in the lifeboat.
Do this for each example.

10 After each group of possibilities, invite the students to speculate in pairs or groups.
i.e. After No 7 of 'Why the crew abandoned the ship'
    After No 5 of 'What about the lifeboat?'
    After No 4 of 'One or all of them went mad'
    After No 7 of 'Crime'
    After No 4 of 'Outside Forces'
The pair or group should decide which explanation they prefer in each group and why.
Each pair or group reports its choice to the class. They should try and justify it, and attack alternative choices by other pairs or groups.

11 Drill:
T: *They launched the lifeboat. They wanted to escape the explosion.*
C: *They launched the lifeboat to escape the explosion.*

Continue:
They wanted to save the child.
They wanted to explore an island.
They wanted to escape a disease.
They wanted to tow the ship.
They wanted to save their lives.

12 Having gone through the explanations, each pair or group should choose their favourite explanation of all (as in 29.10).

13 Ask for other ideas. Refer back to the project set at the end of the previous lesson. Discuss the ideas.

14 Homework. Write an account of what happened, based on one of the explanations in the lesson, or another explanation which the student has thought of. Ask them to read the dialogue again first.

Unit 29

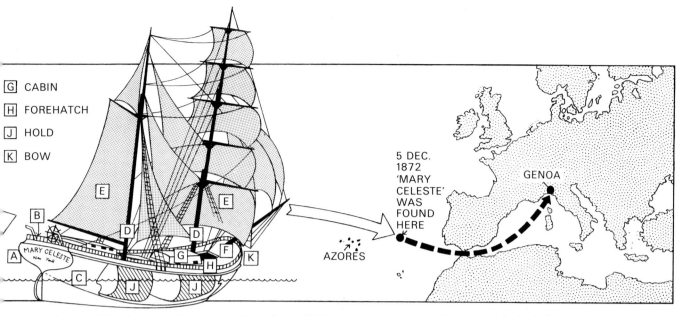

G CABIN
H FOREHATCH
J HOLD
K BOW

5 DEC. 1872 'MARY CELESTE' WAS FOUND HERE

AZORES

GENOA

What do you think happened?

Sarah I don't know what happened, but it must have happened suddenly.

Mark Why do you think that?

Sarah Think about it. There were toys on the captain's bed, weren't there? The child must have been playing, and they must have interrupted her suddenly.

Mark Yes, that's true. And the food was on the table. They must have been eating, or getting ready to eat.

Sarah I'll tell you my theory. The lifeboat was missing, right? They could have been practising their emergency drill. They must have got into the boat, and launched it.

Mark All right, but what happened to the boat?

Sarah Ah! They may have been rowing the lifeboat round the ship, and there must have been a gust of wind, then the ship could have moved forward and run down the lifeboat. That explains the marks on the bows!

Mark Come on! They can't all have been sitting in the lifeboat. What about the captain? He should have been steering the ship!

Sarah Ah, he might have been watching the drill, and jumped in to save the others!

Some possible explanations of why the crew abandoned the ship.

Amazingly, all of these have been suggested at some time.

1 There was water in the hold. The crew panicked and abandoned the ship because they thought it was going to sink. (Why? The captain was very experienced, and the ship was in good condition. The water-pumps were working.)

2 The child fell into the sea. The mother jumped in to save her. They launched a lifeboat to rescue her. (All of them? Why?)

3 One of the barrels of alcohol was damaged. Perhaps there was a small explosion. The hatch cover was off, either because of the explosion or to let the gas escape. They thought all the cargo might explode. (But not much evidence of an explosion.)

4 The last log entry was 1000 km west, near Santa Maria Island. Maybe the ship was in danger of running aground on the island. The crew left the ship in a storm. (How did the ship continue in a straight line for eleven days?)

5 There was no wind, so they got into the lifeboat to tow the ship. The rope broke. (Why were the woman and child in the lifeboat? Surely the ship was too heavy?)

6 They saw an island which was not on the map, and went to investigate. (All of them?)

7 One of the crew had a terrible, infectious disease. The others left to escape from it. The one with the disease killed himself.

What about the lifeboat?

If the crew left the ship by lifeboat, what happened to them?

1 It could have sunk in a storm.

2 The ship itself could have run down the lifeboat.

3 It could have drifted away, and all of them could have died of hunger and thirst.

4 They might have reached land. They were robbed and killed there.

5 A whale or sharks might even have overturned the boat!

One, or all of them, went mad.

1 They drank some of the commercial alcohol. There was a fight. Some were killed, the others left. (But commercial alcohol is very poisonous.)

2 The cook was crazy and poisoned everybody. Then he killed himself after throwing the bodies into the sea.

3 The captain had an attack of religious mania, killed everybody, then himself.

4 There was a fungus called 'ergot' in the bread. This is a fungus which can grow on rye bread. It is very similar to the drug LSD. Whole villages had been poisoned in this way in medieval Europe.

Crime.

1 The 'Dei Gratia' attacked the 'Mary Celeste' and killed everybody.

2 Pirates attacked and killed them.

3 There was a mutiny (a revolution against the captain of a ship). Two of the crew were criminals. There was a fight. Some were killed. The others left.

4 Mrs Briggs fell in love with one of the crew. Again there was a fight.

5 The crew of the 'Mary Celeste' attacked and robbed another ship, and left on the other ship with its cargo. (Which other ship? There are no records.)

6 They found an abandoned ship with a valuable cargo, and stole it.

7 Captain Briggs and Captain Moorhouse planned everything together, for the salvage money. The ship was never abandoned. None of the story was true.

Outside forces.

1 A spaceship from another planet took everybody away.

2 A giant wave knocked them all from the deck, or a tornado.

3 A sea monster (a giant octopus or sea serpent) attacked the ship.

4 Men living below the sea attacked the ship, when it passed over the old site of Atlantis.

SPECULATION

1△

Look at this

He	must	be	crazy.
She	could	have been	at home.
They	may		
It	might	be doing	something.
	might even	have done	
	can't	have been	
	couldn't	doing	

Make as many sentences as possible about each of the pictures.

2△

3△

4△

Unit 30

Teaching points

▶ Speculating about the past and present
Revision of Units 20–29, contrasting:

He She They It	must could may might might even can't couldn't	be have been be doing have done have been doing	crazy. at home. something.

Key vocabulary

As the aim of this unit is speculation by the students, the vocabulary is unpredictable.

1 Ask the students to study the 'Look at this' section on the first page.

2 For each of the pictures, follow this procedure.
   a) Focus attention on the picture. Ask *What can you see in Picture x ?* Get students to describe the picture.

   b) Ask questions:
   Who do you think they are?/What do you think it is?
   Where do you think they (might) be?
   What (might) they be doing?
   What (might) be happening?
   What (might) have just happened?/What (might) have been happening?
   What (might) happen next?

   c) Pair Work. Students draw up a list of possibilities in pairs. Discuss their suggestions.

THESE NOTES MAY HELP: Students should be encouraged to speculate freely about each picture and will come up with other ideas.

Picture 1

Why have the cars been put there?
Someone must have dug holes and buried them. They must have used a crane. It might be a work of art/the work of a lunatic.
Someone might be going to jump over them in a car/on a motor-cycle.
Perhaps someone's going to ride between them.
Maybe it's a fence of cars. It could be an advert for a car-breaking company.
The cars must be old/American.

Picture 2

Who/where might they be?
They may be telephone engineers/telephone salesmen. It may be a telephone museum. They may collect telephones.
They may be buying and selling by telephone. It may be an import/export company/a currency exchange. A lot of the telephones are off the hook. Why? People must be waiting on the other end.
If they're international telephones, people may have called from New York/Tokyo/Sydney, etc.
They must have received a big phone bill last month!

Picture 3

Are the legs real? They're very long. They may be dummies/people.
They must be tall people. Are they men or women?
They may be advertising something. (Tights?/shoes?)
They may be making a film/an advert.
They must have taken a long time to prepare. How could they have done it? They must have used real leaves and branches.
How did they stick them on? They could have made a frame.
What are they going to do?
Are there two legs or one leg in each 'tree'?
Are they right legs or left legs? If there's only one, where's the other leg? They must have taken the photograph very carefully.

Picture 4

What are they holding? They could be driving something/getting an electric shock/moving something/switching something on/shooting something.
They must have just seen something. It must have been exciting/shocking/amazing/horrific, etc.
They could be sitting in a golf trolley/a dodgem car at a fair/a railway engine/an aeroplane/a ship.

Picture 5

Which country might the photo have been taken in?
What's the building? It might be a house/church/country school/part of a film set.
How did it get on the truck? They must have used a crane. They might have dug a tunnel under the building.
It must be a special truck. Why might they be moving it? Perhaps they're going to build a dam/new road/airport.
They might be moving it to a museum. Someone famous might have lived there.

Picture 6

They must be watching something/waiting for somebody to pass along the street. It must be someone important.
They might be waiting for a king/queen/president/football team/pop star/astronauts, etc.
The boy's holding a periscope. It says 'London Broadcasting'.
The picture must have been taken in England/London.
What's the lady holding? It may be a mirror/some slides.
She must be trying to see something. One man is looking to the right. Why? He may not be interested/He may be a security guard/Someone might have called his name/He might be looking for a friend/Someone might have stepped on his foot.
A man's wearing a bowler hat. He must be English/a businessman.

Picture 7

They might be businessmen/journalists/students/politicians/people at a sale or auction/detectives.
They're taking notes ... Why? They may be watching something/listening to something/drawing something.
If they're journalists, it may be a press conference.
Who might they be interviewing? The man in front looks surprised/worried. What might he have just heard/seen?
If it's an auction, what might they be buying/selling?

Picture 8

It must be an advert.
It could be a pyramid/a billboard/the side of a building/a wall.
They might be workmen/soldiers.
They might be putting it up/taking it down/painting it/cleaning it.
What language is it? Do you know? If not, speculate.
What do you think it's advertising? What do you think it says?
Is the man at the top stuck/on a ladder/on the side/on the roof of a building?
Why might they have climbed up there?
They might have climbed up to paint/repair/finish/clean it/put it up/take it down.

Picture 9

Where might it be? It might be a dancing school/film studio/mental hospital/health farm/private house.
The man in white looks like an instructor. The other two may be students/a married couple/patients.
They may be dancing/doing exercises/practising for a show/trying to lose weight.
They must be rich/The sun must be shining outside.
If it's a health farm/dancing school, they must have paid a lot of money.

Picture 10

Where might they be? A pop concert/a sports event/a parade/a political meeting/a demonstration.
They might be watching a group/an air display/a motor race/a royal wedding/a carnival/an important visitor/a golf tournament, etc.
Why have they got umbrellas? They could be for the sun, or for the rain.
The weather forecast might have been good/bad. The sun must be shining at the moment.
They're standing in rows. Why?
Someone might have told them to. There might be lines on the ground.

Picture 11

They could be watching a football match/political speech/parade/the news/a visitor to their town/country.
Why aren't they watching it indoors? There might be only one T.V.
It might be a campsite. It must be warm. It must be very interesting.
There are more men than women. Why?
It may be in a park/a forest/someone's garden.
If it's the news, something important must have happened.
A war might have started/The election results may have been announced/Taxes may have changed/Someone important may have been assassinated/married.

Picture 12

The water must be shallow/It can't be very deep.
The people on the bench are wearing summer clothes. It must be summer/It must be a warm day.
It might be a river/It might be a lake/It can't be the sea.
The man's a frogman. He might be diving for sport. He might be a policeman/a scientist/studying the river/lake. He might be looking for a dead body/a diamond ring/a weapon/fish.
Someone might have fallen in the water/dropped something in the water/thrown something in the water.
There's a line attached to the frogman. It can't be an air line. (He's got air tanks.) It may be for safety. He might be an actor/making a film.
There are some feathers on the water. Some birds must have been there. They might have been ducks/swans. People might have been feeding them.
What's the diver saying?
He might be showing the size of something/He might be clapping/He might be talking about a fish.

5△

6△

7△

8△

9△

11△

10
◁

12△

Unit 30

APOLOGIES

C Excuse me.
D Yes?
C Would you mind putting out your cigarette?
D I beg your pardon?
C This is a 'no smoking' compartment!
D Is it? I didn't see a sign.
C There it is. On the window.
D Oh, yes. I'm terribly sorry.

G Oi! You!
H Me?
G Yes, you. What do you think you're doing?
H Pardon? I'm just waiting for the bus.
G Well, there's a queue, you know.
H Is there? Sorry ... I didn't mean to push in. I didn't realize there was a queue.

A Hello. Derek Moore speaking.
B Oh, hello, Derek. This is Clive.
A Ah, yes. Did you get home all right?
B Yes, thanks, but I just wanted to apologize for last night.
A Don't worry about it. It really doesn't matter.
B But the carpet, it must be ruined. It was so silly of me to put the cup on the floor.
A Forget it, Clive. It's all right now.
B But it must have made an awful stain.
A Look, it's nothing. I was annoyed last night, but it doesn't look so bad this morning.
B Anyway, you must let me pay for the cleaning.
A Listen, Clive. Accidents happen. They always do at parties. I don't want to hear any more about it. Right?
B All right. I really am very sorry.
A See you on Monday. Bye.

E Oh! Good morning, Mrs Newbury.
F Good afternoon, Sharon. Late again?
E Oh, yes. I'm ever so sorry. I couldn't find a parking place.
F Perhaps you should have left home earlier.
E Yes, I know. It won't happen again.
F It'd better not, Sharon. This is the third time this week!

I Are you OK?
J Yes, I'm all right, but what about my car?
I There's not too much damage.
J What! Just look at it! I only bought it last week. You shouldn't have been going so fast.
I Well, I'm sorry, but it wasn't my fault.
J Wasn't your fault? What do you mean? I had right of way.
I I'm afraid you didn't. You shouldn't have come out like that.
J Why not? There's no sign.
I What's that there then?
J Oh, yes. A 'stop' sign. I must have missed it.
I Well, you should be more careful. You could have killed us all!
J Yes ... I'm sorry. What more can I say?
I All right ... all right. At least nobody's hurt. Here come the police. You'd better explain it to them.

Unit 31

Teaching points

▶ Apologies, and accepting apologies

Sorry.
I'm terribly sorry.
I really am very sorry.
I'm ever so sorry.
I just want(ed) to apologize.

Don't worry about it.
It really doesn't matter.
Forget it.
It's all right.
It's nothing.
I don't want to hear any more about it.

I didn't mean to do it.
I didn't realize . . .
It was so silly of me to do it.
It won't happen again.
It wasn't my fault.
What more can I say?

Revision points

must/should(n't) do
must/should/shouldn't/could have | *done.*
                                    | *been doing.*

Expressions

See above, plus:
What do you think you're doing?
There it is.
Accidents happen.
It'd better not!
Just look at it!
What's that there, then?
Here come the police.
Keep off the grass.
No smoking.

Key vocabulary

cleaning	*taxi rank*	*realize*
compartment	*– – – – –*	*ruin*
damage	*come out*	*push in*
grass	*give way*	*put out*
right of way	*keep off*	*– – – – –*
stain	*mean to*	*at least*

1 Dialogue – A and B. Focus attention on the picture. Set the situation. Ensure the text is masked. Play the cassette.

2 Listen and repeat.

3 Silent reading.

4 Pair work. Students read the dialogue in pairs.

5 Act out the conversation with one or two individuals, playing both parts and substituting items.

6 Focus attention on the pictures. Say *What can you see? What might have happened?* (e.g. *Someone might have stepped/fallen on the guitar.*) Ask students to make parallel conversations in pairs.

7 Dialogue – C and D. Follow the same procedure, 31.1–31.5.

8 Focus attention on the four signs. Ask *Where might you see these signs?* Ask each other '*Who might tell you not to do these things?*' (e.g. *A traffic warden/park keeper/zoo keeper*). Ask students to make parallel conversations, in pairs, e.g.
A: *Excuse me?*
B: *Yes?*
A: *Would you mind not walking on the grass?*
B: *Pardon?*
A: *You mustn't walk on the grass.*
B: *Really? I didn't see a sign.*
A: *There it is. Over there.*
B: *Oh, yes. I'm very sorry.*
Get one or two pairs to demonstrate.

9 Dialogue – E and F. Follow the same procedure, 31.1–31.5.

10 Focus attention on the prompts. Ask students to make parallel conversations in pairs.

11 Dialogue – G and H. Follow the same procedure, 31.1–31.5.

12 Focus attention on the signs. Ask *Where might you see these signs? What might you be queuing for?* Ask students to make parallel conversations in pairs.

13 Dialogue – I and J. Follow the same procedure, 31.1–31.5.

14 Focus attention on the signs. Ask students to make parallel conversations in pairs.

15 Transfer:
Imagine you are late for work. What do you say?

Continue:
You bump into someone in the street.
You have forgotten to do your homework.
You stand on someone's foot.
You pick up the wrong bag/coat.
You don't remember someone's name/miss an appointment/ sit in somebody else's place.
Ask *Have you ever done this? Ask each other.*

16 Role-play. Students make a conversation in pairs using one of these ideas. One or two pairs demonstrate their conversations.

Teaching points

▶ Verb + -ing form compared with verb + infinitive

stop	doing	stop	to do
remember		remember	
		forget	

Revision points

▶ Verb + infinitive

try/manage/decide to do

▶ *might/could/must have done*

Expressions

to keep an eye on something
I bet it wasn't!
on the increase
on this occasion

Key vocabulary

cab door	Road Transport	extra
case	Industry	marketable
cash desk	service area	well-informed
diesel	sunset	well-organized
hijacking	– – – – – –	– – – – – –
hitch-hiker	concentrate	definitely
load	concern	increasingly
M6	propose to	
puddle	– – – – – –	

Note: *lorry* and *truck* are used as direct alternatives. The use of *truck* has increased in British English, particularly among *truck* drivers.

1 Classroom set.
Write something on the board.
Say *What am I doing?* to elicit *You're writing.*
Stop writing, say *I'm going to sit down.*
Say *What have I stopped doing?* to elicit *You've stopped writing.*
Say *Why did I stop? I stopped because I wanted to sit down. I stopped to sit down.*
Do the same with:
I stopped reading. I stopped to ask a question.
I stopped cleaning the board. I stopped to open my book.
I stopped listening to the cassette. I stopped to write on the board.

2 Newspaper extract. Focus attention on the picture. Ensure the text is masked.

3 Silent reading.

4 Question and answer:
What is the Road Transport Industry becoming concerned about?
What do the gangs concentrate on?
What have drivers been forbidden to do?
What have they been warned to do?
What happened at Burnham Wood yesterday? It wasn't the first time, was it?

5 Dialogue. First part. Ensure the text is masked. Play the cassette.

6 Selective repetition.

7 Play the cassette, pausing to ask questions at the appropriate points.
Does he want a cigarette? Ask 'Why not'?
Where was he driving from? He stopped driving, didn't he?
Where did he stop? Why did he stop? (to elicit: He stopped to get diesel/He stopped to have a coffee.)
Why did he sit by the window? (He sat there to keep an eye on the truck.)
He was watching the truck, wasn't he? Why did he stop?
(He stopped to make a phone call.)
Why did he stop at the cash desk? (He stopped to get some change.)
Who was he talking to? Why did he stop?
Why did he drop the phone? (He dropped the phone to run outside.)

8 Silent reading.

9 Pair work.

10 Written phase:
He stopped driving to get some diesel.
What did he stop doing? He stopped driving.
What did he stop to do? He stopped to get some diesel.

11 Dialogue – second part. Ensure the text is masked. Play the cassette.

12 Selective repetition.

13 Play the cassette, pausing to ask questions at the appropriate points.
What does he always remember to do?
Is he sure? What does he remember doing?
Does he actually remember checking the passenger door?
He might have forgotten, mightn't he?
It could have been open, couldn't it?
They must have had keys, mustn't they?
He doesn't know how they got the keys, does he?
They didn't stop to tell him, did they?

14 Silent reading.

15 Pair work.

16 Ask students to speculate on how the hijacking happened.
How do you think they got the keys?
(to elicit Mr Fletcher might have given them the keys/They might have stolen them/They might not have had the keys/He might have left the door open/etc)
Where do you think they took the truck?
Where do you think they sold the whisky?

17 Go through. 'Look at this' and Exercise 1.

18 Go through. 'Look at this' and Exercise 2.

19 Transfer:
Tell me some of the important things in your life/things that you can remember doing for the first time.
(Prompt if necessary: First day at school/having your first English lesson/going to your first dance/having your first cigarette/etc.)

20 Ask questions (and *Ask me/him/her/each other.*): *Do you always remember to brush your teeth/set the alarm/do your homework/send birthday cards?* etc.

THEY DIDN'T STOP TO TELL ME!

LORRY HIJACKINGS ON THE INCREASE

The Road Transport Industry is becoming increasingly concerned about the number of lorry hijackings.

The hijackers seem to be both well-organized and well-informed. The gangs concentrate on trucks carrying high-value marketable loads, for example cigarettes, alcohol, or electrical goods. Drivers have now been forbidden to pick up hitch-hikers, and have been warned to take extra care when parking in motorway service areas. Yesterday's hijacking at Burnham Wood on the M6 was the fourth in the area this month.

Inspector Waterman is interviewing Stan Fletcher, the driver of the hijacked truck.

Inspector Sit down, Mr Fletcher. Cigarette?

Stan No, thanks. I'm trying to stop smoking.

Inspector Now, Mr Fletcher. How did you manage to lose your truck?

Stan You know the story already.

Inspector Well, tell us again.

Stan OK. I was driving down the M6 from Scotland carrying whisky ... in cases.

Inspector Hmm.

Stan I decided to stop at Burnham Wood.

Inspector Why Burnham Wood?

Stan I stopped to get some diesel and I needed a coffee. I'd been driving for three hours.

Inspector Go on.

Stan After I'd filled the tank, I parked outside the café.

Inspector Yes.

Stan I got my coffee and sat by the window to keep an eye on the truck.

Inspector Did you see anybody near the lorry?

Stan No, nobody. Then I went to make a phone call.

Inspector A phone call?

Stan Yes, you can check. I stopped to get some change at the cash desk.

Inspector OK. Then?

Stan Well, I was talking to my wife on the phone when I saw the lorry going past the window. I couldn't believe my eyes. I dropped the phone and ran outside ... but it was too late!

Inspector Had you remembered to lock the cab door?

Stan Yes, I always remember to lock it. I'm not stupid, you know!

Inspector All right. All right. But can you actually remember locking it on this occasion?

Stan Yes, definitely.

Inspector How can you be so sure?

Stan Well, I remember putting the key in the lock. It was all wet and dirty. It was raining, you see, and I'd dropped it in a puddle.

Inspector And the passenger door? Did you remember to check that?

Stan I don't actually remember checking it. But I'm sure I must have done. It locks from the inside, and I never use that door.

Inspector But you don't remember checking it?

Stan No, not really. But you can't remember everything, can you? I might've forgotten to check it.

Inspector So it could've been open.

Stan Yes ... yes, it could've been. But I bet it wasn't!

Inspector Well, what's your theory, Mr Fletcher?

Stan They must've had keys, mustn't they? They started the engine, didn't they?

Inspector How did they get the keys?

Stan Don't ask me. I've got no idea. They didn't stop to tell me!

Look at this

He was driving. He stopped. He got some petrol.

A *What did he stop doing? He stopped driving.*
B *What did he stop to do? He stopped to get some petrol.*

Exercise 1
Now make questions and answers from these sentences.
1 He was driving. He stopped. He had a cup of coffee.
2 He was watching the truck. He stopped. He made a phone call.
3 He was talking to his wife. He stopped. He ran outside.

Look at this

I proposed to my wife on the beach at sunset. I can see it now!
I remember proposing to my wife.

I was told to post this letter. I've still got it.
I didn't remember to post it.
I forgot to post it.

Exercise 2
Make sentences.
1 I should have closed the window, but it's still open.
2 I once met the Queen. I can remember it very clearly.
3 There's a film on television. I saw it at the cinema ten years ago.
4 He ought to have done his homework. The teacher's very angry.

Unit 32

Unit 33

Teaching points

▶ Reading comprehension from notes.

Key vocabulary

appeal	permission	pray
aunt	popularity	replace
autograph	relationship	separate
brain tumour	riddle	shoot dead
cold store	rumour	stalk
departure	special edition/issue	weep
grief	spirits	— — — — — —
fur coat	Top 20	avant-garde
hero	— — — — —	exclusive
human race	break up	hit (record)
idol	bring up	incredible
MBE (Member of	evoke	solo
the Order of the	execute	— — — — —
British Empire)	form	RIP (rest in
media coverage	found	peace)
meditation	gather	yeah (=yes)
overdose	hang around	
overtime	plot	

Note:
a) 'Sean' can be spelled 'Shaun' and is pronounced in this way.
b) 'Starting over' (Am. E.) = starting again (Br. E.).

1 Focus attention on the Newspaper Headlines. Ensure the text on the right is masked. Silent reading.

2 Say *From the headlines, what are the facts?*
Who was John Lennon? How did he die? Who killed him?
When, where and how? How did people feel about his death?

3 Check the vocabulary. Ask students to paraphrase the headlines and deduce the meaning of new words. Point out the 'note' style used in headlines, e.g. 'Grief for murder of Lennon'.

4 Silent reading of the introductory text.

5 Free reproduction: *Tell me how it happened.*

6 Biographical notes.
Section One 1940–62. Silent reading.

7 Ask students to expand the notes into full sentences, orally, e.g.
What happened in 1940?
John Lennon was born in Liverpool.
What happened in 1942?
The Lennon family was deserted by his father. His mother left home.
John was brought up by his Aunt.
Go through 1940–62 in this way. Insist on full expansion, transforming into simple past and past passive.

8 Pair work. Students do the same in pairs.

9 Ask students to comment on the facts:
Why do you think his father might have left home?
Why might his mother have left him with an aunt?
How do you think he formed a group?
What do you think he studied?
etc.

10 Section Two 1963–69. Silent reading.

11 Ask students to expand the notes into full sentences as in 33.8.

12 Pair work as in 33.9.

13 Transfer (*Ask me/him/her/each other.*):
Have you heard any Beatles records? Can you remember the titles?
What's your favourite?
Have you seen any Beatles films? Which ones?
Which is your favourite group now? Why? Which of their songs do you like best? Are they as famous as the Beatles?

14 Section Three 1970–81. Silent reading.

15 Ask students to expand the notes into full sentences as in 33.8.

16 Pair work as in 33.9.

17 Ask students to comment on the facts:
Why do you think McCartney left the Beatles?
Why might John have gone to Los Angeles?
etc.

18 Written work. Ask students to choose one of the three sections. They should write a paragraph in connected prose, from the notes. (For homework.)

19 Transfer/Pair work.
Students ask each other about each other's biographical details and make notes.
When were you born? Where were you born?
Where were you brought up?
When did you start school?
When did you come to this school?
etc.

20 Extension. If available, a John Lennon or Beatles record might provide additional discussion points. A suitable record would be 'Imagine'.

21 Extension/Homework. Students might enjoy writing out the lyrics of one of their favourite British pop songs.

Unit 33

JOHN LENNON 1940-1980

John Lennon was murdered just before 11 pm on the 8th December 1980 outside his home in the Dakota Apartment Building in New York City. He had just got out of a car, and was walking to the entrance when a voice called 'Mr Lennon'. Lennon turned, and was shot five times. The killer threw his gun down, and stood there smiling. 'Do you know what you just did?' shouted the doorman. 'I just shot John Lennon,' the killer replied. Lennon was rushed to hospital in a police patrol car, but it was too late. The killer was 25 year-old Mark Chapman from Hawaii. Earlier the same evening he had asked Lennon for his autograph. In fact, he had been hanging around outside the apartment building for several days. Chapman was a fan of the Beatles and Lennon, and had tried to imitate him in many ways. It is said that he even believed that he was John Lennon.

Biographical notes

1940 Born Liverpool
1942 Lennon family deserted by father. Mother leaves. John brought up by aunt.
1956 Forms pop group at school.
1957 Student at Liverpool College of Art.
1958 Mother killed in road accident.
1960 Goes professional as one of 'The Beatles' (Lennon, McCartney, Harrison, Best, Sutcliffe). Plays in Hamburg, Germany.
1961 Plays in Hamburg and Liverpool. Sutcliffe (Lennon's best friend) dies of a brain tumour. Brian Epstein begins to manage the Beatles.
1962 Ringo Starr replaces Pete Best as Beatles drummer. Married Cynthia Powell, an art student. Beatles' first record 'Love me do'. First TV appearance.

1963 Three records Number 1 in British Top 20. Incredible popularity. Son, Julian, born.
1964 First hit record in USA 'I want to hold your hand'. Two US tours. In April, Beatles records at Number 1, 2, 3, 4, and 5 in US Top 20. First film 'A Hard Day's Night'. First book.
1965 'Help!' Beatles' second film. Beatlemania at its height. US tour. Huge audiences in football stadiums. Beatles receive MBE (special honorary award) from Queen Elizabeth.

1966 Lennon in film 'How I won the War' – not a musical. Meets Yoko Ono, Japanese avant-garde artist.
1967 'Sergeant Pepper' – Beatles' most famous LP. All the Beatles interested in meditation. Manager Brian Epstein found dead from sleeping-pill overdose.
1968 In India with Beatles for meditation. Beatles' company 'Apple' founded. Lennon art exhibition 'You are here'. Lennon divorced by wife.
1969 Beatles' film 'Let it Be'. Rumours of quarrels about money. Talk of Beatles' break up. Beatles' last performance on roof of Apple Building. Lennon and Yoko Ono marry. He 29. She 36. Lennon still recording with Beatles but some work solo.

1970 McCartney leaves Beatles. Others start solo careers.
1971 Lennon LP 'Imagine' – most successful LP. Lennon and Yoko Ono in New York one-room apartment.
1972 Charity concerts.
1973 Lennon and Yoko Ono separate. Lennon in Los Angeles. Lennon ordered to leave USA – protests and appeals.
1974 Drink problem – one and a half bottles of spirits a day. Still fighting deportation.
1975 Lennon and Yoko Ono together again in New York. Permission to stay in USA. Son Sean born October 9th (Lennon's birthday).
1976 Retires from public life. Extensive travel. Business affairs managed by Yoko Ono.
1976 Full-time father. Very close rela-
–80 tionship with son. Owns seven apartments in same block – one as a cold-store for fur coats.
1980 First record for six years. LP 'Double Fantasy'. Single 'Starting Over'. Good reviews from critics. Many said it was 'a new beginning'. Dec 8th Lennon murdered. Massive media coverage. TV and radio programmes interrupted to give news. Record companies on overtime to produce records.
1981 In January and February three records at Number 1 in British Top 20: '(Just Like) Starting Over', 'Imagine' and 'Woman'.

Beatle Lennon dies in a hail of bullets

...EY LOVED HIM, YEAH YEAH YEAH

...GES 14 and 15

A STUNNED generation of Beatles fans was in mourning for their murdered idol John Lennon last night.

From IAIN WALKER in New York

...friend after the shooting

...yed for the human
... same for him '

Yoko Ono yesterday

...AND FRANKLIN–Page 6 ● LENNON'S CASTLE–Centre Pages

...day December 10 1980   18p

... murder of Lennon

Yoko Ono is comforted by a record producer, David Geffen, as she leaves Roosevelt Hospital after Lennon's death

Unit 33

KIDNAPPED

Hugh Rolan is a wealthy businessman. His wife phoned him an hour ago to tell him that their daughter hadn't returned home from school. He told her not to worry and came home at once. He's just arrived to find his wife in tears.

Hugh Pamela, what's wrong? Is it Caroline?

Pamela Yes. This note came through the door. She ... she ... she's been kidnapped!

Hugh Kidnapped! Oh, my God, no! Have you phoned the police?

Pamela No, no. Don't touch the phone! Read the note first.

Hugh Half a million pounds! It'll take me a few days to get that much cash together.

Pamela How long?

Hugh I don't know. I just can't put my hands on that much money. Not immediately. Maybe we should phone the police.

Pamela No, not the police! If the kidnappers find out, they'll kill her.

Hugh But I'll have to borrow the money. If I don't tell the police, the bank won't let me have it.

Pamela Oh, Hugh! Unless we do exactly what they say, we may never see her again.

Hugh Hugh Rolan.

Voice Did you get our note?

Hugh Yes.

Voice Have you told the police?

Hugh No ... not yet.

Voice You'd better not. When can you get the money?

Hugh I need a few days.

Voice You've got one day.

Hugh How do we know that Caroline is still alive?

Voice You don't. You'll have to trust us. Get the money by tomorrow evening. You'll hear from us again.

Hugh If you harm a hair on her head, I'll ... I'll ...

We have got your **daughter**

She is safe and well

We want **£500,000** If you **give** us the **money** she will be **OK**

don't phone the POLICE or we'll **KILL** her If you **try** to contact them, **We'll** know

If you **don't** follow our INSTRUCTIONS your **daughter** will *DIE* UNLESS **you** pay up you'll **never** see her again.

Exercise 1

1 If you were Hugh, would you telephone the police?
2 If you were the kidnappers, how would you arrange to get the money?
3 If you were Hugh and Pamela, what would you do?
4 If you were the police, what would you do?

Exercise 2

A *Give me the money!*
B *Why?*
A *If you don't give me the money, I'll kill you.*
B *What? You're joking!*
A *No, I'm not. Unless you give me the money, I'll kill you.*

Now look at the pictures, and make similar conversations.

Exercise 3
Look at Exercise 2.
What would you do in these situations?
If I were him, I'd give him the money.
If I were him, I'd run away.
If I were him, I'd hit the robber with the briefcase.

Teaching points

▶ Conditional sentences (Type 1) with *unless*

If you do this, I'll do that.
If you don't do this, I'll do that.
Unless you do this, I'll do that.

▶ Revision of conditional sentences (Type 2) with *If I were ...*

Expressions

I can't put my hands on that much money.
If you harm a hair on her head, I'll ...

Key vocabulary

kidnapper	find out	trust
– – – – –	harm	– – – – –
contact	kidnap	wealthy
fail	pay up	– – – – –
		in tears

1 Introduction/first part of dialogue. Set the situation. Ensure the text is masked. Play the cassette.

2 Silent reading.

3 Question and answer:
What does Hugh do? Is he rich? Ask 'How rich?'
Who phoned him? Ask 'When?/Why?'
What did he tell her to do? What did he do?
What was his wife doing when he arrived home?
What's happened to Caroline?
Has Pamela phoned the police? Ask 'Why not?'

4 Focus attention on the note. Silent reading.

5 Question and answer:
How much do they want? What will happen if they give them the money?
What will happen if they phone the police?
What will happen if they don't follow the instructions?
What will happen unless they pay up?

6 Ask the students to write out the note neatly, with correct use of capital letters.

7 Dialogue – second part. Ensure the text is masked.
Play the cassette.

8 Selective repetition.

9 Silent reading.

10 Question and answer:
Can he get the money immediately? Ask 'How long?' Why do they think he can't put his hands on that much money?
What does he think they should do? Do you agree? What'll the kidnappers do if they find out?
What will happen if he doesn't contact the police?
What will happen if they don't do exactly what they say?

11 Pair work.

12 Drill:
T: *If you don't follow our instructions, your daughter will die.*
C: *Unless you follow our instructions, your daughter will die.*

Continue:
If you don't pay up, you'll never see her again.
If you don't follow the instructions, the kidnappers will be angry.
If I don't tell the police, the bank manager will be suspicious.
If they don't get the money in time, Caroline will die.
If the kidnappers don't phone, Hugh won't know what to do.
If he doesn't phone the police, he won't get any help.

13 Drill:
T: *Unless you follow our instructions, your daughter will die.*
C: *If you don't follow our instructions, your daughter will die.*
Continue: use the responses from Drill 34.12 above as prompts.

14 Dialogue – third part. Ensure the text is masked.
Play the cassette.

15 Listen and repeat.

16 Silent reading.

17 Pair work.

18 Exercise 1. Ask individuals orally. Get them to do it in pairs.

19 Exercise 2. Read out the mini-dialogue. Get them to read the mini-dialogue in pairs, and construct parallel dialogues for Pictures 1–5. Get one or two pairs to act out the situations without using the book.

20 Exercise 3. Ask individuals orally. Get them to do it in pairs.

Teaching points

▶ Revision: conditional sentences (Type 1) to contrast with conditional sentences (Type 2)

▶ Introduction of *unless* with Type 2 conditionals

If you did this, I'd do that.
If you didn't do this, I wouldn't do that.
Unless you did this, I wouldn't do that.
Not unless you did this.

Expressions

Expressions for directing attention:
Have you seen this?/Take a look at this./What do you think of this?
Did you see this?/Look at this./There's something in the paper.
It's a waste of time.
I wasn't born yesterday!
I'm prepared to do it. I wouldn't dream of doing it.
I didn't say that.
It's slave labour!
Commission only basis.
Salary negotiable.
all day   every day

Key vocabulary

ad	enthusiasm	negotiate
advert	fortune	provide
advertisement	hairstyle	– – – – –
basis	model	ambitious
challenge	nanny	keen
commission	security	one-way
disadvantage	volunteer	
energy	– – – – –	

1 'Want a new hairstyle?' Focus attention on the advertisement. Silent reading.

2 Question and answer:
What do they require? Ask 'Why?/When?/Where?'
What will the volunteers get?
What qualification do they need?

3 Dialogue 1 – Stephen/Wendy. Focus attention on the advertisement. Ensure the text is masked. Play the cassette.

4 Selective repetition.

5 Silent reading.

6 Question and answer:
Is Wendy interested in the advert?
She phoned them, didn't she? Ask 'When?'
Is her hair long?
What'll they do, if they want her?
What'll she get if she goes? (Three things)

7 Pair work.

8 Dialogue 2 – Mandy/Andrew. Follow the procedure 35.3–35.7, but ask the questions:
Has Mandy phoned?
Her hair isn't long enough, is it?
What would she do if she had longer hair?

9 Transfer:
If you lived near London, would you phone them? Ask 'Why?/Why not?'
What would you get, if you went? (Three things)
If you went, would you be worried about anything?
Would you mind green hair?

10 'Are you ambitious?' Focus attention on the advertisement. Silent reading.

11 Question and answer:
What kind of people are they looking for?
Is there a salary?
How are they paid?
What do applicants need?

12 Dialogue 3 – Louise/Colin. Follow the procedure 35.3–35.7, but ask these questions:
Is he interested in the job?
Is he going to apply for the job?
Is he prepared to try it?
Have they got a phone?
He's worried about phone bills, isn't he? What will he do, if they don't pay the phone bills?

13 Dialogue 4 – Roger/Sandra. Follow the procedure 35.3–35.7, but ask these questions:
Is he interested in the job? Ask 'Why not?'
Why wouldn't he take the job? (Prompt: security/money/car)
Would Sandra take the job? Why not?

14 Transfer:
Would you apply for this job? Why? Why not?

15 'Are you fond of children?' Focus attention on the advertisement. Silent reading.

16 Question and answer:
What do they want?
Where do they live?
Are they American?
Ask 'How many children?' Ask 'How old?'
Do they want someone with a driving licence? Ask 'Why?'
What are they offering? (Three things)
What about salary?

17 Dialogue 5 – Rachel/Helen. Follow the procedure 35.3–35.7, but ask these questions:
Has she applied for the job? When is the interview?
Does she think she'll get the job?
Will she take the job?
Make two sentences with *unless.*

18 Dialogue 6 – Jane/Tina. Follow the procedure 35.5–35.7, but ask these questions:
Is she going to apply for the job? Why not?
Why wouldn't she take the job?
Make four sentences with *unless.*

19 Write the sentences with *unless* elicited in 35.17 and 35.18 on the board in two columns. (One for Type 1 and one for Type 2.) Students copy it.

20 Transfer:
Would you apply for the job? Why? Why not?

21 Focus attention on 'Look at this'. Silent reading.

22 Exercise. Go through orally asking individuals. Then students do it in pairs.

Unit 35

HAVE YOU SEEN THIS ADVERT?

Stephen Wendy, have you seen this advert?

Wendy Mmm. It looks great, doesn't it? I phoned them an hour ago. They'll ring me back if they want me.

Stephen Oh, they'll want you. I mean you've got beautiful long hair.

Wendy I hope so! If I go, I'll get a new hairstyle … and a day out in London.

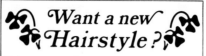

Want a new Hairstyle?

Volunteer models required for national hairstyling competition.

Wednesday 28th January
Carlton Towers Hotel, London

* Free dinner
* Rail fares paid

Only qualification needed is long hair (at least 20 cm)

Tel: 01-129 7880

Mandy Hey, Andrew. Look at this ad.

Andrew It looks fun. Why don't you ring?

Mandy I'd love to, but it's a waste of time. My hair's far too short.

Andrew Well, I like it the way it is. Anyway, you don't know what they might do. Blue and green hair's fashionable at the moment.

Mandy Oh, Andrew, I wouldn't mind that. If I had longer hair, I'd phone them.

Louise Colin, take a look at this.

Colin Oh, yes, I've seen it. I'm going to phone tomorrow.

Louise It sounds very exciting, and you've got a decent car.

Colin Hmm. There are some disadvantages.

Louise Every job's got disadvantages, but you're always complaining about your present job.

Colin I know. I'm prepared to try it. But we haven't got a phone. I won't take it if they don't pay the phone bills!

ARE YOU AMBITIOUS?

– are you aged 22–35?
– do you need a challenge?
– tired of your present job?

Some of our sales representatives earn more than the Prime Minister!!!

All you need is energy, enthusiasm, and your own car and telephone. No salary. Commission only basis.

Contact: **DIRECT SALES LTD.**, Suite 34, Plaza Hotel, Liverpool   051-174 2330

Roger Sandra, did you see this?

Sandra Yes. You aren't interested, are you?

Roger What? Me? I wasn't born yesterday! There are far too many things wrong with it.

Sandra What do you mean?

Roger I wouldn't take a job like that! You wouldn't have any security. You wouldn't earn anything if you didn't work all day, every day. And I wouldn't take a sales job if they didn't provide a car.

Sandra Yes, look at the address. It's a hotel room. I certainly wouldn't work for a company if they didn't even have an office!

Rachel Helen, what do you think of this advertisement?

Helen Didn't I tell you? It was in last week's paper too. I applied. I've got an interview tomorrow.

Rachel Do you think you'll get it?

Helen They seemed very keen on the phone. I think they'll offer me the job.

Rachel So, you're going to California!

Helen I didn't say that. I won't take the job unless they agree to pay my return fare. It'll be hard work with five kids, and I won't go unless they offer me a good salary!

ARE YOU FOND OF CHILDREN?

Nanny wanted for British family living in L.A., California, with 5 children aged between 1 and 8. Must have driving licence. Own room/bathroom. One way air fare paid. Two weeks holiday a year. Tuesday evenings free. Salary negotiable.

Write to BOX NO. 3/646.

Jane There's a job in America in the paper.

Tina Yes, I know. I wouldn't dream of applying for it.

Jane Why not? You've been looking for a job in the States.

Tina It's slave labour, isn't it? Five kids, and one evening off a week.

Jane But the money might be very good.

Tina Huh! I wouldn't take it unless they paid me a really good salary with longer holidays and more free time. And I certainly wouldn't go anywhere abroad unless they paid my return fare!

Look at this

I'm interested. I've applied.	I'm not interested. I haven't applied.
If they offer enough money, I'll accept the job.	If they offered more money, I'd apply.
If they don't pay more, I won't accept the job.	If they didn't offer enough, I wouldn't accept the job.
Unless they pay more, I won't accept the job.	Unless they offered more, I wouldn't accept the job.

Exercise

Could you ever kill a person?
Not unless they tried to kill me.
I wouldn't do it unless they tried to kill me.
What about these things?
Would you ever steal food?/rob a bank?/hit someone?/eat a cat?/jump from a high building?/take your clothes off in the street?/jump with a parachute?/have a heart transplant?

Unit 35

'Good evening, and welcome again to the 'Michael Parkhurst Talkabout'. In tonight's programme, we're looking at the problem of energy. The world's energy resources are limited. Nobody knows exactly how much fuel is left, but pessimistic forecasts say that there is only enough coal for 450 years, enough natural gas for 50 years and that oil might run out in 30 years. Obviously we have to do something, and we have to do it soon!

I'd like to welcome our first guest, Professor Marvin Burnham of the New England Institute of Technology. Professor Burnham.'

'Well, we are in an energy crisis and we will have to do something quickly. Fossil fuels (coal, oil and gas) are rapidly running out. The tragedy is that fossil fuels are far too valuable to waste on the production of electricity. Just think of all the things you can make from oil! If we don't start conserving these things now, it will be too late. And nuclear power is the only real alternative. We are getting some electricity from nuclear power-stations already. If we invest in further research now, we'll be ready to face the future. There's been a lot of protest lately against nuclear power – some people will protest at anything – but nuclear power-stations are not as dangerous as some people say. It's far more dangerous to work down a coal-mine or on a North Sea oil-rig. Safety regulations in power-stations are very strict.

If we spent money on research now, we could develop stations which create their own fuel and burn their own waste. In many parts of the world where there are no fossil fuels, nuclear power is the only alternative. If you accept that we need electricity, then we will need nuclear energy. Just imagine what the world would be like if we didn't have electricity – no heating, no lighting, no transport, no radio or TV. Just think about the ways you use electricity every day. Surely we don't want to go back to the Stone Age. That's what will happen if we turn our backs on nuclear research.'

'Thank you, Professor. Our next guest is a member of CANE, the Campaign Against Nuclear Energy, Jennifer Hughes.'

'Right. I must disagree totally with Professor Burnham. Let's look at the facts. First, there is no perfect machine. I mean, why do aeroplanes

ENERGY CRISIS

crash? Machines fail. People make mistakes. What would happen if there were a serious nuclear accident? And an accident must be inevitable – sooner or later. Huge areas would be evacuated, and they could remain contaminated with radioactivity for years. If it happened in your area, you wouldn't get a penny in compensation. No insurance company covers nuclear risks. There are accidents. If the nuclear industry didn't keep them quiet, there would be a public outcry. Radioactivity causes cancer and may affect future generations.

Next, nuclear waste. There is no technology for absolutely safe disposal. Some of this waste will remain active for thousands of years. Is that what you want to leave to your children? And their children's children? A reactor only lasts about 25 years. By the year 2000 we'll have 'retired' 26 reactors in the UK.

Next, terrorism. Terrorists could hold the nation to ransom if they captured a reactor. In the USA the Savannah River plant, and Professor Burnham knows this very well, lost (yes, 'lost') enough plutonium be-

tween 1955 and 1978 to make 18 (18!) atom bombs. Where is it? Who's got it? I consider that nuclear energy is expensive, dangerous, and evil, and most of all, absolutely unnecessary. But Dr Woodstock will be saying more about that.'

'Thank you Jennifer. Now I'm very pleased to welcome Dr Catherine Woodstock. She is the author of several books on alternative technology.'

'Hello. I'd like to begin by agreeing with Jennifer. We can develop alternative sources of power, and unless we try we'll never succeed. Instead of burning fossil fuels we should be concentrating on more economic uses of electricity, because electricity can be produced from any source of energy. If we didn't waste so much energy, our resources would last longer. You can save more energy by conservation than you can produce for the same money. Unless we do research on solar energy, wind power, wave power, tidal power, hydroelectric schemes etc, our fossil fuels will run out, and we'll all freeze or starve to death. Other countries are spending much more than us on research, and don't forget that energy from the sun, the waves and the wind lasts for ever. We really won't survive unless we start working on cleaner, safer sources of energy.'

'Thank you very much, Dr Woodstock. Our final speaker, before we open the discussion to the studio audience, is Charles Wicks, MP, the Minister for Energy.'

'I've been listening to the other speakers with great interest. By the way, I don't agree with some of the estimates of world energy reserves. More oil and gas is being discovered all the time. If we listened to the pessimists (and there are a lot of them about) none of us would sleep at night. In the short-term, we must continue to rely on the fossil fuels – oil, coal and gas. But we must also look to the future. Our policy must be flexible. Unless we thought new research was necessary, we wouldn't be spending money on it. After all, the Government wouldn't have a Department of Energy unless they thought it was important. The big question is where to spend the money – on conservation of present resources or on research into new forms of power. But I'm fairly optimistic. I wouldn't be in this job unless I were an optimist!'

Unit 36

Teaching points

▶ Revision: conditional sentences (Type 1) and (Type 2) with *if not* and *unless*

▶ *begin by doing*

▶ *instead of doing*

Expressions

I'd like to welcome ... /I'm very pleased to welcome ...
sooner or later
By the way ...
In the short term ...
There are a lot of them about!
to keep something quiet
to turn one's back on something

Key vocabulary

coal mine	risk	survive
compensation	solar energy	waste
conservation	source	– – – – – –
crisis	Stone Age	active
estimate	Third World	alternative
fact	tidal power	evil
forecast	waste	flexible
form	wind power	inevitable
fossil fuel	– – – – – –	limited
generation	conserve	optimistic
hydroelectric scheme	contaminate	pessimistic
nuclear reactor	cover	strict
oil rig	create	– – – – – –
optimist	evacuate	fairly
outcry	face	instead of
pessimist	hold to ransom	lately
plant	invest	obviously
reserve	run out	rapidly
resource	starve	totally

1 Introductory text. Ensure the text is masked. Set the situation. Play the cassette.

2 Silent reading.

3 Question and answer:
What's the name of the programme?
Have you heard one of these programmes before? What was it about?
What's this one about?
What are the pessimistic forecasts?
When might coal/gas/oil run out?

4 Professor Burnham. Ensure the text is masked. Set this listening task:
What would he choose as an alternative to fossil fuels?
Play the cassette (twice). Check the answers.

5 Silent reading.

6 Question and answer:
Who is he?
What'll happen if we don't start conserving fossil fuels now?
What'll happen if we invest in further research now?
If we spent money on research, what could we develop?
What would they be able to do?

7 Free reproduction.

8 Transfer (*Ask me/him/her/each other.*):
What things can be made from coal/oil?
What have you got? What's in this room?
Imagine a world without electricity. What wouldn't we have?
What wouldn't we be able to do?
Are you worried about nuclear power? Does anybody know how it works?

9 Jennifer Hughes. Follow the procedure 36.4–36.8. Set this listening task:
Try and list the things she's worried about.

10 Question and answer:
Who is she?
What would happen if there were a serious nuclear accident?
Would people get compensation? Why not?
Why does the nuclear industry keep accidents quiet?
What does radioactivity cause? Why is nuclear waste dangerous?
How long does a reactor last?
What could terrorists do?
What happened in the USA?
What's her opinion of nuclear energy?

11 Transfer:
What do you think would happen if there were a serious accident?
How would it affect people? Do you think an accident is inevitable?
Do you think terrorists would attack a nuclear reactor? Why?
How do you think the power station 'lost' plutonium?
Who would want it? Why?

12 Dr Woodstock. Follow the procedure 36.4–36.8. Set this listening task:
What alternative sources of power does she mention?

13 Question and answer:
Who is she? What has she done?
What'll happen unless we try to develop new sources of power?
What would happen if we didn't waste so much energy?
What should we do research on? What will happen unless we do?

14 Transfer:
How do we waste energy? Give examples. In your country, what kind of power do you use?
How do you make electricity?
How do most people cook? Gas? Electricity? Coal? Wood? Butane?
How do they heat/cool their homes?

15 Charles Wicks, MP. Follow the procedure 36.4–36.8. Set one of these listening tasks:
Is he an optimist or a pessimist?
What does he think about the short term?

16 Question and answer:
Who is he?
What does he think about the estimate of world energy resources?
Why doesn't he agree with them?
What would happen to us all if we listened to the pessimists?
There's a Department of Energy; the government is spending money on research. Why do you think they are doing this?

17 Transfer:
Are you an optimist or a pessimist? Why?
Where have oil and gas been discovered recently?
Does your country import or export oil? Where to? Where from?

18 Role–play.
a) Each student chooses one of the four characters and makes notes. Individuals make a short speech based on their notes.
b) Group work – students role-play the four guests with a chairman.
c) Set up a panel of four, plus a chairman. The rest of the class forms a studio audience and questions the panel.

Teaching points

▶ *Would you have said anything?*

What would you have done?

I	'd	have	said	something.
	would		done	
	wouldn't			anything.

Expressions

That's my (something) . . . that was!
in deep water (= in serious trouble)
Honesty is the best policy.
I was scared stiff!
I was trembling with fear!
I couldn't say a word!

Key vocabulary

bishop	short cut	step off
boxer	tinkle	– – – – –
burglary	– – – – –	innocent
flat tyre	heat up	naughty
householder	clear off	saucy
loft	come over	strong
picnic	creep up	– – – – –
pie	dip	innocently
sand	hand over	– – – – –
sauce	insulate	in sight
scratch	relax	
swimming-costume	spot	

1 Introduction. Play the cassette. Silent reading.

2 'That's my beer . . . that was!' Ensure the text is masked.
Play the cassette.

3 Silent reading.

4 Free reproduction. *Tell me the story*. (Prompt/ask questions
where necessary.)

5 Transfer:
What would you have done?
For this story only give an example:
I wouldn't have done anything!
I'd have complained to the landlord!
Get pairs to note their suggestions, and report back to the class. List
the suggestions on the board, in two columns, affirmative and
negative. Get the students to copy them.

6 'In deep water'. Follow the procedure 37.2–37.5.

7 'Naughty Bishop!' As above.

8 'Strangers in the night'. As above.

9 'A saucy thief'. As above.

10 'Unless!!!' As above.

11 'Honesty is the best policy'. As above.

12 Ask individuals to choose a story for reading aloud, prepare it,
and practise reading it aloud to their partners in pairs. Check a few
individuals.

13 Focus attention on 'Look at this'. Silent reading.

14 Exercise 1. Set in class or for homework.

15 Exercise 2. Get students to tell you about their experiences in
class or for written homework.

Unit 37

WHAT WOULD YOU HAVE DONE?

YOUR LETTERS

What would you have done?

Last week we invited readers to write and tell us about things that had happened to them, or things that they had heard about. We wanted stories where people just didn't know what to do next! Here are the stories that interested us most!

That's my beer . . . that was!

I was in a small country pub. I had just sat down with a pint of beer. Suddenly this huge man – he looked like a boxer – came over, picked up my beer, drank it, banged the glass down on the table, stared at me, and then walked away without saying anything. I suppose I should have said something, but I was scared stiff! I didn't know what to do! What would you have done?

Mr A Watney, Hull.

In deep water

I was on a touring holiday in France. It was a very hot day and I stopped at a small deserted beach. I hadn't got my swimming-costume with me, but it was early in the morning and there were no people or houses in sight. So I took off all my clothes and swam out to sea. I'm a very strong swimmer. I lay on my back, closed my eyes, and relaxed in the water. When I looked back at the beach, a coach had arrived and there were thirty or forty people sitting on the sand having a picnic! What would you have done?

Mr T Horniman, Ipswich.

Naughty Bishop!

I was told a lovely story about the Bishop of Fleetwood.

He'd gone to New York for a church conference. Anyway, when he stepped off the plane there were a lot of journalists and cameramen. The first question one of the journalists asked was 'Do you intend to visit any nightclubs in New York?' Well, the Bishop was 85 years old. 'Are there any nightclubs in New York?' he answered innocently. The next morning the headline in one of the New York papers was 'Bishop's first question on arrival in New York – Are there any nightclubs?' How would you have felt?

Reverend Simon Fisher, Exeter.

Strangers in the night

My story isn't at all funny. It was a very frightening experience. You see, one night I woke up suddenly. I heard the tinkle of broken glass from downstairs, and I heard the window opening. Then I heard two voices! My wife had woken up, too. She told me to do something. A couple of days before, there had been a report about a burglary in the local paper. The burglars had been interrupted and they had beaten up the householder. They'd nearly killed him. I was trembling with fear. I just didn't know what to do. In the end, I didn't go down and they stole the silver tea-service I'd inherited from my mother. Was I right? What would you have done?

Mr D Boswell, Edinburgh.

A saucy thief

I had parked my car in a multi-storey car park and I was taking a short cut through the side door of the restaurant in a large store. Half-way across the restaurant I spotted my father eating pie, chips and peas – he often eats there. I crept up behind him, put my hand over his shoulder, took a chip off the plate, dipped it in the tomato sauce and ate it. Then I realized that the man was not my father! I was so embarrassed! I couldn't say a word! What would you have done?

Miss H P Branston, Cardiff.

Unless!!!

I'd just parked my car in the street near a football stadium in Liverpool. It was ten minutes before the start of the match and I was in a hurry. Two little boys came up to me and said 'Give us 50p and we'll look after your car while you're at the match.' I told them to clear off, and one of them looked at me with big, round, innocent eyes and said 'Unless you give us the money, something might happen to your car while you're away. You know, a scratch or a flat tyre. Something like that.' I was furious! What would you have done!

Mr D Revie, Birkenhead.

Honesty is the best policy

I couldn't believe a story I heard the other day. It seems that a couple had just bought a house in Manchester. They wanted to insulate the roof, so they climbed up into the loft. There, under the water tank, was £20,000 in cash! They handed over the money to the police. Would you have reported the find? What would you have done?

Mrs B Leyland, Birmingham.

Look at this

Would you have said anything?
What would you have done?

I	'd would	have	said done	something.
	wouldn't			anything.

Exercise 1
Make sentences like this about each of the seven stories.

Exercise 2
Tell the story of an interesting, surprising or embarrassing experience you have had, or heard about.

A BAD DAY AT THE OFFICE

Bob What was wrong with you this morning?

Debbie Wrong with me? Sorry, Bob, I don't know what you mean.

Bob You walked straight past me. You didn't say a word!

Debbie Really? Where?

Bob It was just outside the newsagent's in the High Street.

Debbie I'm terribly sorry, Bob. I just didn't see you.

Bob Come on, Debbie. You must have done! I was waving!

Debbie No, honestly. I didn't see you. If I had seen you, I would have said 'Hello'.

Exercise 1

She didn't see him. She didn't say 'Hello'.

If she had seen him, she would have said 'Hello'.

Do the same.

1 She didn't notice him. She didn't stop.
2 She didn't recognize him. She didn't speak to him.
3 She didn't see him waving. She didn't wave back.

Mrs Lewis Debbie, have you sent that telex to Geneva?

Debbie No, I haven't.

Mrs Lewis Why haven't you done it yet? It's urgent.

Debbie Because you didn't ask me to do it.

Mrs Lewis Didn't I?

Debbie No, you didn't. If you'd asked me, I'd've sent it!

Exercise 2

Have you sent the telex?

If you'd asked me, I would have sent it.

Do the same.

1 Have you posted the letters?
2 Have you photo-copied the report?
3 Have you typed the contract?

Gordon Did you see a letter from Brazil on this desk?

Debbie Yes, it's here.

Gordon Oh, good. Where's the envelope?

Debbie I threw it away. Why?

Gordon It had some nice stamps on it. I wanted them for my son. He collects stamps.

Debbie Oh, Gordon! If only I'd known!

Gordon It doesn't matter.

Debbie No, I'd have kept it if I'd known.

Exercise 3

I didn't keep it.

I'd have kept it if I'd known.

Do the same.

1 I didn't do it.
2 I didn't give it to you.
3 I didn't put it in the drawer.

Debbie What's the matter, Jeff? You don't look very well.

Jeff No. I've had a terrible cold. I've been in bed all weekend, but it's better today.

Debbie Mm ... I had a bad cold last week.

Jeff I know, and you gave it to everyone in the office. I wouldn't have come to work if I'd had a cold like that.

Exercise 4

She had a bad cold, but she came to work.

I wouldn't have come to work if I'd had a cold.

Do the same.

1 She had a headache. She stayed at work.

---

2 He had a sore throat. He worked all day.
3 She had toothache. She didn't go to the dentist.

Mrs Lewis Debbie.

Debbie Yes.

Mrs Lewis Did you type this letter?

Debbie Yes. Why? Is there something wrong with it?

Mrs Lewis Have a look. This should be £400.00. You've typed £40,000.

Debbie Oh, yes. I'm ever so sorry.

Mrs Lewis And you've also misspelt the customer's name. It should be 'Snelling' not 'Smelling'.

Debbie Hee-hee!

Mrs Lewis It's not funny, Debbie. If I hadn't noticed it, we could have lost the order.

Exercise 5

She noticed the error. They didn't lose the order.

If she hadn't noticed the error, they could have lost the order.

Do the same.

1 She noticed the spelling mistake. They didn't upset the customer.
2 She saw it in time. They didn't send the letter.
3 She checked the letter. They didn't post it.

Ruth Hi, Debbie. Did you have a good day, today?

Debbie No, I didn't. I'm glad today's over! Everything went wrong!

Ruth Really?

Debbie Yes, I made a lot of typing errors, then I forgot to send a telex and I offended Bob because I ignored him in the street.

Ruth Why was that?

Debbie It was that party last night. If I hadn't gone to bed late, it wouldn't have been such an awful day. I'm having an early night tonight!

Exercise 6

I went to a party./I went to bed late./I forgot to set the alarm./I got up late./I missed the bus./I was late for work./I've had a bad day./I forgot to send a telex./I made a typing error.

If I hadn't gone to the party, none of these things would have happened.

If I hadn't gone to a party, I wouldn't have gone to bed late.

Make eight sentences.

Teaching points

▶ Conditional sentences (Type 3)

If	I he she we you they	'd had hadn't had not	done (this), seen (that), known (that),

I he she we you they	'd would wouldn't would not	've have	done (that). seen (this). known (this).

Expressions

You didn't say a word.
No, honestly....
If only I'd known!

Key vocabulary

drawer	collect	wave
order	ignore	– – – – – –
stamp	misspell	urgent
telex	offend	
– – – – – –	throw (it) away	

1 Dialogue 1. Focus attention on the picture. Ensure the text is masked. Play the cassette.

2 Selective repetition.

3 Drill:
T: *I*
C: *If I had seen you, I would have said 'Hello'.*

Continue: *he/they/she/we/Debbie*

4 Silent reading.

5 Ask *Did Debbie see Bob in the street? What would she have done, if she had?*
Go through Exercise 1. Get students to do it in pairs. Set it for homework.

6 Pair work. Students read the dialogue in pairs, substituting items from Exercise 1.

7 Dialogue 2/Exercise 2. Follow the procedure 38.1–38.6, but include the following drill, after the repetition phase.

8 Drill:
T: *Me*
C: *If you'd asked me, if I'd've sent it.*
Continue: *him/us/them/her/Debbie*

9 Dialogue 3/Exercise 3. Follow the procedure 38.1–38.6.

10 Dialogue 4/Exercise 4. Follow the procedure 38.1–38.6, but include the following drill, after the repetition phase.

11 Drill:
T: *I*
C: *I wouldn't have come to work, if I'd had a cold like that.*
Continue: *she/us/they/he/John*

12 Dialogue 5/Exercise 5. Follow the procedure 38.1–38.6, but include the following drill.

13 Drill:
T: *She*
C: *If she hadn't noticed it, we could have lost the order.*
Continue: *I/they/you/he/we/Mrs Lewis*

14 Dialogue 6/Exercise 6. Follow the procedure 38.1–38.6. Write up the language summary in Teaching points above. Get students to copy it.

15 Transfer. Make statements, and get students to ask you questions.
I didn't go to the film ... I didn't know about it.
Would you have gone if you had known about it?

Continue:
I didn't watch that programme on TV.
I didn't listen to that radio programme.
I didn't go to the concert.
I didn't read that article in the paper.
Get students to do the same in pairs. Write up the questions on the board; students copy it.

Teaching points

▶ Revision and consolidation

Expressions

A lovely day, isn't it?
She found it hard to believe.
If I'd had my way ...
to have one's way
to keep something quiet

Key vocabulary

atmosphere	*direct*	*locked up*
column	*to have one's way*	*long-stay*
complexion	*let (somebody) out*	*mentally ill*
corridor	*pause*	*mild-mannered*
drive	*persuade*	*ornamental*
file	*set fire to*	*pinkish*
flower bed	*wave through*	*proud*
incident	*whistle*	*relaxed*
mansion	*wonder*	*surrounding*
mental institution	*write up (results)*	*uneasy*
neighbourhood	$-----$	*withdrawn*
panama hat	*curious*	$-----$
parkland	*depressed*	*extremely*
staff	*determined*	*particularly*
type	*exclusive*	*slightly*
$-----$	*imposing*	$-----$
burn down	*impressed*	*a number of*
certify	*insane*	*on time*

1 Section 1. Ensure the text is masked. Play the cassette.

2 Silent reading.

3 T: *Some of these statements are true and some are false.*
Correct the false ones.
She felt rather ill.
The porter stopped her coming in.
It was a hospital for poor people.
She left her car outside the main entrance.
It was an ugly modern building.
She stopped to look at the gardens.
The old man was from Panama.
He was crying in the flower bed.

4 Question and answer:
Describe the hospital/the gardens/how Gillian felt/the patients.

5 Section 2. Procedure 39.1.

6 Drill:
T: *Lovely day!*
C: *Lovely day, isn't it?*
T: *Not very nice!*
C: *Not very nice, is it?*

Continue: *Cold again!/beautiful weather!/not very nice!/not too bad!/not too cold!*

7 Silent reading.

8 Pair work.

9 Transfer. Ask students to direct you to other locations in the building. Get them to do the same in pairs.

10 Section 3. Procedure 39.1–39.2.

11 Question and answer:
What was the doctor looking forward to?
What had he always been interested in?
What was he proud of?
What was she impressed by?
How did she spend her time?
What were the patients like?
Describe the old man. How did he spend his time?
She became curious about him, didn't she? Ask 'Why?'

12 Section 4. Procedure 39.1.

13 Drill:
T: *I*
C: *If I'd had my way, I'd've let him out years ago.*
Continue: *he/they/we/she/the doctors*

14 Silent reading.

15 Question and answer:
Explain why Maurice is in the hospital. (What had he done?)
Had he started a fire at St Alfred's? Could he have done?

16 Pair work.

17 Section 5. Procedure 39. 1–39.2.

18 Question and answer:
After she'd heard the story, how did she feel?
What did she become determined to do?
What did she do?

19 Section 6. Procedure 39.1.

20 Silent reading.

21 Pair work.

22 Section 7. Procedure 39.1–39.2.

23 Question and answer:
What did she arrange to do?
Where did Maurice go? What time did he leave?
He was excited, wasn't he?
When did they expect him to return?
What had the cook done?
What had the staff done?
He was early, wasn't he?
Where was Gillian standing when she saw him? What was he doing?
What did Gillian see behind him?
What do you think he might have done?
Why do you think he might have done it?

24 Play the complete cassette.

A SATURDAY AFTERNOON

Gillian felt slightly uneasy as the porter unlocked the gates and waved her through. St Alfred's Hospital was not an ordinary mental institution. It was the most exclusive institution of its type in the country. You had to be not only mentally ill, but also extremely wealthy to be accepted as a patient. She parked her car outside the main entrance of the imposing eighteenth century building. She paused on the steps to look at the superb ornamental gardens and surrounding parkland. An old man in a white panama hat was watering the flowerbed beside the steps. He smiled at her.

Old man Good afternoon, miss. A lovely day, isn't it?

Gillian Yes, it certainly is.

Old man Are you a new patient?

Gillian Oh, I'm not a patient. I'm just here to do some research.

Old man Will you be staying long?

Gillian I really don't know. I wonder if you could direct me to Dr Carmichael's office?

Old man Certainly, miss. Just go through the main door, turn left, walk down to the end of the corridor, and it's the last door on the right.

Gillian Thank you very much indeed.

Dr Carmichael was waiting for her. He had been looking forward to meeting his new research assistant. He himself had always been interested in the special problems of long-stay patients. Dr Carmichael was very proud of his hospital and she was impressed by the relaxed and informal atmosphere. She spent the mornings interviewing patients, and the afternoons writing up the results of her research in the gardens. Some of the patients were withdrawn and depressed, some seemed almost normal. Only one or two had to be kept locked up. She found it hard to believe that all of them had been thought too dangerous to live in normal society. She often saw the old man in the panama hat. He spent most of his time working in the gardens, but he always stopped to speak to her. She found out that his name was Maurice Featherstone. He was a gentle and mild-mannered old fellow,

with clear, blue, honest eyes, white hair and a pinkish complexion. He always looked pleased with life. She became particularly curious about him, but Dr Carmichael had never asked her to interview him, and she wondered why. One night, at dinner, she asked about Mr Featherstone.

Dr Carmichael Ah, yes, Maurice. Nice old chap. He's been here longer than anybody.

Gillian What's wrong with him?

Dr Carmichael Nothing. His family put him here thirty-five years ago. They never come to visit him, but the bills are always paid on time.

Gillian But what had he done?

Dr Carmichael I'll show you his file. It seems that he burnt down his school when he was seventeen. His family tried to keep the incident quiet. Over the next few years there were a number of mysterious fires in his neighbourhood, but the family did nothing until he tried to set fire to the family mansion. He was in here the next day. Maurice never protested.

Gillian And that was thirty-five years ago!

Dr Carmichael I'm afraid so. If I'd had my way, I'd have let him out years ago.

Gillian But he can't still be dangerous!

Dr Carmichael No. He's had plenty of opportunities. We even let him smoke. If he'd wanted to start a fire, he could have done it at any time.

Gillian was shocked by the story. She became determined to do something about it. She wrote letters to Maurice's family, but never received a reply. He had never been officially certified as insane, and legally, he could leave at any time. Dr Carmichael was easily persuaded to let her talk to Maurice.

Gillian Maurice, have you ever thought about leaving this place?

Maurice No, miss. I'm very happy here. This is my home. And anyway, I've got nowhere to go.

Gillian But wouldn't you like to go into the village sometimes ... to walk around, to buy your own tobacco?

Maurice I've never thought about it, miss. I suppose it would be nice. But I wouldn't want to stay away for long. I've spent twenty years working on this garden. I know every flower and tree. What would happen to them if I weren't here?

Gillian realized that it would be unkind to make him leave the hospital. However, she found out that the next Saturday was his birthday. She arranged with the staff to give him a party. They wanted it to be a surprise and Dr Carmichael agreed to let him go out for the afternoon. There was a flower show in the village. Maurice left at two o'clock. He seemed quite excited. They expected him to return about four o'clock. The cook had made a birthday cake and the staff had decorated the lounge.

Gillian was standing in the window when she saw him. He was early. He was walking up the drive towards the house, whistling cheerfully. Behind him, above the trees, several thick black columns of smoke were beginning to rise slowly into the clear blue sky.

Transatlantic Airways
The Golden West 14 days   San Francisco 6 nights   Las Vegas 2 nights   Los Angeles 6 nights

HOLIDAY USA

Can you see yourself riding a cable-car in San Francisco, eating fresh crab and lobster at Fisherman's Wharf, winning a fortune in the casinos of Las Vegas or walking with the stars along Hollywood Boulevard? Transatlantic Airways invite you to spend two unforgettable weeks in the cities of California and Nevada and enjoy the glitter and the glamour of the Golden West.

Every city has it own character – San Francisco with the Golden Gate Bridge, Chinatown, cable-cars climbing up the steep hills, restaurants serving food from every country in the world. You'll be offered tours to see the scenery of Monterey and Carmel, and the breathtaking views from the Pacific Coast Highway.

Then you join in the razzamatazz of Las Vegas, the gambling capital of the world, set in the Nevada Desert. Las Vegas never sleeps and the entertainment is the finest in the world. And from Las Vegas there's an optional flight over the spectacular Grand Canyon.

Finally you arrive in Los Angeles, home of the movie industry. Sunset Strip, Beverly Hills and Hollywood all wait to welcome you. You'll be able to choose any number of excursions – the wonderful world of Disneyland, Universal Film Studios or even a shopping trip to Mexico.

This exciting three-centre tour offers you a golden opportunity to experience the special atmosphere of the Golden West.

Mark and Emma Austin are a young couple in their late twenties. Emma was interviewed about the holiday.

'On the whole we enjoyed it very much, but it was pretty tiring. We went on most of the excursions, because we didn't want to miss anything. We really felt we needed more time. If we went again, we'd stay longer. We would have spent more time in San Francisco and less time in Los Angeles if we'd known more about the cities. Los Angeles was a bit disappointing. We went on a tour of Beverly Hills to see the 'houses of the stars'. Unless you'd studied film history, you would never have heard of most of them! Generally speaking, the

hotels, food and service were excellent. We found Americans particularly friendly. We probably took too much luggage. Clothes in the States were so cheap! It would have been a good idea to take empty suitcases! If we'd done that, the savings on clothes would almost have paid for the air fare!'

Jack and Vera Drake are a retired couple. Jack was asked about the holiday.

'We'd been looking forward to this trip for years, and it was the holiday of a lifetime. I think we liked Las Vegas most, but two nights were

probably enough! If we'd stayed there much longer, we'd have lost all our money! We saw Tom Jones at the Desert Inn. I've never seen anything like that place! Disneyland is a 'must' for anyone with children. If only we'd had our grandchildren with us! They would have loved it! We went on some of the excursions, and we could have gone on more, but you can't see everything, can you? I didn't think much of American beer, but Californian wine was a nice surprise. We wouldn't have chosen this tour unless it had been escorted. We're both in our seventies and we couldn't have managed on our own. Everybody was so helpful to us!'

Unit 40

Teaching points

▶ Extension of conditional sentences (Type 3) with *unless* and *if only*.

Unless you'd studied film history, you would never have heard of them.
We'd never have gone fly-drive, unless we'd had the kids with us.
If only we'd had our grandchildren with us!

Expressions

Can you see yourself doing this?
in their late twenties/in our seventies/in their early thirties
We took it in turns to drive.
On the whole . . .
Generally speaking . . .
loads of
The town is set in the Nevada desert.
It is a must for anyone with children.
any number of

Key vocabulary

autumn (Br. E.)	variety	golden
cable car	view	helpful
chain (of motels)	voucher	infinite
character	wild flower	logical
couple	– – – – –	optional
crab	cover (distances)	retired
distance	deliver	rocky
fall (Am. E.)	escort	rolling
glamour	experience	sandy
glitter	explore	spectacular
lifetime	pre-pay	unbelievable
lobster	supply	unforgettable
movie-industry	tour	well-equipped
resort town	– – – – –	– – – – –
saving	breathtaking	absolutely
starting point	disappointing	finally
steeple	fine	
razzamatazz	flexible	

1 'The Golden West'. Ensure the text is masked. Play the cassette. Ask students to read it silently and compile a list of things you can do in each of the three cities.
Ask them to report back to the class.

2 Ask *Which of the three towns would you like to visit most? Why? What could you do, if you were in San Francisco?/Las Vegas? Los Angeles?* (to elicit *If I were in San Francisco, I could ride a cable car.*)
Ask me/him/her/each other.
Which excursions would you choose?

3 Mark and Emma. Set the situation. Ensure the text is masked. Pre-questions:
Which town did they like best?
Which town didn't they like?
Play the cassette. Check the answers.

4 Selective repetition (focus on target structure).

5 Silent reading.

6 Question and answer:
Did they enjoy most things?
Why did they go on most of the excursions?
They needed more time, didn't they?
What would they do if they went again?
What would they have done, if they'd known more about the cities?
What was wrong with the tour of Beverly Hills?
What did they think of the food/hotels/service/people?
They took too much luggage, didn't they?
Why would it have been a good idea to take empty suitcases?

7 Jack and Vera. Ensure the text is masked. Pre-questions:
Which town did they like best?
How old are they?
Play the cassette, check the answers.

8 Selective repetition (focus on target structure).

9 Silent reading.

10 Question and answer:
How long did they stay in Las Vegas? What would have happened if they'd stayed there longer?
Who did they see there? Ask 'Where?'
What did they think about Disneyland?
They would have liked their grandchildren with them, wouldn't they? Ask 'Why?'
Did they go on all of the excursions? Why didn't they go on more?
What did he think of the wine and the beer?
Would they have gone on an unescorted tour? Ask 'Why not?'

11 Written phase:
Unless you'd studied film history, you would never have heard of them.
We wouldn't have chosen this tour, unless it had been escorted.

12 Transfer:
If you'd gone on that tour, what would you have done?
What wouldn't you have done?
What would you have seen?
Which excursions would you have taken?
Do you think you would have liked it?

continued

13 'East Coast fly-drive'. Ensure the text is masked. Play the cassette. Ask students to read it silently, and write down why America is a good country for drivers. Ask them to report back to the class.

14 Ask *If you went on the holiday, where would you go from Boston? What would you see? Would you choose that direction? Do you like driving? Would you go on a fly-drive holiday? What do you think the problems might be?*

15 Matthew and Polly. Set the situation. Ensure the text is masked. Play the cassette.

16 Selective repetition (focus on target structure).

17 Silent reading.

18 Question and answer:
What's Matthew's job?
Was it really a holiday for him?
Why did they go fly-drive?
Would they have chosen this holiday if they hadn't had children?
Had they realised how great the distances were?
What wouldn't they do, if they went to the States again?
What would they do?
What did they think of the motels? Why were they pleased that every room had TV?
What did they think of New England?

19 Ian and Chris. Ensure the text is masked. Pre-questions:
How often did they sleep in the car?
What did they buy?
Play the cassette.

20 Selective repetition (focus on target structure).

21 Silent reading.

22 Question and answer:
Why didn't the distances seem too great?
What did they think of the cars?
Why did they sleep in the car?
Why did they buy a lot of records and clothes?
What time of year was it? What do they call it in the United States?
Would they have chosen the holiday if they hadn't liked driving?
Where do they intend to go next year?

23 Written phase:
We'd never have gone fly-drive unless we'd had the kids with us.
We wouldn't have chosen this holiday unless we'd liked driving.

24 Transfer:
If you'd gone on this holiday, where would you have driven from Boston?
What would you have seen to the south-east/north/west/south?
Would you have preferred the holiday in 'The Golden West' or 'The Fly-Drive'? Why?
Have you ever been to the States? Tell us about it.

25 Homework. Write a short paragraph on a holiday you have had.

26 Extension. Students could be asked to bring in holiday brochures and to plan a holiday in groups.

Unit 40

HOLIDAY USA

Fly-drive means freedom – the freedom of the road to explore this exciting country. Fly-drive must be the logical way of seeing the land of the motel and the freeway. America is made for drivers. American cars are easy to drive, comfortable, and petrol is much cheaper than in Europe. A flexible timetable is the ideal way of getting the most out of your holiday. We book your first night's accommodation in a hotel near the airport and deliver your car in the morning. Then you are as free as a bird – go anywhere, stay anywhere. If you wish to pre-pay your accommodation before departure, we can supply accommodation vouchers for one of the large chain of motels.

Boston is the ideal starting-point to explore New England. To the southeast are the rocky cliffs and sandy beaches of beautiful Cape Cod, ideal for swimming, sailing and fishing. To the north is New Hampshire with its green valleys, white steepled churches and infinite variety of wild flowers. Drive up into Maine, a land of forests and mountains with a spectacular coastline. Drive west across New York State to Niagara Falls or south through the beautiful rolling hills of Connecticut to a coastline of resort towns and fishing ports.

Matthew and Polly Winthrop took their two children on the fly-drive holiday. Polly's talking about it.

'We'd never have gone fly-drive unless we'd had the kids with us. Matthew is a bus-driver and it wasn't much of a holiday for him! But I think it's the only way to travel with young children. The distances were much greater than we had imagined. If we had another holiday in the States, we wouldn't try to drive so far. I think we'd cover the longer distances by plane, and then hire a different car in each place. The motels were very well equipped and the children were always made welcome. The motels didn't have much character, but when you're touring you just need somewhere to sleep. Every room had TV; for us that was marvellous. We wouldn't have been able to leave the children if there hadn't been a TV in the room. We would never have left them alone for too long of course, but it was nice for us to go down to the bar for a drink. New England was absolutely fantastic and we'd recommend it to anyone!'

Ian and Chris are in their early twenties. Chris spoke about their holiday.

'It was really great. We took it in turns to drive, so the distances didn't seem too long. American cars are tremendous. They're so big. One night we couldn't find a motel, and we slept in the car. We bought loads of records and clothes. If we'd bought them in England, they'd have cost twice as much. We went in the autumn, they'd call it 'fall' in the States, and the colours on the trees in New England were unbelievable! We wouldn't have chosen this holiday unless we'd liked driving. You spend a lot of time in the car. We intend to go again next year, but we'll go to Miami or San Francisco, if we can afford it!'

Unit 40

FOOD FOR THOUGHT

"One man's meat is another man's poison."
English proverb.

There is a wide range of nutritious foods in the world. However, eating habits differ from country to country. In some societies certain foods are taboo. An eccentric millionaire once invited guests from several countries to a banquet and offered them this menu. All the foods are popular in some parts of the world, but are not eaten in others.

STARTERS	
Snails	100-year-old eggs
Frogs' legs	Tripe (cow's stomach)
Pigs' feet	Black pudding (made from
Shellfish	blood)
Caviare	

SOUPS
Bird's nest soup
Shark fin soup
Sea-weed soup

FISH
Octopus
Jellied eels

MAIN COURSES	
Brains	Whale
Whole stuffed camel	Roast dog
Grilled songbirds	Pork
Roast snake	Beef
Bat stew	Lamb
Horsemeat	Veal
Kangaroo	

DESSERT
Chocolate-covered ants
Salad of flower petals

If you had been there, which items could you have eaten? Which items would you have eaten? Which items couldn't you have eaten? Why not?

Do you know which countries they are popular in? Would you eat them, if you were starving?

What unusual things are eaten in your country? Has your country got a national dish? How do you make it?

"Part of the secret of success in life is to eat what you like, and let the food fight it out inside you."
Mark Twain.

Here are some common ideas about food: Eating carrots is good for the eyes.
Fish is good for the brain.
Eating cheese at night makes you dream.
Garlic stops you getting colds.
Drinking coffee stops you sleeping.
Yoghurt makes you healthy.
An apple a day keeps the doctor away.
A hot milky drink helps you go to sleep.
A cup of tea revives you.
Guinness is good for you.
Crusty bread makes your hair curl.
Brown eggs taste better than white ones.

Have you heard similar expressions?
Do you agree or disagree with them?

"More die in the United States of too much food than too little."
J. K. Galbraith.

At different times in different countries there have been different ideas of beauty. The rich would always want to look fat in a society where food was scarce and to look thin in a society where food was plentiful. The current interest in slimming is because of fashion as well as health. However, overeating causes a variety of illnesses.

Do you know what they are? Are you overweight/average/underweight? Does it worry you? Have you ever been on a diet? What did you eat? What foods should you eat if you want to lose weight? What should you eat if you want to put on weight?

"One should eat to live, not live to eat."
Molière.

"When we consume a large steak we are eating something that may have used up enough grain to keep a family in the drought-stricken areas of Africa for a week."
Kenneth Mellanby, Can Britain Feed Itself?

"Year by year, while the world's population has increased, the food supply has increased more. (But)... supplies of nourishing food could be enormously increased if, in the richer countries of the world, people were prepared to eat some of the food they feed to their pigs and cattle... and to their pet dogs and cats."
Dr Magnus Pyke, Hunger and Humanity.

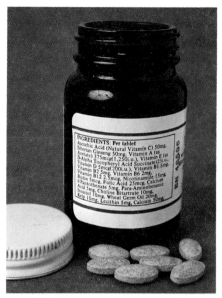

Teaching points

▶ Guided discussion

Expressions

See Section 2 of student's page.

Key vocabulary

ant	range	eccentric
banquet	seaweed	jellied
bat	secret	milky
beauty	shark fin	nourishing
bird's nest	slimming	nutritious
black pudding	snail	overweight
brain	snake	pet
camel	songbird	plentiful
cattle	tripe	scarce
frog	yoghurt	short
garlic	– – – – –	slim
grain	cheer up	stuffed
horsemeat	consume	taboo
item	differ	underweight
kangaroo	dream	– – – – –
octopus	fancy	enormously
petal	– – – – –	
poison	current	
proverb	drought-stricken	

1 'One man's meat is another man's poison.' Silent reading of introductory text. Check vocabulary.

2 Ask students to study the menu. Explain vocabulary items.

3 Ask *Have you ever eaten snails? When did you eat snails? Did you like them?* Get them to go through the menu in pairs asking these questions.

4 Ask individuals the questions in the student's book. (*Ask me/him/her.*) Get them to ask each other the same questions in pairs.

5 'Part of the secret of success in life . . .' Silent reading. Students study the expressions. Explain where necessary.

6 Ask individuals the questions in the student's book. (*Ask me/him/her.*) Get them to ask each other the same questions in pairs.

7 Ask students to think of expressions about food in their own language and translate them into English.

8 'More die in the United States of too much food than too little.' Silent reading of introductory text. Check vocabulary.

9 Ask individuals the questions in the student's book. (*Ask me/him/her.*) Get them to ask each other the same questions in pairs.

10 'One should eat to live, not live to eat.' Silent reading of the two quotations. Check vocabulary.

11 Ask *What do you think of the quotations? Do you agree? Do you think they're nonsense? Have you heard similar ideas before?* Discuss.

12 Focus attention on the photographs. Ask students to describe them, and to comment on them first in pairs, and then in general discussion.

13 Transfer. Ask about eating/cooking habits. (*Ask me/him/her/each other.*)
Can you cook?
Do you like cooking?
What do you eat a lot of?
What would you eat on a special occasion? (i.e. birthday, Christmas)
Ask about strong likes and dislikes. *What's your favourite food?*
How do you usually cook meat/vegetables/fish/eggs?
Do you prefer tinned/frozen/fresh food?
What are 'convenience foods'? Do you use them?

Teaching points

▶ Wishes

I wish I	was there.			I wish I	could do it.	
	wasn't here.				'd	done it.
	was working there.				had	
	wasn't working here.				hadn't	
	had	a car.			worked	there.
	didn't have	to do it.			didn't work	here.

Expressions

I know what you mean.   It can't be bad!
You know what they say.
pouring with rain
end up as a cleaner
The grass is always greener on the other side of the hill.

Key vocabulary

chance	line (telephone)	pour
choice	– – – – – –	– – – – – –
cocoa	get soaked	chauffeur-driven
double yellow line		

1 Dialogue 1. Ensure text is masked. Play cassette.

2 Selective repetition.

3 Drill:
T: *I*
C: *I wish I wasn't here.*
Continue: *she/they/he/we/John*

4 Drill:
T: *I*
C: *I wish I was at home.*
Continue: *she/they/he/we/Mary*

5 Silent reading.

6 Question and answer:
Who is he? Where is he?
Is he busy?
It's late, isn't it?
He'd rather be somewhere else, wouldn't he?
What does he say?

7 Pair work.

8 Exercise 1. Go through orally. Students do it in pairs.

9 Written phase:
I'm at work now. I wish I wasn't here. Where do you wish you were? I wish I was at home.

10 Transfer:
T: *I'm not rich.*	T: *I'm weak.*
C: *Do you wish you were rich?*	C: *Do you wish you were strong?*
T: *Yes, I do.*	T: *Yes, I do.*

Continue:
I'm not fit. I'm fat.
I'm not handsome/beautiful. I'm ugly.
etc.
Get students to do it in pairs.

11 Dialogue 2. Procedure 42.1–42.7, with these questions:
What's the weather like?
What has Paula got to do?
Has Mr Mannering got to walk to the station? Ask 'Why not?'
She's going to get soaked, isn't she?
She hasn't got a car, has she?
What does she say?

12 Exercise 2. Go through it orally. Students do it in pairs.

13 Written phase:
I haven't got a car. I wish I had a car.

14 Transfer (act out):
T: *I haven't got a hi-fi.*
C: *Do you wish you had one?*
T: *Yes, I do.*
C: *Why do you wish you had a hi-fi?*
T: *Ah, if I had a hi-fi, I could listen to my favourite music.*

Continue: *T.V./video recorder/a gun/a boat/a cassette recorder/etc.*
Get students to do it in pairs.

15 Dialogue 3. Procedure 42.1–42.7, with these questions:
Where's James? Ask 'Why?'
Does he usually work in the evenings? Is he working this evening?
Does he want to work this evening?
What does he say?
Why does he wish he wasn't working?

16 Exercise 3. Go through orally. Students do it in pairs.

17 Written phase:
I'm working today. I wish I wasn't working today.

18 Dialogue 4. Procedure 42.1–42.7, with these questions:
Has she finished?
What does she say?
Can she go home now?
Can she do the report tomorrow?
What does she say?

19 Written phase:
| *I haven't finished yet.* | *I wish I had.* |
| | *I wish I had finished.* |

| *I can't do it tomorrow.* | *I wish I could.* |
| | *I wish I could do it tomorrow.* |

20 Transfer:
T: *I can't swim.*
C: *Do you wish you could swim?*
T: *Yes, I do.*

Continue: *ski/dance/cook/sew/speak French/type*
Get students to do it in pairs.

21 Dialogue 5. Procedure 42.1–42.7, with these questions:
Is she working tonight?
Does she like working?
Does she have to work?
What does she say?
Can Joan type? Did she ever learn?
What does she say?
When did Shirley leave school?
What does she say?

22 Exercise 4. Go through this orally. Students do it in pairs.

23 Written phase:
| *She didn't learn to type.* | *She wishes she had.* |
| | *She wishes she had learnt to type.* |

| *She left school at fourteen.* | *She wishes she hadn't.* |
| | *She wishes she hadn't left school at fourteen.* |

24 Transfer:
Tell me some things that you didn't do when you were younger, that you wish you had done.

25 Dialogue 6. Procedure 42.1–42.7.

26 Play complete cassette. Students note sentences with *wish*.

Unit 42

I WISH...

Mr Mannering J. C. Mannering.

Secretary Your call from New York's on line one, sir. Paris has just come through on line two and I've got a call from Tokyo on line four.

Mr Mannering Ask them to ring back tomorrow, Judy. Tell them ... tell them I'm not here. It's far too late. I wish I wasn't here. I've had enough today.

Secretary But sir, they're urgent, all of them.

Mr Mannering Do you know something, Judy? I wish I was at home now, in front of the television with a cup of cocoa!

Paula Look at that! It's pouring with rain again, and I've got to walk to the station.

Diane Typical British weather!

Paula It's all right for old Mannering. His Rolls-Royce is downstairs waiting to take him home.

Diane Mmm. I wish I had a chauffeur-driven Rolls.

Paula I wish I had a car, any car. I'm going to get soaked tonight!

Tony Hello, James. still here?

James Yes. I'm waiting to see Mr Mannering.

Tony You don't usually work in the evenings.

James I wish I wasn't working this evening. There's a good concert on.

Tony Oh well. Perhaps he'll call you soon.

James I hope he does!

Alan Haven't you finished yet?

Lorraine No. I wish I had. I can't go until I've completed this report.

Alan Can't you do it tomorrow?

Lorraine I wish I could, but Mannering wants it tonight.

Shirley Evening, Joan.

Joan Evening, Shirley. I don't feel like working tonight.

Shirley Neither do I. I hate this kind of work.

Joan Why do you do it then?

Shirley I wish I didn't have to! But we need the money. My husband's out of work again.

Joan I know what you mean. I wish I'd learnt to type, or something like that.

Shirley We can all wish! I left school at fourteen. I wish I hadn't, but there was no choice in those days. Youngsters have so many opportunities nowadays. I wish we'd had the chances. I'd never have ended up as a cleaner.

Joan Come on Shirley, let's have a cup of tea.

PC Look at that, Sergeant. There are still lights on in the insurance company again.

Sergeant Yes, it looks nice and warm, doesn't it? I sometimes wish I worked there.

PC Do you really?

Sergeant Mmm. Sometimes. A nice office, a desk, secretaries everywhere. It can't be bad.

PC And the boss's Rolls outside!

Sergeant Still, you know what they say: 'the grass is always greener on the other side of the hill.'

PC I suppose you're right, Sarge. Hey, that Rolls is on a double yellow line.

Sergeant Oh, yes. Give him a parking ticket. He can afford it!

Exercise 1
1 I wish I was on holiday.
  I wish I was in Hawaii.
  Where do you wish you were now?
  Do you wish you were in bed?/at home?/on the beach?
2 I'm a student.
  I wish I was an actor.
  What do you wish you were?

Exercise 2
I haven't got a car. *I wish I had a car.*
Make five sentences.

Exercise 3
It's raining.
I wish it wasn't raining.
He's working.
He wishes he wasn't working.
Continue.
1 The phones are ringing.
2 It's snowing.
3 She's sitting in an office.
4 He's waiting.

Exercise 4
He hasn't finished yet.
He wishes he had finished.
I didn't learn to type.
I wish I had learnt to type!
Continue.
1 They haven't done their homework.
2 She left school at fourteen.
3 I haven't seen that film.
4 He lost his wallet.

Unit 42

THE HAPPIEST DAYS OF YOUR LIFE?

Some people say that your schooldays are the happiest days of your life. Here are six people talking about their schooldays.

Sally Jennings works in an advertising agency.

'I went to the local grammar school. It was an all-girls' school, and we all had to wear uniform. That uniform! I really hated it! We had to wear white socks, white blouses, matching blue skirts and blazers, and one of those ... you know ... funny little hats. Ooh! And we had to wear ties, really! We didn't mix much with children from other schools. It was a bit snobbish, I suppose. The syllabus was very academic. We never did things like cookery or needlework. I was glad at the time but I wish they'd taught us a few ... a few basics. I can't even make a decent omelette. I didn't like games, either – a lot of girls running round a hockey field on a freezing cold January afternoon. I hated it! Oh and another thing I regret ... I wish the school had been co-educational. I was terribly shy of boys for a couple of years after I left school ... simply because I hadn't met many.'

Freddie Tapper is a successful self-employed builder. He went to a secondary modern school.

'School? I left when I was 15, and I was glad to get out. I knew exactly what I wanted to do. I wanted to start earning a living as soon as possible ... in the real world. Most of the teachers were boring, and they didn't seem to understand us. They lived in a different world. They couldn't understand that we didn't want the things they wanted – you know, Shakespeare and all that rubbish! I'd have left earlier if I could. I think teachers are overpaid, and their holidays are too long. I don't know what they're always complaining about. I'm sorry I had to go to school at all!'

Samantha Wharton is the personnel manager of a department store.

'I was at a big comprehensive – nearly 2000 students. Because it was so big there was a wide choice of subjects and I liked that. I suppose it was a bit impersonal sometimes. I often wished it had been smaller, but the teaching was very good and there were lots of extra activities. I played in the school orchestra – not very well – and helped to produce the school newspaper. I think comprehensives could be improved. A lot of my friends left at 16, and they now regret leaving so early. Some of them would have done very well academically, if they had been encouraged enough. Still, maybe things are different now.'

William Bunter is a civil servant. He's a senior official in the Foreign Office.

'I went to Eton, actually. I suppose I had a very privileged education. Academic standards were very high and I was able to go on to Oxford. The thing I remember most is the comradeship. The friendships I made there have lasted through my life. Sports were very important for me – I believe that team games teach people to work together, and we played every afternoon. There's been a lot of bad publicity about corporal punishment in schools. I was often beaten but it didn't do me any harm. Maybe young people would be better behaved these days if there were more discipline in schools. My only regret about boarding-school is that I didn't get to know my parents very well. I didn't see much of them after the age of eight. I've thought a lot about the problems, but I'd like to send both of my sons to Eton. I've already reserved their places.'

Joyce Brown is a housewife.

'I was brought up in the country and I went to the little village school. We were all together – boys and girls of all ages. It was like one big, happy family. It was difficult for the teacher of course – different ages and abilities – but the older children helped the younger ones. I think it was a good preparation for life. I wish they'd never closed it. My children have to travel four miles by bus to the school in town. My schooldays were very happy. I never passed any exams, but I don't regret going to my little village school.'

Darren Andrews was at a comprehensive school. He's unemployed.

'I left last year when I was 18. I passed all my exams, but I still haven't been able to find a job. I wish I'd applied for university, but even with a degree, there's no guarantee of work nowadays. I wish I'd chosen different subjects. I specialized in English Literature, History, and Latin. I enjoyed doing them, but you see ... most of the jobs these days are on the technical side. I think schools ought to give more advice on careers and there should be more specific job preparation. If I'd known more about job possibilities, I'd've done other subjects.'

Some types of secondary school found in England.

Grammar school: State or independent secondary schools. They are selective and take more academically able children, up to the age of 16 or 18. There are state grammar schools in only a few areas now.

Secondary modern: State schools in areas which also have grammar schools. The pupils usually leave at 16, or transfer to a grammar school or college.

Comprehensive: Nowadays the normal secondary school in most areas. They take pupils of all abilities, and have replaced both grammar and secondary modern schools.

Public schools: Independent, private schools, taking pupils from 13–18 years. Most of the pupils are boarders. (They live in the school.) Eton is the most famous.

Exercise
What about your schooldays?
What do/did you like?
What don't/didn't you like?
What about uniforms? games? punishment? subjects? teachers? extra activities? travel?
Is/Was it co-educational or single-sex?
What changes would you make/would you have made?

Teaching points

▶ Expressing regret

I wish they │ had │ done it.
              │ hadn't │

If I'd (done this), (that) would have happened.
I'm sorry (it happened).

I regret │ (it).
          │ (doing it).

My only regret is . . . .

▶ Expressing opinions about past experiences

Key vocabulary

basics	harm	able
blazer	hockey field	academic
boarder	preparation	co-educational
boarding school	schooldays	gifted
civil servant	secondary modern	impersonal
comprehensive	standard	privileged
school	– – – – – –	selective
comradeship	beat	self-employed
corporal punishment	last	single-sex
department store	mix with	snobbish
the Foreign Office	overpay	specific
friendship	regret	– – – – –
games	transfer	on the technical side
grammar school	– – – – –	

1 Set the situation. During the lesson refer students to the 'notes' as necessary. Sally Jennings. Ensure the text is masked. Play the cassette.

2 Play the cassette again, pausing to ask these questions:
What kind of school was it?
Describe the uniform. Did she like wearing it?
Why does she say the school was snobbish?
What didn't she study? What does she wish they'd been taught?
It was an academic syllabus. What do you think she studied?
What did she think about compulsory games?
Why does she wish the school had been co-educational?

3 Drill:
T: *She didn't like wearing white socks.*
C: *She wishes she hadn't had to wear them.*

Continue: *She didn't like wearing a white blouse/a blue skirt/a matching blazer/a funny hat/a tie.*

4 Silent reading.

5 Listen and read.

6 Freddie Tapper. Follow the procedure 43.1–43.5.
Pause to ask these questions:
How did he feel when he left school? Why?
What did he think about the teachers at his school?
What would he have done if he could?
What's his opinion of teachers?
What's he sorry about?

7 Samantha Wharton. Follow the procedure 43.1–43.5.
Pause to ask these questions:
Describe her school. What did she like about it?
Why did she wish it had been smaller?
Why do you think that her friends regret leaving early?

8 William Bunter. Follow the procedure 43.1–43.5. Pause to ask these questions:
Tell me about his education.
What does he remember most? Why?
What's his opinion of team games?
What about corporal punishment?
What's his only regret?

9 Joyce Brown. Follow the procedure 43.1–43.5. Pause to ask these questions:
Tell me about her school. What happened there?
Why does she wish they hadn't closed it?
Does she regret going to a village school?

10 Darren Andrews. Follow the procedure 43.1–43.5. Pause to ask these questions:
Why does he wish he'd applied for university?
Why does he wish he'd chosen other subjects?
What subjects do you think he could have done?

11 Transfer (Ask me/him/her/each other.):
Do/did you have to wear a school uniform? Would you like to?
Why/Why not? Why do you think some children have to in England?
What are the advantages/disadvantages?
What subjects do/did you study?
Do you prefer academic or practical subjects? Why?
What's your favourite?
Should everybody learn to cook/type/sew/do simple electrical repairs? Why?/Why not?
What would you have liked to study (that you didn't study)? Why?
Are/Were games compulsory? Which games do/did you play?
What's your favourite sport? Which sports would you have liked to play?
Is/Was your school co-educational or single-sex? Which would you prefer? Why? What are the advantages/disadvantages?
Is/Was your school state or private? Selective or comprehensive? Which do you prefer? Why?
Does/Did your school/country have corporal punishment? What do you think about it? Were you ever beaten?
How far do/did you have to travel to school?
What extra activities do/did/would you like to do?
If you have children, what kind of school would you send them to: private/state/religious/day/boarding/single-sex/co-educational/selective/comprehensive? Why?

12 Exercise. Get students to ask each other in pairs. Open out into general discussion.

13 Homework. Ask students to write a short paragraph about their schooldays for homework.

Teaching points

▶ Listening

▶ Wishes

What would you wish for?
If you could make a wish, what would it be?
I'd wish for peace/health/fame/happiness/good luck/ a long life.

Revision points

▶ Personal details, hobbies and ambitions

▶ -ing form and infinitive

I like cooking.
I'd like to work with children.

Expressions

I don't take them seriously.
It's like a cattle market.
Beauty's only skin deep.

Key vocabulary

astronomy	intelligence	values
beauty consultant	judo	– – – – –
beauty contest	luck	insult
charm	make-up	judge
dressmaking	peace	– – – – –
fame	personality	degrading
fashion model	primary school	false
happiness	self respect	harmless
health	stage	irritated

Note: A full text of the listening passages can be found in the appendix to the student's book. There are eight sections.

1 Introduction. With the text masked, set the situation. Play the cassette.

2 Silent reading.

3 Explain they're going to listen to the interviews, and complete the chart. Focus attention on the example. Play Section 1. They fill in the numbers of each contestant. Play the section again.

4 Play Section 2. Students look at completed examples on chart.

5 Play Sections 3–7. Students listen only.

6 Play Sections 3–7 again. Students make notes, and complete the chart.

7 Focus attention on the Exercise. Students work in pairs, asking each other the questions and comparing their completed charts. Each pair works on a final version, of the chart.

8 Ask questions about each contestant to elicit the correct version, which is printed below:

9 Play the cassette of Sections 1–7 again, pausing to indicate correct answers.

10 Pair work. If you were a judge, who would you choose, and why? Make up a list of the first three. Report back to the class.

11 Focus attention on the Results chart. Play Section 8. Play it again; students complete the chart, and compare their answers in pairs. The correct version is:

Place	Name	Prize Money	Holiday
3rd	Victoria Hardy	£5 000	Paris
2nd	Myfanwy Lloyd	£10 000	Spain
1st	Dawn Munro	£20 000	California

12 Discussion: *Do you agree with the judges' choice? Why? Why not?*
How would you spend £20,000? Where would you go? What would you buy? etc.
Would you have chosen the same three girls? Why? Why not?

13 'Beauty contests: points of view'. Ensure the text is masked. Play the cassette.

14 Silent reading.

15 Discussion: *Which ones do you agree with? Why? Why not? What do you think about beauty contests?*

16 Pair work. Refer back to the exercise. Students ask each other the questions and answer about themselves.

17 Role–play. Set up a contest in groups (or with the whole class). 'Miss World', 'Mr Universe' or 'Student of the Year'. The announcer uses the Exercise as a guide for questions. Students act out a competition. (You could also use a panel of judges.)

Contestant	Number	Age	Occupation	Hobbies	Ambitions	Wish
Miss Lancashire Grace Field	14	17	shop assistant	dressmaking cooking	to work with children	world peace
Miss Dorset Victoria Hardy	13	25	beauty consultant	sailing horseriding	to sail across the Atlantic	a long life
Miss Norfolk Lynn King	50	21	primary school teacher	astronomy playing the piano	to go to the moon	happiness
Miss Gwent Myfanwy Lloyd	6	19	university student	judo drama	to be an actress	health
Miss Strathclyde Dawn Munro	30	23	fashion model	photography dancing	to become Miss World	fame
Miss Warwickshire Kerry Talbot	40	18	typist	reading swimming	to have a large family	good luck

Announcer This is the third and final stage of the 'Miss Britain' competition. We have seen all the contestants in bathing-costumes and in evening dresses, and the judges have selected our six finalists. The last stage is the interview, and in this stage our contestants will be judged on charm, intelligence and personality.

Listen to the interviews, and complete the chart at the bottom of the page.

MISS BRITAIN

Exercise

Ask and answer about each of the contestants:
Where's she from? How old is she? What does she do? What are her hobbies? What's her ambition? If she could have one wish, what would she wish for?

If you were a judge, which would you choose, and why? Listen to the results, and complete this chart:

Place	Name	Prize-money	Holiday
3rd			
2nd			
1st			

Beauty contests: points of view

'I never watch beauty contests. They're like a cattle market! I think they insult the intelligence of women. No woman with any self-respect would ever enter a competition like this. I find them totally degrading!'

'I certainly don't take them seriously. They're harmless fun, really. I mean, you see prettier girls every day in shops and offices. But people earn a living from their intelligence, or from their abilities. Why shouldn't they make money from their appearance?'

'I occasionally watch them, but I don't think I'd like them if I were a woman. After all, a lot of girls would look just as good with the make-up, clothes and lights. Anyway, beauty's only skin deep. I often feel irritated when I'm watching a beauty contest. The values are false.'

'I always watch them. I like looking at pretty girls. I'd rather watch a beauty contest than a programme about politics. There isn't enough glamour in the world. If you don't like it, you can always switch off the television!'

Contestant	Number	Age	Occupation	Hobbies	Ambition	Wish
MISS LANCASHIRE Grace Field	14	17	shop assistant	dressmaking cooking	to work with children	world peace
MISS DORSET Victoria Hardy						
MISS NORFOLK Lynn King						
MISS GWENT Myfanwy Lloyd						
MISS STRATHCLYDE Dawn Munro						
MISS WARWICKSHIRE Kerry Talbot						

OPERATION IMPOSSIBLE

Teaching points

▶ Defining relative clauses

He	is the one	who	does	it.
She		that	did	
It		which		
That		that		

Those	are the ones	who	do	it.
They		that	did	
		which		

He's	the one.		him.	He's	the one I saw.
She's		I saw	her.	She's	
It's			it.	It's	
They're	the ones.	I saw them.		They're	the ones I saw.

Key vocabulary

air-to-air missile	launch pad	defend
assassin	mini-submarine	dye
bodyguard	mission	track
complex	orbit	transport
controller	pipeline	vanish
crime syndicate	plastic surgery	– – – – – –
crocodile	radar scanner	charming
defector	rocket	expert
gorilla	satellite	legitimate
guy	superstructure	undersea
inventor	– – – – – –	
laser	defect	

1 Set the situation.
Have you ever seen a spy film? When? Where? Who was the hero?
Have you ever heard of James Bond? Have you read any books/seen any films? What can you remember about them?
Tell the class.
Do you like them? Why? Why not?
What number did James Bond use?
This is a story about another secret agent, 006.

2 Section 1. Focus attention on the picture. Ensure the text is masked. Play the cassette.

3 Selective repetition.

4 Drill:
T: *He's the one. He ordered the murder of 003.*
C: *He's the one that ordered the murder of 003.*

Continue:
He's the one. He planned the hijacking.
He's the one. He organized the drug smuggling operation.
He's the one. He wants to control the world.
He's the one. He uses false names.
He's the one. He went to Vienna.
He's the one. He stayed in Bangkok.

5 Repeat the above drill, eliciting *who* instead of *that*.

6 Drill:
T: *He's the one. We've been after him for years.*
C: *He's the one we've been after for years.*

Continue:
That's the name. He uses it in business.
That's the name. He was using it in Vienna.
That's the signature. He left it in a hotel register.
He's the man. We must stop him.
They're the people. We're looking for them.

7 Silent reading.

8 *Tell me what you know about Otto Krugerand.*

9 Pair work. Students read the dialogue in pairs.

10 Section 2. Focus attention on the picture again. Ensure the text is masked. Play the cassette.

11 Selective repetition.

12 Drill:
T: *Who's that gorilla? He's standing behind Krugerand!*
C: *Who's that gorilla standing behind Krugerand?*

Continue:
Who's that woman? She's standing on his left.
Who's that man? He's wearing thick glasses.
Who's that man? He's standing in the middle.
Who are those people? They're standing outside a building.
Who's that woman? She's wearing dark glasses.

13 Drill:
T: *He's the one. He travels everywhere with Krugerand.*
C: *He's the one who travels everywhere with Krugerand.*

Continue:
Slojob's the man. He threw 004 into a tank full of crocodiles.
Heidi's the one. She met 006 in Beirut.
She's the woman. She arranged the pipeline explosion.
He's the one. He defected from Moldania.
Beratski's the scientist. He was able to perfect a laser weapon.

14 Repeat the above drill replacing *who* with *that*.

15 Silent reading.

16 *Tell me what you know about Slojob, about Heidi, and about Beratski.*

17 Pair work. Students read the dialogue in pairs.

18 Section 3. Focus attention on the second picture. Ensure the text is masked. Play the cassette.

19 Selective repetition.

20 Drill:
T: *It carries air-to-air missiles. They could destroy any aircraft.*
C: *It carries air-to-air missiles which could destroy any aircraft.*

Continue:
They're building a rocket. It could put a satellite in orbit.
That's the superstructure. It conceals the launch pad.
That's the radar scanner. It can track the rocket.
That's the helicopter. It carries air-to-air missiles.
That's the oil rig. It conceals a vast undersea complex.

21 Repeat the above drill, eliciting *that* instead of *which*.

22 Silent reading.

23 *Tell me what you know about the rig.*

24 Pair work. Students read the dialogue in pairs.

25 Play the complete cassette.

26 Exercises 1–3. Go through these orally, then get students to do them in pairs.

27 Homework. Write out the answers to Exercises 1–3.

28 *If you were 006, how would you stop Krugerand?* Discuss in pairs. Report back to the class.

Unit 45

M Now, 006. I want you to look at these pictures carefully. This could be the most important mission of your life. At last we've got the chance to break the biggest crime syndicate in the world – SMASH. Look at the man on the right. He's the one we've been after for years.

006 Who is he?

M We think he's the one that controls SMASH. He's certainly the one that ordered the murder of 003, the one that planned the hijacking of the jumbo jet full of world leaders, and he organizes the biggest drug-smuggling operation in the world.

006 Do we know his name?

M We know some of them. Otto Krugerand, that's the name he uses in legitimate business. Dr Nada, that's the name he was using in Vienna last year. John Smith, that's the signature he left in a hotel register in Bangkok.

006 Who's the gorilla standing behind him?

M Ah, Slojob. He's the bodyguard who travels everywhere with Krugerand, and the only person he trusts. He's an expert assassin. He's the one who fed 004 to the crocodiles.

006 How charming! What about the woman?

M Don't you recognize her?

006 No, I've never seen her before.

M You would have recognized her, if she hadn't had plastic surgery, and dyed her hair. Think back to Beirut.

006 Not Heidi Schwartz! She's the one who arranged the pipeline explosion, and then vanished into thin air!

M She's also Krugerand's wife, and the only pilot he allows to fly his private plane.

006 Who's the little guy wearing thick glasses?

M That's Professor Beratski, the mad scientist who defected from Moldania. He's an expert on laser technology, and the first man who's been able to perfect a space laser weapon. Krugerand is planning to build a private space-rocket which could put a satellite into orbit. Do you understand the importance of this, 006? If they got a laser weapon into space, they could hold the world to ransom. That's something which must not happen, 006!

M Take a look at this picture, 006.

006 It's an oil-rig.

M It looks like it, doesn't it? It belongs to Krugerand's oil company. It's a rig that's supposed to be drilling for oil in the Indian Ocean. Below it, there's a vast undersea complex.

006 The superstructure looks odd.

M In fact it conceals the launch-pad they're going to use for the rocket.

006 That must be a radar scanner, there.

M Yes. It's the scanner they'll use to track the rocket, but they can also see anything that tries to get near the rig. It's going to be very difficult to get you in, 006.

006 There's a helicopter pad.

M We think that would be too dangerous. Look at the helicopter closely. It carries air-to-air missiles which could destroy any aircraft approaching the rig.

006 How are we going to do it then?

M Go home and pack. We're flying you to Scotland tonight for two weeks of intensive mini-submarine training.

006 That sounds fun!

M And 006, try not to be late for the plane this time.

Exercise 1

```
            TOP SECRET
SMASH AGENTS


KRUGERAND
controller of oil company/
millionaire/leader of SMASH

SLOJOB
killer of 004/expert assassin/
black belt karate

BERATSKI
defector from Moldania/laser
expert/inventor, space weapon

HEIDI
plastic surgery/pilot/married
Krugerand/met 006, Beirut
```

Krugerand's the | *who   controls an oil*
one | *that   company.*
He's the one | *who* | *'s a millionaire.*
               | *that* |

Make more sentences like this.

Exercise 2

```
                     TOP SECRET
DETAILS:OIL-RIG

SUPERSTRUCTURE
for hiding rocket

SCANNER
for tracking rocket

LAUNCH PAD
for launching rocket

PIPES
for rocket fuel

HELICOPTER
for transporting supplies/
people, defending rig

LIFT
for reaching undersea complex

PRIVATE ARMY
for defending rig
```

What's that? It's the radar scanner
| *which* | *they'll use for tracking*
| *that* | *the rocket.*

Make more sentences.

Exercise 3

She's the woman. He met her in Beirut.
She's the woman he met in Beirut.

Continue.

1 003 was the agent. Slojob killed him.
2 Krugerand's the leader. We've been trying to catch him.
3 Smith was the name. He used it in Bangkok.
4 Heidi's the woman. Krugerand married her.
5 Beratski's the scientist. SMASH recruited him.
6 They're the people. 006 must stop them.

OPERATION ACCOMPLISHED

Exercise 1
Look at the itinerary opposite.

He went to Scotland, where he learnt to handle a mini-sub.

He went to London, where he was given a transmitter.

He was given a transmitter, which was put into the heel of his shoe.

Make complete sentences, using 'where' and 'which' about 006's itinerary.

When 006 reached the rig he climbed up one of the towers. He was looking for someone whose uniform he could steal, but the rig seemed deserted. He went into an empty cabin. As he was looking for a change of clothes, the guard, whose cabin he was searching, came in. He was surprised to see 006 in his black frogman's suit and 006 had no difficulty in silencing him with one blow to the neck. Fortunately the guard was about the same size as 006, and the uniform fitted perfectly. There was a pass in the pocket. The pass operated the lift which went down to the undersea complex.

Exercise 2
Look at the diagram opposite.

This is where 006 left the mini-sub. Look at the diagram, and make ten more sentences like this.

006 woke up with his hands tied behind his back. His head was throbbing. He was not alone. In the room were Krugerand, Slojob, Heidi, and the guard whose clothes he was wearing. And a beautiful girl, whose hands were also tied, was lying beside him. 006 recognized her instantly. She was Pip Kingsley, an American agent he'd met in Washington. 006 looked at his watch. The explosive device he'd put on the rig was timed to explode in 45 minutes. Krugerand noticed that 006 was awake.

'Welcome, Commander Fleming. We've been expecting you,' he said smiling. 'Unfortunately we haven't got time to show you around. Blast-off is in forty minutes. Slojob will take you to feed the sharks ... they must be very hungry by now.'

'I'm delighted to meet you, Krugerand. I've been looking forward to it. Thank you for your invitation. I've always been interested in big fish. See you later.'

'I don't think so, Commander. This will be your last mission. Slojob! Take Commander Fleming and Miss Kingsley to the aquarium.'

Slojob escorted them to Krugerand's private apartment. One wall was made of thick glass and behind it 006 could see the dark shapes of the sharks, cruising around. Slojob pushed them up a spiral staircase to a platform above the shark tank.

'Ladies first,' 006 said politely.

'No, no. After you,' replied Miss Kingsley with a smile on her face.

'You wouldn't refuse us a last cigarette, would you, Slojob?' 006 asked.

'I don't smoke,' Slojob grinned. 'And you should give up smoking, it's bad for your health.'

'Now, come on, Slojob. There are some cigarettes and a lighter in my pocket.' 006 indicated his jacket pocket.

'OK. But don't try anything.' Slojob reached into 006's pocket and took out the cigarettes and lighter. He was careful to keep his gun trained on 006 all the time. He took a cigarette out of the packet and pushed it into 006's mouth. He pressed the lighter with his thumb. The sudden force of the flame took him by surprise. At that moment 006 kicked him in the stomach. He fell backwards and disappeared into the tank. Within

seconds all that remained of him was a red pool of blood on the surface.

The lighter had dropped to the floor and was still burning and 006 was able to burn through the ropes which held his hands. He quickly released Miss Kingsley. He glanced at his watch.

'We haven't got much time,' he said. 'Can you fly a helicopter?'

'I can fly anything if I have to,' she replied calmly.

'Good. Go and get the engines started and be ready to go. If I'm not there in exactly ten minutes, go without me.'

006 ran back to the control room and walked calmly in. 'Good evening, gentlemen,' he said. Krugerand turned, and he was moving his hand towards his pocket when a jet of flame from 006's lighter threw him back across the room. 006 pointed the lighter at Beratski and Heidi while he pulled every switch on the control panel until it exploded and burst into flames. 006 ran quickly to the lift but it was on fire. He had five minutes left and he started to climb the ladder in the lift shaft. He was halfway up when he felt a hand grabbing at his ankles. It was Krugerand! 006 gripped the ladder tightly, turned and kicked Krugerand hard in the face. He fell back, screaming, into the flames below. The helicopter was already in the air, hovering about a metre above the pad. 006 leapt onto a wheel, shouting 'Take it up! Take it up!' The helicopter soared into the sky. A few seconds later there was a massive explosion as the rig went up. 006 managed to climb into the helicopter cabin. He sat back, reached into his pocket and took out his cigarettes. He put one in his mouth, 'Oh blast!' he said. 'I seem to have forgotten my lighter. You haven't got a light, have you?'

Teaching points

▶ Relative clauses with *where* and *whose*

He went to Scotland, where he did this.
This is where it happened.

He was looking for someone whose uniform he could steal.
A girl, whose hands were tied, was lying beside him.

Expressions

Ladies first!
After you.
take someone by surprise
You haven't got a light, have you?
Oh, blast!

Key vocabulary

aircraft carrier	shape	show (you) around
aquarium	staircase	silence
anti-submarine net	surface	throb
blast-off	thumb	time
blow	tower	tried
change (of clothes)	transmitter	—————
commander	—————	dark
design	board	massive
device	fit	spiral
flame thrower	get started	sudden
freight	grab	tiny
frogman	grip	—————
guard	handle	backwards
heel	hover	instantly
jet	indicate	perfectly
lift shaft	leap	
neck	operate	
pass	release	
ropes	rendezvous	
sea bed	service	

1 Briefly review the previous lesson.
(Who's Krugerand/006/M/Slojob/Heidi/Beratski? What's Krugerand trying to do? Where is the oil-rig?)

2 Itinerary for 006. Silent reading.

3 Exercise 1. Go through this orally. Get students to do it in pairs. Check answers.

4 Section 1. Focus attention on the diagram. Ensure the text is masked. Play the cassette.

5 Silent reading.

6 Question and answer:
What did 006 do when he reached the rig?
What was he looking for?
Where did he go? What was he searching for?
Which of the guards came in?
What was 006 wearing?
How did 006 silence him?
Why did the uniform fit perfectly?
Which man had a pass in his pocket? Which pass was it?
Which lift did it operate?

7 Written phase:
He was looking for someone. He wanted to steal his uniform.
He was looking for someone whose uniform he could steal.
The man had a pass. 006 had stolen his uniform.
The man whose uniform he'd stolen had a pass.

8 Diagram. Ask students to study it silently.

9 Exercise 2. Go through orally. Get students to do it in pairs. Check answers.

10 Section 2. Ensure the text is masked. Play the cassette.

11 Silent reading.

12 Question and answer:
How did he feel? What had they done to him?
Who was there?
Who was Pip Kingsley?
When was the device timed to explode?
What was 006's name?
How did they intend to kill him?

13 Pair work. Get students to act out the dialogue section.

14 Section 3. Ensure the text is masked. Play the cassette.

15 Silent reading.

16 Reproduction:
Describe Krugerand's private apartment.
Describe how 006 killed Slojob.
How did 006 free his hands?
What did he tell Miss Kingsley to do?

17 Section 4. Ensure the text is masked. Play the cassette.

18 Silent reading.

19 Question and answer:
What happened in the control room?
What happened in the lift shaft?
How did 006 escape from the rig?
What was the first thing he did when he got into the helicopter cabin?
Why was he annoyed?

20 Play the complete cassette. Students listen.

21 Free reproduction: the whole story from 006's itinerary to the end.

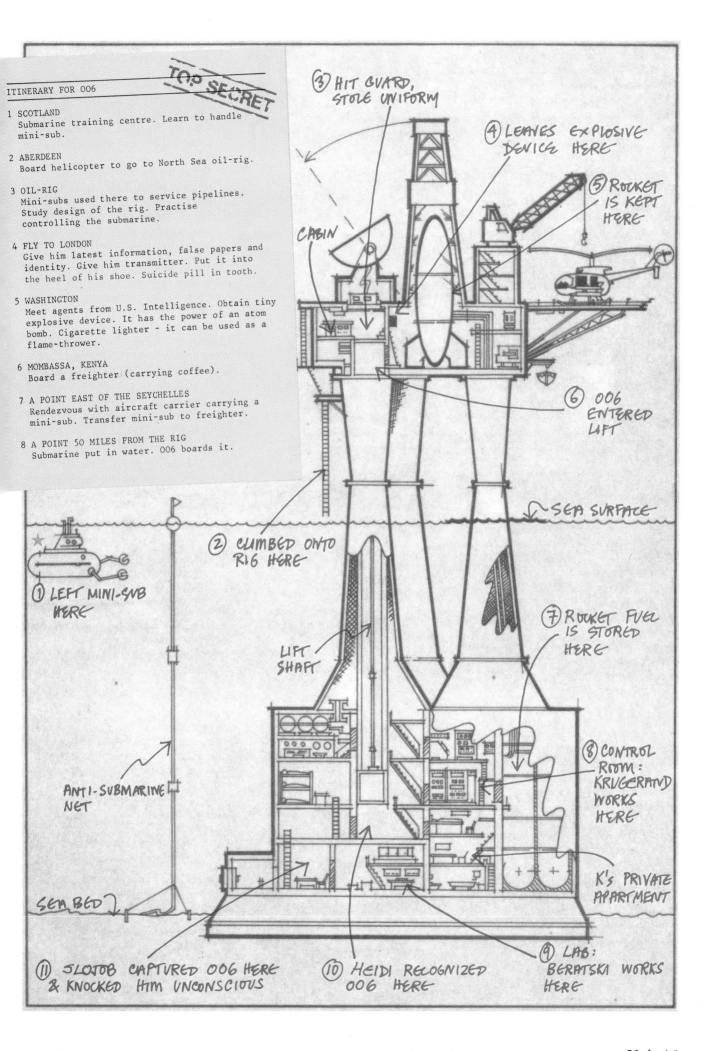

ITINERARY FOR 006

~~TOP SECRET~~

1 SCOTLAND
  Submarine training centre. Learn to handle mini-sub.

2 ABERDEEN
  Board helicopter to go to North Sea oil-rig.

3 OIL-RIG
  Mini-subs used there to service pipelines. Study design of the rig. Practise controlling the submarine.

4 FLY TO LONDON
  Give him latest information, false papers and identity. Give him transmitter. Put it into the heel of his shoe. Suicide pill in tooth.

5 WASHINGTON
  Meet agents from U.S. Intelligence. Obtain tiny explosive device. It has the power of an atom bomb. Cigarette lighter - it can be used as a flame-thrower.

6 MOMBASSA, KENYA
  Board a freighter (carrying coffee).

7 A POINT EAST OF THE SEYCHELLES
  Rendezvous with aircraft carrier carrying a mini-sub. Transfer mini-sub to freighter.

8 A POINT 50 MILES FROM THE RIG
  Submarine put in water. 006 boards it.

③ HIT GUARD, STOLE UNIFORM

④ LEAVES EXPLOSIVE DEVICE HERE

⑤ ROCKET IS KEPT HERE

CABIN

⑥ 006 ENTERED LIFT

SEA SURFACE

② CLIMBED ONTO RIG HERE

① LEFT MINI-SUB HERE

LIFT SHAFT

⑦ ROCKET FUEL IS STORED HERE

ANTI-SUBMARINE NET

⑧ CONTROL ROOM: KRUGERAND WORKS HERE

K's PRIVATE APARTMENT

SEA BED

⑪ SLOJOB CAPTURED 006 HERE & KNOCKED HIM UNCONSCIOUS

⑩ HEIDI RECOGNIZED 006 HERE

⑨ LAB: BERATSKI WORKS HERE

Unit 46

Quiz master Our next contestant on 'Student Mastermind' is Victoria Bamber, who is a student at Sandpool Comprehensive. I'll just remind you of the rules, Miss Bamber. You have two minutes in which to answer as many questions as possible. If you do not know the answer, you should say, 'Pass'. I shall then go on to the next question. If you answer incorrectly, I shall then give the correct answer. You will get one point for each correct answer. If two contestants have the same number of points at the end, the one who has the fewest number of passes will be the winner. Are you ready?

Victoria Yes.

QM Can you name the President of the United States whose early career was in Hollywood?

Victoria Er ... Reagan. Ronald Reagan.

QM Correct. What is an instrument which shows the direction of north?

Victoria A compass?

QM Correct. Can you tell me the name of the sea where eels go to breed and die?

Victoria Er ... um ... pass.

QM Name the person who became the first woman prime minister of Britain?

Victoria Mary ... er, sorry ... Margaret Thatcher.

QM I'll accept that. What is the date when the United States celebrates its independence?

Victoria The fourth of July.

QM Correct. What do we call a person who always expects the best to happen?

Victoria Er ... an optimist.

QM Correct. Can you tell me the language which was spoken in the Roman Empire?

Victoria Italian?

QM No, wrong. The correct answer is Latin. What is the office people visit when they want advice about their marriage?

Victoria Pass.

QM Who was the Egyptian queen whose beauty was famous throughout the world?

Victoria Cleopatra.

QM That's correct. What's the newspaper column where jobs are advertised?

Victoria Er ... the job adverts?

QM Can you be more exact?

Victoria No. I can't think of it.

QM I'm afraid I can't give you that. We were looking for 'Situations Vacant'. Now can you tell me ...

STUDENT MASTERMIND

(DING) I've started, so I'll finish. Can you tell me the name of the French Emperor whose final battle was at Waterloo?

Victoria Napoleon Bonaparte.

QM Correct. And at the end of that round Victoria Bamber has scored seven points. You passed on two. The sea where eels go to breed and die is the Sargasso Sea, and the office people visit when they want advice about their marriage is the 'Marriage Guidance Council'. Thank you. Can we have our next contestant, please?

Exercise 1
Now practise the game with a partner.

Questions
1 What's a person who breaks into a house and steals things?
2 Who was the boxer whose most famous words were 'I am the greatest'?
3 What do we call a shop where bread is sold?
4 What is the day when Christians celebrate the birth of Jesus?
5 What's the place where you stand and wait for a train?
6 What's a tool which is used for digging?
7 Can you tell me the unusual public transport which is used in San Francisco?
8 Can you name the American president who was assassinated in 1963?
9 What do the British call the time of year when leaves fall from the trees?
10 Name the two young lovers whose tragic story was made into a play by Shakespeare.

Answers: burglar / Muhammed Ali / baker's / Christmas Day / platform / spade / cable-car / John F. Kennedy / autumn / Romeo and Juliet

Exercise 2
Work with a partner. One of you uses List A, the other uses List B. Each of you writes down ten questions, using the words *who/which/where/when/whose* given in brackets in the list. Your question must give the answer provided in the list. For example:

Neil Armstrong (who)
Q *Can you tell me the name of the first man who walked on the moon?*
A *Neil Armstrong.*

widower (whose)
Q *What do you call a man whose wife has died?*
A *A widower.*

Now, with books closed, ask your partner the questions you have prepared. Your partner will then ask you to answer the questions he or she has prepared.

List A
Neil Armstrong (who)
sailor (who)
receipt (which)
submarine (which)
newsagent's (where)
casino (where)
golden wedding (when)
careers advisory service (when)
widow (whose)
Josephine Bonaparte (whose)

List B
widower (whose)
Columbus (who)
sleeping-pill (which)
driving licence (which)
left-luggage office (where)
butcher's (where)
job centre (when)
silver wedding (when)
Yoko Ono (whose)
pilot (who)

Unit 47

Teaching points

▶ Revision of defining relative clauses introduced by *who/which/where/whose/when*

▶ *You have two minutes in which to answer the questions.*

Key vocabulary

Note: The vocabulary items defined in the game can be found in Units 1–46, with the exception of *orphan*, *butcher's* and *baker's*.

Christian	*winner*	*exact*
contestant	– – – – –	*tragic*
instrument	*assassinate*	– – – – –
leaves	*celebrate*	*wrongly*
orphan	*name*	– – – – –
quiz master	*pass*	*throughout*
Roman Empire	– – – – –	
tool	*Egyptian*	

Note: This lesson is an oral practice game, which is set by the dialogue. The major part of the lesson will be involved with playing the game. Note that 'passes' count against contestants in the event of a tie. However, it may be foolish to make wild guesses to avoid saying 'pass', because the quiz master will then give the correct answer, thus using up time.

1 Quiz master's introduction. Ensure the text is masked. Play the cassette.

2 Silent reading. Check that the students understand the rules. Ask them to explain them.

3 Dialogue. Ensure the text is masked. Play the cassette, twice if necessary.

4 Selective repetition.

5 Ensure the text is still masked. Go through putting the questions to the class.

6 Silent reading.

7 Pair work. Students read the dialogue in pairs.

8 Exercise 1. Students study it silently. Then play the game in pairs, noting points and 'passes'. They report back to the class.

9 Check through the questions in Exercise 1. Play the game with a student at the front of the class. Get two students to play it in front of the class.

10 Exercise 2. Ensure that students follow the instructions. In each pair one students uses List A, the other List B. They should work alone to prepare questions which will elicit the answers in their list, and then use their list to question their partner. They should note points and passes and report back to the class.

11 Get some 'A' students to play the game with 'B' students from other pairs in front of the class (and vice-versa).

12 For homework each student prepares five questions, one of each type, to bring to a subsequent lesson.

13 If there is time, the teacher may wish to act as quiz master with one or two students. Here are some further questions:

Who

A person who takes photographs. (photographer)
A person who expects the worst to happen. (pessimist)
A person who is having treatment in hospital. (patient)
The actor who wore a bowler hat, baggy trousers and carried a cane. (Charlie Chaplin)
A uniformed person who drives a car for somebody else. (chauffeur)
The secret agent who killed Krugerand. (006 – Unit 46)

Which

The animal which seems to commit suicide by jumping over a cliff. (lemming)
The ship which was found deserted near the Azores in 1872. (Mary Celeste)
The language which is spoken in Brazil. (Portuguese)
Religious songs which are sung in churches. (hymns)
A machine which takes passengers up and down in a building. (lift)
The instrument which measures how much petrol you have. (fuel gauge)

Where

A shop where rings and watches are sold. (jeweller's)
A place where T.V. programmes are made. (studio)
The room on a ship where people sleep. (cabin)
The place on a plane where food is prepared. (galley)
The room where you sit and wait at a station. (waiting room)
The place where the Pope lives. (Vatican)

When

The day when a country celebrates its independence. (Independence Day)
The day when we celebrate the beginning of the year. (New Year's Day)
The time of year when plants begin to grow after the winter. (spring)
A glove worn by boxers when they are fighting. (boxing glove)
A boat you get into when a ship is in danger of sinking. (lifeboat)
A document you carry when you go from one country to another. (passport)

Whose

The American president whose tape recordings became world famous. (Nixon)
The man whose wife became Queen of England in 1952. (Prince Philip)
A country whose football team won the World Cup in 1958, 1962 and 1970. (Brazil)
The Liverpool pop group whose records sold in millions. (The Beatles)
The English dramatist whose most famous play was 'Hamlet'. (Shakespeare)

Teaching points

▶ Non-defining relative clauses

Note: These are much more common in written English. A non-defining clause is separated from its noun by a comma (because it is not a necessary part of the meaning of the noun). If the sentence continues after the clause, there is another comma. The relative pronoun (*who/which*/etc.) can never be omitted.

1) *Robert Gibbs, who escaped from prison, has been recaptured.*
2) *A three year old block of flats, which cost £10 million, is going to be demolished.*
3) *Brian Huff, the Eastfield United FC Manager, who the crowd booed from the field last Saturday, has been sacked.*
4) *The Lanstable self-portrait, which he painted from his death bed, has been sold for £900,000.*
5) *Jim Miles, the racing driver, whose legs were badly injured in last year's Grand Prix crash, will never race again.*
6) *The British Motors 'Calypso', whose success surprised everybody, is now Britain's best selling car.*

(These sentences form the 'Newsguide' section of the paper.)

Expressions

wish to do
the worst in living memory
... and that's that!

Key vocabulary

ageing process	rubble	issue
cable	seafront	make way for
carriageway	senile dementia	observe
chaos	series	prescribe
chemical	side effect	surround by
chimney	speeding	take refuge
clinical trial	stiffening	turn (something
defiance	test well	loose)
encouragement	tide	– – – – –
flash	troops	alarming
gale	wonderdrug	determined
the general public	– – – – –	effective
hair loss	assist	extensive
havoc	base in	miraculous
high-sided vehicle	block	north (bound)
joints	blow down	premature
local authority	blow in	reluctant
loss	blow over	widespread
memory	charge with	– – – – –
mooring	collapse	entirely
painkiller	combine	hastily
redevelopment	demolish	
region	flood	

1 'Newsguide'. Students study it silently. Point out the commas, and read the sentences aloud, omitting the relative clauses. Point out that they still make sense.

2 Question and answer:
T: *What can I find on p.4?*
To elicit *The story about Robert Gibbs who has been recaptured.*
T: *What can I find on p.6?*
To elicit *The story about the block of flats which is going to be demolished.*
Go through items 3–6 in the same way. (The students omit the non-defining clause and reproduce the item with a defining clause.)

3 Drill:
T: *Robert Gibbs escaped from prison last Friday. Robert Gibbs has been recaptured.*
C: *Robert Gibbs, who escaped from prison last Friday, has been recaptured.*
Go through items 2–6 in the same way.

4 '100 mph gales cause widespread chaos' – main text. Silent reading. Check vocabulary.

5 Reproduction from transformations.
T: *Strong winds at times reached speeds of 100 mph. They brought havoc to many parts of Britain yesterday.*
C: *Strong winds, which at times reached speeds of 100 mph, brought havoc to many parts of Britain yesterday.*
Continue through the paragraph in the same way.

6 '100 mph gales' – short news items. Silent reading. Check vocabulary.

7 Ask *What happened in Stoke-on-Trent?/on the M6 Motorway?/in Blackpool?/in Clitheroe?/in Whitehaven?/in the Irish Sea?*

8 Pair work. Students ask each other the questions in 48.7 in pairs.

9 Transfer:
Have you ever been in a strong wind?
Do they cause damage in your country? What about floods?
What would you do if your town were flooded?
etc.

10 'Widow's defiance continues'. Silent reading. Check vocabulary. Point out the relatives. Ask *Which word is missing? Why?*

11 Free reproduction:
What can you remember about this story?

12 Ask *What would you do if you were her? What would you do if you were a council official?*

13 'Kidnap girl found'. Silent reading. Check vocabulary. Point out the relatives.

14 Free reproduction:
What can you remember about this story?

15 'Mystery explosion'. Silent reading. Check vocabulary. Point out the relatives.

16 Free reproduction:
What can you remember about this story?

17 '"Wonderdrug" banned by DoH'. Silent reading. Check vocabulary. Point out the relatives.

18 Free reproduction.

19 Extension. If you can obtain a supply of English newspapers, get students to work in groups to create the front page of a newspaper by cutting out and assembling various articles. Each group would have to discuss their selection.

Unit 48

THE DAILY GAZETTE

Thursday May 27 — No 8158 — Price 30p

100 mph gales cause chaos

Strong winds, which at times reached speeds of 100 mph, brought havoc to many parts of Britain yesterday.

THE GALES, which were the worst in living memory, combined with high tides to cause devastation in some coastal regions. The government has sent troops to assist the emergency services in the North West, which has been hit particularly hard. Sea-walls, which have been broken in many places by unusually high tides, are being repaired urgently. Local authorities hope to contain the situation before the high tides, which are expected this evening. Calls have been issued for volunteers to help local council workmen, who have been working through the night. Many parts of Fleetwood, where the sea-wall collapsed entirely, are under two metres of water. Residents whose homes were flooded took refuge in the upstairs rooms. Men from the Fylde Naval Station, who have rescued hundreds of families, were visited by the Prime Minister during the evening.

● In Stoke-on-Trent, a woman, who was walking to work, was killed by a falling chimney.

● On the M6 Motorway, between Lancaster and Preston, a high-sided vehicle, which was carrying dangerous chemicals, was blown over. The north-bound carriageway was blocked for several hours.

● In Blackpool, hotels and shops which face the seafront are busy repairing windows which were blown in.

● Homes in Clitheroe, where electrical cables were blown down, were without electricity for eight hours.

● In Whitehaven, where fishing boats were torn from their moorings, the damage has been estimated at £200,000.

● A Spanish freighter, which was on its way to Liverpool, is missing in the Irish Sea. Air Sea Rescue helicopters are searching the area.

Mystery explosion in Indian Ocean

AN OIL-RIG in the Indian Ocean mysteriously exploded yesterday. The oil-rig, which had been drilling test wells, belonged to the Krugerand Corporation. A series of bright flashes, which were observed by ships 100 km away, preceded shock waves of unusual force. Several ships, which rushed to the rescue, have been searching for survivors but so far none have been found. It is not known how many people were working on the rig and the Krugerand Corporation, which is based in Switzerland, would not comment on the explosion.

Widow's defiance continues

MRS FLORENCE HAMILTON is still refusing to move from her old home. Tadworth local council, who have been trying to rehouse her for several months, have been unable to gain entry. The house, which the council wish to demolish to make way for redevelopment, now stands alone, surrounded by a mountain of rubble. Two council officials, who were trying to enter the house in the early hours of yesterday morning, were forced to retreat hastily when Mrs Hamilton turned her two pet alsatians loose. The dogs, Caesar and Nero, seem to be as determined as their owner, whose final words to the council were, 'I'm not b... moving, and that's that!' The council are reluctant to call in the police to remove Mrs Hamilton, whose plight has brought in many letters of support and encouragement from the general public.

Kidnap girl found

CAROLINE ROLAN, who police have been looking for since last Monday, has been found safe and well. Fourteen year old Caroline was found in a deserted house in Hackney after extensive police enquiries. A man and woman have been arrested and charged with the kidnapping.

'Wonderdrug' banned by DoH

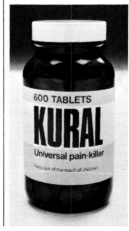

THE so-called wonderdrug 'Kural' which some doctors have been prescribing as a pain-killer, has been banned by the Department of Health. After extensive clinical trials over a number of years the drug has been found to produce alarming side-effects. 'Kural', which the manufacturers say produces almost miraculous results, is certainly very effective as a pain-killer. Unfortunately the drug seems to speed up the ageing process, which leads to premature hair loss, stiffening of the joints, loss of memory and, eventually, premature senile dementia.

Unit 48

FORMAL CORRESPONDENCE

139 Elm Tree Avenue
London SW13
15th August, 1982

Dear Sir,

I am writing to enquire about some items of laundry which were lost in your hotel laundry service. I was staying at the Haughty House Hotel from August 3rd until August 6th. On the morning of the 5th, I handed in my laundry bag and when it was returned the next day, I discovered that two socks were missing. One was brown, the other bright yellow. I also discovered that a shirt, which had also been laundered, had lost all its buttons. The housekeeper, to whom I complained, told me that the items would be posted on to me. I have heard nothing. I would also like to mention the question of compensation for the shirt, which was ruined. I bought it for £15 only a week previously.

Yours faithfully,
Barry Foot

139 Elm Tree Avenue
London SW13
22nd August, 1982

For the personal attention of Sir Basil Haughty.

Dear Sir Basil,

I enclose a copy of a letter, which I sent to your hotel in Torquay. The manager, to whom I addressed it, replied in a most unsatisfactory way. I enclose his reply. I am most shocked that a hotel in which I have stayed on several occasions should reply in such an unhelpful fashion. I hope that you will take this matter up on my behalf.

Yours sincerely,
Barry Foot

42 Winslow Avenue.
Guildford.
Surrey.
3rd March, 1982

Dear Sir,

Exactly one week ago, I purchased a polo-neck pullover from your Guildford store — the one in the High Street. I had worn the pullover only twice when I was amazed to discover a hole in the left sleeve. What is more, the pullover was not cheap. I believe in paying for quality. When I took the pullover back to the salesperson from whom I had bought it, she refused to exchange it and referred me to the manager. She too refused to exchange it. I am writing to you in the hope of gaining satisfaction. I have bought several pullovers from your store recently all of which have developed holes in the sleeves. I enclose the pullover and the receipt which shows the price and the date on which it was purchased.
Yours faithfully
Alfred King (Major retired)

Haughty House Hotel
Cliff Drive, Torquay, Devon

B. Foot Esq.
139 Elm Tree Ave.
London SW13

21st August 1982

Dear Mr. Foot,

Thank you for your letter in which you complained about our laundry service. May we remind you that the form on which you listed the items for laundering, states quite clearly that the hotel can accept no responsibility for lost items of clothing. The bag in which you placed your clothes, has the same warning clearly printed on it. We apologise for the inconvenience and hope that we shall have the pleasure of your custom on future occasions.

Yours sincerely,

Simon Loxenby

Manager

Haughty House Hotels Group
Head Office: Torres St., London W1.

1st September 1982

Dear Mr. Foot,

Thank you for your letter of August 22nd to Sir Basil Haughty, for whom I am replying. Sir Basil is unable to answer personal correspondence about hotels in the group. All correspondence should be addressed to the manager of the hotel concerned, to whom I have passed your letter.

Yours sincerely,

Anna Scales

Private Secretary to Sir Basil Haughty

Sparks & Fraser Ltd.

HEAD OFFICE Butcher Street London W2

Major A. King
42 Winslow Avenue
Guildford

12th April 1982

Dear Major King,

Please find enclosed the pullover about which you complained in your letter of March 3rd. We regret that we cannot exchange it. Our Guildford Manager, to whom you first complained, was perfectly correct in refusing to do so. She was carrying out company policy, which states that goods which have been worn cannot be exchanged. Our quality control department investigated your complaint and came to the conclusion that the sleeve in which the hole appeared, must have been subjected to unusual stress. Perhaps in your work or your leisure you constantly rub your elbows on a rough surface. Perhaps leather patches sewn onto the elbows would extend its life. The leather patches, to which I refer, are on sale at our Guildford branch, the one from which you bought the pullover. I am sure the staff there will be only too ready to help.

Yours sincerely,

Harriet Littlewood (Mrs.)

Unit 49

Teaching points

▶ Formal correspondence

▶ Use of relatives in formal, written style

to/for/from/	which
on/in/about/	whom
of/all of	

Defining relatives

He was the man to whom I spoke. (formal written)

He was the man	*I spoke to.*	(spoken and informal
	who I spoke to.	written style)
	that I spoke to.	

Non-defining relatives

Mr Lazenby, to whom I addressed it, replied in a most unsatisfactory way. (formal)
Mr Lazenby, who I addressed it to, replied in a most unsatisfactory way. (informal)

Expressions

I hope that you will take this matter up on my behalf.
in the hope of gaining satisfaction
For the personal attention of ... only too ready to help
accept no responsibility for come to a conclusion
May we remind you that ... the hotel concerned
Please find enclosed ... in the first place

Key vocabulary

compensation	quality	print
correspondence	quality control	rub
fashion	responsibility	sew
head office	salesperson	subject to
housekeeper	sleeve	– – – – – –
inconvenience	stress	formal
items	– – – – – –	missing
laundry	carry out	rough
leather patch	enclose	ruined
leisure	extend	unhelpful
occasion	hand in	– – – – – –
policy	launder	constantly
polo-neck pullover	list	previously

1 Check through letter format: address of sender, address to which it is being sent, date, beginnings (*Dear Sir/Madam/Sir or Madam, Dear Mr/Mrs/Miss/Ms Smith, Dear Dr/Major/Professor Smith/Sir John*), and endings (*Yours faithfully/truly, Yours sincerely, Yours*). Write the beginnings on the board and get students to tell you the correct endings.

2 Letter 1 – 15th August. Silent reading. Check vocabulary. Point out that *to whom I complained* is now a formal, written style and means *who I complained to*.

3 Drill:
T: *to whom I complained*
S: *who I complained to*

Continue:
to whom I spoke
to whom I gave it
to whom I posted it
to whom I sent it
to whom I addressed the letter

4 Question and answer:
What's he complaining about? What exactly did he lose? Who did he complain to? What do you think he wants?

5 Letter 2 – 21st August. Silent reading. Check vocabulary.

Note:
(a) 'It's the bag in which you placed your clothes' could become either 'It's the bag you placed your clothes in' or 'It's the bag which/that you placed your clothes in'.

(b) 'The bag, in which you placed your clothes, has a warning on it' could become 'The bag, which you placed your clothes in, has a warning on it'. In other words, we cannot leave out *which* in this example.

6 Drill:
T: *on which you listed the items*
S: *which you listed the items on*

Continue:
in which you placed your clothes
on which you put your bag
in which you signed your name
on which you travelled

7 Question and answer:
Which letter are they thanking him for? What was in that letter? Should he have known that the hotel accepts no responsibility? Why?

8 Letter 3 – 22nd August. Silent reading. Check vocabulary.

9 Drill:
T: *I addressed it to the manager. He replied in a most unsatisfactory way.*
S: *The manager, to whom I addressed it, replied in a most unsatisfactory way.*

Continue:
I sent it to the secretary. She didn't reply.
I spoke to the receptionist. She was very rude.
I complained to the housekeeper. She promised to help me.
I went to the porter. He was very helpful.

10 Repeat the Drill in 49.9, this time eliciting *The manager, who I addressed it to, replied in a most unsatisfactory way.*

11 Question and answer:
Who's he writing to? Is he angry? Why? What's he shocked about? What does he hope Sir Basil Haughty will do? Do you think he will?

12 Letter 4 – 1st September. Silent reading. Check vocabulary.

13 Drill:
T: *who I'm replying for*
S: *for whom I am replying*

Continue:
who I'm speaking for
who I'm writing for
who I'm answering for
who I'm phoning for

14 Question and answer:
Did he write to Anna Scales? Ask 'Who?' Why did Anna Scales reply? Who has she passed the letter to?

15 Homework. Ask students to write the reply from Barry Foot to Anna Scales.

16 Letter 5 – 30th March. Silent reading. Check vocabulary.

17 Drill:
T: *I have bought several pullovers. All of them have developed holes.*
S: *I have bought several pullovers, all of which have developed holes.*

Continue:
T: *I bought two cups. Both of them have broken.*
T: *I bought ten plates. Three of them have broken.*
T: *I bought some tomatoes. Half of them were bad.*
T: *I bought some bananas. None of them was fresh.*
T: *I bought two shirts. Neither of them was satisfactory.*

18 Ask students to mark examples similar to the ones they have been practising, and transform them into less formal language.

19 Letter 6 – 12th April. Repeat the procedure 49.16–49.17.

20 Homework. Ask students to write the reply from Major King to Mrs Littlewood.

21 Transfer:
Have you ever bought clothes and been dissatisfied? What was wrong with it/them? Did you complain? What happened?

Teaching points

► Review of relative clauses, introduced by *who, which, that, whose, who*

Examples and further notes on each type are given below.

Note: The lesson consists of a series of exercises. We would suggest that for each exercise the following procedure is adopted.
1 Students study the summary, and ask questions as necessary.
2 Students try to do the exercise in pairs.
3 The teacher asks individuals to answer, and then checks the correct answers.

Some structural notes on the types of relative clause used in the lesson are included below. Each teacher will decide how much grammatical explanation and terminology to use in class.
For further notes on relative clauses, see:
Michael Swan: *Practical English Usage*, Oxford University Press, 1980.
R.A. Close: *A Reference Grammar for Students of English*, Longman, 1975.
Geoffrey Leech and Jan Svartvik: *A Communicative Grammar of English*, Longman, 1975.
This chart may be useful:

RELATIVE PRONOUNS

	DEFINING and NON-DEFINING (sometimes called identifying and non-identifying, or restrictive and non-restrictive)		DEFINING ONLY
	PERSONS	THINGS	PERSONS and THINGS
Subject	*who*	*which*	*that*
Object	*who(m)* *	*which*	*that*‡
Possessive	*whose*	*of which/ whose*	

* '*Whom*' is formal usage, and does not normally occur in conversation. We have used it only with prepositions in formal written style.
‡ In defining clauses the object pronoun is often omitted.

The categories used in this lesson are:
Exercise 1 – Defining, subject
Exercise 2 – Defining, object
Exercise 3 – Non-defining, subject
Exercise 4 – Non-defining, object
Exercise 5 – Defining, possessive
Exercise 6 – Non-defining, possessive
Exercise 7 – Relative pronoun as the object of a preposition in formal style
Exercise 8 – Mixed examples

Unit 50

WHO, WHICH, THAT, WHOSE, WHOM

Exercise 1
He's the man. He saw Mary.

| He's the man | who that | saw Mary. |

That's the car. It crashed.

| That's the car | which that | crashed. |

1 She's the swimmer. She's just won the gold medal.
2 They're the keys. They open the drawers.
3 That's the travel agency. It sells cheap tickets.
4 Those are the astronauts. They were in orbit for six months.

Exercise 2
He's the man. Mary saw him.
He's the man Mary saw. or

| He's the man | who that | Mary saw. |

That's the car. He bought it yesterday.
That's the car he bought yesterday. or

| That's the car | which that | he |

bought yesterday.

1 These are the books. I use them in class.
2 They're the spies. The police have been watching them.
3 He's the criminal. The police are looking for him.
4 That's the name. I couldn't remember it yesterday.

Exercise 3
Mr Cox is the manager. He saw Ann.
Mr Cox, who saw Ann, is the manager.

The blue car crashed. It was a Ford.
The blue car, which was a Ford, crashed.

1 Those men saved my life. They pulled me from the burning car.
2 That woman travels everywhere by private plane. She's a millionairess.
3 That hotel's near the beach. It's the most expensive.
4 Those birds migrate to Antarctica. They breed near the North Pole.

Exercise 4
Ann has got the job. Mr Cox saw her.
Ann, who Mr Cox saw, has got the job.

The car crashed. He had only bought it the day before.
The car, which he had only bought the day before, crashed.

1 My parents send their best wishes. You met them last month.
2 The parcel contained a bomb. They had opened it carefully.
3 The match will be shown on TV tonight. They filmed it this afternoon.
4 His sisters are identical twins. I saw them last year.

Exercise 5
The book is about Dennis Thatcher. His wife became Prime Minister.
The book is about Dennis Thatcher whose wife became Prime Minister.

1 The film is about two people. Their plane crashed in the jungle.
2 The play is about a king. His ambition was to rule the world.
3 The ballet is about a princess. Her step-mother hated her.
4 The song is about two young lovers. Their romance ended happily.

Exercise 6
My neighbour gave me some theatre tickets. Her brother is an actor.
My neighbour, whose brother is an actor, gave me some theatre tickets.

A man from our village was on TV last night. I teach his children.
A man from our village, whose children I teach, was on TV last night.

1 Charlie Chaplin died in 1977. His films amused millions.
2 Rod Lee, the actor, has just won an Oscar. I know his sister.
3 Our teacher speaks English perfectly. Her parents are Greek.
4 The Taylor family now live in America. We bought their house.

Exercise 7
She's the woman. I wrote to her.
She's the woman to whom I wrote. (Very formal.)
She is the woman who I wrote to.

That's the hotel. I stayed in it.
That is the hotel in which I stayed. (Very formal.)
That's the hotel which I stayed in.

Transform these sentences, first in a formal style, then in an informal style.
1 They are the people. I was talking about them.
2 That is the dog. I was afraid of it.
3 Mr Cox is the manager. I am telephoning for him.
4 That is the tunnel. He went through it.
5 She is the lady. He argued with her.
6 She is the policewoman. The driver spoke to her.
7 That is the mistake. I am complaining about it.
8 He is the man. The novel was written by him.
9 There is the shop. I bought my radio from it.

Look at this.

The Pickwick School of English, London
Class: 7 (intermediate)   Date: 1st July

Name	From	Mother tongue	Age	Arrival date	Leaving date
Hans Schmidt	Zurich, Switzerland	German	18	30/6	29/7
Maria Perez	Monterrey, Mexico	Spanish	17	31/5	30/8
Paola Rossi	Turin, Italy	Italian	16	15/6	15/8
Rodrigo Cabral	São Paulo, Brazil	Portuguese	20	30/6	31/9

Exercise 8
1 *Hans is the one who comes from Zurich.*
2 *He's the one who speaks German.*
3 *He's the one who's leaving on July 29th.*
4 *Hans, who's from Zurich, speaks German.*
5 *Hans, who speaks German, is Swiss.*
6 *Hans, who's Swiss, is 18.*
7 *Hans, who's 18, arrived on June 30th.*
8 *Hans, who arrived on June 30th, is leaving on July 29th.*
9 *Hans, whose mother tongue is German, comes from Zurich.*
10 *Zurich, which is in Switzerland, is Hans' home town.*

Make sentences about all the students.

DESCRIBING THINGS

Lost property

A British Rail Lost Property, Waterloo.

B Oh, good morning. I left my briefcase on the train this morning. I wondered if it had been handed in.

A Which train, sir?

B Sorry, the 7.47 from Bournemouth.

A Can you describe the briefcase, sir?

B Er ... yes. It's sort of a ... well, an average-sized, rectangular, black leather briefcase with brass locks.

A We've got rather a lot like that, sir. Did it have your name on it?

B No, not my name. But it's got the initials 'J.R.' near the handle.

A Hang on, then, sir. I'll just go and have a look.

Exercise 1
Imagine you have lost something. Describe it to your partner without telling him what it is. Your partner has to guess.

Stolen car

A Metropolitan Police.

B My car's been stolen! It's gone!

A Calm down, sir. Could I have your name and address?

B Yes, Richard Lockwood, 3 Park Terrace, W.C.13.

A May I have a description of the vehicle, sir?

B It's a 1982 Escort, a silver-blue, four-door 1300GL model. Oh, and it's got a dark blue stripe along the sides, and a dent in the nearside front wing.

A But what's the registration, sir?

B PSV 439Y.

A I've got good news for you, sir. It hasn't been stolen. It's been towed away. It was parked on a double yellow line. You can collect it from the Police Compound, and you'd better bring your cheque-book with you!

Exercise 2
Describe somebody's car. Describe a car you would like to own.

The estate agent

A Rebecca Trueman speaking.

B Ah, Mrs Trueman. This is Fox and Connor, the estate agents. I think we've found a house that you may be interested in.

A Could you tell me something about it?

B It's in Redhill, near the station, as you requested. It's a rather attractive four-bedroomed 1930s red-brick property. It's in very good decorative order, with a fitted kitchen.

A And the garden?

B There's a large, mature garden. Would you like to view it?

A Yes, I think it's worth a look. Could you put the details in the post?

Exercise 3
Describe somebody's house. Describe a house you would like to live in.

Exercise 4
Describe these rooms. Describe your ideal room. Describe the furniture you would put in it, and where you would put it. Describe a café or a restaurant that you have visited. Describe a room or office in the school.

Exercise 5
Try and describe an object to a partner using the diagram below. Your partner guesses what it is.

Note: This diagram shows the usual order of Adjectives. You won't often find them all in one sentence.

How much/ many?	What's it like?	How big?	What shape?	How old?	What colour?		What's the pattern?	Where's it from?	What's it made of?	What is it?
a/an	beautiful	little	square	old	pale	red	check	French	silk	scarf
one	nice	small	round	new	light	yellow	striped	English	cotton	blouse
three	ugly	medium-sized	oval	modern	bright	green	plain	Japanese	wooden	desk
some	clean	average-sized	rectangular	antique	dark	blue	flowered	German	leather	car
a few	dirty	large	pointed	19th century		brown	spotted	Italian	gold	house
several	cheap	big	triangular	1930s		black		Roman	metal	box
a lot of	expensive	long	flat	1982		white		Parisian	paper	

Unit 51

Teaching points

▶ Describing things

▶ Ordering of adjectives (see diagram on student's page)

Key vocabulary

compound (for cars)	describe	mature
dent	tow away	oval
description	– – – – –	painted
initials	average-sized	pale
model	brass	plain
registration number	checked	redbrick
stripe	decorative	striped
wing	flowered	triangular
– – – – –	nearside (opposite	
calm down	offside)	

Note: Although not essential, a set of flashcards would be very useful in this lesson for generating paired practice. One student describes the picture on his flashcard, the other has to guess what it is. Pictures cut from magazines and stuck on to card would be an excellent way of building a set of cards for this purpose.

1 Classroom set. Ask students to close their eyes. Get one or two students to describe the room, or the objects on their desk, from memory.

2 'Lost property'. Set the situation. Ensure the text is masked. Set these pre-questions:
What did he lose?
Where did he lose it?
What was it like?

3 Selective repetition.

4 Silent reading.

5 Pair work. Students read the dialogue in pairs, substituting other items of vocabulary.

6 Exercise 1. Pair work. Change the students to different partners. They then describe what they were told about.

7 'Stolen car'. Follow the procedure 51.2–51.5, asking these pre-questions:
What's his name?
What was the registration of his car?
What was the year and type?
What did it look like?

8 Exercise 2. Pair work as in 51.6.

9 'The estate agent'. Follow the procedure 51.2–51.5, asking these pre-questions:
Where's the house?
What was it like?

10 Exercise 3. Pair work as in 51.6.

11 Focus attention on the diagram at the foot of the student's page. Ask them to study it silently.

12 Ask each pair of students to use the diagram to draw up a list of five sentences which make sense. Some examples:
Some nice small square checked French silk scarves.
A large oval 19th century English wooden desk.
A cheap modern light blue Italian car.

13 Ask each student to choose a sentence from his or her list. Ask the questions *How many? How big?* etc. to discover what the sentence is. Students say *I don't know* if the question is not relevant.

14 Get students to do the same in pairs.

15 Exercise 4. Students work in pairs. They improvise the conversation.

16 Exercise 5. Students work in pairs. They report back to the class.

17 Get students to describe an object to their partners, who try to guess what it is. (The flashcards would be useful here.)

18 Game: Animal, Vegetable, Mineral.
A student chooses an object and states whether it is animal, vegetable or mineral. Examples:
A sweater is made of wool, wool is from an animal, so it is animal.
A tree is made of wood, wood comes from a tree, so it is vegetable.
The waste-paper bin is steel, which is mineral.
The class have to try and establish what the object is by asking no more than 20 questions. In the original game all the questions elicited *Yes* or *No*. Examples:

Is it square?	Is it made of wool?
Is it English?	Can I eat it?
Does it move?	Do I use it for cooking?
Have I got one?	Do you find it indoors?
Is it made of metal?	

You could however use the open questions on the diagram *(What shape is it? What colour is it?)* to provide practice on adjectives.

Unit 51

Teaching points

▶ Describing people

▶ Listening

Key vocabulary

See the chart in the student's book.
Note that much of this vocabulary will already be familiar.

Note: For teachers working without a cassette, the full text of the listening passages may be found in the appendix. A set of flashcards (see Unit 51) would be useful.

1 Focus attention on the chart at the foot of the student's page. Ask them to study it silently. Check problems about vocabulary.

2 Focus attention on the listening exercise. Ask students to listen. Play the cassette of Donna while students look at the example.

3 'Colin'. Play the cassette once. Students listen. Ask:
What can you remember about Colin?
How old is he?
What sort of build is he?
How tall is he? etc.
The class works together to get down as much information as possible.

4 Play the cassette again. Students work from memory to fill in missing details.

5 Play the cassette, pausing to fill in the chart.

6 'Janet'. Play the cassette once. Students work in pairs to fill in the chart from memory. Follow points 52.4 and 52.5 to complete the chart.

7 'Robert'. Play the cassette once. Students work alone to fill in the chart from memory. Follow points 52.4 and 52.5 to complete the chart.

The completed chart should look like this:

8 Ask students to describe the four people, using their charts, first in pairs, then to the class.

9 Focus attention on the photographs. Students work in pairs, giving a description which their partner must relate to one of the photos. Then get students to describe the people to the whole class. (Flashcards could be used for extra transfer, where only the student giving the description can see the card.)

10 Get students to refer back to previous units and describe the people illustrated. The rest of the class try and guess who they are referring to.

11 Get two students to stand back to back, and describe each other. Repeat with other students.

12 Get students to describe a famous person (adding biographical details if necessary). The rest of the class try and guess who is being described. This could be turned into a game by using a limited number of questions. This could also be done by using members of the class as subjects for the description.

13 Homework/class work. Get students to write a description of themselves. For follow-up, students could mix-up their written descriptions and try to recognize each other from the descriptions.

Name	Donna	Colin	Janet	Robert
Age	*late teens*	*early 30's*	*late 30's–early 40's*	*elderly, early 70's*
Build	*good figure*	*well-built, broad shoulders*	*slim*	*medium, overweight*
Height	*fairly tall*		*average*	
Hair colour	*black*	*fair*	*blonde (dyed?)*	*white*
Hairstyle	*long, wavy*	*short*	*neat, long, expensive*	*receding*
Face	*heart-shaped, turned-up nose, full lips*	*long, thin lips, long straight nose*	*high cheek bones, small chin, attractive*	*high forehead*
Eyes	*blue, long eyelashes*	*thick eyebrows*	*pale grey, thin eyebrows*	*large, brown*
Complexion	*olive-skinned*		*sunburned*	
Distinguishing features	*dimples*	*scar on chin, long sideburns, moustache*	*well made up, beauty spot on left cheek*	*wrinkled eyes. white beard*
Dress			*well-dressed*	
Personality	*lively, talkative*	*reserved, thoughtful, moody*	*sophisticated, calm, reliable, sociable, polite*	*lively, amusing, intelligent*

Unit 52

DESCRIBING PEOPLE

Listen to these people talking about their friends. Look at the example. Complete the other columns.

Name	Donna	Colin	Janet	Robert
Age	late teens			
Build	good figure			
Height	fairly tall			
Hair colour	black			
Hairstyle	long, wavy			
Face	heart-shaped, turned-up nose, full lips			
Eyes	blue, long eyelashes			
Complexion	olive-skinned			
Distinguishing features	dimples			
Dress				
Personality	lively, talkative			

Look at this

Age	Build	Height	Hair colour	Hairstyle	Face	Distinguishing features	Personality
young	fat	1.70 m	black	long	thin	beard (M)	quiet
middle-aged	thin	medium height	brown	short	long	moustache (M)	reserved
elderly	slim	average height	red	straight	round	side-burns (M)	thoughtful
old	plump	below average	fair	wavy ·	oval	unshaven (M)	calm
in his/her 30's	medium-build	tall	blonde	curly	square	clean-shaven (M)	moody
in his/her late teens	well-built (M)	short	grey	neat	heart-shaped (F)	a scar	unsociable
in his/her mid-20's	broad-shouldered (M)	tallish	white	untidy	high cheekbones	a beauty-spot (F)	sociable
in his/her early 40's	overweight	shortish	dyed	with plaits (F)	high forehead	a mole	sophisticated
			a brunette (F)	a fringe	thin lips	with freckles	lively
				swept back	full lips	with dimples	cheerful
			a blonde (F)	in a bun (F)	long nose	with spots	amusing
				pony-tail (F)	straight nose	with wrinkles	polite

Eyes	Complexion	Dress					
blue	pale	smart	a redhead (F)	bald (M)	turned-up nose	with lines	reliable
grey	sunburned/tanned	scruffy		balding (M)	broken nose	with glasses	talkative
brown	olive-skinned	well-dressed	mousey	thinning (M)	a cleft chin	(well) made-up (F)	aggressive
long eyelashes	fair-skinned	casual	dark	receding (M)	a pointed chin		friendly
thick eyelashes	Oriental	conservative			double chin		shy
bushy eyelashes	brown	elegant					
thin eyebrows	black	fashionable					

Describe these people. Describe yourself, another student, a famous person.

Unit 52

BUDGET DAY

The British government normally announces changes in taxation once a year. This usually happens in March when the Chancellor of the Exchequer reads his budget proposals in the House of Commons. He outlines the changes in taxation which will balance government income and expenditure for the next year. Sometimes the changes in indirect taxation take effect immediately. Many people try to 'beat the budget' by guessing which articles will increase in price, and buying them before the Chancellor makes his announcement.

The day before the budget

Julie Hello, darling. You're late.

Graham Yes. I went to the garage to get some petrol.

Julie But that only takes five minutes, doesn't it?

Graham Not today. There was a queue halfway down the road.

Julie Really? Why? There isn't another oil crisis, is there?

Graham No, no. They were all filling their tanks to beat the budget. Everybody expects a big increase in tax on petrol. I bought ten gallons!

Exercise 1

garage
He went to the garage to get some petrol.
Make sentences with:
1 bank
2 chemist's
3 library
4 newsagent's
5 butcher's
6 baker's
7 greengrocer's
8 florist's
9 tobacconist's
10 off-licence

Budget morning

Graham It says in the paper that they might increase taxes on electrical goods.

Julie Perhaps we should buy that new fridge/freezer we were looking at. What do you think?

Graham Yes, we need one anyway.

Julie Can you get to the shop at lunchtime?

Graham I'm afraid not. Look, we know how much it is. Why don't you write a cheque, and send Stuart to buy it?

Julie All right. If you're sure we can afford it.

Graham It was an Electrolux 1241, wasn't it? Send him to get it at the show-room in Highfield Road. They had it on special offer.

Exercise 2

He/her/post office/stamps.
He sent her to the post office to get some stamps.
Continue.
1 They/him/newsagent's/a map.
2 She/them/off-licence/wine.
3 My boss/me/stationer's/paper.
4 We/John/supermarket/fruit.

4.30, Budget afternoon

Julie Stuart, switch on the television, will you? I want to hear the news about the budget.

Stuart Right, Mum.

Newsreader And here are the major points about today's budget again. In order to raise £60 million, the government proposes to increase the duty on tobacco. This will mean an increase of 15p on a packet of cigarettes, which should please anti-smoking campaigners. The Chancellor has also increased the duty on beer, wines, and spirits in order to raise an extra £400 million in revenue. The government has also increased petrol tax by 15% so as to encourage energy saving. Value Added Tax has been reduced by 2% so as to stimulate the economy. This will mean that household goods – televisions, washing-machines, fridges, etc., will go down in price.

Exercise 3

In order to raise £60 million, they increased tobacco duty.
So as to raise £60 million, they increased tobacco duty.
They increased tobacco duty in order to raise £60 million.
They increased tobacco duty so as to raise £60 million.
Make sentences in each of these four ways about each proposal in the table below.

Proposal	Purpose
Increase tobacco duty.	Raise £60 million.
Put up the duty on wines, beers and spirits.	Raise £400 million.
Increase petrol tax by 15%.	Encourage energy saving.
Reduce VAT by 2%.	Stimulate the economy.
Reduce income-tax.	Increase incentives.
Subsidize heavy fuel.	Help industry.
Impose import controls.	Protect home industries.
Sell parts of the steel industry.	Raise £1,000 million.
Give financial help for home insulation.	Encourage energy saving.
Increase old age pensions.	Protect old people from inflation.

Teaching points

▶ Purpose: expressed by the infinitive

He did this to do that.
He sent someone to do that.

Expressed by 'so as to'/'in order to' (more formal)

| *He did this* | *so as to* | *do that.* |
| | *in order to* | |

| *So as to* | *do that, he did this.* |
| *In order to* | |

Expressions

a queue halfway down the road
to beat the budget
on special offer

Key vocabulary

budget	incentive	balance
Chancellor of the	indirect taxation	impose
Exchequer	proposal	outline
(Finance Minister)	purpose	protect
duty	revenue	raise
expenditure	taxation	stimulate
gallon (4.5 litres)	VAT (Value	subsidize
House of Commons	Added Tax)	
import controls	− − − − −	

1 Introductory text. Set the situation. Ensure the text is masked. Focus attention on the picture. On Budget Day, the Chancellor traditionally poses for photographs holding the red attaché case containing the budget proposals. Silent reading.

2 Question and answer:
How often does the government announce changes in taxation?
When does this normally happen?
What kinds of changes does the Chancellor outline?
How do people try to beat the budget?

3 'The day before the budget'. Ensure the text is masked. Play the cassette.

4 Selective repetition.

5 Silent reading.

6 Question and answer:
Where did he go? Ask 'Why?'
How long does it usually take? Why did it take longer tonight?
Why were they all filling their tanks?
How much petrol did he buy?

7 Pair work.

8 Exercise 1. Go through it orally. Set up pair work, based on this model.
A: *He went to the bank.*
B: *Why did he go to the bank?*
A: *He went to get some money.*

9 'Budget morning'. Ensure the text is masked. Play the cassette.

10 Selective repetition.

11 Silent reading.

12 Question and answer:
What does it say in the paper?
What does she think they should do?
Do they know how much it is?
Who are they going to send to buy it?
Who do you think Stuart is?
Where are they sending him to get it?

13 Pair work.

14 Exercise 2. Go through this orally.

15 '4.30, Budget afternoon'. Mask text and play the cassette.

16 Selective repetition.

17 Silent reading.

18 Question and answer:
Why has the government proposed an increase in tobacco duty?
What will this mean? Who should this please?
Why has the Chancellor increased the duty on beer, wines, and spirits?
Why has the government increased petrol tax? Why has Value Added Tax been reduced? What will this mean?

19 Exercise 3. Students study silently the chart 'Proposal, Purpose'.

20 Get them to make sentences in pairs based on the four models. Check orally.

21 Role-play (in pairs). One student is the Chancellor, the other is a journalist. The journalist interviews the Chancellor.

Chancellor:	And	*I have increased*	*tobacco duty.*
		I'm going to increase	
		I propose to increase	

Journalist:	Why	*have you done*	*that?*
		are you going to do	
		do you propose to do	

| Chancellor: | So as to | *raise another £60 million.* |
| | In order to | |

Get one or two pairs to do this in front of the class.

22 Written phase. Write up the summary in Teaching points. Students copy it.

23 Set up this chain drill:
T: *Why do you come to school?*
S1: *To learn English.*
T: *Ask 'Why?'*
S2: *Why do you want to learn English?*
S3: *To pass my examination.*
T: *Ask 'Why?'*
S4: *Why do you want to pass your examination?*
S5: *To go to university/get a better job/please my parents.*
T: *Ask 'Why?'*
S6: *Why do you want to go to university?* etc.

24 Get students to repeat the chain which develops in pairs.

25 The 'Why?' Game.
T: *I went to the bank yesterday. Guess why.*
S1: *To get some money?*
T: *No.*
S2: *To see the manager?*
T: *No.*
S3: *To get a new cheque book?*
T: *No.*
S4: *To open an account?*
T: *No.*
Keep it going until students run out of ideas; then give an unlikely answer such as *To see a friend who was there.*
Other starting points:
T: *He went to Paris./She went to hospital./They went to the police station./He jumped out of the window./She went to school./He went to the shop./She got into her car./They bought some tickets./He went to the station./*etc.
The game could be repeated with *in order to* – but note that it is more formal.

26 Discuss different taxes in Britain and your country. Discuss taxation policy, rates of tax, indirect versus income tax, etc.

Teaching points

▶ Expressing purpose with *so that*

| *I did this* | *so that* | *he* | *could*
couldn't | *do that.* |
| | | *this* | *would*
wouldn't | *happen.* |

| *I do this*
I'm doing this | *so that* | *he* | *can*
can't | *do that.* |
| | | *this* | *will*
won't | *happen.* |

Or

| *So that* | *he* | *could*
couldn't | *do that,* | *I did this.* |
| | *this* | *would*
wouldn't | *happen,* | |

| *So that* | *he* | *can*
can't | *do that,* | *I'm doing this.*
I do this. |
| | *this* | *will*
won't | *happen,* | |

What is the purpose of that?

Expressions

do-it-yourself
a bad state of repair

Key vocabulary

bleeper	*power points*	*impress*
burglar alarm	*precaution*	*install*
carpentry	*ramp*	*level*
corridor	*smoke alarm*	*rewire*
device	*swing door/gate*	*widen*
electrics	– – – – – –	– – – – – –
extension (to a	*affect*	*disabled*
house)	*alter*	*handicapped*
handyman	*convert*	

1 Introductory text. Set the situation. Silent reading.

2 Question and answer:
What kind of competition do they organize? Ask 'When?'
Who's the winner this year?
What does he do?
Who has come to his house? Ask 'Why?'

3 Dialogue. Part 1. Ensure the text is masked. Play the cassette.

4 Selective repetition.

5 Drill:
T: *He wanted to learn carpentry. He went to evening classes.*
S: *He went to evening classes so that he could learn carpentry.*

Continue:
He wanted to learn basic electrics. He went to evening classes.
She wanted to improve her English. She bought this book.
They wanted to improve their pronunciation. They bought some cassettes.
He wanted to get a book about carpentry. He went to the library.
She wanted to learn Spanish. She went to Spain.

6 Silent reading.

7 Question and answer:
When did Mr Miller first become interested in 'do-it-yourself'? Why?
Why did he have to learn to do it himself?
Had he had any experience of this kind of work?
What did he do?
Did the books help him very much? Why not?
Why did he decide to go to evening classes?
What sorts of changes did he make? Why?
What does he say is wrong with most government buildings?
Where did they use to live?
Why did they need a house with a wide corridor?
Why did they have to buy an old house? How old was it?
What condition was it in?
Where did he begin?
Why did he rewire the house?
Why did he go on to do the whole house?

8 Transfer:
Imagine the problems that a disabled person might have in your home. Discuss in pairs. What about the problems in shops?/at the airport?/driving? What could you do to help them?

9 Dialogue. Part 2. Ensure the text is masked. Play the cassette.

10 Selective repetition.

11 Silent reading.

12 Question and answer:
What did he enjoy doing?
What did he install? Ask 'Why?'
How does the front door open?
Why is he going to put a device on Paul's wheelchair?
What kind of device do you think it is?
How has he designed the kitchen?
Why is he building an extension?
What is he hoping to do? Ask 'Why?'

13 Focus attention on 'Look at this'. Ask students to study it silently.

14 Set Exercises 1 and 2. Students do them in pairs. Check the answers with the whole class.

15
T: *I've bought a calculator. Ask 'Why?'*
S1: *Why have you bought a calculator?*
S2: *So that I can do my accounts.*

Continue:
I've bought an electric typewriter/car/tent/washing-machine/cassette player/tumble dryer/alarm clock/dishwasher/video recorder/dictionary/hairdryer/shampoo/electric razor/ladder/mirror/desk lamp/safe/etc.

16 *Imagine that you are converting a house for a) deaf people b) blind people c) physically handicapped people d) very old people e) mentally handicapped people. What changes would you have to make, and why? Discuss in pairs. Report back to the class.*

17 Transfer:
Do you know any handicapped people? Describe their handicaps. How do they overcome them? What could be done to help them?

Unit 54

DO IT YOURSELF

Do It Yourself magazine organizes a competition every summer to find the 'Handyman of the Year'. The winner this year is Mr Roy Miller, a Sheffield postman. A journalist and a photographer have come to his house. The journalist is interviewing Mr Miller for an article in the magazine.

Journalist Well, I'm very impressed by all the work you've done on your house, Mr Miller. How long have you been working on it?

Mr Miller I first became interested in do-it-yourself several years ago. You see, my son Paul is disabled. He's in a wheel-chair and I just had to make alterations to the house. I couln't afford to pay workmen to do it. I had to learn to do it myself.

Journalist Had you had any experience of this kind of work? Did you have any practical skills?

Mr M No. I got a few books from the library but they didn't help very much. Then I decided to go to evening classes so that I could learn basic carpentry and electrics.

Journalist What sort of changes did you make to the house?

Mr M First of all, practical things to help Paul. You never really realize the problems handicapped people have until it affects your own family. Most government buildings, for example, have steps up to the door. They don't plan buildings so that disabled people can get in and out. We used to live in a flat, and of course, it was totally unsuitable. Just imagine the problems a disabled person would have in your house. We needed a large house with wide corridors so that Paul could get from one room to another. We didn't have much money and we had to buy this one. It's over ninety years old and it was in a very bad state of repair.

Journalist Where did you begin?

Mr M The electrics. I completely re-wired the house so that Paul could reach all the switches. I had to lower the light switches and raise the power-points. I went on to do the whole house so that Paul could reach things and go where he wanted.

Journalist What else did you do?

Mr M By the time I'd altered everything for Paul, do-it-yourself had become a hobby. I really enjoyed doing things with my hands. Look, I even installed smoke-alarms.

Journalist What was the purpose of that?

Mr M I was very worried about fire. You see, Paul can't move very quickly. I fitted them so that we would have plenty of warning if there were a fire. I put in a complete burglar-alarm system. It took weeks. The front door opens automatically, and I'm going to put a device on Paul's wheelchair so that he'll be able to open and close it when he wants.

Journalist What are you working on now?

Mr M I've just finished the kitchen. I've designed it so that he can reach everything. Now I'm building an extension so that Paul will have a large room on the ground floor where he can work.

Journalist There's a £10,000 prize. How are you going to spend it?

Mr M I'm hoping to start my own business so that I can convert ordinary houses for disabled people. I think I've become an expert on the subject.

Look at this

| I did this so that | he | could / couldn't | do that. |
| | | this | would / wouldn't | happen. |

| I'm doing this / I do this | so that | he | can / can't | do that. |
| | | this | will / won't | happen. |

or

| So that | he | could / couldn't | do that, | I did this. |
| | | this | would / wouldn't | happen, |

| So that | he | can / can't | do that, | I'm doing this. / I do this. |
| | | this | will / won't | happen, |

Exercise 1

These are some of the things that Mr Miller did. Look at the chart, ask questions with *Why?/What's the purpose of . . . ?* and answer them.

Improvement	Purpose
swing gate, swing doors	Paul wouldn't have to use the handles.
level the path	The wheel-chair would move easily.
widen the doors	The wheel-chair could get through.
phones in every room	Paul could always get to one.
special bathroom	Paul could use it.
lower the light switches	Paul could reach them.
remove the steps, put in ramps	The wheel-chair could get in and out.

Exercise 2

Here are some of the things Mr Miller is going to do. Ask questions and answer them.

Plan	Purpose
a device on his wheelchair	He'll be able to open and close the front door.
install a lift	He'll be able to get upstairs on his own.
build an extension	He'll have a room on the ground floor.
convert mini-bus with a ramp	He'll be able to get in and out.
design a 'bleeper'	He can call me at any time.
build a workshop in the garden	I'll have somewhere to work.

TAKE CARE!

Look at this

Do this	so as in order	not to do that.
Do this	to so as to in order to	avoid	that. doing that.
Do this	to prevent	that. something (from) happening. somebody (from) doing that.

Exercise 1

Look at the expressions in Mandangani. Practise with a partner using:
How do you say (this) in Mandangani?
Can you translate (this) into Mandangani?
What does (that) mean in English?

Exercise 2

Why should we keep plastic bags away from babies?
To avoid the danger of suffocation.
or
To prevent babies from suffocating themselves.
Look at the table above. Ask questions about the warnings, and answer them.

SAFETY FIRST

To avoid danger of suffocation keep this plastic bag away from babies and young children.

Supertrack hi-fi stylus ST800E

Check your stylus regularly to avoid damaging your valuable records. Change it at the first sign of wear.

MACDONALD
CONSTRUCTION (UK) LTD.

River Danga Irrigation Scheme
Advice to employees travelling to Mandanga for the first time.

MEDICAL PRECAUTIONS

1 To avoid the possibility of infection, inoculations against typhoid, cholera, and yellow fever should be given before departure.

2 Mandanga is a malarial area. To prevent malaria, a course of anti-malaria tablets should be started two weeks before departure. In the evenings long-sleeved clothes should be worn to prevent mosquito bites.

3 When in camp always use a net in order to prevent mosquitos biting while you are asleep.

4 A thorough medical examination and a full dental checkup is advised before leaving the UK.

5 A spare pair of glasses is recommended.

6 Mandanga is a tropical country and certain precautions should be taken when working:

a To prevent heat exhaustion, take care to drink adequate quantities of fluid.

b Salt tablets may be taken to avoid dehydration.

c To prevent sunstroke, great care must be taken when working in direct sunlight.

d Sensible, loose-fitting lightweight clothes are recommended. Cotton is the best material.

HYGIENE

1 To avoid infection, water should be boiled or purified with tablets.

2 Fruit and vegetables should be washed thoroughly.

LOCAL CUSTOMS

1 Women should wear hats and long dresses when entering religious buildings. They should particularly avoid wearing trousers, shorts, or mini-skirts.

2 Shoes should be removed when entering private homes, to avoid giving offence to the householder.

3 So as not to cause offence, washing should never be hung out in public view. This particularly applies to underclothes.

4 Women should avoid wearing bikinis on public beaches.

5 In order not to seem rude, we would strongly advise learning a few expressions in Mandangani before arrival.
Here are a few essential expressions:

Whot ho	*Hello*
Tu dalu	*Goodbye*
Yup	*Yes*
Nok	*No*
Ta aw flee	*Thank you*
Ifi	*Please*
Ay up	*Excuse me*
Oop Zee	*Sorry*

CONFIDENTIAL

TEFL
Non-stick frying pan

To avoid scratching this pan, always use a wooden or plastic spatula. Avoid using metal implements at all times.

National Midland
Cheque Card

To prevent the possibility of someone misusing this cheque guarantee card, never keep it in the same place as your cheque-book.

Set of six Irish coffee glasses
Always place a spoon in the glass before pouring hot coffee into it. This will prevent the glass cracking.

Swanham's multigrade oil 20/50

To prevent undue engine wear always change the oil at regular intervals.

Rollalong tyres
To prevent undue wear always check that the tyres are at the correct pressure. Stones should be removed from the tread to prevent them from damaging the tyre. At regular intervals change tyres to different wheels to avoid uneven wear.

Bunter and Farmer
—— BISCUITS ——

In order to keep these biscuits in good condition store in a cool, dry place.

Teaching points

▶ Expressing negative purpose

Do this	so as in order	not to do that.

Do this	to so as to in order to	avoid	that. doing that.

Do this	to prevent	that. something from happening. somebody from doing that.

▶ Asking what something means in a foreign language

How do you say this in . . . ?
Can you translate this into . . . ?
What does that mean in . . . ?

Key vocabulary

bacteria	safety	take care
bite	spatula	– – – – –
bleach	stylus	adequate
cholera	suffocation	confidential
climate	sunstroke	cool
condition	tread (tyre)	direct
custom	typhoid	essential
dehydration	yellow fever	lightweight
discomfort	– – – – –	long-sleeved
exposure	apply to	loose-fitting
fluid	avoid	malarial
heat-exhaustion	cause offence	multigrade
hygiene	crack	non-stick
implement	give offence	rude
infection	hang out	thorough
inoculation	misuse	tropical
interval	offend	undue
irrigation scheme	prevent	uneven
malaria	purify	– – – – –
mosquito	store	thoroughly
net	swallow	

1 Set the situation. A British company is building an irrigation scheme in Mandanga, which is a tropical country. Many employees will be working in a hot climate for the first time. Focus attention on their 'Notes for Employees'.

2 'Medical Precautions'. Silent reading. Check vocabulary.

3 Question and answer:
Why should the employees have inoculations?
Why should they take anti-malarial tablets?
Why should they wear long-sleeved clothes at night?
Why should they use a net at night?
Why do you think they should have a thorough medical examination?/a dental check-up?
What precautions should be taken when working, and why?

4 Transfer (plus *Ask me/him/her/each other.*):
Have you ever had an inoculation? Why? Where? Did it hurt?
Who gave it to you?
Did they sterilise the needle? Why?
Did it leave a scar?
Do you live in a tropical country? A temperate climate?
Are there any mosquitos? Are they malarial?
Have you ever been to a tropical/temperate country?
Have you ever been bitten by a mosquito/insect/snake?
When did you last have a medical examination/dental check-up?
Why?
What did the doctor/dentist do?
What precautions would/do you take if you were/are working in a hot climate? Why?

5 'Hygiene'. Silent reading. Check vocabulary.

6 Question and answer:
What precautions does the company advise? Why?

7 Transfer. (*Ask me/him/her/each other.*)
Can you drink the tap water here? Is it safe? Why/Why not?
Do you drink bottled water? Why?
Is it safe to drink water from rivers/streams?
Do you always wash fruit and vegetables? Why?
Have you had stomach trouble? What caused it?

8 'Local customs'. Silent reading. Check vocabulary.

9 Question and answer:
Why should women wear hats and long dresses when entering religious buildings?
What should they avoid wearing? Why?
Why should shoes be removed when entering private homes?
Why shouldn't washing be hung out in public view?
What should women avoid wearing on public beaches?
Why do they advise learning a few expressions in Mandagani?

10 Transfer. (*Ask me/him/her/each other.*)
Would any of these things cause offence in your country? Why?
Which other things might give offence? Why?
Do you know what things might cause offence in other societies?
Do you know why?
(For example: In England, not queuing might cause offence. A young person not giving his seat to an older person on public transport. Throwing litter in the street. Snapping your fingers at a waiter (or even shouting to a waiter).)

11 Exercise 1. Get students to do it in pairs.

12 'Look at this'. Ask students to study it silently, and look back through the text to find examples. Check through the examples – selective repetition.

13 Exercise 2. Focus attention on the example. Get students to do the exercise in pairs. Then check through the vocabulary.

14 Note that in Exercise 2, only two possible answers are shown. Extra practice could be provided by asking students to generate other examples from the chart.
So as to/In order to avoid the danger of suffocation.
So as to/In order to prevent babies from suffocating themselves.
Go through the warnings again, asking individuals *Why?*

15 Transfer. Students work in pairs and give advice to someone planning a visit to their country.

Teaching points

▶ Result clauses, with *so . . . that* and *such . . . that*

The house was so beautiful that they bought it.

It was such a beautiful house that they bought it.

| *He had so* | *much work* | *that he couldn't sleep at night.* |
| | *many problems* | |

| *He had* | *such a lot of work* | *that he couldn't sleep at night.* |
| | *so many problems* | |

They worked so hard that they hardly ever saw each other.

Expressions

the rat-race
. . . and a good thing, too!
a matter of opinion
a way of life
If you don't mind me asking.

Key vocabulary

assembly line	*pannier*	*solve*
bolt	– – – – –	– – – – –
breakfast cereal	*break up*	*natural*
croft (small	*communicate*	*regular*
Scottish farm)	*give up*	– – – – –
goat	*lead (someone) to do*	*hardly ever*
nut	*set off*	

1 Introduction. Set the situation, ensure the text is masked. Play the cassette.

2 Question and answer:
What's the programme about?
Who interviewed the people?
What had the people decided to do?

3 Dialogue 1. Ensure the text is masked. Play the cassette.

4 Selective repetition.

5 Drill:
T: *hardly ever*
C: *We hardly ever saw each other.*

Continue: *rarely/never/almost never/seldom/hardly ever/occasionally/often/sometimes.*

6 Drill:
T: *We liked it very much. We decided to give up our jobs.*
C: *We liked it so much that we decided to give up our jobs.*

Continue:
We came to live here/We moved to Scotland/We left London/We became farmers/We bought the croft/We sold our house.

7 Silent reading.

8 Question and answer:
Why did they hardly ever see each other?
Why were they afraid to leave their jobs?
Why was their marriage breaking up?
Why did they decide to give up their jobs?
Why did they work from 5 a.m. to 8 p.m.?
Why don't they have time to feel lonely?

9 Transfer. (*Ask me/him/her/each other.*)
Would you like to live on a remote farm? Why/Why not?
What would you like/dislike about it?
Are you happy with your present life?
Would you like to change it? Why/Why not?/How?
Would you like the simple life?
Do you think money/friends is important in life? Why/Why not?

10 Dialogue 2. Ensure the text is masked. Play the cassette.

11 Selective repetition.

12 Drill:
T: *You've had an exciting time. You'll find it hard to settle down.*
S: *You've had such an exciting time that you'll find it hard to settle down.*

Continue:
It was a routine job. He was bored.
He's had a long journey. He must be tired.
It was an interesting journey. He's learnt a lot.
They were friendly people. Problems seemed to solve themselves.
There was a lot of interest in the bike. It was easy to start conversations.

13 Silent reading.

14 Question and answer:
Why didn't he have to think in his old job?
Why did problems seem to solve themselves?
Why was it easy to start a conversation?
Why did he have to go to hospital?
Why will he find it difficult to settle down?

15 Transfer. (*Ask me/him/her/each other.*)
Would you like to travel round the world?
Would you like to do it on a motorbike? Why/Why not?
How would you prefer to do it?
Would you like to work on an assembly line?
How do you think you would feel?
Would you like a job as a fruit picker/washing up? Why/Why not?
Would you like to work as a mechanic?
Would you like to travel alone? Why/Why not?
How would you feel if you were alone in a strange country?
And you couldn't speak the language?
And you had no money?
And you were ill?
What would you do?

16 Exercises 1–3. Go through orally. Students do them in pairs. Check the answers. Set for homework.

17 Invention. Complete these sentences:
T: *He was so rich . . . .*
S1: *He was so rich that he could buy anything.*
S2: *He was so rich that he could go anywhere.*
S3: *He was so rich that he had a private plane/two houses/a Rolls-Royce.*

Continue:
They were so poor . . . ./He was so hungry . . . ./They were so thirsty . . . ./She was so tired . . . ./He was so angry . . . ./They were so excited . . . ./She was so intelligent . . . ./He was so crazy . . . ./He was so stupid . . . ./He was so afraid . . . ./He was so strong . . . ./He was so ugly . . . .

18 Complete these sentences:
T: *She was such a good student . . . .*
S: *She was such a good student that she passed the exam/got 100%/learnt very quickly/answered everything correctly./etc.*

Continue:
He was such a good player . . . ./She was such a beautiful girl . . . ./They were such hard workers . . . ./He was such a strong man . . . ./She was such an important person . . . ./They were such nice people . . . ./ etc.

Unit 56

Announcer On 'TV Magazine' tonight we're looking at people who have given up regular jobs and high salaries to start a new way of life. First of all, we have two interviews with people who decided to leave the 'rat race'. Nicola Burgess spoke to them.

Nicola This is the Isle of Skye. Behind me you can see the croft belonging to Daniel and Michelle Burns, who gave up their jobs to come to this remote area of Scotland. Daniel was the sales manager of Hi-Vita, the breakfast cereal company, and Michelle was a successful advertising executive. Michelle, can you tell us what made you give up everything to come here?

Michelle Everything? That's a matter of opinion. A big house and two cars isn't everything! Dan and I both used to work long hours. We had to leave so early in the morning and we came home so late at night, that we hardly ever saw each other. We should have come here years ago, but we were earning such big salaries that we were afraid to leave our jobs. In the end we had so little time together that our marriage was breaking up. So two years ago, we took a week's holiday in the Scottish Highlands. We saw this place and we both fell in love with it. It was for sale, and we liked it so much that we decided to give up our jobs, and here we are!

Nicola How do you earn a living? If you don't mind me asking.

Michelle We don't need very much. We keep sheep and goats, grow our own vegetables. We've got a few chickens. It's a very simple life, and we're not in it for profit. We're still so busy that we work from five in the morning until eight at night, but we're together. We're happier than we've ever been and we're leading a natural life.

Nicola There must be some things you miss, surely.

Michelle I don't know. We knew such a lot of people in London, but they weren't real friends. We see our neighbours occasionally and there's such a lot to do on the farm that we don't have time to feel lonely. At least we see each other now.

A NEW WAY OF LIFE

Nicola The motor-bike I'm sitting on is a very special one. Special because it's been all the way round the world. It belongs to Luke Saunders, who has just returned to England after a three-year motor-cycle journey. Luke, what led you to leave your job and make this trip?

Luke I worked in a car factory on the assembly line. All I had to do was put four nuts on the bolts that hold the wheels on. It's done by robots now, and a good thing too! The job was so routine that I didn't have to think at all. I bought this Triumph 750 cc bike second-hand, fitted two panniers on the back and just set off for Australia.

Nicola What did you do for money?

Luke I had a bit of money to start with, but of course it didn't last long and I had to find work where I could. I've done so many different things – picked fruit, washed up, worked as a mechanic.

Nicola How did people react to you? In India, for example.

Luke Everywhere I went, the people were so friendly that problems seemed to solve themselves. There was such a lot of interest in the bike that it was easy to start a conversation. You know, often you can communicate without really knowing the language.

Nicola Did you ever feel like giving up, turning round and coming home?

Luke Only once, in Bangladesh. I became so ill with food poisoning that I had to go to hospital. But it didn't last long.

Nicola You've had such an exciting time that you'll find it difficult to settle down, won't you?

Luke I'm not going to. Next week I'm off again, but this time I'm going in the opposite direction! See you in about three years' time!

Exercise 1

The people were very friendly. He felt welcome.

The people were so friendly that he felt welcome.

Continue.

1 He was very old. He couldn't walk.
2 She was very busy. She didn't stop for lunch.
3 He was very late. He missed the train.
4 She's was very ill. She couldn't go out.
5 He had spent too much money. He couldn't buy a ticket.
6 There were too many people on the boat. It sank.

Exercise 2

The house was so beautiful that they bought it.

It was such a beautiful house that they bought it.

Continue.

1 The book was so interesting that she couldn't stop reading it.
2 The problems are so difficult that nobody can solve them.
3 The man was so friendly that everybody liked him.
4 The dog was so savage that the postman refused to deliver the letters.
5 The box was so heavy that she couldn't lift it.
6 The trip was so exciting that he's going again.

Exercise 3

He was such a good boxer that nobody ever beat him.

The boxer was so good that nobody ever beat him.

Continue.

1 It was such a dangerous job that nobody would do it.
2 She was such a good dancer that she won the prize.
3 They were such boring films that nobody watched them.
4 It was such a crazy story that nobody believed it.

LAST OF THE AIRSHIPS?

At 7.20 pm on May 6th 1937, the world's largest airship, the Hindenburg, floated majestically over Lakehurst airport, New Jersey, after an uneventful crossing from Frankfurt, Germany. There were 97 people on board for the first Atlantic crossing of the season. There were a number of journalists waiting to greet it. Suddenly radio listeners heard the commentator screaming 'Oh, my God! It's broken into flames. It's flashing ... flashing. It's flashing terribly.' 32 seconds later the airship had disintegrated and 35 people were dead. The Age of the Airship was over.

The Hindenburg was the last in a series of airships which had been developed over 40 years in both Europe and the United States. They were designed to carry passengers and cargo over long distances. The Hindenburg could carry 50 passengers accommodated in 25 luxury cabins with all the amenities of a first class hotel. All the cabins had hot and cold water and electric heating. There was a diningroom, a bar and a lounge with a dance floor and a baby grand piano. The Hindenburg had been built to compete with the great luxury transatlantic liners. It was 245 metres long with a diameter of 41 metres. It could cruise at a speed of 125 km/h, and was able to cross the Atlantic in less than half the time of a liner. By 1937

it had carried 1000 passengers safely and had even transported circus animals and cars. Its sister ship, the Graf Zeppelin, had flown one and a half million kilometres and it had carried 13,100 passengers without incident.

The Hindenburg was filled with hydrogen, which is a highly flammable gas, and every safety precaution had been taken to prevent accidents. It had a smoking room which was pressurized in order to prevent gas from ever entering it. The cigarette lighters were chained to the tables and both passengers and crew were searched for matches before entering the ship. Special materials, which were used in the construction of the airship, had been chosen to minimize the possibility of accidental sparks, which might cause an explosion.

Nobody knows the exact cause of the Hindenburg disaster. Sabotage has been suggested, but experts at the time believed that it was caused by leaking gas which was ignited by static electricity. It had been waiting to land for three hours because of heavy thunderstorms. The explosion happened just as the first mooring rope, which was wet, touched the ground. Observers saw the first flames appear near the tail, and they began to spread quickly along the hull. There were a

number of flashes as the hydrogen-filled compartments exploded. The airship sank to the ground. The most surprising thing is that 62 people managed to escape. The fatalities were highest among the crew, many of whom were working deep inside the airship. After the Hindenburg disaster, all airships were grounded and, until recently, they have never been seriously considered as a commercial proposition.

Airships – achievements and disasters.

1852 1st airship (43.8 m long) flew over Paris.

1910 Five Zeppelin airships operated – 14 commercial flights within Germany, carrying 35,000 people without injury.

1914 Military Zeppelins took part in – 18 53 bombing raids on London, during First World War.

1919 British 'R34'. First transatlantic crossing. Both directions (10,187 km in 183 hours).

1921 British 'R38' broke up over Yorkshire, killing 15 passengers, 29 crew.

1925 US 'Shenandoah' (first helium airship) destroyed in a storm over Ohio. Heavy loss of life.

1926 Italian airship, the 'Norge', flew over North Pole.

1929 German Graf Zeppelin flew round the world. Began commercial transatlantic flights.

1930 British 'R101' (236 m long) crashed over Beauvais, France. Killed 48 out of 54 on board. British airship programme cancelled.

1931 US 'Akron' in service in USA – could carry 207 passengers.

1933 'Akron' wrecked in a storm.

1935 Sister ship, US 'Macon' wrecked.

1936 Hindenburg built. Carried 117 passengers in one flight.

1937 It crashed.

1938 'Graf Zeppelin II' completed. It never entered service.

1940 Both Graf Zeppelins scrapped.

1958 US Navy built a radar airship, the 'ZPG3–W'. (123 m long, 21 crew.)

1960 June. 'ZPG3–W' crashed in the sea.

1961 US Navy airship programme ended.

1975 US Goodyear company operating small airship fleet. The 'Europa' (58 m long) carries a pilot and six passengers.

Revision points

▶ Use of *with* in place of relative clause

There was a lounge | *which had a dance floor.*
                     | *with a dance floor.*

▶ *They heard him. He was screaming.*
They heard him screaming.

▶ *many* | *of whom*
some
half
thirteen

▶ Purpose expressed by the infinitive

Key vocabulary

(the) age (of the ...)	*mooring rope*	*float*
achievement	*piston engine*	*ground*
advantage	*running cost*	*ignite*
airship	*sabotage*	*leak*
amenity	*series*	*minimize*
baby grand piano	*sister ship*	*pressurize*
bombing raid	*spark*	*– – – – – –*
commentator	*static electricity*	*accidental*
diameter	*tail*	*bulky*
flame	*– – – – – –*	*conventional*
fleet	*accommodate*	*flammable*
forward propulsion	*break into*	*luxury*
helium (He)	*break up*	*uneventful*
hull	*cancel*	*– – – – – –*
hydrogen (H)	*chain*	*fatally*
incident	*cruise*	*majestically*
liner	*disintegrate*	*– – – – – –*
means	*flash*	*among*

1 Paragraph I. Set the situation. Ensure the text is masked. Play the cassette.

2 Silent reading.

3 Question and answer:
What time was it? What was the date? What was the name of the airship? What was special about it? Where had it come from? How many people were there on board? What were the journalists doing? What did the radio commentator say? How did he say it? What happened to the Hindenburg? How many people died?

4 Drill:
T: *They heard the commentator. He was screaming.*
C: *They heard him screaming.*

Continue:
They saw the airship. It was waiting to land.
He saw the airship. It was flashing.
He saw the airship. It was disintegrating.
They saw the people. They were jumping from the window.

5 Drill:
T: *The journalists were waiting. They wanted to greet the airship.*
C: *The journalists were waiting to greet the airship.*

Continue:
Some people were waiting. They wanted to film it.
Some people were waiting. They wanted to see it.
Some people were waiting. They wanted to meet friends.
The commentator was waiting. He wanted to describe the arrival.

6 Paragraph 2. Ensure the text is masked. Play the cassette.

7 Silent reading.

8 Question and answer:
Where had airships been developed? What were they designed to do? How many cabins were there? How many passengers could it accommodate? Describe the cabins. Describe the other amenities. Why had the Hindenburg been built? How long was it? What was the diameter? How fast could it cruise? How long did it take to cross the Atlantic? What had it done by 1937? What had the Graf Zeppelin done?

9 Drill:
T: *There were 25 cabins which had all the amenities of a first class hotel.*
C: *There were 25 cabins with all the amenities of a first class hotel.*

Continue:
There was a lounge which had a dance floor.
There were 25 cabins which had electric heating.
There was a lounge which had a baby grand piano.
There were luxury cabins which had hot and cold water.

10 Paragraph 3. Ensure the text is masked. Play the cassette.

11 Silent reading.

12 Question and answer:
Why is hydrogen dangerous? Why did they take so many safety precautions? Why was the smoking room pressurized? Why were the cigarette lighters chained to the table? Why were the passengers and crew searched for matches? Why did they use special construction materials?

13 Paragraph 4. Ensure the text is masked. Play the cassette.

14 Silent reading.

15 Question and answer:
Does anybody know the exact cause of the disaster? What did some people suggest? What did the experts believe? How long had it been waiting to land? Why? When exactly did the explosion happen? What did observers see? What happened then? How many people escaped? Why did so many of the crew die?

16 Drill:
T: *There were 50 passengers. Some of them died.*
C: *There were 50 passengers, some of whom died.*

Continue:
There were 50 passengers. Most of them escaped.
There were 50 passengers. 13 of them died.
There were 47 crew. About half of them escaped.
There were 47 crew. 22 of them died.

17 Play the complete cassette.

18 Drill:
T: *The journalists were waiting so that they could greet the Hindenburg.*
C: *The journalists were waiting to greet the Hindenburg.*

Continue:
The airships were designed so that they could carry cargo and passengers.
The airships were built so that they could compete with the liners.
Precautions had been taken so that they could prevent accidents.
The smoking room was pressurized so that gas could not enter it.
Special materials had been chosen so that they could minimize the possibility of a spark.

19 'Airships – achievements and disasters'. Ask students to study it silently and ask as many questions as possible about it.
Which was the earliest airship? When did it fly? Where did it fly?

20 Check through, asking individuals.

21 Questions:
Have you ever seen an airship? a film? a photograph?
Would you like to go in an airship? Why/Why not?
Why do some scientists believe they will become the cargo transporter of the future? Discuss.

Unit 57

Teaching points

▶ Clauses of reason, introduced by *because*
It was raining. He took his umbrella.
He took his umbrella because it was raining.

▶ Clauses of contrast, introduced by *although/though/even though*
It wasn't raining. He took his umbrella.

Although	*it wasn't raining, he took his umbrella.*
Though	
Even though	

▶ Clauses of reason, introduced by *as*
I chose the house wine, as this is often the best way to judge a restaurant's wine list.

Expressions

We were made very welcome.	*a delight to see*
speciality of the day	*a second helping*
for our taste	*go wrong with*
luckily	*Have a nice day! (Am.E.)*

Key vocabulary

chain	oz (ounce) (=	run
cherries	28.35g)	– – – – – –
cinnamon	port	acceptable
corn on the cob	portion	antiseptic
delight	quality	brightly-lit
establishment	quay	family-run
fast food	relish	French-bottled
French fries	rosemary	fresh
grapefruit	shoulder of lamb	futuristic
helping	trout	generous
herb	– – – – – –	newly-opened
house wine	bake	overcooked
milkshake	cater for	spotlessly clean
mill	eat out	tasteless
nourishment	overlook	time-consuming
		underdone

1 'Eating out'. Set the situation. Silent reading. Check vocabulary.

2 Drill:
T: *We'd been advised to book early. We managed to get a good table.*
S1: *Because we'd been advised to book early we managed to get a good table.*
T: *Or ... ?*
S2: *We managed to get a good table because we'd been advised to book early.*

Continue:
The service was excellent. It was a small family business.
A large menu worries me. It often means a large freezer.
The steak was almost perfect. It was cooked just long enough.
The bread was fresh. It had been baked on the premises.
I chose the house wine. This is often the best way to judge a restaurant.
The fruit salad was very good. I had two helpings.

3 Drill:
T: *The choice of items on the menu was very extensive, but it was rather traditional.*
S: *Although the choice of items on the menu was very extensive, it was rather traditional.*

Continue:
The fish was fresh, but it was spoiled by the number of herbs.
The quality of the meat was good, but my wife thought it was a little underdone.
The vegetables were fresh, but they came in very small portions.
The vegetables were fresh, but they were rather overcooked.
It must have been very time-consuming to prepare, but it was a delight to see the fresh fruit salad.
The bill was quite acceptable, but it did not include service.

4 The exercise in 58.3 could be repeated to elicit *though* and *even though*.

5 Pair work:
What did he like about the restaurant?
What didn't he like about the restaurant?
Make a list.
What would you have liked about the restaurant?
What wouldn't you have liked about the restaurant?

6 Focus attention on 'The Old Mill' menu. Silent reading.
T: *Would you have chosen the same as he did?*
What would you have chosen?
Would you have asked for the à la carte menu?
What would you have liked to see on the à la carte menu?

7 Role-play. Order a meal in the restaurant (as customer and waiter). Students work in pairs.

8 'Fast Food'. Set the situation. Silent reading. Check vocabulary.

9 Drill:
T: *There was a long queue, but service was incredibly fast.*
S: *Although there was a long queue, service was incredibly fast.*

Continue:
The burger was rather tasteless, but there was a large selection of relishes.
There were seats available, but many of the customers were standing up.
I'm not very fond of milkshakes, but I felt I should have one.
It's quick and efficient, but it isn't very quiet and romantic.
I wasn't in a hurry, but I was in, fed, and out in ten minutes.
Point out that *although* could be replaced by *though* or *even though*.

10 Pair work. See 58.5.

11 Focus attention on 'Nashville Superburger Bar' menu.
Silent reading.
Explain *oz (ounce)*, which is 28.35 grams. A pound (0.454 kilograms) is divided into 16 ounces. (Abbreviation for a pound weight is lb.)
T: *Would you have chosen the same as she did?*
What would you have chosen?

12 Role-play. Order a meal at the counter. Note that the customer might order by numbers: *I'll have a No. 5.* The waiter might reply *One No. 5.*

13 Exercise. Go through orally. Set for homework.

14 Extend the exercise with these oral prompts:
She took the job. The money was good.
Paul's very stupid. He passed all his exams.
Lisa didn't need a new dress. She bought one.
Anna's very intelligent. She passed all her exams.
Emma was thirsty. She drank two glasses of water.
Peter didn't jump out of the window. The building was on fire.
Barry's afraid of water. He's going by boat.
Mary jumped from the window. The building was burning.

15 Transfer:
Which restaurant would you prefer? Why? When?
If you were going to open a restaurant, what kind of restaurant would you open?
What kind of décor would you have?
What would you have on the menu?
Would you have music? What kind?
Would you have video games/a juke box/a bar/an orchestra/a piano/a singer?
Where would you open it?
What hours would you open?

16 Group work:
Plan a restaurant and its menu. Choose a name.
Write a newspaper advertisement for your restaurant.

Unit 58

EATING OUT

Eating Out
by Clement Harding

The Old Mill, The Quay, Wardleton, Sussex
Open: Tuesday – Sunday 7–11.30 p.m.

This week we decided to look at a small family-run restaurant in the village of Wardleton. 'The Old Mill' is newly opened and overlooks the River Wardle, and we had heard several favourable comments about it. Because we had been advised to book early, we managed to get a nice table with a view of the quay. We were made very welcome and the service was excellent because it is a small family business. The proprietor, Jeff Dean, runs the kitchen himself and his wife, Nelly, showed us to our table.

Although the choice of items on the menu was very extensive, it was rather traditional. A long menu always worries me, because a large menu often means a large freezer! We started with Wardle Trout and although it was fresh, it was spoilt by the number of herbs. For my main course I chose the pepper steak, which was the speciality of the day. I thought it was almost perfect because the chef had chosen excellent meat and it was cooked just long enough.

My wife ordered the roast lamb, and although the quality of the meat was good, she thought it was a little underdone. Though the vegetables were fresh, they came in very small portions and were rather over-cooked for our taste. However, the bread was fresh because it had been baked on the premises. I have often complained in this column about the difficulty of finding any restaurant which serves a fresh fruit salad. Luckily, this one did. Even though it must have been very time-consuming to prepare, it was a delight to see, and I had a second helping.

As usual I chose house wine, as this is often the best way to judge a restaurant's wine list. It was a French-bottled table wine which was quite satisfactory and reasonably priced. The bill, including coffee and brandy, came to £37, which was acceptable for the class of restaurant, although that did not include service.

Fast Food
by Rebecca Mitchell

Nashville Superburger Bar, Leicester Square, London
Open: 7 days a week, 24 hours a day

A new American fast-food chain has just opened its first restaurant in Britain. 'The Nashville Superburger Bar' is just off Leicester Square. Because of the success of McDonald's and Kentucky Fried Chicken, I was interested to see if Nashville had anything new to offer. The restaurant was so brightly-lit that I wished I'd brought my sunglasses. Once I'd got used to the light, I rather liked the green and orange plastic décor, which was very futuristic. The place was spotlessly clean – almost antiseptic! Although there was a long queue, service was incredibly fast. The menu was limited to a variety of hamburgers and prices were very reasonable. I had the 'Giant Superburger' which was served with a generous helping of french fries. Although the burger itself was rather tasteless, there was a large selection of relishes on every table and the french fries were the best I've ever tasted. This kind of establishment obviously caters for young people in a hurry. I was amazed to see that many of the customers preferred to eat standing up even though there were seats available. Most of the customers were under 25 and alone. Everybody seemed to be drinking milk-shakes and although I'm not very fond of them I felt I should have one. Not much can go wrong with a milk-shake and it tasted as good or as bad as any other. Although it's a quick and efficient way of taking nourishment, you wouldn't choose 'The Nashville' for a quiet and romantic evening with a friend. Although I wasn't in a hurry I was in, fed, and out in ten minutes. It reminded me very much of a motorway filling station.

The Old Mill

Specialities of the day

Fresh Wardle Trout	£2.00
Wardle Estuary Oysters (½ doz)	£7.00
Grapefruit with White Port and Cinnamon	£2.00
Old Mill Pepper Steak	£5.95
Roast Shoulder of Sussex Lamb with Rosemary	£5.75
Fresh Fruit Salad	£2.00
Hot Black Cherries in Brandy	£2.00

+ full à la carte menu

Nashville Superburger Bar

1 Straight burger (2oz)	60p		Side orders of French fries:	
2 Big burger (4oz)	90p		7 Small	40p
3 King-size burger (6oz)	£1.20		8 Big	60p
4 Super burger (8oz)	£1.60		Beverages:	
5 Giant super burger (10oz)	£2.00		9 Milk	30p
6 Titanic burger (12oz)	£2.40		10 Selection of milkshakes	80p
			11 Coffee	40p
All served in fresh, toasted buns with a choice of relishes.			12 Coca-cola	40p
			Have a nice day!	

Look at this

It was raining. He took his umbrella.
He took his umbrella because it was raining.

It wasn't raining. He took his umbrella.

Although	it wasn't raining he took his
Though	umbrella.
Even though	

Exercise
Now combine these sentences with 'because' or 'although'.

1 He didn't take the job. The salary was good.
2 Mark wasn't thirsty. He drank some milk.
3 They're afraid of flying. They flew to New York.
4 Sarah needed a new dress. She bought one.

Unit 58

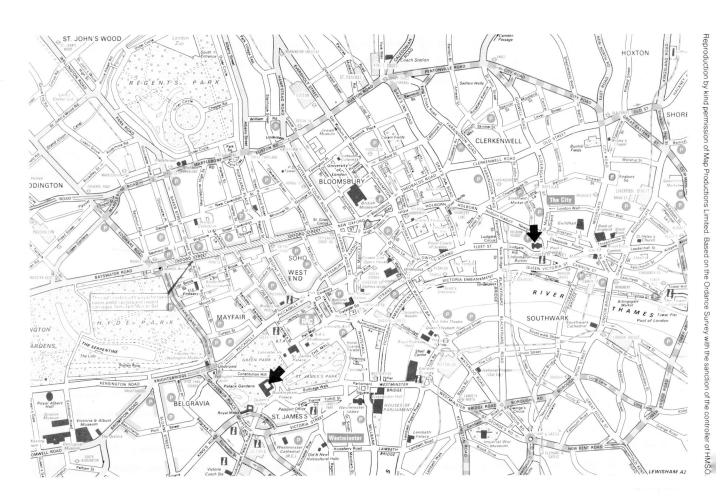

FINDING YOUR WAY AROUND

THE KNOWLEDGE

Becoming a London taxi driver isn't easy. In order to obtain a licence to drive a taxi in London, candidates have to pass a detailed examination. They have to learn not only the streets, landmarks and hotels, but also the quickest way to get there. This is called 'The Knowledge' by London cab drivers and it can take years of study and practice to get 'The Knowledge'. Candidates are examined not only on the quickest routes but also on the quickest routes at different times of the day. People who want to pass the examination spend much of their free time driving or even cycling around London, studying maps and learning the huge street directory by heart.

Monty Hunter is taking the examination now. Listen to the examiner's question and try to follow Monty's directions on the map of London.

Examiner OK, Monty. Ready? You're outside Buckingham Palace and you've just picked up a passenger who wants to go to St Paul's Cathedral. It isn't the rush-hour. Use the most direct route.

Monty I'd go straight along the Mall, round the one-way system at Trafalgar Square, and turn into Northumberland Avenue. I'd turn left along the Embankment and carry on as far as Blackfriars Bridge, turn left into New Bridge Street, then right at Ludgate Circus and up Ludgate Hill to St Paul's.

Exercise 1
Now practise with a partner. Point out your departure point on the map, state your destination and ask your partner to direct you.

Teaching points

▶ Asking for, giving, and following directions

▶ *Not only ... but also ....*

Expressions

Find your way around.
I'd go this way.
straight along
round the one-way system
turn into/left/right
Take a look at this map.
eastbound/westbound/northbound/southbound
There's not much in it.
We've got to get to ...
It looks easy enough.
It doesn't matter which one it is.
up here/top right/bottom left
change from ... to ...
The best/quickest way is ...
We might as well do this.
That goes straight there.
It's the (first) stop.
How do I get to ... ?
Which is the nearest tube station?
Follow the signs for ...
by heart

Key vocabulary

alphabetical order	*route*	*cycle*
automatic barrier	*rush hour*	*present*
cab	*street directory*	*– – – – – –*
(spare) change	*tube*	*(east) bound*
knowledge	*underground*	*colour coded*
landmark	*– – – – – –*	*detailed*
line	*carry on*	

1 Set the situation. (This is a map of the central area of London. London is the capital of the United Kingdom, the largest port and the largest industrial city. London's population is about eight million, but the population of Greater London is twelve million.)
Have you ever been to London?
Would you like to go to London?
What would you like to see?
Have you heard of any places in London?
What are they?
Make a list in pairs. (You can use the map.)

2 'The Knowledge'. Ensure the text is masked. Play the cassette.

3 Silent reading.

4 Question and answer:
What do candidates have to do in order to obtain a licence?
Do they only have to learn the streets?/the landmarks?/the hotels?
What do they also have to learn?
Make a sentence with 'not only ... but also ...'.
Are they only examined on the quickest routes?
Do they also have to know the quickest routes at different times of day?
Make a sentence with 'not only ... but also ...'.

5 Written phase.
They have to learn not only the streets, landmarks and hotels, but also the quickest way to get there.
They do not only (this), but also (that).

6 Dialogue. 'Monty Hunter'. Ensure the text is masked. Play the cassette.

7 Selective repetition.

8 Exercise 1. Students do it in pairs.

9 Role-play. Students repeat Exercise 1 as candidate and examiner and are 'passed' or 'failed' by their partner. They can repeat this with the town they are in, from memory.

continued

Unit 59

10 Focus attention on the Underground map. Explain the key to the lines.
This is a map of the central area only.
Have you been on an underground railway? Ask 'Where? When?'
Do you know which cities have Undergrounds? (Paris – Metro, New York – Subway, Munich, Glasgow, etc.)
What do you think are the advantages of an underground railway? (no traffic/doesn't use up building land/quiet.)
What about the disadvantages? (very expensive to build/you see nothing if you are a tourist.)

11 'The Underground'. Ensure the text is masked. Play the cassette.

12 Silent reading.

13 Question and answer:
Is it easy to find your way around on the London Underground?
Why?
Why should you carry spare change?
How do you know the correct fare?
How do you get on to the platforms?
Why should you keep your ticket?

14 For each of the dialogues, point out the starting point on the map. Play the cassette. Students listen and trace the route.

15 Selective repetition.

16 Pair work.

17 Exercises 2, 3 and 4. Students work in pairs. Get individuals to direct you, using the map.

18 By using the map of London on the previous page, which also has tube stations, Exercise 3 can be extended.

Unit 59

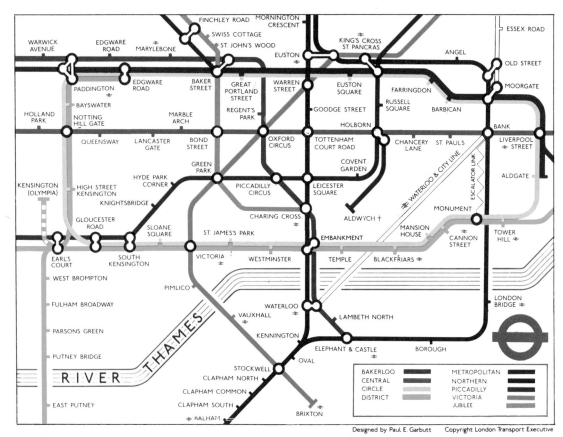

Designed by Paul E. Garbutt   Copyright London Transport Executive

THE UNDERGROUND

Travelling on the London underground (the 'tube') presents few difficulties for visitors because of the clear colour-coded maps. It is always useful to have plenty of spare change with you because there are often long queues at the larger stations. If you have enough change you can buy your ticket from a machine. You will find signs which list the stations in alphabetical order, with the correct fares, near the machines. There are automatic barriers which are operated by the tickets. You should keep the ticket, because it is checked at the destination.

Listen to these people talking about the underground map, and follow their routes on the map.

Peter and Susan have just arrived at Victoria.

Peter Right. We've got to get to Baker Street. Can you see it?

Susan Yes, it's up here. It looks easy enough. We just take the Victoria line to Green Park, then change to the Jubilee line. That goes straight there. It's only the second stop from Green Park.

Laura is at the enquiry office at King's Cross.

Laura Oh, excuse me. How do I get to King's Road, Chelsea. I mean, which is the nearest tube station?

Clerk You want Sloane Square. Take a look at this map. The best way is to take the Victoria line, that's this light blue one, as far as Victoria Station. Then you'll have to change. When you get to Victoria, follow the signs for the Circle and District lines, they're on the same platform. Then take the first westbound train. It doesn't matter which one it is. Sloane Square's the next stop.

Laura Thank you very much indeed.

Simon and Elizabeth are at Waterloo.

Simon Where's a map?

Elizabeth There's one over here. They said the hotel was near Russell Square. Can you see it?

Simon Yes, it's up here. In the top right of the map. Look, I reckon we should take the Bakerloo as far as Piccadilly Circus, then change to the Piccadilly line, that's the dark blue one. It's only four stops to Russell Square.

Elizabeth Are you sure that's the quickest way? We could take the Northern line (it's the black one) to Leicester Square, and join the Piccadilly line there.

Simon There's not much in it, really. We might as well take the Northern. Have you got any change for the ticket machine?

Exercise 2
Practise with a partner. Give directions from:
1 Sloane Square to Marble Arch
2 Baker Street to Russell Square
3 Waterloo to Paddington
4 Victoria to Great Portland Street
5 Pimlico to Russell Square
6 Great Portland Street to St Paul's

Exercise 3
Here are some famous London landmarks with their nearest tube stations. Make conversations about getting to them from: a Sloane Square, b St Paul's, c Marble Arch.
1 Buckingham Palace (St James's Park)
2 British Museum (Russell Square)
3 National Gallery (Trafalgar Square)
4 Houses of Parliament (Westminster)
5 Tower of London (Tower Hill)
6 Madame Tussaud's (Baker Street)

Exercise 4
Practise with a partner. State a departure point and destination. Your partner has to give you directions.

Unit 59

Good evening, and here is the Eight O'Clock News.

Five thousand people marched through the streets of Chesilworth today protesting against plans for a new international airport near the town. Although there was such a large number of demonstrators, there was no trouble. The demonstrators marched to the town hall, where a public enquiry into the plans was taking place, and handed in a petition to the chairman of the enquiry. A new airport is needed because the other airports in the London area are over-crowded. Several sites for the new airport have been suggested, and Chesilworth was considered because it is near both a major motorway and a railway line. Although it was a protest march, there was almost a carnival atmosphere, and both demonstrators and police remained good-humoured.

Families were evacuated from four streets in the centre of Glasgow today, because of a gas explosion. The explosion occurred at ten a.m. in a deserted house in Mickle Street. Gas Board officials believe that the explosion was due to leaking gas. The house had been empty for several months, and they suspect that a gas main had cracked because of vibration from road-works in the street. Windows 100 metres away were broken by the blast. The police have forbidden anyone to enter the area until the Gas Board has completed tests.

Air-sea rescue helicopters from RAF Sopworth were called out after a yacht capsized in a storm off the Devon coast. Despite high seas the helicopters lowered rescue teams to try and save the crew. Two men and a girl were pulled to safety. Unfortunately, the other two crewmembers died in spite of the rescue team's efforts. One was lost at sea. The other was rescued and taken to hospital, but was dead on arrival. The coastguard had warned small boats to stay in the harbour, but the yacht, the 'Neptune III' from Poole, had set out for France despite the warnings.

Fernside Engineering announced today that they are closing their plant in Tadworth. Three hundred jobs will be lost because of the closure, which is due to a sharp decline in orders for their products. There have been

THE EIGHT O'CLOCK NEWS

rumours for several weeks that the plant might be closed, and in spite of lengthy discussions between unions and management, closure became inevitable because of the cancellation of several major orders. As well as the three hundred redundancies at Tadworth, union leaders predict further redundancies in the area, in firms which supply Fernside Engineering with components.

Reports are coming in of a 100 mph car chase through the roads of Hampshire. Police disturbed a gang of men who were breaking into a chemist's in Lyndford. However, the men escaped in a stolen Jaguar saloon, and the police chased them through the New Forest at high speed. The Jaguar was forced off the road near Bransley. The men were armed with shot-guns, but nevertheless police-officers chased them across a field. Several shots were fired. Fortunately, however, no one was injured, and the men were taken into custody.

Brighton Belle XIV, a four-year-old Dalmatian bitch, became the 'Supreme Champion Dog' at Cruft's Dog Show in London. There were almost

10,000 dogs on show, worth around £8,000,000. There were 120 judges looking at 144 different breeds of dog. Brighton Belle XIV is expected to earn up to £100,000 in breeding and advertising fees.

And lastly, sport. Eastfield United are through to the next round of the European Cup after an exciting match in Scotland. Dunromin Rangers scored twice in the first half, and although Eastfield were two down at half-time, they went on to win with a hat trick by Trevor Franklin in the second half. Towards the end of the second half, Franklin was limping because of a knee injury, but nevertheless managed to score the winning goal one minute from time. The game was stopped twice because of fighting in the crowd, but in spite of the trouble, and in spite of the appalling weather, both teams played well. Viewers will be able to see highlights of the match after the news.

Look at this

It was snowing so she wore a coat.

or

| She wore a coat | because it was snowing. |
| | because of the snow. |

or

| Because it was snowing, | she wore a coat. |
| Because of the snow, | |

It was snowing, but she didn't wear a coat.

or

She didn't wear a coat	although it was snowing.
	in spite of	the snow.
	despite	

or

Although it was snowing,	she didn't wear a
In spite of	the snow,	coat.
Despite		

It was difficult, but he managed to do it.

or

| It was difficult. | However, | he managed |
| | Nevertheless, | to do it. |

or

| It was difficult. He managed to | however. |
| do it | nevertheless. |

Exercise
Now write the news for today.

Teaching points

▶ Expressing reason and contrast
See 'Look at this' section in Student's Book.

▶ *due to*
The explosion was due to leaking gas.
The closure is due to a sharp decline in orders.

Key vocabulary

bitch	*gas main*	*capsize*
blast	*harbour*	*distort*
cancellation	*hat trick* (three goals	*evacuate*
carnival	scored by one	*hand in*
chase	player)	*limp*
closure	*highlight*	*march*
coastguard	*knee*	*predict*
components	*petition*	– – – – –
custody	*road works*	*appalling*
decline	*shotgun*	*good-humoured*
demonstrator	*vibration*	*lengthy*
Gas Board	– – – – –	*overcrowded*

1 Section 1. Ensure the text is masked. Set the situation. Play the cassette. Set these pre-questions:
How many people were there? What were they protesting about? Was there any trouble?

2 Silent reading. Check pre-questions.

3 Drill:
T: *There were a lot of people. There was no trouble.*
S1: *Although there were a lot of people, there was no trouble.*
T: *Or ...?*
S2: *There was no trouble, although there were a lot of people.*

Continue:
A new airport is needed. The other airports are overcrowded.
Chesilworth was considered. It's near a motorway and a railway.
It was a protest march. There was almost a carnival atmosphere.

4 Question and answer:
Were there a lot of people at Chesilworth today? Ask 'How many?'
What were they doing? There was no trouble, was there? Where did they march to? What was happening there? What did the demonstrators do when they arrived? Why is a new airport needed? Why was Chesilworth considered? What was the atmosphere like?

5 Transfer:
Do you live near an airport? Would you like to? Why/Why not?
Would you protest if an airport were planned for your town?
Why/Why not?
What do you think the advantages/disadvantages might be?

6 Section 2. Ensure the text is masked. Set the situation. Play the cassette.

7 Silent reading. Mark the sentences with *because of* and *due to*.

8 Question and answer:
Why were families evacuated from the centre of Glasgow today?
When and where did the explosion occur? What was the explosion due to? Was the house empty? Ask 'How long?' What was cracked? Ask 'Why?' What broke the windows? What have the police done?

9 Point out the difference between *because* and *because of*. (See 'Look at this'.)

10 Section 3. Ensure the text is masked. Play the cassette.
Set these pre-questions:
How many people were on the boat? How many were rescued? How many survived?

11 Silent reading. Check pre-questions.

12 Point out the difference between *although* and *in spite of/despite*. Get the students to say these sentences another way using *in spite of/despite*:
Although the seas were high, the helicopters lowered rescue teams.
The other two died, although the rescue team tried hard to save them.
The yacht had set out for France, although the coastguard had warned small boats to stay in harbour.

13 Section 4. Ensure the text is masked. Play the cassette.

14 Silent reading.

15 Question and answer:
What was announced today? Who by? How many jobs will be lost?
Ask 'Why?' Was it unexpected? How do you know? Why did the closure become inevitable? What will be the results of the closure?

16 Section 5. Ensure the text is masked. Play the cassette.

17 Silent reading.

18 Question and answer:
Why did the police chase the men? Where did they chase them? How did they chase them? What kind of car were the thieves in? How fast did they drive? How did the police stop the car? Were the men armed? Ask 'What with?' Where did the police chase them? How many shots were fired? Was anybody injured? What happened in the end?

19 Point out *however* and *nevertheless*.

20 Transfer:
Note that English policemen do not usually carry guns, and often have to tackle armed criminals. However, as a result, fewer criminals carry guns. What do you think of this? If you were a policeman, would you want to carry a gun? Why/Why not?

21 Section 6. Ensure the text is masked. Play the cassette.

22 Silent reading.

23 Question and answer:
How many dogs were there? How many breeds were represented?
How many judges were there? How much were the dogs worth?
Which dog became 'Supreme Champion'? What kind of dog was it?
It's worth a lot of money, isn't it? Why?

24 Transfer:
Would you pay a lot of money for a dog?
What kind of advertising do you think the dog does?
What products have you seen animals advertising?

25 Section 7. Ensure the text is masked. Play the cassette.

26 Silent reading.

27 Question and answer:
It was a European Cup match, wasn't it? Where was it played? What was the final score? Who won? Who lost? Why was it an exciting match? Why was Trevor Franklin mentioned especially? What was the weather like? Why was the game stopped twice? What's on television after the news?

28 Focus attention on 'Look at this'. Run through. Set the exercise for homework.

29 Play the complete cassette.

30 Get individuals to role-play the newsreader and to read out a news item without hesitating.

Unit 60

Teaching points

▶ Reading comprehension

▶ *It's worth fifteen million pounds. It's a fifteen million pound contract.*

Expressions

for a change
double the number
without incident
telling the right time
with the minimum effort
No news is good news.

Key vocabulary

auctioneer	*seedling*	*exhibit*
cereal	*trade fair*	*ordain*
chunk	*treatment*	*plough*
death rate	– – – – –	*print*
decade	*auction*	*sow*
first-class mail	*award*	– – – – –
harvest	*benefit*	*congenital*
heart defect	*conduct* (a religious	*gurgling*
loan	service)	*leading*
Press Awards	*deliver*	*undreamed of*
registry office	*emerge*	
schedule	*enable*	

1 Set the situation. Ask *What was on the news this morning? Was it mainly good news or mainly bad news? What about the news in Unit 60? It was nearly all bad news, wasn't it? How do you usually find out about the news? From a newspaper?/on the radio?/on television? Ask him/her/each other.*

2 Set the situation. *Prince Charles was talking at a Press Awards Lunch (where prizes are given for the best journalism of the year).*

3 Silent reading.

4 Set Exercises 1–3. Students work in pairs. Check through, getting pairs to report to the class.

5 Go through the text checking vocabulary.
First class mail: in Britain there are two classes of letter post. First class is more expensive, but faster (usually arriving the next day).
The River Thames: the river which runs through London; it used to be so polluted that nothing could live in it.
Canterbury Cathedral: traditionally the most important place of worship for the Church of England.
Big Ben: the famous clock in the Houses of Parliament.
House of Commons: there are two 'houses' in parliament.
The House of Commons is the elected one. The other is the House of Lords.
Rugby League Football: there are two types of rugby, 'Union' with 15 players in a team, and 'League' with 13 players. The rules differ as well. It is traditionally a 'men only' sport. Liz was a 13-year-old girl who took legal action to be allowed to play the game.

6 Discussion points. Go through *(Ask me/him/her/each other).*

7 Project. Get students to work in groups to create a newspaper front page, with headlines and reports, dedicated entirely to good news. Each member of the group takes responsibility for one news item. They should be encouraged to make the page look as authentic as possible.

Unit 61

ALL THE GOOD NEWS

Our news present to Charles

Prince Charles, speaking at a Press Awards lunch, once asked why newspapers only printed the bad news. 'Why don't they, for a change, tell us how many jumbo jets landed safely at Heathrow Airport?' Later the same year a leading British newspaper published a column of 'good news' as a birthday present for Prince Charles. Here are some of the news items.

♛ Last week 330 jumbo jets landed or took off without incident at Heathrow, the world's leading international airport, with 20 million international passengers, which is double the number at New York's Kennedy Airport, the world's second busiest international terminal.

♛ Approximately 12,200 happy, gurgling babies were delivered to British mothers last week.

♛ 92 per cent of the first class mail was also delivered on time.

♛ The government received its first chunk of petroleum revenue tax last week – £176 million from BP's successful 'Forties' oil-field. The first oil from the Ninian group of oil-fields was moving through the pipeline towards its terminal in the Shetland Islands, part of the riches undreamed of a decade ago of 1,100,000 barrels a day from North Sea oil.

♛ The battle to clean up the River Thames is being won. Species of fish, which even ten years ago could not have survived in the polluted water, are being caught in increasing numbers.

♛ About 6,500 couples emerged happily from churches and registry offices.

♛ Last week was 'National Tree Planting Week'. Thousands of seedlings were planted.

♛ British Rail carried two million passengers each working day with 88 per cent of express trains arriving within ten minutes of schedule.

♛ Canterbury Cathedral was conducting services in its 798th year.

♛ At the Houses of Parliament, where Big Ben was telling the right time, the House of Commons resumed its 306th Parliament since 1213.

♛ Britain's ladies won the Wightman Cup tennis tournament.

♛ Two women clerks won equal pay for 14,000 young women at Lloyds Bank.

♛ Despite the example of the Church of England, which is still refusing to ordain women priests, Liz Beal, aged 13, won permission to play Rugby League Football.

♛ Five children at the Great Ormond Street Hospital for Sick Children were successfully operated on for congenital heart defects – some of the 2,000 babies now benefiting from the treatment each year.

♛ Britain's gold and currency reserves amounted to £15,977 million, and this year we have repaid foreign loans to the value of £3,500 million.

♛ Sotheby's, the auctioneers, auctioned a cello for a record £144,000.

♛ By the end of this year, 30,000 home students will have been awarded degrees by the Open University, which operates through post, television, radio, and short summer courses to enable people to get a university degree at home.

♛ Bovis, the construction company, won a £15 million contract to build three schools in Saudi Arabia. 47 British companies were exhibiting at a trade fair in Peking, and over 200 at a trade fair in Mexico City.

♛ Even farmers were smiling last week. At the beginning of the good weather they were able to bring in a record cereal harvest with the minimum effort. Since then, there has been no rain and autumn ploughing and sowing is going wonderfully well.

PS: The death rate from suicide is going down.

Exercise 1
Find words in the text which mean:
1 A period of ten years. *Decade*
2 A place where people can marry without a religious ceremony. *Registry office*
3 A young newly grown tree. *Seedlings*
4 A programme of pre-arranged times. *Schedule*
5 A contest of skill between a number of players. *Tournament*
6 Groups of animals or plants (which are able to breed together). *species*
7 A formal legal agreement. *Contract*
8 Firms which sell goods at a public sale to the person who offers most money. *Auctioneers*
9 The collection of fruit, grain or vegetables made by a farmer. *harvest*
10 A standard measurement for oil. *barrels*

Exercise 2
Find expressions which mean:
1 twice as many as *double the number*
2 with no unusual occurrences *without incid*
3 showing the time correctly *telling the right time*
4 with as little work as possible *with the minimum effort*

Exercise 3
There are five examples of the use of 'to win'. What are they? ✱

Discussion points

❝ When a dog bites a man, that is not news, but when a man bites a dog that is news. ❞

❝ No news is good news. ❞

What do you think these sayings mean? Discuss.
Prince Charles said that newspapers always print the bad news. Is that true?
Why do you think newspapers might concentrate on 'bad' news?
Would you buy a newspaper which only reported 'good' news? Why? Why not?
Did you hear the news yesterday? What was it? Was it all bad?
Give some examples of 'good' news.

THE ANNUAL DINNER AND DANCE

Every year, 'Continental Computers' holds an annual dinner and dance, to which all employees and their husbands and wives are invited. It is the only time of the year when all the employees get together socially.

Christopher Simpson is a young accounts clerk. He's speaking to Edward Wallis, the Chief Personnel Officer.

Chris Mr Wallis? Can I buy you a drink?

Mr W Oh, that's very kind of you, Christopher. I'll have a scotch, a large one.

Chris Ice?

Mr W No, no, no. Just a splash of soda, please. Thank you.

Chris Er ... I wanted to ask you what was happening about the job in Sheffield.

Mr W It's being advertised next week. Are you interested?

Chris I might be. I really don't know what to do. I'm quite happy here, but it would be a promotion. Do you think I should apply?

Mr W Why not? There's no harm in trying. I'll tell you what to do. Pop up and see me on Monday, and I'll tell you what I can about the job.

Martin Webber is a computer programmer. He's at the dance with his wife, Melanie.

Martin Melanie, do you have to flirt with Philip every time we come to a dance?

Melanie We were only dancing. There's no need to get jealous.

Martin I saw what he was doing! He was whispering to you!

Melanie Oh, Martin! You don't know what you're talking about. He had to speak into my ear because of the music! How many drinks have you had?

Martin Oh, come on! That's got nothing to do with it!

Melanie Do you want to hear what he said?

Martin I don't care what he said, I...

Melanie He was asking me what he should buy for his wife's birthday, that's all!

Jacqueline Dibben works in the Marketing Department. She's just met Fiona Johnson, who's in charge of advertising.

Fiona Ah, Jacky! So you're back from New York.

Jacky Yes, Fiona. I've been doing market research there.

Fiona I know. How did you get on?

Jacky Well, what I saw in the States astonished me ... really! I think there'll be a lot of demand for our new 2CL home computer.

Fiona That's very interesting.

Jacky Yes. What I heard was very encouraging. We've got just what they're looking for.

Sir Joseph Lennox is the Managing Director. He's just run into Alex Fielding, one of the union representatives.

Sir Joseph Good evening, Mr Fielding.

Alex Good evening, Sir Joseph.

Sir Joseph Did you get my message about the meeting on Monday?

Alex Yes, I did, but I'm still not absolutely sure what the meeting's about. Not bad news, I hope.

Sir Joseph No, no. Don't worry. It's good news, in fact. What we'd like to do is expand production of the new home computer. Either we'll have to increase overtime working or take on new staff.

Alex That sounds promising. What we'll need to know is exactly how much more work will be created.

Sir Joseph I'll give you all the facts and figures on Monday. But let's forget about all that now. We don't want to talk shop all night, do we? That's not what this evening's all about. Another drink?

Alex Please.

Kelly's a secretary and Teresa works in the Data Processing Department.

Kelly Hey, Teresa. Wasn't that Neil Pincher you were dancing with?

Teresa Yes. Do you know what he asked me?

Kelly No.

Teresa He invited me out for dinner.

Kelly You're not going, are you?

Teresa No fear! I've heard all about him. I wouldn't go out with him if he was the last man on earth.

Kelly So what did you say?

Teresa What I wanted to say was, 'Go to hell', but I just told him I was busy.

Look at this

I don't know *what* to do.
I'll tell you *what* I can.
What I saw astonished me.

Teaching points

▶ Structures with *what*

I don't know what to do.
I'll tell you what I can.
What I saw astonished me.

Expressions

There's no harm in trying.
Pop up/in and see me.
There's no need to get jealous.
That's got nothing to do with it!
That sounds promising.
You're back from New York.
We don't want to talk shop (talk business).
I wouldn't go out with him if he was the last man on earth!
('Was' often replaces 'were' in conditional sentences, particularly in spoken English.)

How did you get on?
We've got just what they're looking for.
Not bad news, I hope.
all the facts and figures
No fear!
Go to hell!

Key vocabulary

computer	splash	whisper
programmer	– – – – –	– – – – –
home computer	create	encouraging
overtime working	expand	promising
soda	pop up/in	– – – – –
		socially

1 Introduction and Dialogue 1. Ensure the text is masked. Set the situation. Play the cassette.

2 Selective repetition.

3 Drill:
T: *Do something!*
C: *I don't know what to do.*
Continue:
Say/Drink/Write/Buy/
Eat something!

4 Drill:
T: *What can you tell me about the job?*
C: *I'll tell you what I can about the job.*

Continue:
What did you see?/What will you do?/What are you going to do about it?/What do you know about it?/What did you say to him?/What should you be doing?

5 Silent reading.

6 Question and answer:
What did Chris want to know? What is happening about it? Can Chris decide what to do about the job? Why not? What will Mr Wallis tell Chris on Monday?

7 Pair work. Encourage students to substitute other vocabulary items and to role-play the characters of Chris and Mr Wallis.

8 Dialogue 2. Mask text, set the situation and play the cassette.

9 Selective repetition.

10 Drill:
T: *Do you want to hear what he said?*
T: *I don't care what he said.*
T: *Do you want to know what she wrote?*
T: *I don't care what she wrote.*
T: *Do you want to hear what she said?*
C: *I don't care what she said.*

Continue:
Do you want to know what he wrote?
Do you want to know what he did?
Do you want to know what they're going to do?
Do you know what I've just done?

11 Silent reading.

12 Question and answer:
Why is Martin angry? What did he see Philip doing? Does Martin want to hear what he said? What was Philip asking Melanie?

13 Pair work. (See 62.7.)

14 Dialogue 3. Mask text, set the situation and play the cassette.

15 Selective repetition.

16 Drill:
T: *What did you see?*
C: *What I saw astonished me.*

Continue:
What did he do?/What did you hear?/What did they say?/What did she ask?/What did you notice?

17 Question and answer:
Where's Jackie been? What's she been doing? What astonished her? What was encouraging? Why?

18 Pair work. (See 62.7.)

19 Dialogue 4. Ensure the text is masked. Set the situation. Play the cassette.

20 Selective repetition.

21 Drill:
T: *We'd like to expand production.*
T: *What we'd like to do is expand production.*
T: *We'll have to increase overtime.*
T: *What we'll have to do is increase overtime.*
T: *We'd like to expand production.*
C: *What we'd like to do is expand production.*

Continue:
We'll have to increase overtime.
We'll probably sell more computers.
We'll need to know how much work there'll be.
We should discuss future plans.
We must employ more salesmen.

22 Question and answer:
What isn't Alex sure about? What would Sir Joseph like to do? What will they have to do? What will they need to know? Why doesn't he want to talk shop?

23 Pair work. (See 62.7.)

24 Dialogue 5. Ensure the text is masked. Set the situation. Play the cassette.

25 Selective repetition.

26 Drill:
T: *'Go to hell!' I wanted to say.*
T: *What I wanted to say was 'Go to hell!'*
T: *'Go away!' I should have said.*
T: *What I should have said was 'Go away!'*
T: *'Go to hell!' I wanted to say.*
C: *What I wanted to say was 'Go to hell!'*

Continue:
'Shut up!' I nearly said./'Get lost!' I almost said./'Drop dead!' I felt like telling him./'Jump in the river!' I wanted to say.

27 Pair work. (See 62.7)

28 Focus attention on 'Look at this'.

29 Role-play – groups. 'The annual dinner and dance'. Use the characters in the unit and get the students to act out the conversations as in Unit 62, then to improvise the conversations which occur as the characters 'circulate' (e.g. Mr Wallis and Jacqueline Dibben, Sir Joseph and Chris Simpson).

Unit 62

Teaching points

▶ *Whatever, whichever, whoever, whenever, wherever, however*

When shall I do it? I don't mind. Do it whenever you like./Whenever you like.

What shall I do? It doesn't matter. Do whatever you want./Whatever you want.

Where shall I go? I don't know. Go wherever you want./Wherever you want.

Who shall I ask? I don't care. Ask whoever is there./Whoever is there.

Which shall I take? I'm not sure. Take whichever you like./Whichever you like.

How shall I do it? It isn't important. Do it however you like.

▶ Expressing surprise with *What ever, Which ever, Who ever, Where ever, When ever, Why ever, How ever.*

What ever are you talking about?

▶ *It's time for the tea-break.*

Expressions

You can call me Bert.	*Know what I mean?*
Any questions?	*Another thing . . .*
son/lad	*Just stop and think.*
I'll give you a tip! (=some advice)	

Key vocabulary

apprentice	*numbered space*	– – – – –
bench (= work bench)	*row*	*pass (it) on*
bucket	*storeman*	– – – – –
locker	*stores*	*left-handed*
National	*tea-break*	*right-handed*
Insurance card	*white spirit*	

Note: It is a convention in British factories to play mild tricks on new employees by sending them to get ridiculous objects. (Other popular 'objects' are tartan paint, glass nails, some holes for the washers.)

1 Introduction and Dialogue 1. Ensure the text is masked. Set the situation. Play the cassette.

2 Selective repetition.

3 Drill:
T: *I'll show you what to do.* Continue:
T: *He* *me*
T: *He'll show you what to do.* *tell*
T: *me* *her*
T: *He'll show me what to do.* *I*
T: *tell* *show*
T: *He'll tell me what to do.* *they*
T: *I'll show you what to do.* *them*
T: *He* *say*
C: *He'll show you what to do.*

4 Pair work.

5 Dialogue 2. Mask text, set the situation and play the cassette.

6 Selective repetition.

7 Drill:
T: *It doesn't matter which locker you take.*
T: *Take whichever one you want.*
T: *It doesn't matter which cup you use.*
T: *Use whichever one you want.*
T: *It doesn't matter which locker you take.*
C: *Take whichever one you want.*

Continue:
It doesn't matter which cup you use/record you play/tie you wear/programme you watch/colour you choose.

8 Drill: Continue:
T: *Who should I give it to?* *Who should I ask?/speak to?/*
C: *Give it to whoever is there.* *work with?/tell?*

9 Drill:
T: *When can I do that?*
C: *Do it whenever you like.*

Continue:
When can I go?/stop?/have a break?/open it?/see the boss?

10 Pair work.

11 Dialogue 3. Mask text, set the situation and play the cassette.

12 Selective repetition.

13 Drill:
T: *Where can I leave my motorbike?*
C: *Leave it wherever there's room.*

Continue:
Where can I park my car?/sit?/put my bag?/hang my coat?

14 Drill:
T: *What shall I do?*
C: *Do whatever I tell you.*

Continue:
What shall I say?/take?/answer?/bring?

15 Pair work.

16 Drill:
T: *How should I clean them?*
C: *Clean them however you want.*

Continue:
How should I open it?/do it?/finish it?/make it?/spend my money?

17 Pair work.

18 Dialogue 4. Mask text, set the situation and play the cassette.

19 Selective repetition.

20 Pair work.

21 Dialogue 5. Mask text, set the situation and play the cassette.

22 Selective repetition.

23 Drill:
T: *A tin of striped paint, please.*
T: *A what? What ever are you talking about?*
T: *A tin of striped paint, please.*
C: *A what? What ever are you talking about?*

Continue:
A rubber hammer, please.
A glass nail, please.
A left-handed screwdriver, please.
A bucket of steam, please.

24 Drill: Continue:
T: *A tin of striped paint, please.* *A rubber hammer, please.*
T: *What? Who ever told you that?* *A glass nail, please.*
T: *A tin of striped paint, please.* *A left-handed screwdriver, please.*
C: *What? Who ever told you that?* *A bucket of steam, please.*

25 Pair work.

26 Get students to go through Exercises 1–3 in pairs. Then go through with the whole class.

27 Transfer:
Do tricks like this happen in your country? /in school?/in offices?/in factories? Have you heard of any tricks like this? What are they? Describe one. Has it ever happened to you? Have you ever done it to anyone?

Unit 63

THE APPRENTICE

It's Alan Newman's first day in his first job. He's started work in an electrical components factory. The Personnel Officer, Mrs Vaughan, is introducing him to Bert Hogg, who has worked there for thirty years.

Mrs Vaughan Alan, this is Bert, Bert Hogg. You'll be working with him.

Alan Morning, Mr Hogg.

Bert You can call me Bert, son. Don't worry. I'll show you what to do.

Mrs Vaughan Can I leave him with you then, Bert?

Bert Oh, yes, Mrs Vaughan. I'll look after him. Follow me, son.

Bert Right, son. Any questions?

Alan Er . . . yes. Where can I leave my coat and things?

Bert There's a row of lockers over there. It doesn't matter which one you use. Take whichever one you want.

Alan Oh, thanks. And I've got my National Insurance card here. Who should I give it to?

Bert You should have given it to Mrs Vaughan. I don't suppose she asked you for it. Just take it up to the office. You can give it to whoever is there. They'll pass it on to her.

Alan When can I do that?

Bert It doesn't matter really. Take it whenever you like, lad, but I'll give you a tip. Don't take it during the tea-break. You know what I mean?

Alan Right. Thanks.

Alan Oh, another thing. Where can I leave my motor-bike?

Bert There's plenty of room in the car-park. Just don't put it in a numbered space. They're reserved for the directors' cars. But apart from that, you can leave it wherever there's room. Come on, I'll show you where you'll be working. Right, this is our bench. Just watch me, and do whatever I tell you, OK?

Alan OK.

Bert First of all, you can clean these tools. There's a bottle of white spirit on the shelf.

Alan All right. Is there any special way of doing it?

Bert Eh? Special way? No, son, no. Clean them however you want. There's no special way.

10.30.

Bert Oi! Alan, you can stop work for a bit. It's time for the tea-break.

Alan Thanks.

Bert Don't thank me, son. You've done well. You'll need a cup of tea. Oh, look . . . after the tea-break I want you to go to the stores and get me a few things. Is that all right?

Alan Oh, yes. I'll get whatever you want.

Bert Good lad. Now, I'll need a tin of striped paint, a rubber hammer and a glass nail, a left-handed screw-driver, and a bucket of steam. Oh, and tell them Bert sent you.

At the stores.

Alan Morning.

Storeman Morning.

Alan I've come to get a tin of striped paint.

Storeman A what? What ever are you talking about, son?

Alan A tin of striped paint. I want a tin of striped paint.

Storeman Who ever told you to come and get that?

Alan Bert . . . er, Bert Hogg.

Storeman Oh, Bert Hogg! What colour stripes would you like, son?

Alan I'm not sure. Perhaps I'd better ask him.

Storeman I suppose he asked you to get a right-handed screw-driver, as well.

Alan No, he wants a left-handed one.

Storeman Just stop and think for a minute, lad! Just stop and think!

Exercise 1

A What do you fancy doing this evening?

B *I don't mind. Whatever you like.*

1 Well where shall we go then?
2 How shall we go there?
3 Which would you prefer, bus or taxi?
4 When do you think we should leave?
5 Which pub would you like to go to?
6 What shall we have to drink?
7 Where shall we go for a meal?
8 Who shall we invite to the party?
9 What shall we give them to eat?

Exercise 2

A What shall I do with these old newspapers?

B *It doesn't matter. Do whatever you want.*

1 Which of these books can I borrow?
2 Who shall I give my ticket to?
3 When can I come to see you?
4 How should I do it?
5 Where can I park my car?

Exercise 3

A He's talking about something. Nobody knows what!

B *What ever is he talking about?*

1 They found out about it. Nobody knows how!
2 She's been somewhere. Nobody knows where!
3 He gave it to someone. Nobody knows who!
4 She found time to do it. Nobody knows when!
5 They jumped in the river. Nobody knows why!

A CHANGE FOR THE BETTER?

Newspapers and magazines are full of advertisements which try to persuade people to change their appearance in one way or another. Look at these advertisements, and discuss them.

Teaching points

▶ Guided discussion

▶ Revision and consolidation

Expressions

a change for the better	*in complete confidence* (privately)
While you wait.	*as used by models*
No appointment necessary.	*to suit every pocket* (=budget)
the world of entertainment	*surgeons of international repute*
I owe it all to . . .	*in one way or another*
Do yourself a favour!	

Key vocabulary

bald patch	*needle*	*touch up*
body building	*optician*	*tremble*
booklet	*pattern*	------
client	*procedure*	*custom-made*
confidence (belief in	*relocation*	*dietary*
yourself)	*reshaping*	*discoloured*
confidence (privacy)	*sauna*	*disfiguring*
consultation	*slimming*	*facial*
contact lens	*solarium*	*greying*
contouring	*stud*	*healthy*
cosmetic surgery	*supplement*	*hygienic*
denture	*tattoo*	*inferior*
design	*toupée*	*non-toxic*
dye	*transplant*	*optical*
earring	------	*painless*
filling	*blush*	*plain*
finish	*brush on*	*premature*
gymnasium	*consult*	*scaled*
hair loss	*ensure*	*sparkling*
hair restorer	*lack*	*thinning*
lettering	*owe*	*unique*
massage	*pierce*	
medical practitioner	*stammer*	

1 Set the situation. *A lot of advertisements try to persuade people to change their appearance. Can you think of any examples? Discuss in pairs. Make a list.* (Books closed.)

2 Focus attention on Unit 64. Silent reading (of the whole page). Students compare with their lists.

3 'Ears pierced'. Focus attention. Silent reading. Ask questions. (*Ask him/her/me/each other.*) *What do you think that 'pierce' means? What's a stud? What's an earring? Why do they say 'while you wait'? What does it mean? Have you had your ears pierced? Would you? Ask 'Why?/When?' How is it done? Does it hurt? Why/Why not? In some countries girls have their ears pierced when they are very young. What happens in your country? Some men have one ear pierced. Why do they do it? Do you like it? Why/Why not? Would you have your nose pierced? Why/Why not?*

4 'Tattoo Artist'. Focus attention. Silent reading. Ask questions. (*Ask him/her/me/each other.*) *What do you think 'non-toxic' dye and 'hygienic' mean? How is tattooing done? Do you think it's painless? Have you seen any interesting tattoos? Describe them. Where were they? Have you seen any women with tattoos? Would you have one? If you had to have one, what would you have? Where would you have it? Why do you think people have tattoos? Why do you think sailors and soldiers often have tattoos?* (Note that Portsmouth has a large naval base.)

5 'Sparta Health and Slimming Club'. Focus attention. Silent reading. Ask questions. (*Ask him/her/me/each other.*) *What do 'sauna', 'solarium' and 'gymnasium' mean? What kinds of exercises might they have? What kind of dietary advice might they give? What kinds of 'electronic slimming aids' might they use? Do you worry about your weight? Why? Do you think people should have to worry about their weight? Have you ever been on a diet? What was it? Did you lose weight? Would you like to go to a clinic like this? Why/Why not? Do you think women worry more than men about their weight? Is this because advertisements usually show 'thin' women?*

6 'Would you like a body like mine?' Focus attention. Silent reading. Ask questions. (*Ask him/her/me/each other.*) *Would you like a body like this? Why/Why not? Do you think big muscles are attractive? Would you like to change your body? How? Do you believe Ed Sampson? Why/Why not?*

7 'Bald? Balding?' Focus attention. Silent reading. Ask questions. (*Ask him/her/me/each other.*) *What do you think these words mean: bald/balding/receding/greying/hair restorer/toupée/hair replacement/hair transplant/in confidence? Have you ever worried about your hair/hair loss? Do you think it matters? Some actors shave their heads completely. Do you like this? Would you do it? Would you prefer to wear a toupée or to shave your head completely? Some people have lots of wigs of different styles and colours. If you were going to buy one, what colour and style would you choose?*

8 'Harley Manor'. Focus attention. Silent reading. Ask questions. (*Ask him/her/me/each other.*) *What do you think these words mean: cosmetic surgery/disfiguring/scar/medical practitioner/international repute/confidence? Cosmetic surgery is often used because of accidents or burns. Sometimes it is used for purely cosmetic reasons. Would you like to change the shape of your features? How? Why? Would you like a new nose, for example? Would you have it done if you were rich? Do you know anybody who's had cosmetic surgery? A lot of actors/actresses have 'face lifts'. What do you think is done?*

9 'New super tooth make-up'. Focus attention. Silent reading. Ask questions. (*Ask him/her/me/each other.*) *What do you think these words mean: model/quizmaster/discoloured/denture/filling/touch up? Why do you think models and quizmasters might use 'Blanche'? Would you?*

10 'Be taller'. Focus attention. Silent reading. Ask questions. (*Ask him/her/me/each other.*) *What do you think these words mean: custom-made/unique/confidence? Would you like to be taller/shorter/fatter/thinner/younger/older? Why/Why not? Is it possible? Do some clothes/patterns/colours make you look taller/shorter/etc?*

11 'Do you lack confidence?' Focus attention. Silent reading. Ask questions. (*Ask him/her/me/each other.*) *What do you think these words mean: making dates/inferior/blush/stammer/tremble? Why do you think the booklet is sent in a plain, sealed envelope? Do you lack confidence in these situations? Do you think the booklet would help?*

12 'Wear glasses?' Focus attention. Silent reading. Ask questions. (*Ask him/her/me/each other.*) *What are contact lenses? Do you wear them? Why do sportsmen and sportswomen wear them? What are the problems with contact lenses? Do they take long to get used to? Which do/would you prefer? Glasses or contact lenses?*

13 Discussion: *Do you think many young people believe such adverts? Are some of them more 'genuine' or 'truthful' than others?*

Unit 64

Teaching points

▶ Listening

▶ Vocabulary and expressions associated with medical treatment

Expressions

* = Appendix only
What seems to be the trouble? *
I haven't been feeling too well. *
There's a lot of it going round at the moment. *
What are the symptoms? *
Let's have a look at you. *
Say 'Aah'. *
The best thing is to ..... *
We'll take a look at you.
It looks worse than it is.
Does it hurt anywhere else?
They don't seem to be doing me any good.
You're doing very well.
A touch of 'flu.

Key vocabulary

appetite *	symptom *	vomit *
dressing	thermometer *	– – – – –
fluid *	– – – – – –	dizzy
gland *	ache *	feverish *
graze	breathe *	inflamed *
legionnaire's	bruise	sore
disease¹ *	hurt	stiff
rash	sneeze *	swollen *
sore throat *	sting	
stitches	unbutton *	

See also: 'Parts of the Body' diagram in student's book and specific illnesses on the insurance form.
¹Legionnaire's disease became famous when several members of the American Legion (ex-soldiers) died in a hotel from it. It has since appeared in various hotels, and is a type of virus infection.

---

1 Exercise 1. Ensure that students' books are closed. Ask students in pairs to make three lists of: a) illnesses
b) medical treatment c) parts of the body. Check the vocabulary.

2 Play the cassette of the listening passage. Students tick any items on their list that they hear in the passage.

Mr Williams *Good morning, doctor.*
Doctor *Hello, Mr Williams. Take a seat. What seems to be the trouble?*
Mr Williams *I'm not sure, doctor. But I haven't been feeling too well. I think I must have a touch of flu.*
Doctor *Mm. There's a lot of it going round at the moment. What are the symptoms?*
Mr Williams *I'm feeling very tired, and I'm aching all over. I've been sneezing a lot, and feeling pretty feverish, hot and cold all the time. Oh, and I've got a sore throat.*
Doctor *Any vomiting?*
Mr Williams *No, but I don't feel very hungry. I've got no appetite at all.*
Doctor *Well, let's have a look at you. Open your mouth. 'Aah.' Yes, your throat's a bit inflamed, and the glands in your neck are swollen. Can you just unbutton your shirt? I want to listen to your chest. Breathe deeply. Right. I'll just take your temperature. Don't say anything for a minute, just keep the thermometer under your tongue. I'll write out a prescription for you, but you know the best thing is just to go home, go to bed, and take plenty of fluids.*

3 Play the cassette again for selective repetition. Check against the lists.

4 Write up new vocabulary items and explain them. (These are marked * in the lists above.)

5 Focus attention on the illustration. Silent reading. Check vocabulary.

6 Dialogue – Wayne/Dr Singh. Set the situation. Play the cassette.

7 Selective repetition.

8 Drill:
T: *I fell off. I was going round a corner.*
C: *I fell off going round a corner.*

Continue:
I grazed my knee. I was climbing a tree.
I bruised my leg. I was playing football.
I cut my thumb. I was slicing bread.
I broke my arm. I was playing rugby.
I burnt myself. I was cooking.

9 Silent reading.

10 Pair work. Encourage students to substitute other vocabulary items.

11 Transfer. (*Ask him/her/me/each other.*)
Have you ever cut yourself? When? Where? How?
Have you ever had stitches? Why? When? Where? How? How many?
Have you ever broken a bone? Why? When? Where? How?
Have you ever been to a casualty department? Why? When? Where?

12 Dialogue – Mrs Mallard/Dr Gillespie. Set the situation. Play the cassette.

13 Selective repetition.

14 Drill:
T: *Are the pills doing you any good?*
C: *They don't seem to be doing me any good!*

Continue:
Is the medicine helping your cold?
Are the tablets curing your cough?
Is the treatment doing your back any good?
Are the capsules helping your sore throat?
Is the cream doing your rash any good?

15 Silent reading.

16 Pair work. Encourage the students to substitute other vocabulary items.

17 Transfer:
Do you think Mrs Mallard is really ill?
What does Dr Gillespie think?
A lot of people take a lot of pills. Do you think they're always necessary?

18 Exercise 2. Set the situation. *Have you ever had a check-up? What sorts of questions did they ask? Make a list in pairs.*

19 Focus attention on the form. Run through, asking individuals the questions.

20 Pair work. Students role-play Doctor and Rosemary Key and ask each other the questions, completing the questionnaire for their partners.

21 Ask individuals about their partners.

22 Role-play (in groups). A doctor's waiting-room. Students choose characters and ailments (e.g. an old man who is a hypochondriac, a businessman in a hurry who needs an injection for travel, a pregnant lady, a girl with a terrible cold who keeps sneezing over the others, a man who needs a certificate showing that he is too ill to work because of a bad back, etc.). They then role-play the situation which might develop in the waiting-room.

GOING TO THE DOCTOR'S

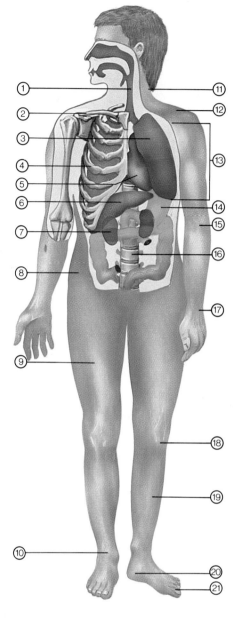

Exercise 1
List as many words as you can about:
a illness
b medical treatment
c parts of the body.
Listen to the conversation and tick any words in your list that are used in the conversation.

Craig Williams has gone to see Dr Casey at the Health Centre. He's in his surgery now.

Wayne fell off his bicycle. He's in the casualty department at the local hospital. Dr Singh is examining him.

Doctor Hello, Wayne, isn't it? You've had a bit of a fall. What were you doing? Going too fast?

Wayne Yes, doctor. I fell off going round a corner.

Doctor You'd better get undressed then, and we'll take a look at you. Mm. That's a nasty cut. I'll have to put a couple of stitches in that.

Wayne I've got a cut here too, doctor.

Doctor It looks worse than it is. It's only a graze. The nurse will clean it up for you. It'll sting, but that's all. Now, does it hurt anywhere else?

Wayne I've got a pain in my arm. It's very sore, and it feels stiff.

Doctor Well, there's nothing broken, but you've bruised your shoulder. It'll be sore for a few days. Now, did you bang your head at all?

Wayne Yes, I did. I fell onto the bike. But it doesn't hurt now.

Doctor Did you feel dizzy?

Wayne No, not at all.

Doctor Look up there, I'm just going to shine this light in your eye. No, that's fine. I'll just do the stitches, and the nurse will put a dressing on it. Then you can go home.

Mrs Mallard has gone to see Dr Gillespie, her family doctor.

Mrs Mallard Good morning, doctor.

Doctor Ah, good morning, Mrs Mallard. What can I do for you this time?

Mrs Mallard It's those pills, doctor. They don't seem to be doing me any good.

Doctor Really? What's wrong?

Mrs Mallard What isn't wrong with me, doctor! It's old age, I suppose.

Doctor You're doing very well, Mrs Mallard! You'll live to be a hundred!

Mrs Mallard I've got this terrible cough, doctor, and I've still got that rash on my hands. And the backache! I can hardly walk sometimes. You don't think it's that legionnaire's disease, do you? I've been reading about it in the paper.

Doctor No, no ... no chance of that. You're very fit for your age.

Mrs Mallard Pardon? Anyway, I've nearly finished the old pills, doctor. Can you give me a different colour next time?

① throat	⑧ hip	⑮ elbow
② collar bone	⑨ thigh	⑯ spine
③ lung	⑩ ankle	⑰ wrist
④ rib	⑪ neck	⑱ knee
⑤ heart	⑫ shoulder	⑲ shin
⑥ liver	⑬ chest	⑳ heel
⑦ kidney	⑭ stomach	㉑ toe

Exercise 2
Rosemary Key wants to take out a life insurance policy. The insurance company has sent her to see a doctor for a check up. This is part of the form he has to complete.
Practise their conversation. (*Can I take your ...?/Have you ever had ...?/Have you been vaccinated against ...?* etc.)

FRIARY INSURANCE NORWICH   CONFIDENTIAL

Name ....   Children ....   Address ....
Marital status ....   Occupation ....
Date of birth ....

Measurements

Height ....   Chest (a) normal ....   Waist ....
Weight ....   (b) expanded ....   Hips ....
Blood pressure ....   Pulse rate ....   Vision ....

Medical history (*please give approximate dates where possible*)

Measles	**Vaccinations and inoculations**	Please give details of any hospital
Mumps	Polio	treatment or operations (not including
Rubella (German measles)..........	Scarlet fever	normal pregnancy)
Chicken-pox	Diphtheria	....
Whooping cough	Whooping cough	....
Other serious illnesses (*give details*	Measles	....
below)	Tetanus	....
....		....
....		....
....		....

A MESSAGE TO THE STARS

Teaching points

▶ Revision and consolidation

▶ Guided discussion

Expressions

There is no reason why they should not use a different type of communication.
Suppose this were done . . . .
so far without success
Ranging in style from . . . to . . .
It could be better spent . . . .

Key vocabulary

being	plague	revolve
billion (one thousand million)	planet	– – – – –
	radio frequency	alien
	radio telescope	dramatic
civilization	response	gold-sprayed
friendship	solar system	man-made
galaxy	spacecraft	naked
gesture	star	outer
impression	universe	pictorial
life form	wave	scientific
light year	– – – – –	slow-moving
location	interpret	unknown
outer space	range	

1 Text 1. Set the situation. Silent reading. (In astronomy 'billion' carries the meaning 'one thousand million'.)

2 Ask students to read through the text again, and make three questions with *How many?*, two questions with *How long?*, and one question each with *How far?* and *How fast?* They should each put the questions to a partner. Check by getting individuals to ask you the questions.

3 Children often write long, complicated addresses for fun such as: *10 Mill Lane, Accrington, Lancashire, England, The United Kingdom, Europe.* Ask students to write down their complete addresses including these items in the correct order: *the Universe, the Solar System, Earth, the Milky Way Galaxy.*

4 Discussion: *Earth is sending out radio and television signals into space all the time. The first signal an alien civilization might get from us would be the early radio broadcasts of the 1900s. They would have to wait over 40 years to receive TV signals. What kind of picture of life on earth would they get from our radio and television broadcasts? Would it be an accurate one?*

5 Text 2. 'Pioneer 10'. Silent reading.

6 *Find words in the text which mean:*
a) a flat metal plate with something written or drawn on it,
b) without clothes on,
c) place or position,
d) a drawing which explains or illustrates something,
e) to understand the meaning of something,
f) a movement used to express meaning.

7 Reproduction. *Tell me about Pioneer 10.*

8 Focus attention on the diagram of the Solar System. Ask students to study it briefly. Ask a few questions, such as
Which is the biggest planet? (Jupiter)
Which is the smallest? (Mercury)
Which is the nearest to the sun?
Which is the furthest from the sun?
Which is the nearest to the Earth? (Venus)
Which is the furthest from the Earth?

9 'The Voyager Mission'. Silent reading.

10 Reproduction. *Tell me about the Voyager Mission.*

11 Exercise 1. Students work in pairs or groups to draw up a list, then report back to the class, with their reasons for their choices.

12 Exercise 2. Discussion.

Unit 66

Our planet Earth is one of nine planets revolving around the Sun, a fairly small and ordinary star, which lies in the outer areas of the Milky Way galaxy. There are about 250 billion stars in our galaxy, and billions of galaxies in the universe. People have always wondered about the possibility of intelligent life forms on other planets. In recent years this has become serious scientific speculation. Some scientists believe that there must be large numbers of stars with planets which could support living intelligent beings. Perhaps we shall never know. The nearest star is 4.3 light years away. A light year is the distance covered by light (travelling at almost 300,000 kilometres a second) in one year. It would take the fastest Earth spacecraft about 40,000 years to reach the nearest star.

For a number of years radio telescopes have been trying to pick up signals from outer space, so far without success. There are, however, millions of possible radio frequencies, and there is no reason why a completely alien civilization should not use a different type of communication, such as X-rays or even a type of wave we have not yet discovered. Suppose contact were made with beings 300 light years away. By the time we had sent our reply, and received their response, the earth would be 600 years older. It would be an interesting, but rather slow-moving, conversation!

Pioneer 10

The first man-made object to leave our solar system was the Pioneer 10 spacecraft. It was launched from Cape Kennedy on March 3rd, 1972. It was designed to pass close to the planet Jupiter and then continue into deep space. A gold plaque, about 15cm by 22cm, was placed on the spacecraft. On the plaque is a dia-

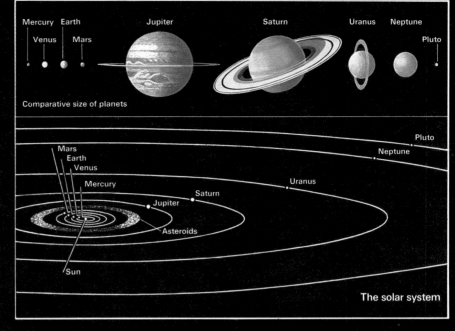

Comparative size of planets

The solar system

gram showing the solar system, and its location in the galaxy. There is also a drawing of a naked man and woman, standing in front of a picture of the spacecraft. The man's right hand is raised in a gesture of friendship. It is unlikely, however, that the plaque will ever be seen again. If it were found by an alien civilization it seems improbable that they would be able to interpret it.

The Voyager mission

Every 175 years the large outer planets – Jupiter, Saturn, Uranus, and Neptune – are in such a position that a spacecraft from Earth can fly past all of them. The two Voyager spacecraft were launched in 1977 to photograph and investigate these planets. Voyager I passed Jupiter in December 1978 and reached Saturn in November 1980. It sent back dramatic pictures of the rings of Saturn and discovered previously unknown moons. It then left the solar system. Voyager II was designed to reach Saturn in

July 1981, Uranus in January 1986 and Neptune in August 1989 before leaving the solar system to travel silently through space forever.

As well as a pictorial plaque, Voyager II carries a gold sprayed disc. The disc contains greetings in 60 languages, 140 photographs, and one and a half hours of music and songs, ranging in style from Beethoven and Mozart to the Beatles and Chuck Berry.

Exercise 1

Imagine you could send objects, weighing up to five kilos which would give an impression of civilization on Earth. This would include a record and a video tape with photographs and film. What would you choose to send and why?

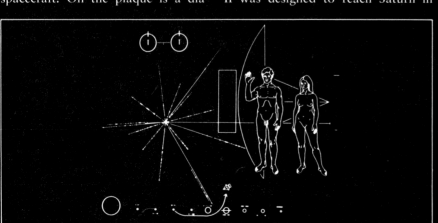

Exercise 2
Space research costs billions of dollars. Some people think that the money would be better spent on more practical projects here on Earth. What do you think?

IT'S ABOUT TIME

Janet and Bruce live in London. Janet's younger sister, Pam, who lives in Edinburgh, is flying down to spend the weekend with them.

Janet Bruce, I think it's time to go and meet Pam at the airport.

Bruce Oh, no, we've no need to hurry. There's plenty of time. It's only half past eight. There won't be much traffic at this time of night.

Janet You never know, and I think your watch must be slow. I make it 8.40, and you'll have to stop for petrol. I'd sooner we were too early than too late!

Bruce It'll take her a while to get her luggage.

Janet Oh, come on, Bruce! It's time we were leaving. We can always have a coffee at the airport. Anyway, I like watching people at the airport.

Bruce I'd rather see the end of the football match, but never mind, we'd better go.

Bruce Janet! Hold on a minute, there's the phone.

Janet You haven't got time to answer it now. Ignore it.

Bruce No, I'd better see who it is. It might be important. Bruce McGregor speaking . . . oh, Pam, we were just on our way to fetch you. Oh, no! Hold on, I'll get Janet.

Janet Pam! Where are you?

Pam I'm still in Edinburgh. The flight's been delayed.

Janet You caught us just in time. We were about to leave for the airport.

Pam I know, Bruce said so. I'm glad I phoned. You'd have had a long wait otherwise.

Janet When will you be leaving, do you think?

Pam Oh, not for an hour at least. Look, don't bother to come out to the airport.

Janet It's no trouble. We'll meet you.

Pam No, I'd rather you didn't. Honestly.

Janet Now, don't be silly, Pam. We'll collect you.

Pam No, Janet, I'd rather get a taxi.

Janet We'll be there, Pam! See you later.

Bruce It's nearly 12.30.

Janet Well, we couldn't let her find her own way. Not at this time of night!

Bruce She knows how to look after herself. That plane landed half an hour ago. It's about time she was here.

Janet It always takes ages to get your luggage.

Bruce I know. It's about time they did something about it. Last time, it took me longer than the flight!

Janet Oh, Bruce, there she is!

Bruce About time, too.

Janet Pam! Pam! Over here!

Bruce I'll go and bring the car round. I won't be long.

Janet Well, Pam, what would you rather do tomorrow morning, lie in or go shopping?

Pam This morning, you mean! I'd rather go shopping, but there's no need for you to get up and come with me. I'd rather you had a lie in. You must be tired out!

Janet I am a bit tired. But I'll meet you for lunch. There's a new restaurant just off Kensington High Street. Do you think you'll be able to find your way there?

Pam Oh, Janet! It isn't as if this were my first visit to London! You can tell me where it is in the morning.

Look at this

| I'd | rather | go there. |
| | sooner | |

I'd	rather	you	went there.
	sooner	he	didn't go there.
		she	
		we	
		they	

It's time to go.

| It's (about) time | we left. |
| | we were leaving. |

| It isn't as | if | this were my first visit. |
| | though | he didn't know. |

Exercise 1

The baggage handling is slow. They should do something about it.
It's about time they did something about it.
Continue.
1 It's late. We should go to the airport.
2 She's getting tired. She should go to bed.
3 He coughs a lot. He should stop smoking.
4 The windows are dirty. We should clean them.
5 The bus is late. It should be here.
6 He's bored. He should find an interesting job.

Exercise 2

Are you going to do it?
No, I'd rather not do it. I'd rather you did it.
Continue.
1 Are you going to write to her?
2 Would you like to drive?
3 Do you want to ask him?
4 Would you like to choose?
5 Do you want to arrange it?
6 Are you going to see the manager?

Unit 67

Teaching points

▶ Expressions with *rather/sooner*

$$\text{I'd} \left| \begin{array}{l} \textit{rather} \\ \textit{sooner} \end{array} \right| \textit{go there.}$$

$$\text{I'd} \left| \begin{array}{l} \textit{rather} \\ \textit{sooner} \end{array} \right| \left| \begin{array}{l} \textit{you, he, she} \\ \textit{we, they} \end{array} \right| \left| \begin{array}{l} \textit{went there.} \\ \textit{didn't go there.} \end{array} \right.$$

▶ Time expressions

It's time to go.

$$\textit{It's about time} \left| \begin{array}{l} \textit{we left.} \\ \textit{we were leaving.} \end{array} \right.$$

▶ $\textit{It isn't as} \left| \begin{array}{l} \textit{if} \\ \textit{though} \end{array} \right| \left| \begin{array}{l} \textit{this were my first visit.} \\ \textit{he didn't know.} \end{array} \right.$

Expressions

There's no need to hurry.
There's plenty of time.
I make it 9.40.
You never know.
Your watch must be slow.
I'd sooner/rather we were
    too early than too late.
Not for an hour at least.
See you later!
It always takes ages.
last time
honestly
It'll take her a while to do it.

We were just on our way.
Hold on a minute.
just in time
You haven't got time to do it.
We were about to do it.
have a long wait
Don't bother to do it.
Not at this time of night.
About time, too.
I won't be long.
tired out
It's just off the High Street.

Key vocabulary

delay	tie in	otherwise
need	– – – – – –	

1 Dialogue – Part 1. Set the situation. Play the cassette.

2 Listen and repeat.

3 Drill:
T: *Let's go.*
C: *Yes, it's time to go.*

Continue:
Why don't we go home?
I think we should start.
We ought to go to bed.
Shouldn't we finish?
Shall we begin?

4 Drill:
T: *We should have left 5 minutes ago.*
C: *Yes, it's time we were leaving.*

Continue:
We should have gone 10 minutes ago.
We're late. We ought to have started 5 minutes ago.
Is that the time? We should have finished 10 minutes ago.
It's nearly ten. We ought to have stopped 15 minutes ago.

5 Silent reading.

6 Question and answer:
Why does she say that his watch must be slow?
What time does he make it?
What time do you make it now? Ask each other.
Do you think your watch is fast or slow?
Would she sooner they were too early or too late?
What does she like doing at the airport?
What does she say they can do at the airport?
What would he rather do?

7 Pair work.

8 Dialogue – Part 2. Play the cassette.

9 Listen and repeat.

10 Silent reading.

11 Pair work.

12 Dialogue – Part 3. Play the cassette.

13 Listen and repeat.

14 Drill:
T: *Pam doesn't want Janet to meet her.*
C: *She'd rather she didn't meet her.*

Continue:
Pam doesn't want Janet to drive out to the airport.
Pam doesn't want Janet to collect her.
Pam doesn't want Janet to come to the airport.
Pam doesn't want Janet to have to wait for her.

15 Silent reading.

16 Question and answer:
Where is Pam? Ask 'Why?'
Why does Janet say 'You caught us just in time'?
Why is Pam glad she phoned?
When does she think she'll be leaving?
Does she want them to meet her?
What would she rather do?

17 Pair work.

18 Dialogue – Part 4. Play the cassette.

19 Listen and repeat.

20 Drill:
T: *She isn't here.*
C: *It's about time she was here.*

Continue:
They aren't here.
He isn't here.
Pam isn't here yet.
Mr and Mrs Davis aren't here yet.
The train isn't here yet.

21 Silent reading.

22 Question and answer:
What's the time? Has the plane landed yet? Ask 'How long ago?' Why couldn't they let her find her own way?

23 Pair work.

24 Dialogue – Part 5. Play the cassette.

25 Listen and repeat.

26 Silent reading.

27 Question and answer:
Where has Bruce gone?
What would Pam rather do, lie in or go shopping?
What would Pam rather Janet did? Ask 'Why'?
Does Pam think she'll be able to find the restaurant?
What does she say?

28 Pair work.

29 Play the complete cassette.

30 Focus attention on 'Look at this'. Go through. Get the students to do Exercises 1 and 2, a) in pairs b) as a class.

31 Ask students to look back through the unit and mark expressions which are about time. Get them to compose mini-dialogues in pairs using the expressions they have found.

Unit 67

Teaching points

▶ Reading comprehension

Expressions

only too happy to do it
It's no bed of roses. (It isn't easy.)
It isn't fit to print. (It's too obscene to print.)
to measure up to a job (to be capable of doing a job)
a sense of fair play/sense of humour
the stature for the job
for free
Believe us . . .
earn every penny
Thank God!
Clear off!
Fuzz (the police – pejorative)
Copper (a policeman – slang)
Officer (policeman – formal)
Watch it!
for a start
In our view . . .
What's more . . .
no good

Key vocabulary

arson	*paperback*	*anonymous*
budgie (budgerigar)	*pay packet*	*brutal*
calling	*quote*	*cowardly*
christening	*red light*	*drunken*
compensation	*statue*	*errant*
conservation	*victim*	*indifferent*
contraception	*villain*	*missing*
demo	*wallpapering*	*obstinate*
(demonstration)	‒ ‒ ‒ ‒ ‒	*present day*
divorce	*chastise*	*printable*
a drink	*dim*	*random*
enthusiasm	*drop round*	*regardless*
fair play	*handle*	*required*
false alarm	*lose blood*	*threatening*
handicap	*measure up to*	*similar*
humour	*raise (a question)*	*stale*
loneliness	*snatch*	*wayward*
London allowance	*suit*	‒ ‒ ‒ ‒ ‒
O levels (state exam	*turn up*	*'cos* (because)
usually taken at 16)	‒ ‒ ‒ ‒ ‒ ‒	

Note: This page is an authentic recruiting advertisement for the Metropolitan (i.e. London) police force. It can be divided into four sections for exploitation;
a) Section 1 (up to the end of paragraph 4),
b) Section 2 (paragraphs 5 to 11: '. . . it won't be easy.'),
c) Section 3 (up to the end of the text),
d) Section 4 (the picture and captions).

1 Section 1. Set the situation. Explain that it is an advertisement. Silent reading.

2 Ask students to put the passage into their own words.
T: *What do you think 'It's no bed of roses . . .' means?*
S: *It isn't easy being a policeman.*
T: *Try and use the expression in a sentence of your own.*
S: *It's no bed of roses learning English!*
Go through the passage in the same way, asking transfer questions:
What time did you turn up this morning?
What do you think some of the things policemen are called might be?
etc.

3 Section 2. Silent reading.

4 Ask questions:
What are the eight things which a day could bring?
Can you think of any other things?
What are some of the things he was asked about?
What was he called upon to do?
What do you think a drunken husband/errant wife/wayward kid/obstinate grandparent might have done?
What are the things he received?
What does he mean by 'often in that order, particularly among the very young'?
What are the opposites of: 'brutal', 'brave', 'hater'?
(Note: 'villain' is police slang for a criminal.)

5 Section 3. Silent reading.

6 Pair work: *Draw up a list of qualifications (age, height, education) and qualities needed by a policeman. Report back to the class.*

7 Ask questions:
Have you got the qualities and qualifications needed?
Why/Why not?

8 Section 4. The picture and captions. Silent reading.

9 *What do you think might have happened in each situation? How do you think the policeman might reply?*

10 Pair work. Each situation is developed into a mini role-play. Different pairs could work on different situations and demonstrate them to the rest of the class.

11 Role-play. In pairs students role-play the Police Careers Officer and a prospective cadet, and conduct the interview. (Begin with straightforward information questions and move on to *How would you deal with this situation? What would you do if you were attacked by a man with a knife?* etc.)

12 Homework. Students write a short letter giving brief details about themselves and why they would like to join the police force and requesting more information.

Unit 68

THE POLICE

1▶ It's no bed of roses being a police officer in London.

When people need help they're only too happy to call you. But just you turn up when it doesn't suit them and what you can get called isn't fit to print.

After a while, however, the experience can become very printable indeed.

Published recently was a paperback written by a south London copper called "Policeman's Progress."

2▶ Here are some random quotes, by Police Constable Harry Cole:

"It is one of the few occupations left in present day society where a person can arrive for work ... and have no idea what the day will bring. It could be an accident, a murder... an armed robbery, arson or a request for directions. It could be an explosion, a false alarm or a drunk."

"I was asked about holidays, treatment for budgies, wallpapering, social security, conservation, contraception, politics and prison visits. I was called upon to chastise drunken husbands (occasional success), errant wives (hundred percent failure), wayward kids and obstinate grandparents."

"I received anonymous threatening letters (I recognised the writing), anonymous threatening phone calls (I recognised the voice), and an anonymous cake for my... birthday (it was stale)."

"I was invited to christenings, weddings and divorces (often in that order, particularly with the very young)."

"CLEAR OFF FUZZ. THIS IS A PRIVATE QUARREL."

"SHE'S ONLY 3 YEARS OLD. SHE'S BEEN MISSING FOR 3 HOURS."

"OFFICER, YOU DID NOT SEE ME GO THROUGH A RED LIGHT."

"THANK GOD YOU'VE ARRIVED OFFICER. THE DRIVER IS LOSING BLOOD."

"YOU ONLY STOP ME 'COS I'M BLACK."

"WATCH IT COPPER, I'VE GOT A KNIFE."

"TWO MEN HAVE JUST BROKEN INTO MY SHOP."

"MY HANDBAG HAS BEEN SNATCHED."

Could you put up with a calling like ours?

"I rarely completed a Christmas duty without having to report a suicide, usually caused by loneliness."

"The bodies, dogs, demos, drunks and fights; the villains and the victims; the brutal, the gentle, the cowardly and the brave; the haters, the lovers and the just plain indifferent ... One day I shall have to live without them; it won't be easy."

3▶ Any police officer in London could tell you a similar story. But the question it would raise is the same.

What kind of person measures up to such a job?

It isn't enough for a man to reach the required minimum height of 172 cm (5'8"). Or for a woman to make 162 cm (5'4").

Regardless of your height you're obviously no good if you don't have the stature for the job.

This means having a real concern for people. A real sense of fair play.

And a real sense of humour.

Qualities more valuable, in our view, than qualifications.

(If you have a few 'O' levels, fine. A university degree is no handicap either.

But best of all is a degree of common sense.)

If you're under 22 you'll earn £4,956 a year the day you join us.

If you're older you'll start at £5,919.

(What's more you'll pick up London Allowances of £1,482.)

You'll also get somewhere to live for free, if you need it.

Or we'll provide you with a tax-paid Rent Allowance up to £1,457 a year.

Believe us, you'll earn every penny of your pay.

Violent criminals, nasty accidents and freezing weather will all turn up when you least expect them.

But the reward you get as a human being for handling it all is compensation greater than any pay packet.

Still interested in being a Metropolitan Police Officer? You'll have to be over 18½ for a start.

If we haven't dimmed your enthusiasm, why not drop round our Careers Information Centre at New Scotland Yard in Victoria Street?

Or let us know your name, your age and your address and we'll send you the information you need.

The man to write to is The Chief Inspector, Metropolitan Police Careers Information Centre, Department **OUP 15**, New Scotland Yard, London SW1H 0BG.

Or you can phone us. Our number is 01-230 5215 and 5146.

Yours is one call we'll be especially pleased to get.

London needs people like you in the Metropolitan Police.

Gold (Au) is a metallic chemical element. Atomic number 79. Atomic weight 197.2.

Since civilization began gold has been regarded as a symbol of power and wealth. In many societies gold was seen as a magic substance which could protect people against illness or evil spirits. It is the one material that has always been accepted in exchange for goods or services. Mankind never seems to have enough gold and the search for it has driven men mad. The need to search for gold has been compared to a disease, and is called 'gold fever'. In the Middle Ages men called 'alchemists' tried to manufacture gold from other metals. In spite of man's constant search for gold, the amount which has been produced since the beginning of time is only enough to make a solid block of eighteen cubic metres, the size of a large house.

Industrial uses

Because gold is untarnishable, workable, almost indestructible, durable, reflective and conductive, it has a number of industrial uses. About 10% of the annual production is used for industrial processes.

Gold is measured in troy ounces (31.1 grams). One ounce can be drawn into 80 kilometres of wire.

A single grain (0.065 grams) can be beaten down to make a sheet which would cover this page.

Between 20 and 30 ounces are needed for every jet engine.

Gold coatings, 0.000024 mm thick, are used to reflect heat from jet engine exhausts.

The windscreens of Concorde, other high speed aircraft, and some express trains have a gold electric heating element, 0.000005 mm thick, which is used to prevent icing.

Spacecraft are protected against radiation by a thin layer of the metal.

As it conducts electricity well and does not tarnish, gold is used extensively in computers and electric consumer goods.

For many years it has been blended with oils and applied as decoration to china and glass.

Because it is so reflective, it is employed in the manufacture of some roof tiles and glass.

Gold has always been prescribed for various ailments, and is used today to treat cancer and arthritis. It is used extensively in dentistry.

Decorative purposes

Because gold is valuable, bright, rare, attractive, durable and untarnishable it has always been used for decorative purposes.

Gold works of art were created by many of the great civilizations of the past, and may be seen in museums all over the world.

Since time immemorial gold has been coveted and desired. Until recent years it was worn only by the very rich and was considered the ultimate status symbol.

Gold jewellery is made to four standards, 22, 18, 14 and 9 carats. 18 carat gold is 18 parts gold out of 24, which is pure gold. That is, 18 carats is 75% pure gold. 24 carat gold is too soft for most purposes.

Gold jewellery includes rings, earrings, necklaces, bracelets, chains, pendants, armlets, anklets, medals, cuff-links, tie-pins, spectacle-frames and watches. It is also used to decorate pens, lighters, glasses, and books.

In traditional Indian cooking, gold flakes are used to decorate food and are consumed.

In Britain, gold is hallmarked, using a system which dates back to the twelfth century. There are five marks on gold which has been tested for quality in Britain.

The manufacturer's name is shown by a mark like this.

The crown shows that the article is gold, and has been hallmarked in the UK.

This shows the gold content. '375' is 9 carats (i.e. 37.5% pure gold).

The assay mark shows where it was tested. A leopard for London, an anchor for Birmingham, a rose for Sheffield, and a castle for Edinburgh.

A different letter is used for each year. 'J' was 1980.

Financial uses

The first gold coin was issued by King Croesus of Lydia in the sixth century BC. Today gold still plays an important part in the international monetary system.

About thirty years' production of gold is being held by central banks and monetary authorities, in spite of efforts to reduce its importance.

New deposits of gold are being found, and old mines are being reopened and it is likely that gold will always be valued as protection against inflation.

Gold can be bought by private investors in the forms of bars, coins and medals, as well as jewellery.

Gold production

Gold is found on all five continents, but 85% of the annual output of gold is produced by four countries:

South Africa	30 million oz
USSR	5½ million oz
Canada	4 million oz
USA	1½ million oz

In South Africa about three tonnes of gold-bearing rock have to be mined to produce each ounce of gold. Billions of tonnes of gold are suspended in the seas, but this gold is impossible to exploit at the moment.

Look at this
Gold *is used* for many purposes.
It *was produced* in ancient times.
Gold *has been used* for 6000 years.
New deposits *are being* found.
It *will be valued* in the future.
It *can be used* in industrial processes.
It *may be seen* in museums.
Three tonnes of rock *have to be mined* to produce an ounce of gold.

Teaching points

▶ Review of passives

It is done/They are done.	It will be done.
It was done/They were done.	It can be done.
It has been done/They have been done.	It may be done.
It is being done/They are being done.	They have to be done.

Expressions

since time immemorial	to drive someone mad
the ultimate status symbol	a system which dates back to
gold fever	to play a part in

Key vocabulary

ailment	pendant	reflect
alchemist	process	regard
amount	rock	tarnish
anklet	roof tile	treat
armlet	sheet	——————
arthritis	spirit	conductive
article	standard	cubic
Assay Office	substance	decorative
block	symbol	evil
carat	tie-pin	gold-bearing
chain	troy ounce	hallmarked
coating	wealth	indestructible
crown	windscreen	magic
cuff-link	wine	monetary
decoration	——————	pure
effort	apply	rare
exhaust	beat into	reflective
grain	blend	solid
heating element	conduct	suspended
icing	covet	ultimate
investor	desire	untarnishable
layer	draw into (wire)	workable
leopard	exploit	——————
mankind	hallmark	extensively
Middle Ages	mine	
output	plate	

1 Introduction. Silent reading.

2 Transformations:
T: *People have regarded gold as a symbol of power and wealth.*
S: *Gold has been regarded as a symbol of power and wealth.*

Continue:
People saw gold as a magic substance.
People have always accepted gold in exchange for goods and services.
People have compared the need to search for gold to a disease.
Man has produced only enough gold to make an 18 cubic metre block.

3 'Industrial uses'. Silent reading.

4 Exercise:
T: *Gold doesn't tarnish, so . . . .*
S: *It's untarnishable.*
T: *You can work in many ways with gold, so . . . .*
T: *Gold lasts almost for ever, so . . . .*
T: *Gold reflects light, so . . . .*
T: *Gold conducts electricity, so . . . .*

5 Go through, checking vocabulary.

6 Transformations:
T: *We use 10% of the annual production for industrial processes.*
S: *10% of the annual production is used for industrial processes.*

Continue:
We measure gold in troy ounces.
We can draw 1 ounce into 80 km. of wire.
We can beat a single grain to make a sheet the size of the page.

Every jet engine needs between 20 and 30 ounces of gold.
Jet engine exhausts use gold coatings to reflect heat.
We use gold electric heating elements to prevent icing in windscreens.
A thin layer of gold protects spacecraft against radiation.
Computers and electric consumer goods use gold extensively.
We blend gold with oils and apply it as a decoration to china and glass.
We employ gold in the manufacture of some roof tiles and glass.
Doctors have prescribed gold for various ailments.
Doctors use gold to treat cancer and arthritis.
Dentists use gold extensively.

7 If necessary, get students to transform the same sentences from passive to active.

8 Transfer:
Can you think of any other industrial uses of gold?
Have you ever seen gold wire? Where? When? How was it used?
Have you ever seen gold leaf? Where? When? How was it used?
Look back through the passage. Which of the uses of gold did/didn't you know about? (I didn't know gold was used for windscreens. I knew gold was used for decorating china and glass. etc.)

9 'Decorative purposes'. Silent reading. Check vocabulary.

10 Question and answer:
Why has gold always been used for decorative purposes?
How was gold used by great civilizations of the past?
Where may it be seen?
How long has gold been coveted and desired?
Why was gold considered to be the ultimate status symbol?
What are some other status symbols?
Describe the items of gold jewellery. What shape are they?
Where are they worn? Why?
Have you got any of these items? Describe them.
What is a hallmark?
If you have any gold jewellery, is it hallmarked?
What are the marks?
Do you know what they mean?
How is gold used in Indian cookery?
Would you eat gold?
How about a gold sandwich?

11 'Financial uses'. Silent reading. Check vocabulary.

12 Transformations. (See 69.2 and 69.6.)
King Croesus issued the first gold coin.
Central banks are holding about 30 years' production of gold.
People are finding new deposits of gold.
They are re-opening old mines.
People will always value gold as protection against inflation.
Private investors can buy gold in many forms.

13 Transfer:
Does your country issue gold coins?
Can you buy gold in your country?
Can you describe a gold coin?
What's it worth?
Can you spend it in the shops?
Would you buy gold as an investment?
What other things can you buy as protection against inflation?

14 'Gold production'. Silent reading. Check vocabulary.

15 Question and answer:
Where is gold found?
How much gold is produced by South Africa? the USSR? Canada? the USA? your country?
How much gold rock has to be mined in South Africa to produce an ounce?
How much gold might be suspended in the seas?

16 Focus attention on 'Look at this'. Run through.

Teaching points

▶ Review of passives (continued) to include
It was being done./It had been done.

Expressions

gold-rush
by whatever means they could
to strike it rich
to brave the winter
They kept on going.
£500 worth of gold
to lay the foundation for
(See 70.13 below, for explanation of the 'gold' expressions)

Key vocabulary

colonization	prospector	soar
creek	river bed	squeeze
dirt	settlement	– – – – –
donkey	soil	frozen
gambler	speculation	irrational
gold dust	stampede	massive
gravel	trapper	risky
investor	tributary	
law and order	uncertainty	– – – – –
mountain pass	– – – – –	fabulously
nugget	abandon	historically
outlaw	anchor	hysterically
pan	brave	overland
preacher	leak out	therefore

Note: A world map might be a useful visual aid.

1 Briefly revise the previous lesson, checking through active – passive transformations.

2 'California'. Silent reading.

3 Question and answer:
What happened in 1848 at Sutter's Mill?
What kind of people went to California?
How did they get there?
How many travelled overland?
What did they leave behind?
Why were so many ships anchored in San Francisco Bay in 1850?
Why was it a dangerous place at that time?
Why was gold fever an important part of the colonization process?

4 'Australia'. Silent reading.

5 Question and answer:
What happened in 1851 in Australia?
What do you think 'stampede' means?
Some people were very lucky. Why?

6 'The Yukon'. Silent reading.

7 Question and answer:
Why were conditions worse than in the earlier gold rushes?
What do you think a 'creek' is?
How did they get gold in the Yukon?
How quickly did Dawson grow? Why did it grow so quickly?
Describe what a man had to do to reach the Klondike.
How many set out? How many arrived? How many found gold?
Are these figures exact?
Why has there been a new rush to the Klondike?
What has happened to Dawson?
Who do you think 'Diamond Tooth Gertie' was?
How did she get her name?
What is happening to the mountain outside Dawson? Why?

8 'South Africa'. Silent reading.

9 Question and answer:
When was gold found in South Africa?
What has happened there since?
How is the gold obtained?

10 'Twentieth-century gold-rush'. Silent reading.

11 Question and answer:
Where are new finds being made?
What happens in a modern day 'gold-rush'?
When do these happen?
What usually happens to the price?
Why has gold always held its value?

12 Ask students to re-read the unit, marking passive constructions and transforming them. Point out 'It was being done' and 'It had been done'.

13 Expressions which use the words 'gold' or 'golden'.
Ask students to speculate on the meaning, before giving the explanation.
T: *What do you think a golden handshake might mean?*
S1: *Is it a friendly greeting?*
T: *No.*
S2: *Is it a very strong handshake?*
T: *No.*
S3: *Is it a bribe?*
T: *No. Any other ideas?*
S4: *Is it a present?*
T: *It's a kind of present. It's a sum of money given to someone who is leaving a job.*
The other expressions are:
The golden rule: any important rule of conduct.
A golden age: A period in a nation's history which is remembered as a particularly good era (e.g. *The late sixteenth century was the golden age of English drama*).
The golden gates: the 'gates' of heaven.
A golden wedding: fiftieth wedding anniversary.
A golden opportunity: a once in a lifetime chance (to be successful).
As good as gold: well-behaved (e.g. *The children were as good as gold*).
Everything he touches . . ./The Midas Touch: refers to someone who is always both lucky and successful. The story of King Midas in Greek mythology is about a king who was given a wish. He wished that everything he touched would turn into gold. In the original story his children were turned into gold as well.
All that glitters is not gold: because something is attractive on the surface, it does not mean that it is good (or valuable).
Don't kill the goose . . . : refers to the goose in Aesop's fable which laid golden eggs. It was killed by its owner, who was greedy and wanted even more gold.
A heart of gold: refers to someone who is very kind and generous.
A gold digger: someone who marries a rich person for their money.
A gold disc: is awarded to performers who sell 1 million 'single' records, or $1 million worth of 'LP' records.

Unit 70

GOLD RUSH!

California

In 1848 gold was discovered at Sutter's Mill, about 100 miles east of San Francisco, and the first great gold-rush began. When the news leaked out, farmers, trappers, lawyers, preachers, sailors, soldiers and school teachers rushed to California by whatever means they could. Within a year 100,000 people, only 8,000 of whom were women, had reached the coast of California. More than half of them had travelled overland across the American continent. 'Gold fever' began to spread. Settlements throughout the United States were deserted. Homes, farms and stores were abandoned as everybody raced for California. Many came by sea, and in July 1850 more than 500 ships were anchored in San Francisco Bay, many of which had been deserted by gold-hungry sailors. A few people became fabulously rich, but it was a risky business. Law and order broke down. Even if a miner 'struck it rich' there were always those who would try to take it away: gamblers, outlaws, thieves and saloon keepers. Gold and silver were discovered in Nevada a few years later, and 'gold fever' was an important part of the colonization of the western United States.

Australia

The next major gold-rush occurred in 1851, when gold was struck in New South Wales, Australia. This led to another stampede and many rich finds were made. Other discoveries were made in Victoria and Kalgoorlie, Western Australia. In some places massive nuggets of gold were found accidentally, just lying about on the ground. The 'Welcome Stranger' nugget, which was found in 1869, weighed 78.37 kilos.

The Yukon

Perhaps the most difficult conditions were experienced by those prospectors who braved the Canadian winters to win gold from the Yukon and Klondike rivers. On August 16th 1896 three prospectors struck gold in Bonanza Creek, a tributary of the Klondike River, and then in a second creek which was named 'Eldorado'. In the Yukon, gold was obtained by washing gravel from river-beds, and soon as much as $800 worth of gold was being taken from a single pan of dirt. Within a year, Dawson had grown from nothing to a town of 30,000 people. Every man who entered the country had to carry a year's supply of food and mining equipment over steep and frozen mountain passes. To do this, each man had to carry 25 kilos of stores about 10 kilometres, leave it there, and return for another load. Therefore to move all his stores less than 80 kilometres, each man had to walk nearly 1500 kilometres. Horses and donkeys died in the ice and snow, but the men kept on going. It is estimated that of the 100,000 men who set out for the Klondike, fewer than 40,000 actually arrived. Only 4000 ever found gold, and very few of these became rich.

The rising price of gold in the late 1970s started a new rush to the Klondike. Dawson is still there, and 'Diamond Tooth Gertie's', the only legal gambling hall in Canada, remains in business. Just outside Dawson a mountain is actually being moved to find gold. The whole mountain is being washed down for gold-dust. It is believed to contain at least $80 million worth of gold.

South Africa

By the turn of the century gold had been found in South Africa and this laid the foundation for the world's largest goldmining industry. Today South Africa accounts for 70% of world gold production. Vast sums of money are being invested, and modern mining technology is being used to squeeze gold from the rock.

Twentieth-century gold-rush

New finds are being made in the Soviet Union, Saudi Arabia and the United States. The largest single mine in the world was discovered in Uzbekistan, USSR, in 1958. However, in spite of recent finds, modern day 'gold-rushes' are usually confined to speculation on the gold markets of Zurich, London and New York. At times of economic uncertainty investors rush hysterically to buy gold, and the price soars, often only to fall back again. Gold fever is in many ways irrational, but historically gold has always held its value, and it is likely that in an uncertain world, it will continue to do so.

Look at these expressions. What do you think they might mean?

A golden handshake.
The golden rule.
A golden age.
The golden gates.
A golden wedding.
A golden opportunity.
As good as gold.
Everything he touches turns to gold (or He's got the Midas touch).
All that glitters is not gold.
Don't kill the goose that lays the golden eggs.
A heart of gold.
A gold digger.
A gold disc.

THE CIRCUS IS COMING

Announcer This is RW2, Watermouth's own independent radio station. In the studio with me this morning is Sally Farnham, the daughter of circus owner, Bertie Farnham. Farnham's circus will be here in Watermouth for two weeks. That's right, isn't it, Sally?

Sally Yes, that's right. We open tomorrow for two weeks.

Announcer Has the circus arrived yet, Sally?

Sally No, no. Not yet. It's on the road somewhere between Sandpool and here.

Announcer I suppose there's a lot to be done between now and the first show.

Sally Yes, that's right. I've already been here for three days. There were all the advance arrangements to be made. It's like preparing for a small invasion.

Announcer What sort of things have you done?

Sally Oh, there are so many things to be done, you know. There are posters to be put up, newspaper ads to be arranged, casual labour to be hired and so on.

Announcer When will the circus actually arrive?

Sally In the next hour or so. The first trucks should be arriving any time now, and then the hard work really begins.

Announcer Most people love the circus, don't they? But not many realize how much work there is, do they?

Sally That's right. We'll be working all day and half the night. It's a bit like moving a small army. But, fingers crossed, by tomorrow morning everything will have been set up in time for the afternoon performance. Oh, there's the grand parade through the town centre at 11.30, so don't forget to come and see us.

Announcer Thank you, Sally, for coming in to talk to us. Now don't forget, folks. The grand circus parade will start from the pier at 11.30, go along the promenade, through the gardens and finish in Jubilee Park. Farnham's Circus will be in town for two weeks until 28th August. Now for some music.

Exercise 1

This is Sally's checklist of arrangements:

1 consult police about car parking (Wessex police)
2 arrange telephone lines (British Telecom)
3 connect water supply (Wessex Water Authority)
4 place ads (Watermouth Echo, Wessex Advertiser, Radio Watermouth)
5 order food supplies for animals (Wessex Meat Company)
6 arrange for fire inspection (Wessex Fire Brigade)

All of these things will have been done before the circus arrives. Make sentences.
A telephone line will have been arranged.
She'll have asked British Telecom.

Exercise 2

Sally's brother, Freddie Farnham, is in charge of the menagerie. This is his checklist:

1 unload animals
2 collect meat supplies
3 water animals
4 feed animals
5 check sanitary arrangements for animals
6 provide straw for animals

The animals have to be unloaded.
Make sentences.

Exercise 3

It's eleven o'clock on Sunday morning. There's a lot to be done. Sally's father, Bertie Farnham, is in charge of the arrangements.

1 erect big top
2 set up ticket office
3 park caravans
4 put up seating
5 erect cages
6 connect generators
7 put up safety net
8 set up high wire
9 put up trapezes
10 set up bandstand
11 place loudspeakers in tent
12 connect amplifiers
13 set up and connect lights
14 connect microphones
15 check everything

There's the big top to be erected.
Make sentences.

Teaching points

▶ Extension of passives

There's a lot to be done.
It will have been done before the circus arrives.

Expressions

and so on
fingers crossed (superstition – crossed fingers are for good luck)
folks

Key vocabulary

acrobat	horse troop	trapeze artist
amplifier	invasion	zebra
bandstand	llama	– – – – – –
bear	loudspeaker	consult
big top	pier	erect
box office number	pony	unload
caravan	promenade	– – – – – –
casual labour	safety net	precisely
generator	seal	
highwire act	straw	

1 Focus attention on the circus poster. Get students to speculate on what might happen in each of the various acts and on what other acts there might be. Focus attention on the small advertisement. Silent reading.

2 Dialogue. Set the situation. Ensure the text is masked. Play the cassette.

3 Selective repetition.

4 Drill:
T: *We have to do a lot.*
T: *There's a lot to be done.*
T: *We have to make arrangements.*
T: *There are arrangements to be made.*
T: *We have a lot to do.*
C: *There's a lot to be done.*

Continue:
We have to make arrangements.
We have to do so many things.
We have to put up posters.
We have to arrange newspaper ads.
We have to hire casual labour.

5 Silent reading.

6 Question and answer:
When will the circus arrive?
How long will the circus be in Watermouth?
What should be happening any time now?
What will be happening all day and half the night?
What will have happened by tomorrow morning?

7 Pair work.

8 *Sally says 'fingers crossed' to bring good luck. Do you do or say or wear anything to bring good luck?*
Sally compares moving the circus and preparing for its arrival in military terms. What does she actually say?

9 Run through the exercises. Students do them in pairs. Repeat with the class.

10 Transfer:
Are there any circuses in your country? Are they popular?
Have you ever seen a circus? When? Where?
Do you like circuses?
Describe some of the acts you've seen.
How do they train the animals?
Do you think it's cruel?
Would you like to work in a circus?
What would you like to do?

11 Written phase:
We have to do a lot of things.
There's a lot to be done.
We will have done a lot of things.
A lot of things will have been done.

Unit 71

Teaching points

▶ Listening

▶ *to have/get something done*

▶ *It needs doing.*

▶ *It needs to be done.*

Expressions

It's getting on my nerves.
I'm not very good with my hands.
Oh, my God!
The sooner the better, if you ask me.
to give somebody a lift
to pick somebody up
to drop somebody off

Key vocabulary

aerial	washer	replace
brake	– – – – –	restyle
bulb holder	adjust	rewrite
electrician	convert	shampoo
element	double glaze	tile
enthusiast	drip	– – – – –
grant	fix	keen
kitchen unit	mention	thorough
plumber	neglect	reasonable
ring	perm	
tap	redecorate	

1 Dialogue 1. Set the situation. Ensure the text is masked. Play the cassette.

2 Selective repetition.

3 Silent reading.

4 Question and answer:
What's the problem?
Can Tim do it? Why not?
What are they going to do about it?

5 Pair work.

6 Transfer pair work. Using Exercise 1, get the students to construct parallel dialogues and practise in pairs. Get some students to act out the dialogues in front of the class.

7 Dialogue 2. Set the situation. Ensure the text is masked. Play the cassette.

8 Selective repetition.

9 Silent reading.

10 Pair work.

11 Exercises 2 and 3. Run through orally. Set in class, or for homework.

12 Exercise 4. Focus attention on the 'House for Sale' and get the students collectively to draw up a list of what might need doing.

13 Exercise 5. Listening. Set the situation. Play the cassette (students listen). Play the cassette again and students tick off items on their lists that are mentioned in the conversation.

Estate Agent *I'm afraid it's been rather neglected. The present owner is in his eighties. He's just gone into an old people's home.*
Robin *Yes. It looks as though a lot needs doing to it.*
Estate Agent *That's true, but the price is very reasonable. It would be ideal for a do-it-yourself man.*
Robin *Mm. I'm not very good with my hands, I'm afraid. We'd have to get most things done for us, wouldn't we, Jean?*
Jean *Oh, I don't know. Could we see inside?*
Estate Agent *Of course. I'll show you the kitchen first.*
Jean *Oh dear! Just look at that sink. It must have been there since the house was built.*
Robin *It's a nice large room, though, and there's plenty of light. We'd have to have kitchen units put in, and we'd need to get it tiled.*
Jean *But you could do the ceiling yourself, couldn't you? And the painting.*
Robin *Is that the only power-point there?*
Estate Agent *I'm afraid so.*
Robin *It looks pretty old. I'm sure the whole place would need rewiring. We certainly couldn't do that ourselves and we'd need to have more points put in at the same time.*
Estate Agent *Would you like to see the lounge? It's through here.*
Jean *Oh my God! It'd certainly need redecorating. I suppose we could do the painting and wallpapering. What's it like upstairs?*
Estate Agent *Pretty bad, really. It obviously hasn't been decorated for years, and as I told you on the phone, it hasn't got a bathroom. But you could have the small bedroom converted into a bathroom and get a grant towards the cost. All the other houses in the street have had that done.*
Robin *What about the toilet?*
Estate Agent *I'm afraid that's outside, but you could get one put in the new bathroom. And of course, you'd get a grant for that as well.*
Jean *Is there anything else that needs doing?*
Estate Agent *Well, you'd probably have to get the roof repaired pretty soon.*
Robin *The sooner the better if you ask me. It looks as though water's been coming in over there. And, of course, we'd want to have central heating put in, and the windows double glazed, it's a very noisy street. I couldn't do any of that myself.*
Estate Agent *Of course not.*
Robin *Anyway, thank you for showing us around. But really I think the best thing would be to knock it down and start all over again!*

14 Play the cassette again, this time pausing for repetition whenever something is suggested that needs to be done.

15 Exercise 6. Explain the exercise. Play the cassette, twice if necessary. Check through the answers by playing the cassette and pausing where the answers occur. Then get students to say what they could do themselves, and what they would have done.

Unit 72

GETTING THINGS DONE

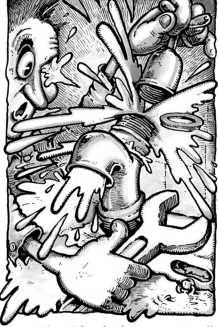

Anne Tim! That bathroom tap's still dripping. It's getting on my nerves! I thought you said you were going to fix it.

Tim Oh, yes ... the washer needs replacing.

Anne Why don't you replace it then?

Tim It's not as easy as that. I'll try and do it next week.

Anne But you said that last week.

Tim I know. I think you'd better phone for a plumber and get it done. I'm not really quite sure how to do it.

Exercise 1
Make conversations using the following:
1 That light's still broken/bulb holder/electrician
2 The stop light on my car's not working/bulb/take it to the garage
3 The record-player sounds terrible/stylus/take it to the shop
4 One of the rings on the cooker isn't working/element/electrician
5 The television reception's very poor/aerial/TV engineer

Adrian and Susannah are going on a touring holiday of France next week. They're taking their own car. Adrian always gives Susannah a lift to work. He's dropping her off outside her office.

Adrian Oh, Susannah! I won't be able to pick you up from work tonight. I'm having the car serviced. I thought we'd better have it done before we go.

Susannah That's all right. When are you collecting it?

Adrian Not till quarter to six. Why?

Susannah Well, I want to have my hair done before the holiday. I'll try and make an appointment to get it done after work. Then you can pick me up from the hairdresser's.

Adrian OK. Can you ring me at work and let me know what time?

Susannah Right, I'll call you later. Bye.

Exercise 2

HOLIDAY ADVICE
Before taking your car abroad, don't forget to:
- have a thorough service
- change the oil
- check the battery
- test the brakes
- check the tyres carefully and change if necessary
- have the lights adjusted for driving on the right

Adrian hasn't got time to do any of these things himself.
He's going to have the car serviced.
Make five more sentences.

Exercise 3
Susannah's going to have her hair done.
Make sentences with:
wash/shampoo/re-style/dye/cut/perm

Exercise 4

HOUSES FOR SALE

TERRACED house. Built 1872. 3 bedrooms. Needs some attention. Ideal for keen do-it-yourself enthusiast. Very reasonable price. Gatsby & Stahr, Estate Agents.

Look at the advertisement. This house is old, and is in very bad condition. Imagine you were interested in buying it. What do you think might need to be done to the house?
The house might need repainting.
Make a list.

Exercise 5
Listen to the conversation between an estate agent and Robin and Jean Harvey, who are looking at the house. Tick any items on your list that are mentioned in the conversation.

Exercise 6
When Robin and Jean are talking about the house, they mention some things that they could do themselves, and some things they would have to have done. Look at the chart below, and the example: they would have to have kitchen units put in. Listen to the conversation again, and complete the chart.

	Do it themselves	Have it done by someone else
Put in kitchen units		✓
Do kitchen ceiling	✓	
Paint kitchen	✓	
Rewire house		✓
Put in more power-points		✓
Redecorate lounge	✓	
Convert small bedroom into bathroom		✓
Put toilet in bathroom		✓
Repair roof		✓
Put in central heating		✓
Double-glaze windows		✓

What could you do yourself, and what would you have done by someone else?

KEEPING FIT

QUESTIONNAIRE

1 Would you describe yourself as:
   □ Very fit   □ Average
   □ Quite fit   □ Unfit

   Do you think physical fitness is important?
   □ Yes   □ No

2 □ Do you ever get out of breath?
   □ Can you touch your toes (without bending your knees)?
   □ Can you run for 1 km?
   □ Can you hang from a bar, supporting your own weight for 20 seconds?

3 Does your daily routine involve any physical exertion?
   □ Yes   □ No

4 Do you take regular exercise?
   □ Yes   □ No

5 If you take regular exercise, how often do you take it?
   □ Every day   □ More than once a week
   □ Every other day   □ Once a week   □ Less

6 If you take regular exercise, in which of the following ways do you take it?
   □ Sport   □ Dance   □ Yoga
   □ Jogging   □ Cycling   □ Walking
   □ Swimming   □ Keep-fit exercises
   □ Other (What other ways? ....)

7 If you play a sport, is it:
   □ A team game   □ Amateur
   □ Competitive   □ Professional
   □ Organised

8 Do you possess any sports equipment?
   □ Yes   □ No

   If so, what? ....

9 Do you/Did you have to play any sports at school?
   □ Yes   □ No

   If so, which ones? ....

   How often? ....

10 Do you/Did you have P.E. (Physical Education) classes at school?
   □ Yes   □ No

   If so, how often? ....

11 Do you think sports or P.E. should be a compulsory part of the school curriculum?
   □ Yes   □ No

12 Why?/Why not? ....

Here are instructions for two keep-fit exercises:

Warming up exercise
Raise hands above head, feet apart. Bend forward slowly and touch ground in front of toes, then between feet. Don't worry if you can't reach the floor at first. Repeat 10 times the first day, and build up over 5 days to 20.

Exercise for bottom and hips
Sit on floor, legs outstretched, ankles crossed. Lean back slightly supporting weight on palms of hands. Lifting right arm above head, bend to left, keeping knees straight. Roll over until upper knee touches floor. Repeat to the right. Do it ten times in each direction. Cross ankles other way and repeat whole procedure.

If you do exercises, describe how to do them in detail. Get someone to follow your instructions. If you play a sport, describe the sport and briefly explain the rules, without mentioning the name of the sport. See if people can guess which sport you have described.

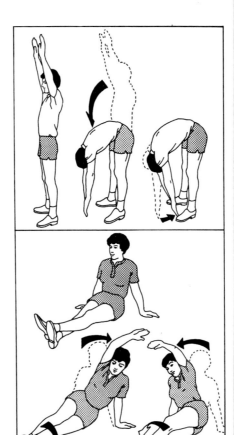

5,300 WIN MARATHON

One million people turned out to watch Britain's biggest-ever sporting event. The most amazing sporting event Britain has ever seen turned out to have 5,300 winners yesterday.

Around that number finished out of 6,700 who officially started in the first London Marathon and were cheered by a million people as they ran through the streets.

The first and last to complete the 26 miles and 385 yards symbolized in their different ways the spirit of the occasion.

At the front, Dick Beardsley from the United States and Inge Simonsen from Norway linked hands to run the last few yards and staged a dead heat for first place.

'What does it matter who wins?' said 24-year-old Beardsley. 'Every runner who finishes this race is a winner.' Some four hours later, last man home was the oldest competitor 78-year-old Bob Wiseman. 'I feel good. It's great to be alive,' he said.

The leaders made it an event of the highest athletic quality. At 2 hours, 11 minutes, 48 seconds, the joint winners ran the fastest marathon ever in Britain – and 142 runners finished under 2 hours 30 minutes.

Race director Chris Brasher, said: 'It went like a dream.'

St John Ambulance crews treated hundreds of runners for exhaustion, but the worst damage reported was a broken leg. 'We are surprised there weren't more casualties – everyone was very fit,' a spokesman said.

The drizzly conditions were ideal for marathon running – and competitors praised the camaraderie of those taking part and the encouragement given them by the spectators.

This aspect was summed up by 29-year-old jogger Ron Crowley, from Liverpool. Four miles from the finish he was on the point of quitting after stumbling to a halt.

Then, he said, he heard the crowd yelling out his number. 'No one has ever cheered like that for me before,' he said. 'They gave me heart to go on.'

Unit 73

Teaching points

► Revision and consolidation

► Reading comprehension

► Oral practice

► Giving and following instructions

► *Do you do this? If so, when?*

Expressions

It's great to be alive.
It went like a dream!
They gave me the heart to go on.
a dead heat
out of breath

Key vocabulary

ankle	*spirit*	*stumble*
bottom	*spokesman*	*sum up*
camaraderie	*toes*	*symbolize*
casualty	*yoga*	*warm up*
exertion	– – – – –	*yell*
halt	*bend*	– – – – –
keep-fit exercises	*hang*	*amateur*
jogger	*keep fit*	*drizzly*
jogging	*link hands*	*fit*
marathon	*possess*	*ideal*
palm	*praise*	*organized*
PE (Physical	*quit*	*outstretched*
Education)	*roll over*	*professional*
physical fitness	*stage*	*unfit*

1 Focus attention on the newspaper headline and the picture. Get the students to describe the picture and speculate about what is going on.

2 Reading. Pre-questions. Write these questions on the board or dictate to the class:
How many people took part in the race?
How many finished?
Who won?
Who came last?
How old was the oldest competitor?
What was the worst accident?
What was the weather like?

3 Get students to read the text silently, then to read it again, answering the questions. Check the answers.

4 Ask them to find these expressions in the text, and to mark them.
'the spirit of the occasion'
'a dead heat'
'It went like a dream.'
'The drizzly conditions were ideal.'
'the camaraderie of those taking part'
'on the point of quitting'
'They gave me heart to go on.'
Ask them to read through and to try and deduce the meaning. Check through.

5 Focus attention on the 'Questionnaire'. Check through the questions, explaining any difficult vocabulary.

6 Pair work. Students interview each other, fill out the questionnaire, and report back to the class.

7 Discuss the results. *How many people do regular exercise? Which is the most popular way?* etc.

8 Focus attention on the keep-fit exercises. Ask students to study the instructions carefully.

9 Pair work. Students give instructions to their partners, who carry them out.

10 Transfer. (See notes below the exercises.)
Get students to describe an exercise in detail. Get someone to follow the instructions.
Get students to describe a sport and to explain the rules, without naming the sport. The other students try to guess which sport has been described.

Unit 73

Teaching points

▶ Reporting (1)

▶ verb + *someone* + infinitive

Tell/ask/remind/invite/	*someone*	*to do something*
advise/promise/help/		*not to do something*
refuse/warn/instruct/		
order/urge/force/		
beg/threaten		

Expressions

You can make it!
Don't panic.
Whatever you do, don't ...

Key vocabulary

chute	*plug*	*adjust*
emergency	*turbulence*	*proceed*
procedures	*warning light*	*– – – – – –*
headset	*– – – – –*	*duty-free*

1 Classroom set. Revise orders and requests.
T: *Stand up!*
T: *What did I tell him?*
C: *You told him to stand up.*
T: *Would you open the window, please?*
T: *What did I ask him?*
C: *You asked him to open the window.*
T: *Don't forget to do your homework.*
T: *What did I remind him to do?*
C: *You reminded him to do his homework.*
T: *Would you like to come to a party?*
T: *What did I invite him to do?*
C: *You invited him to come to a party.*
T: *If I were you, I'd see a doctor.*
T: *What did I advise him to do?*
C: *You advised him to see a doctor.*
T: *I won't help you.*
T: *What did I refuse to do?*
C: *You refused to help him.*
T: *Stand up straight!*
T: *What did I order him to do?*
C: *You ordered him to stand up straight.*
T: *I'll definitely meet you.*
T: *What did I promise to do?*
C: *You promised to meet him.*

2 Listening. (Books closed.) Set the situation for 'Don't panic'. Play the cassette.

3 Play the cassette again, pausing after each announcement. Get the students to transform each announcement, using the prompts given in Exercise 1.
Don't forget to fasten your seat belts.
T: *What did she remind them to do?*
C: *She reminded them to fasten their seat belts.*
Note that number 10 'Don't panic' is not recorded.

4 Play the cassette again. Students follow the text in their books.

5 Pair work. Student 1 tells Student 2 to make the announcements.
S1: *Remind them to fasten their seat belts.*
S2: *Don't forget to fasten your seat belts.*
Students refer to Exercise 1 to find the correct verbs.

6 Role-play. Set up a passenger compartment. Student 1 is a trainee hostess. Student 2 is training the hostess, other students role-play passengers and can respond at random. (It would greatly help to re-arrange classroom furniture, if possible.)

7 Exercise 1. Get students to go through in class. (74.5 uses 'remind', this will use 'reminded'.) Set for homework.

8 Exercise 2. Go through orally. Get students to complete the exercise in pairs. Set for homework.

9 Exercise 3. Get students to go through in pairs. Check by indicating students, and saying:
(S1) ask (S2) to meet you tonight.
(S2) promise to meet (S1).
(S3) advise (S4) not to smoke so much. etc.

10 Transfer. Divide the class into groups of three. S1 tells S2 what to say to S3. S3 can respond freely.

Unit 74

DON'T PANIC

1 Don't forget to fasten your seat-belts!
2 Please do not leave your seat while the warning light is on.
3 May we remind passengers to read the emergency procedures.
4 Please do not smoke in the aisles or in the toilets.

5 Would you like to see the flight deck?

6 I'm busy now but I'll bring you a drink in a minute.

7 I'm afraid I can't give you another drink sir.

8 Here's the headset. Let me help you.

9 Please keep your belts fastened. We're going through turbulence.

10 Don't Panic!

11 Remove your shoes and proceed at once to the emergency exits.

12 Come on dear... you can make it! Just slide down the chute.

13 I'll have to push you.

Exercise 1

1 remind
She reminded them to fasten their seat-belts.
2 warn
She warned them not to leave their seats.
Continue.

3 remind	10 warn
4 tell	11 tell
5 invite	12 instruct
6 promise	13 order
7 help	14 urge
8 ask	15 force
9 refuse	

Exercise 2

Look at these sentences.
1 He said, 'No, no ... please don't shoot me.'
2 She said, 'Whatever you do, don't go to that dentist.'
3 He said, 'If I were you, I'd travel by train.'
4 He said, 'Would you like to come to a party on Saturday?'
5 She said, 'Don't forget to go to the bank today.'
6 The policeman said, 'Switch off the engine, and get out of the car.'
7 The old man said, 'Certainly not, I won't sell it at that price.'
8 She said, 'Don't worry. I'll definitely meet you at six o'clock.'
9 The attendant said, 'Would you mind moving your car?'
10 She said, 'I'm too busy now. Come back later.'

1 *He begged them not to shoot him.*

Continue, using these words:
refuse/ask/tell/warn/order/remind/advise/promise/invite.

Exercise 3

Practise with a partner (one is Student A, the other is Student B).

Student A	Student B
Ask B to meet you tonight.	Promise to meet A.
Advise B not to smoke so much.	Tell A to mind his own business.
Ask B to write a letter from your dictation.	Ask A to speak more slowly.
Invite B to a party.	Refuse politely.
Order B to be quiet.	Tell A not to talk to you like that.
Remind B to repay the money you lent him.	Promise to pay tomorrow.
Threaten to kill B.	Beg A not to do it.
Order B to jump out of the window.	Tell A not to be so silly.
Warn B not to exceed the speed-limit.	Tell A to watch out for police cars!

MESSAGES

Amanda Hayward is a secretary at Standard Security Systems. Her boss, Peter Dawson, was away on business on Monday. She took several messages for him. Listen to the conversations and look at the notes.

MESSAGES FOR MR DAWSON - MONDAY

9.00 Jenny phoned. Won't be in till Friday - flu.

9.40 Mr Watkins. Can't make the meeting Tues. pm. Will ring Wed.

11.30 Godfrey wants Fri. off. Grandmother died Sun. Will have to go to funeral.

12.15 Wadley's Garage called. New car not ready yet. Strike at factory.

2.10 Miss Dobson (Western Video) must cancel order. Customers have changed their minds.

3.20 Mr. Gonzalez. May be in London 21st-25th. Wants to see you then.

4.35 Samantha Ellis. Please phone her as soon as possible. Very urgent.

4.55 Mr Berry rang. Don't supply Mason and Co! Will explain later.

It's Tuesday morning. Peter Dawson has just returned to the office after his business trip to Lyon. Look at the notes and listen to her report.

Peter Good morning, Amanda. Could you come in for a minute, please?

Amanda Good morning, Mr Dawson. Did you have a good trip?

Peter Yes, thank you. Were there any messages for me yesterday?

Amanda Yes, quite a few. Shall I just run through them?

Peter Please.

Amanda Jenny phoned. She said she wouldn't be in till Friday.

Peter Oh. Why's that?

Amanda She said she had 'flu. She'd seen the doctor.

Peter Right. Go on.

Amanda Then Mr Watkins called. He said he couldn't make the meeting this afternoon but would ring you on Wednesday.

Peter OK.

Amanda Godfrey came in looking for you. He said he wanted Friday off.

Peter Did he?

Amanda Yes. He told me his grand-mother had died and he'd have to go to the funeral.

Peter Oh dear. I'd better see him later.

Amanda And Wadley's Garage called. They said your new car wasn't ready.

Peter Oh, no ... why on earth not?

Amanda They said there was a strike at the factory yesterday.

Peter Again!

Amanda After lunch Miss Dobson phoned. She said that Western Video Systems had to cancel their last order because their customers had changed their minds.

Peter Pity!

Amanda Mr Gonzalez called from Mexico to say he might be in London from 21st – 25th. He said he wanted to see you then.

Peter Oh, good. I hope he can make it.

Amanda Then a lady phoned. Samantha Ellis. She asked you to phone her as soon as possible. She said it was urgent.

Peter Ah, Samantha. I wonder what she wants.

Amanda Oh and just before five, Mr Berry phoned. He told us not to supply Mason & Co. until further notice. He said it was important and that he would explain later.

Peter Anything else?

Amanda No. That's it. Coffee?

Peter Please. That would be nice.

Exercise

Janice Taylor is personal assistant to Heather Bates, who is the chief fashion buyer for Sparks & Fraser, a chain of department stores. Heather was away yesterday visiting a supplier in Manchester. Janice took these messages.

Messages

9.10 Mr. Foster. Wants to see you Wed. Will be here at 10am.

10.25 Alan Moore, International Denim. Can't supply order for jeans. Their shipment from Hong Kong hasn't arrived.

11.05 Madame Bourvil called from Paris. She's sending photos of spring collection.

12.10 Miss Noris, Brighton store, rang. Monogram blouses are selling very well. Has nearly run out of stock. Wants 1000 as soon as possible.

13.45 Angela called. Got back from Florence yesterday. Saw lots of interesting things. Will discuss possible purchases.

14.50 Mr. Collins Wigan Textiles. May be able to supply new pullover range. Can't confirm order yet. Must discuss prices.

Janice reported the messages to Heather.

9.10 *Mr Foster called. He said he wanted to see you on Wednesday and that he would be here at ten o'clock.*

Report the other messages.

Look at this

am/is → was		'It's important.' She said (that) it was important.
are → were		'They're going to be late.' She said (that) they were going to be late.
have/has → had		'I've done the letters.' She said (that) she had done the letters.
don't → didn't		'I don't know.' She said (that) she didn't know.
want → wanted		'I want a day off.' She said (that) she wanted a day off.
didn't do → hadn't done		'I didn't finish it.' She said (that) she hadn't finished it.
saw → had seen		'I saw him.' She said (that) she had seen him.
was/were → had been		'I wasn't there.' She said (that) she hadn't been there.
will/won't → would/wouldn't		'I won't do it.' She said (that) she wouldn't do it.
can/can't → could/couldn't		'I can't do it.' She said (that) she couldn't do it.
may → might		'I may do it.' She said (that) she might do it.
had done/would/could/should/ought/might		No change

When you are reporting, you may also need to change these words:

this → that
these → those
here → there
now → then
yesterday → the day before
tomorrow → the next day
this (week) → that (week)
last (month) → the (month) before
next (year) → the next (year)

Teaching points

▶ Reporting (2)

▶ Listening

▶ Notetaking

▶ See student's book 'Look at this'

Expressions

* = in listening passages only
Mr Dawson's office *
Something important's come up. *
Can you put me through to . . . ? *
Shall I just run through them?
Why on earth not?
Pity!
I hope he can make it.
I wonder what she wants.
out of stock

Key vocabulary

denim	spring collection (of fashion)	change (their) minds
fashion buyer		— — — — —
range (of pullovers)	trade fair	chief
shipment	— — — — —	

1 Listening passages. Set the situation. Ensure that all the books are closed. Play the first telephone message. Stop the tape and ask what the message was. Write up: *Jenny phoned. Won't be in till Friday. 'Flu.*

9.00
Amanda *Mr Dawson's office.*
Jenny *Oh, it's Jenny. Can you give Mr Dawson a message? I won't be in till Friday, I've got flu. I saw the doctor this morning.*
Amanda *OK, Jenny. I'll pass the message on. I hope you feel better soon.*

2 Go through the other phone messages. Pause after each to give students time to try and write the messages.

9.40
Amanda *Mr Dawson's office. Can I help you?*
Mr Watkins *May I speak to Mr Dawson, please?*
Amanda *I'm afraid he's away on business. He'll be back tomorrow. Can I take a message?*
Mr Watkins *Please. It's Tom Watkins here. Look, I can't make the meeting on Tuesday afternoon. Something important's come up. I'll ring Peter on Wednesday.*

11.30
Amanda *Hello, Godfrey. What can I do for you?*
Godfrey *Mr Dawson isn't here, is he?*
Amanda *No, not till tomorrow.*
Godfrey *Ah . . . it's just that I want Friday off. You see, my grandmother died yesterday. I'll have to go to the funeral.*
Amanda *Oh, I am sorry. How old was she?*
Godfrey *92.*

12.15
Amanda *Mr Dawson's office.*
Salesman *Can you put me through to Mr Dawson?*
Amanda *I'm afraid he isn't here today. Would you like to leave a message?*
Salesman *Oh, right. Wadley's Garage here. It's about his new car. It isn't ready yet. There's a strike at the factory today.*

2.10
Amanda *Good afternoon. Mr Dawson's office.*
Miss Dobson *Good afternoon. this is Juliet Dobson from Western Video Systems. Mr Dawson's at the trade fair in Lyon, isn't he?*
Amanda *Yes, that's right. He should be here tomorrow.*
Miss Dobson *Well, can you give him this message first thing in the morning? I'm afraid we must cancel our last order. The customers have changed their minds, again!*

3.20
Amanda *Good afternoon. Mr Dawson's office.*
Mr Gonzalez *Hello, this is Miguel Gonzalez speaking. Is Peter there?*
Amanda *No, I'm afraid he's away on business today. Can I pass on a message, Señor Gonzalez?*
Mr Gonzalez *Yes. I may be in London from the 21st to the 25th. I want to see Peter then, if possible. It's about the agency in Mexico.*

4.35
Amanda *Mr Dawson's office.*
Mrs Ellis *My name's Samantha Ellis. Can you get Mr Dawson to phone me as soon as he gets back from Lyon? It really is very urgent.*

4.55
Amanda *Mr Dawson's office.*
Mr Berry *Ah, Miss Hayward. This is Charles Berry.*
Amanda *Oh, good afternoon, sir.*
Mr Berry *I've got an important message for Mr Dawson. Give it to him the minute he comes in. Just say, 'Don't supply Mason and Company until further notice'. I'll explain later.*

3 Open books. Focus attention on 'Messages for Mr Dawson'– Monday'. Ask students to compare the notes with their own.

4 Play all the phone messages again. Students look at the notes. Point out the different registers Jenny uses: 'Godfrey', 'Señor Gonzalez', 'Sir'. (Note the use of 'Señor', 'Monsieur', 'Herr', etc. when addressing foreigners.) Ask *Why do you think she calls Charles Berry 'sir'? What is his position in the company?*

5 Dialogue. Focus attention on the messages. Ensure the dialogue is masked. Play the cassette.

6 Silent reading.

7 Pair work. Ensure the dialogue is masked. Students use the messages as a basis for a role-play of the conversation between Peter and Amanda. Get one or two pairs to demonstrate. If they have difficulty with the transformations, refer them to the 'Look at this' section.

8 Exercise. Silent reading.

9 Role-play. Students use the 'Message for Heather Bates', and role-play Janice reporting the messages to Heather Bates.

10 Check through the messages again, getting individuals to report the statements. Set it as a written homework.

11 Focus attention on 'Look at this'; go through. If more practice is needed, students can mask the reported element, and it may then be done as an exercise.

Teaching points

▶ Reporting (3)

He asked me if he could come in.
He asked me where I was last night.

Expressions

Open up!
Hold on a minute.
Let me think.
I'll be seeing you.
inside (=in prison)
fire away
Bloody hell!
closing time (the time at which pubs must close)
Think before you drink before you drive.
That's what I always say.
Fair enough!
They've just been round.

Key vocabulary

detail	*remission*	*routine*
influence	*search-warrant*	– – – – –
mate (slang for	– – – – –	*in case*
friend)	*satisfy*	
	– – – – –	

1 Dialogue 1 – Harry and Grimes. Set the situation. Ensure the text is masked. Play the cassette.

2 Selective repetition (focusing particularly on Grimes' questions).

3 Dialogue 2 – Harry and Tommy. Ensure the text is masked. Play the cassette.

4 Selective repetition.

5 Focus attention on Exercise 1. Go through the examples.

6 Ensure Dialogue 1 is still masked; go through the cassette, pausing after each of Grimes' questions. Get students to report the questions.

7 Silent reading of Dialogues 1 and 2.

8 Pair work. Students role-play the two dialogues.

9 Exercise 1. Students go through in groups of three, reporting both Grimes' questions and Harry's answers.

10 Get students to repeat 76.9 as a conversation between Harry and Tommy.

11 Exercise 2. Set the situation. Students do the exercise in pairs. Check with the whole class.

12 Exercise 3. Students report the conversation which developed in Exercise 2.

A FEW QUESTIONS

Harry Who's there?

Grimes The police. Open up!

Harry Er ... hold on a minute. I'm in the bathroom.

Grimes Come on! Open up!

Harry Oh, Sergeant Grimes. What can I do for you? Is this a social call?

Grimes Very funny, Harry. I've got a few questions to ask you. Can I come in for a minute?

Harry Have you got a search-warrant?

Grimes No. Why? Do I need one? Have you got anything to hide then, Harry?

Harry No, no. Nothing at all. Come in. Questions, you said. Well ... fire away.

Grimes Just a routine check, Harry. That's all. Just a routine check. Were you in the Mile End Road last night?

Harry No.

Grimes Mm, hm ... have you been there recently?

Harry No, no, I haven't. Why? Has there been any trouble?

Grimes I think I'll ask the questions, Harry. Where were you last night?

Harry I was in the pub, the 'Pig and Whistle'.

Grimes Did anybody see you?

Harry Oh, yes. I've got plenty of witnesses.

Grimes Witnesses, Harry? You haven't been accused of anything ... yet. Why do you need witnesses?

Harry I don't, Sergeant. I don't. Er, I was with some of my mates.

Grimes I didn't know you had any, Harry. Who were they?

Harry Er, let me think ... Tommy Ferrett, Albert Bloggs, and ...

Grimes What, Albert 'the boot' Bloggs? I thought he was still inside.

Harry No, they let him out last week. He got two years' remission for good behaviour. Oh, yes, Sid Parker was there too.

Grimes What time did you get there, and what time did you leave?

Harry I suppose I got there about seven, and left at closing time.

Grimes Did you come straight home?

Harry Yeah.

Grimes How did you get here? Did you drive?

Harry Oh, no. I'd had a few drinks. I'd never drive under the influence of alcohol, Mr Grimes, you know me. 'Think before you drink before you drive'. That's what I always say.

Grimes Very good, Harry. Very good. By the way, is that your car outside? The red Granada?

Harry That's right. I've got all the papers. I can prove it's mine.

Grimes Nice car. Especially as you're out of work.

Harry Oh, yeah. Well, my grand-mother died. Left me some money.

Grimes I see. You don't mind my asking, do you?

Harry Not at all. I mean, it's your job, isn't it?

Grimes Well, how did you get that dent in the front wing, then?

Harry Oh. It happened in a car park. I wasn't there. Someone must have run into it.

Grimes Fair enough, Harry. Well, I'll be seeing you. That's all for now.

Tommy Tommy, here.

Harry Tommy, listen. It's me, Harry. The police have just been round. It was Grimes, again. I don't think he knows anything, but he asked a lot of questions. Er ... I told him I was with you.

Tommy Bloody hell! Harry! Did you have to mention me?

Harry I'm sorry, Tommy, really I am. Look we'd better check the details in case they come to see you.

Tommy What do you mean, 'in case they come to see me'? If I know Grimes, he'll be here any minute. Come on, Harry. Tell me exactly what he asked you, and what you told him.

Exercise 1

'Can I come in for a minute?'

He asked if he could come in, so I asked him if he'd got a search-warrant.

'Where were you last night?'

He asked me where I'd been, and I told him I'd been in the pub.

Look at the conversation between Harry and Sergeant Grimes. Report all the questions and answers.

Look at this

'What's your name?'

She asked me what my name was.

'Are you married?'

She asked me if I was married.

Exercise 2

At Watermouth College of Education, students who wish to follow an examination preparation course have to have a short interview, to satisfy the college authorities that their English is good enough to follow the course. These are the notes which the examiner uses during the interview.

Practise with a partner; one is a student, the other is the examiner.

Examiner *What's your name?*

Student *My name's ....*

Watermouth College of Education
Department of English

Exam English as a Foreign Language (*Pre-course entry questionnaire*)

1 Name?
2 Nationality?
3 Home town?
4 Marital status?
5 Brothers and sisters?
6 Years of English?
7 Length of time spent in England?
8 Occupation? Tell me about it.
9 Hobbies? Tell me about them.
10 Reason for learning English?
11 Exams passed (if any)?
12 Accommodation–flat, landlady or hotel?
13 What would you do if you won £10,000?
14 Other languages?
15 What do you think about England?
16 What major differences have you noticed between England and your country?

Exercise 3

Imagine you are a student who has just had the interview. Report to a friend.

Friend *What did they ask you?*

Student *They asked me if I had any brothers or sisters. I told them I had one brother and two sisters.*

TRUST THE HEART

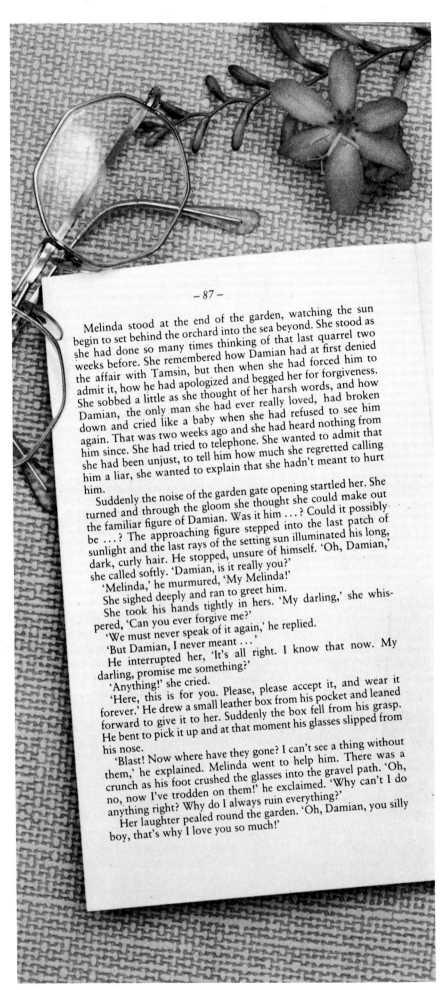

— 87 —

Melinda stood at the end of the garden, watching the sun begin to set behind the orchard into the sea beyond. She stood as she had done so many times thinking of that last quarrel two weeks before. She remembered how Damian had at first denied the affair with Tamsin, but then when she had forced him to admit it, how he had apologized and begged her for forgiveness. She sobbed a little as she thought of her harsh words, and how Damian, the only man she had ever really loved, had broken down and cried like a baby when she had refused to see him again. That was two weeks ago and she had heard nothing from him since. She had tried to telephone. She wanted to admit that she had been unjust, to tell him how much she regretted calling him a liar, she wanted to explain that she hadn't meant to hurt him.

Suddenly the noise of the garden gate opening startled her. She turned and through the gloom she thought she could make out the familiar figure of Damian. Was it him . . . ? Could it possibly be . . . ? The approaching figure stepped into the last patch of sunlight and the last rays of the setting sun illuminated his long, dark, curly hair. He stopped, unsure of himself. 'Oh, Damian,' she called softly. 'Damian, is it really you?'

'Melinda,' he murmured, 'My Melinda!'

She sighed deeply and ran to greet him.

She took his hands tightly in hers. 'My darling,' she whispered, 'Can you ever forgive me?'

'We must never speak of it again,' he replied.

'But Damian, I never meant . . .'

He interrupted her, 'It's all right. I know that now. My darling, promise me something?'

'Anything!' she cried.

'Here, this is for you. Please, please accept it, and wear it forever.' He drew a small leather box from his pocket and leaned forward to give it to her. Suddenly the box fell from his grasp. He bent to pick it up and at that moment his glasses slipped from his nose.

'Blast! Now where have they gone? I can't see a thing without them,' he explained. Melinda went to help him. There was a crunch as his foot crushed the glasses into the gravel path. 'Oh, no, now I've trodden on them!' he exclaimed. 'Why can't I do anything right? Why do I always ruin everything?'

Her laughter pealed round the garden. 'Oh, Damian, you silly boy, that's why I love you so much!'

Exercise

Here are some notes about what happened on page 32 of 'Trust the heart', when Melinda and Damian met for the first time at a party. Read the notes and construct their conversation.

Mrs Blaze introduced her to Damian. *'Oh, Melinda . . . I'd like you to meet Damian.'*

Continue.

1 They greeted each other.
2 He offered to get her a drink.
3 She thanked him, and asked him to get her a dry sherry.
4 He brought her a martini, and apologized because they'd run out of sherry.
5 She replied that it didn't matter, and told him not to worry about it.
6 He asked her if she would like to dance, and she accepted.
7 He said how much he liked the music and she agreed.
8 He complimented her on her dress, and she thanked him, and added that she had made it herself.
9 He invited her to watch the sunset on the terrace, and she accepted.
10 He suggested dinner the next evening.
11 She agreed and promised to meet him.
12 He suggested 'The Old Stable' restaurant and explained that the owner was an old school friend.
13 He arranged to collect her at eight o'clock.

Teaching points

▶ Reporting (4) – conversations
The use of reporting verbs other than *say, ask, tell*, e.g. *think, remember, deny, admit, apologize, beg, refuse, hear, want, regret, explain, mean, call, murmur, whisper, reply, interrupt, cry, exclaim, greet, offer, thank, accept, agree, compliment, add, invite, suggest, promise, arrange*

Expressions

Blast!
You silly boy!
my darling

Key vocabulary

affair	*break down*	*tread*
crunch	*draw*	– – – – – –
forgiveness	*forgive*	*familiar*
grasp	*illuminate*	*harsh*
gravel path	*lean*	*unjust*
laughter	*peal*	*unsure*
liar	*ruin*	– – – – – –
orchard	*set*	*beyond*
patch	*sigh*	*forward*
ray	*slip*	*tightly*
– – – – – –		

1 Set the situation. *Have you ever read any romantic novels? Do you like them? Can you remember the titles of any of them?*
Say: *This is an extract from 'Trust the heart'. It's page 87, in the middle of the book.*

2 Focus attention on the text. Play the cassette. Students follow the text.

3 Silent reading. Check vocabulary.

4 *Damian had denied the affair with Tamsin. What do you think he said?* Give examples:
I didn't have an affair with her. or *I haven't had an affair with Tamsin.* or *I'm not having an affair with her.* or *We're just good friends.* or *It's not true!* or *Who told you that? It's all lies!* etc.
Get students to speculate on what was actually said, giving these prompts:
She forced him to admit the affair.
He admitted it, and apologized.
He begged her for forgiveness.
She thought of her harsh words. What might she have said to him?
She refused to see him again.
He broke down and cried like a baby.
She wanted to admit she had been unjust. What did she want to say?
She wanted to tell him she regretted calling him a liar.
What did she want to say?
She wanted to explain that she hadn't meant to hurt him.
What did she want to say?

5 Role-play. Students act out the original argument between Damian and Melinda. Then they imagine that she had managed to telephone him, and role-play the conversation which might have followed.

6 Get students to read the rest of the page again, and then act out the meeting in pairs in direct speech. Point out that they should follow the 'instructions' in the text on how to say the sentences. That is, they should say 'Oh, Damian' softly, and reply 'Melinda' in a murmur!

7 Get one or two pairs to demonstrate.

8 Exercise. Focus attention on the notes about p.32 of 'Trust the heart'. Go through them initially as an exercise.

9 Get students to repeat the exercise in pairs, and then to role-play the meeting, again following the notes.

10 Get students to do the exercise in writing, for homework.

Unit 77

Teaching points

▶ Listening comprehension

▶ Describing events

Expressions

the whole works
the full treatment
You should have seen . . .
at my best
stag party
well off
cost a packet
our place

Key vocabulary

bridesmaid	tin can	elaborate
bumper	top hat	religious
ceremony	tradition	vulgar
hangover	waste	– – – – – –
honeymoon	– – – – – –	recently
lipstick	bother	somehow
page	get engaged	
tail	– – – – – –	

1 Set the situation. Books closed. Ask *Have you been to a wedding? What was it like?*

2 Listening. 'A church wedding'. Set these pre-questions:
How long ago did they meet?
Who were the bridesmaids?
How old was the page?
What was the weather like?
Where was the reception?
Where was their honeymoon?

'Our wedding was a pretty typical one, really. Caroline and I met about three years ago, and we got engaged last summer. We both wanted a traditional wedding. I suppose it's expensive, and some people say it's a waste of money, but it is a day to remember all your life. Anyway, we wanted to please our parents, and we both wanted to get married in church. Caroline's father hired a white Rolls-Royce to bring her to the church, we wanted the whole works! You know, top hat, tails, champagne – the full treatment. The men rented their morning suits for the day. Caroline had three bridesmaids – her sister and two of her cousins, and a page. The page was her nephew. He's only three and he made a lot of noise during the ceremony. I didn't feel my best that day because my stag party went on until five o'clock in the morning. I do remember the photographs, though. We seemed to be waiting around for ages. Although it was a very sunny Saturday – it was in May – there was a pretty cold wind. The reception was at the Carlton Hotel, it must have cost Caroline's dad a packet. The speeches went on a bit too long, I think . . . and of course some of them were a bit vulgar, but I suppose that's a tradition. It took twenty minutes just to read out all the telegrams. I'd been very careful, and I'd parked my car round the corner, but of course they somehow managed to find out where it was. You should have seen what they'd done to it! It was covered with lipstick, and they'd tied cans to the bumper. But anyway, they didn't find out where we were having our honeymoon. We went to Scotland.'

3 Play the cassette twice. Go through, pausing to check answers to pre-questions.

4 Play the cassette again, pausing to ask these questions:
Why was the wedding 'a pretty typical one'?
What does 'the whole works' mean?
What about 'the full treatment'?
What does 'I didn't feel at my best' mean?
What do you think 'a stag party' is?
What does 'cost a packet' mean?
What about 'a bit vulgar'?
What happened to their car?

5 Get students to describe the wedding in their own words.

6 Listening. 'A Registry Office wedding'. Set these pre-questions:
Where's Stuart from?
Where's Ann from?
Where did they meet?
Who was at the wedding?
Where did they go after the wedding?

'Stuart and I met last year. We were both working in Birmingham, although Stuart comes from Leeds and I'm from London. We didn't want an elaborate wedding and neither of us are particularly religious, so we got married in the registry office. Another thing is that neither of our families are very well off, and it seemed silly to go to all the expense, when you need the money to set up a new home. We just invited our parents and a couple of friends, who were the witnesses. It was all very simple. We didn't have a reception or anything. We just had a few drinks round at our place. We didn't even bother with a cake. We didn't have a honeymoon, because Stuart's just started his own business and we couldn't afford the time.'

7 Play the cassette twice. Go through, pausing to check answers to pre-questions.

8 Play the cassette again, pausing to ask these questions:
Why did they choose a registry office?
What does 'an elaborate wedding' mean?
What about 'not particularly well off'?
What about 'all very simple'?
What does 'our place' mean?
Why couldn't they afford the time?

9 Get students to describe the wedding in their own words.

10 Ask students to compare the weddings and say which they would have preferred, and why.

11 Focus attention on the pictures. Go through picture by picture, getting students to describe what's happening and who they think the people are.

12 Discuss English wedding customs and traditions, and compare them with those in the students' own countries.

13 Ask students to write a brief description for homework.

Unit 78

WEDDINGS

Listen to two people talking about their weddings.
Adrian had a traditional church wedding. Ann was married in a registry office.
Compare their weddings with customs and traditions in your country.
Tell the story of the wedding in the pictures.

History

Two thousand years ago the British Isles were inhabited by speakers of Celtic languages. These languages still survive in parts of Wales, Scotland, Ireland, and Brittany in France. The Celts were conquered by the Romans, and from 43 BC to about AD 410 the areas which are now England and Wales were part of the Roman Empire, and Latin was the language of government. Between the fourth and seventh centuries A.D., the Anglo-Saxons arrived from what is now northern Germany, Holland and Denmark, and occupied most of England, and parts of southern Scotland. In some parts of Wales, Scotland and Ireland, people still speak Celtic languages. The Anglo-Saxons spoke a Germanic language which forms the basis of modern English. This language was modified by the arrival of Viking invaders in the north and east of the country, who came from Norway and Denmark between the eighth and eleventh centuries. These Scandinavian settlers spoke Old Norse, which was related to Anglo-Saxon, and which is the parent language of modern Danish. The mixing of the two languages greatly enriched the vocabulary of English. By the middle of the tenth century England had become a unified country under one king.

In 1066 England was conquered by the French-speaking Normans, and French became the language of government. For the next three hundred years three languages co-existed. The aristocracy spoke French, the ordinary people spoke English, while Latin was used in the church. Modern English evolved from the mingling of the three tongues. Today English vocabulary is approximately half Germanic (from the Saxons and Vikings) and half Romance (from French and Latin). There are however considerable borrowings from other languages.

Some derived words

Old English	shirt, life, death, heaven, earth, love, hate
Old Norse	skirt, birth, window, ugly, wrong, they, their, them
French	boil, roast, veal, beef, pork, village, painter, tailor
Latin	index, item, major, memorandum

THE ENGLISH LANGUAGE

Features of the English language

English has changed so much in the last 1500 years that it would now be hardly recognizable to the Anglo-Saxons who brought the language across the North Sea. Although they would be able to recognize many individual words, they would not recognize the way those words are put together to make sentences. Old English, like modern German, was a highly inflected language, i.e. most words changed their endings or forms to show their relationship to other words in the sentence according to number (singular, plural), gender (masculine, feminine, neuter), case (subject, object), tense (past, future) etc. Some modern English words still inflect, but much less so than in other European languages. The English verb 'to ride' inflects into five forms (ride, rides, riding, rode, ridden) whereas the equivalent German verb has sixteen forms. The English word 'the' has only one form, whereas other European languages would have several different forms. The trend towards simplicity of form is considered to be a strength of English. Another strength is the flexibility of function of individual words. Look at these uses of the word 'round':

There was a *round* table. (adjective)

He bought a *round* of drinks. (noun)

He turned *round*. (adverb)

He ran *round* the field. (preposition)

The car tried to *round* the bend too quickly. (verb)

This flexibility, together with a flexibility towards the assimilation of words borrowed from other languages and the spontaneous creation of new words have made English what it is today, an effective medium of international communication. English has achieved this in spite of the difficulties caused by written English, which is not systematically phonetic.

Some loan words

Arabic	*admiral, algebra, mattress*
Spanish	*mosquito, cigar, canyon*
Italian	*piano, violin, spaghetti*
Dutch	*yacht, boss, deck*
Hindi	*pyjamas, shampoo, bungalow*
Turkish	*yoghurt, kiosk*
Japanese	*tycoon, karate*
Malay	*bamboo, compound*
Nahuatl (Aztec)	*tomato, chocolate*
Quechua (Inca)	*coca, quinine*
Hungarian	*coach, paprika*
Classical Greek	*theatre, astronomy, logic*
Gaelic	*whisky*
Russian	*vodka, sputnik*
Finnish	*sauna*
Chinese	*tea, silk*
Portuguese	*marmalade*
Eskimo	*anorak*
Czech	*robot*
Farsi (Iranian)	*lilac*
Basque	*bizarre*
Carib	*canoe*
Australian Aborigine	*kangaroo boomerang*
Modern French	*rendezvous, café*
Modern German	*kindergarten*

Some 'created' words

xerox, to xerox, xeroxed
a hoover, to hoover, hoovered
mackintosh, sandwich, submarine, helicopter, pop, rock'n roll, x-ray, astronaut, hot dog.

English today

Approximately 350 million people speak English as their first language. About the same number use it as a second language. It is the language of aviation, international sport and pop music. 75% of the world's mail is in English, 60% of the world's radio stations broadcast in English and more than half of the world's periodicals are printed in English. It is an official language in 44 countries. In many others it is the language of business, commerce and technology. There are many varieties of English, but Scottish, Texan, Australian, Indian and Jamaican speakers of English, in spite of the differences in pronunciation, structure and vocabulary, would recognize that they are all speaking the same basic language.

Teaching points

▶ Reading comprehension

▶ Revision and consolidation

Key vocabulary

aristocracy	structure	effective
assimilation	technology	equivalent
aviation	tongue	Germanic
Baltic	trend	individual
Black Sea	– – – – –	inflected
borrowing	achieve	Indo-European
British Isles	co-exist	official
creation	conquer	Old Norse
culture	descend	phonetic
ending	enrich	recognizable
feature	evolve	related
flexibility	inflict	Scandinavian
function	inhabit	spontaneous
invader	modify	unphonetic
mingling	occupy	unified
nomad	remain	Viking
North Sea	roam	– – – – –
periodical	settle	fully
plain	survive	highly
relationship	– – – – –	systematically
simplicity	Celtic	
strength	considerable	

1 'History'. Set the situation. Say they are going to read a short history of the English language. They should make a short chronological table, e.g.
Before 43 BC Celtic
Silent reading. Students make notes.
Model:

Before 43 BC	*Celtic*
43 BC – approx. 410 AD	*Latin*
4th – 7th centuries	*Anglo-Saxon*
8th – 11th centuries	*Old Norse*
1066 – approx. 1350	*French, English and Latin*

2 Check through the notes on the board.

3 Question and answer:
Where are Celtic languages still spoken?
Where did the Anglo-Saxons come from?
Where did they settle?
What about the Vikings?
When had England become a unified country?
When did your country become unified?
Which people spoke which languages between 1066 and 1350?

4 Focus attention on the words derived from Old English (Anglo-Saxon), Old Norse, French and Latin. Silent reading. Check vocabulary.

5 'Features of the English language'. Silent reading. Check through.

6 T: *English has four main strengths. What are they?* Read through and list the four. *(Simplicity of form, flexibility of function, easy assimilation of borrowed words, spontaneous creation of new words.) There is one great weakness. What is it? (It's not systematically phonetic.) What do you think that means?* Demonstrate by dictating a few homonyms:
T: *Each of these sounds has two spellings. Write them both down.*
Dictate:

blue/blew	*wait/weight*
knows/nose	*here/hear*
son/sun	*threw/through*
weak/week	*aloud/allowed*
meet/meat	*higher/hire*
wood/would	*steal/steel*
flour/flower	*see/sea*
piece/peace	

Get students to use them in sentences to distinguish the meanings. Check through.

7 Discuss briefly differences between the students' own language(s) and English.

8 Focus attention on 'Some loan words'. Go through. Ask students which, if any, of these words are used in their language. Ask them which loan words from English are used.

9 Go through 'Some "created" words' in the same way.

10 'English today'. Silent reading.

11 Discuss the role and importance of English. *Why are you learning English? Will it ever be the world language? Why/Why not? Would this be a good or a bad thing?*

Teaching points

▶ Making arrangements

▶ Expressing thanks

▶ Saying goodbye

▶ Expressions with *case: in case/in case of/in any case*

Expressions

Take a seat.
It sounds OK.
I'll pay cash.
That's all together.
We'll be sorry to lose you.
Call in and see us.
Have a safe journey.
Thanks for everything.
I'm glad I haven't missed you.
Give me a call.
You can be sure of that.
Look after yourself.
Have a nice trip.
It was nice meeting you.
Keep in touch.
£35 between us
If you're ever in . . .
fully booked
local time
a time difference
check-in time
half eleven
to hit traffic

Key vocabulary

course	share
reservation	– – – – –
– – – – –	available

1 Dialogue 1. Set the situation. Ensure the text is masked. Play the cassette.

2 Selective repetition.

3 Silent reading.

4 Pair work. Encourage students to substitute other items.

5 Dialogue 2. Set the situation. Ensure the text is masked. Play the cassette.

6 Selective repetition.

7 Silent reading.

8 Pair work. Encourage students to substitute other items.

9 Point out 'in case'. (Common sign on fire extinguishers: 'In case of fire'.)
Compare:
because/because of
although/in spite of
in case/in case of
Say: *The taxi's leaving early in case they hit traffic.*

10 Situation. *The taxi driver carries several things in the boot of the taxi. He carries a can of petrol in case he runs out of petrol. Why does he carry: a can of water/a can of oil/a fire extinguisher/a first aid box/a spare tyre/a pump/a tool kit?*

11 Dialogue 3. Ensure the text is masked. Play the cassette.

12 Selective repetition.

13 Silent reading.

14 Pair work. Encourage the students to substitute other vocabulary items.

15 Dialogue 4. Ensure the text is masked. Play the cassette.

16 Selective repetition.

17 Silent reading.

18 Pair work. Encourage the students to substitute other vocabulary items.

19 Get students to circulate round the class, saying 'goodbye', using their own words.

20 Dialogue 5. Ensure the text is masked. Play the cassette.

21 Selective repetition.

22 Silent reading.

23 Pair work. Encourage the students to substitute other vocabulary items.

24 Ask *On what occasions would you hear these expressions?*
Make mini-dialogues in pairs using them.
What can I do for you?
Each . . . or between us?
We'll be sorry to lose you.
I hope to come back next year.
Call in and see us.
Have a safe journey.
I'm glad I haven't missed you.
I don't suppose I'll see you again.
Keep in touch.
If you're ever in . . . , give me a call.
Look after yourself.
Have a nice trip.

DEPARTURES

Gina has been studying English at a language school in England. Her course finishes at the end of this week and she's returning home on Saturday. She's in a travel agency now.

Travel agent Take a seat, please. I'll be with you in a minute. Yes, what can I do for you?

Gina I want to fly to Rome. Are there any seats available on Saturday?

Travel agent Just a moment and I'll check ... Rome ... what time of day are you thinking of going?

Gina Well, I'd rather not arrive too late. How about late morning or early afternoon?

Travel agent The 12.10's fully booked, I'm afraid. There are seats available on the 14.55 or the 16.30. Is that too late for you?

Gina The 14.55 sounds OK. What time does that get in?

Travel agent 18.15 local time; there's a one hour time difference, you know.

Gina OK. That'll be fine. I'll pay cash but I'll have to go to the bank and come back.

Travel agent That's all right. I'll hold the reservation for you.

Streamline Taxis Streamline Taxis.

Gina I'd like to book a taxi for Saturday morning, please.

Streamline Taxis Where are you going?

Gina London Airport, Heathrow. There'll be three of us sharing. How much will it be?

Streamline Taxis £35.

Gina £35! Each or between us?

Streamline Taxis Oh, that's all together. What time do you want to leave?

Gina The check-in time is five to two but I don't know how long it takes to get there.

Streamline Taxis Well we'd better pick you up about half eleven, in case we hit traffic. Can I have your name and address?

Gina Yes. It's Gina Castelli ... two 'I's. 32, Seaport Road.

Streamline Taxis 32, Seaport Road. OK. 11.30 Saturday morning. Thank you.

Mr Jenkins Come in!

Gina Oh, hello, Mr Jenkins.

Mr Jenkins Hello, Gina. What can I do for you?

Gina I've just come to say goodbye.

Mr Jenkins Oh yes, of course. You're leaving, aren't you? When?

Gina I'm flying tomorrow morning. I'm back at work on Monday morning.

Mr Jenkins Well, I must say Gina, we'll be sorry to lose you.

Gina I don't really want to go but ... well, I just wanted to thank you and all the other teachers.

Mr Jenkins Oh, that's all right, Gina.

Gina I've really learnt a lot. I hope to come back next year ... for a holiday.

Mr Jenkins Don't forget to send us a card, and if you do come back, call in and see us.

Gina No, I won't forget.

Mr Jenkins Well, there's the bell. Goodbye then, and have a safe journey.

Gina Goodbye and thanks for everything.

Gina Jacques! I'm glad I haven't missed you.

Jacques Hello, Gina. When are you leaving?

Gina Tomorrow morning. I don't suppose I'll see you again. So, goodbye. It was nice meeting you.

Jacques And you. But you will keep in touch, won't you?

Gina Yes, I will. You've got my address, haven't you?

Jacques Yes, and remember, if you're ever in Cherbourg, give me a call. I'd be so pleased to see you again.

Gina Oh, I will. You can be sure of that. And you must do the same if you're ever in Rome.

Jacques Well. Goodbye then.

Gina Goodbye ... and look after yourself.

Mrs Sharples Gina! The taxi's outside. Are you ready? Have you got everything?

Gina Yes, thank you, Mrs Sharples. And ... thank you again.

Mrs Sharples Thank you, Gina, for the flowers. Now don't forget to phone us when you get home. Just to let us know that you've arrived safely.

Gina No, I won't forget. I don't know whether I'll be able to phone tonight or not, but in any case, I'll ring you in the morning whatever happens.

Mrs Sharples Well, goodbye then, dear. You'd better not keep the taxi waiting. Have a nice trip. Bye-bye.

Gina Bye. And look after yourselves. And thank Mr Sharples for me.

APPENDIX

Material recorded on cassette but not included in the text of the units is printed below.

Unit 1

1 The train now standing at Platform 5 will be the 10.25 to Exeter St David's, calling at Reading, Pewsey, Westbury and Taunton.
2 The train now standing at Platform 3 is the 10.20 Inter-City service to Bristol.
3 The train now arriving at Platform 2 is the 9.12 from Oxford.
4 The next train leaving from Platform 9 will be the 10.25 Inter-City service to Plymouth and Penzance. The train will be divided at Plymouth. Passengers for stations to Penzance should take the front six carriages.
5 The train now arriving at Platform 12 is the 7.10 from Swansea. Trains from Swansea are running approximately 15 minutes late due to maintenance work between Swansea and Cardiff.

Unit 13

A Airport announcements
1 This is the last call for the twelve o'clock British Airways flight BA 412 to Amsterdam. Would passengers for this flight please proceed without delay to Gate 17.
2 Scandinavian Airlines announce the departure of the 12.05 flight SK 526 to Stockholm. This flight is now boarding at Gate 8.
3 Would passengers for the 12.10 Iberia flight IB 341 to Madrid please go at once to Gate 16 where this flight is now boarding.
4 Alitalia regret to announce that their 12.15 flight AZ 281 to Rome will be delayed for approximately 30 minutes.
5 Olympic Airways announce the departure of the 12.30 flight OA 260 to Athens. Would passengers on this flight please proceed to Gate 19.
6 This is a call for Mr Gaston Meyer. Would Mr Gaston Meyer travelling on the 12.45 Sabena flight SN 604 to Brussels report to the airport information desk, please.

B In-flight announcements
1 Good afternoon, ladies and gentlemen. Captain Perez and his crew welcome you aboard Iberia flight IB 341 to Madrid. I am sorry to announce a slight delay. We are still waiting for clearance from Air Traffic Control. The delay won't be too long and we hope to arrive in Madrid on time.
2 This is your captain speaking. We are now passing over the English coast. Our Boeing 727 is cruising at a height of 30,000 feet and our speed is approximately 560 miles per hour. The temperature in Madrid is 18°C and it is a clear and sunny day. We expect to pass through some slight turbulence and would recommend passengers to remain in their seats and keep their belts fastened.
3 We are now beginning our descent to Madrid. Would passengers please make sure that their seat-belts are fastened and extinguish all smoking materials. We would like to remind passengers that smoking is not permitted until you are in the airport building.
4 We hope you had a pleasant and enjoyable flight. We would like to thank you for travelling on Iberia, and we hope to see you again soon. Would passengers please remain seated until the plane has come to a complete stop and the doors have been opened.

Unit 15

Bargaining
Lucy Excuse me.
Stallholder Yes, miss?
Lucy How much do you want for this plate?
Stallholder Let me see. Oh, yes ... that's a lovely example of Victorian brass. It's worth twenty quid.
Lucy Twenty pounds! Oh, that's too much for me. It's a pity. It's really nice.
Stallholder Ah, I said it's worth twenty quid. I'm only asking fifteen for it.
Lucy Fifteen pounds?
Stallholder Yes. It's a real bargain.
Lucy Oh, I'm sure it is ... but I can't afford that!
Stallholder Well, look ... just for you ... I'll make it fourteen quid. I can't go any lower than that.
Lucy I'll give you ten.
Stallholder Ten! Come on, love. You must be joking! I paid more than that for it myself! Fourteen. It's worth every penny.
Lucy Well, perhaps I could give you eleven.
Stallholder Thirteen. That's my final offer.
Lucy Twelve.
Stallholder Twelve fifty?
Lucy All right, twelve fifty.
Stallholder There you are, love. You've got a real bargain there!
Lucy Yes, thank you very much.

Unit 44

1
Our six finalists are No 14 Miss Lancashire, No 13 Miss Dorset, Miss Norfolk No 50, Miss Gwent No 6, No 30 Miss Strathclyde and Miss Warwickshire No 40. Would the first contestant please come forward.

2
Announcer This is 17-year-old Grace Field from Lancashire. Just stand there, Grace. You're a shop-assistant, aren't you?
Grace Field Yes, I am.
Announcer What kind of shop is it?
Grace Field It's a clothes shop. We sell children's clothes. It's only a temporary job, actually.
Announcer Now, first of all: what do you do in your spare time?
Grace Field Well, I like dressmaking, I make all my own clothes ... and cooking. I do a lot of cooking.
Announcer That's a beautiful dress you're wearing, did you make it?
Grace Field Yes, with a little help from my mother.
Announcer Now, Grace. You said your job was a temporary one. What would you really like to do?
Grace Field Oh, to work with children. Definitely.
Announcer Uh huh. Last question. If you could have one wish, what would it be?
Grace Field I've thought about that a lot ... world peace.
Announcer Thank you, Grace.

3
Announcer Our next contestant is a beauty consultant from Dorset, Victoria Hardy. Victoria's 25. Hello, Victoria.
Victoria Hardy Good evening, Terry. It's lovely to meet you.
Announcer Mmm. Thank you. Have you got any great ambitions, Victoria?
Victoria Hardy Yes. I'd like to sail across the Atlantic.
Announcer The Atlantic! Alone?
Victoria Hardy No, no.
Announcer Have you any experience of sailing?
Victoria Hardy Yes, I go sailing every weekend.
Announcer Is that your only hobby?
Victoria Hardy It's my favourite one, but I like horseriding too.
Announcer Good. Good. What about one wish?
Victoria Hardy I'd wish for a long life.
Announcer Very nice. Thank you very much, Victoria.

4
Announcer The third finalist is Lynn King, a primary school teacher from Norfolk. You look too young to be a teacher, Lynn. None of my teachers looked like you.
Lynn King I'm 21, this is my first year.
Announcer I see. Tell me about your hobbies.
Lynn King I'm very interested in astronomy ... and playing the piano.
Announcer Ah, music and the stars! How very interesting! Have you got any great ambitions?
Lynn King You'll laugh ... but my ambition is to go to the moon ... seriously.
Announcer Do you think you ever will?
Lynn King Who knows?
Announcer And if you could make a wish?
Lynn King I'd just wish for happiness.

5
Announcer Next we have Myfanwy Lloyd, a nineteen year old brunette from Gwent in Wales. What do you do, Myfanwy?
Myfanwy Lloyd No , Myfanwy. We pronounce it 'Myfanwy'. I'm still at university.
Announcer What are you studying?
Myfanwy Lloyd Drama ... it's also my hobby.
Announcer Any other hobbies, Myfanwy?
Myfanwy Lloyd Well, I'm a black belt in judo.
Announcer Oh, dear ... I'd better pronounce your name correctly, hadn't I?
Myfanwy Lloyd It's all right.
Announcer What do you hope to do when you leave university?
Myfanwy Lloyd To be an actress.

Announcer I'm sure you'll be successful. Would you like to make a wish?

Myfanwy Lloyd Yes. I'd wish for health ... I think it's the most important thing in life.

6

Announcer Our next finalist, from Scotland, is Miss Strathclyde, a twenty-three year old fashion model ... Dawn Munro. Hello, Dawn.

Dawn Munro Hello, Terry.

Announcer What are your interests?

Dawn Munro Er ... dancing ... and ... er ... photographic work.

Announcer So you're a keen amateur photographer?

Dawn Munro No, no ... I'm more interested in modelling.

Announcer I see. What about your ambitions?

Dawn Munro I'd like to become Miss World.

Announcer Really? You are ambitious, aren't you? And your wish?

Dawn Munro I've always wanted one thing ... fame ... I'd like to see my face on magazine covers.

Announcer Well, it's certainly pretty enough. Thank you, Dawn.

7

Announcer Finally, Kerry Talbot ... Miss Warwickshire. How old are you, Kerry?

Kerry Talbot Eighteen.

Announcer Don't be nervous. Speak up a bit. And do you work?

Kerry Talbot I'm a typist.

Announcer What do you like doing in your free time?

Kerry Talbot Reading ... I like reading ... and swimming.

Announcer What's your ambition?

Kerry Talbot To have a large family. I love children.

Announcer And if you had one wish, what would you ask for?

Kerry Talbot It sounds silly, but I'd ask for good luck. I'm very superstitious. Look ... my fingers are crossed.

Announcer Thank you, Kerry. Now while our judges are making their final decision, we'll take a short break.

8

Announcer Now, here to announce the results of our contest is Mr Derek Chorley, the Chairman of EBC. Mr Chorley ...

Derek Chorley Thank you, Terry. I'm going to read the results in reverse order. Third, for a prize of £5,000 and a weekend in Paris, is Number 13, Victoria Hardy from Dorset! Second, with a prize of £10,000 and a holiday in Spain, is Number 6 ... Myfanwy Lloyd! And now ... Miss Britain ... with a holiday in California and £20,000 ... yes, £20,000 is ... Number 30 ... Dawn Munro from Strathclyde!

Unit 52

Donna

Well, she's quite a lively, talkative person in her ... in her late teens. She's fairly tall with a ... a good figure. She's got a heart-shaped face with a small, sort of turned-up nose. It's very attractive really. She's got long, black wavy hair and er ... blue eyes with very long eyelashes. Her complexion is ... well, she's olive-skinned. Her lips are very full ... and she's got dimples ... dimples in her cheeks.

Colin

He's a very big guy, you know, well-built with very broad shoulders. Not fat, really, really ... just well-built. He's in his early thirties. He's got a long face with thin lips. Oh, and a small scar on his chin. He's got very short, fair hair but with long sideburns and a moustache. Eyes ... I haven't really noticed the colour, he wears glasses. He's got thick eyebrows and a kind of a long, straight nose. He's fairly reserved, thoughtful, sometimes even moody.

Janet

She's sophisticated. Well-dressed, expensive hairstyle and so on. I'd say she was in her late thirties or early forties, but she looks younger. She's about average height and very slim. Her hair's very blonde, dyed, I think, but I'm not sure about that. It's always very neat, not long. She's got pale grey eyes with thin eyebrows. Her face is always sunburned and very well made up. It's an attractive face ... not really beautiful, but very attractive, you know what I mean. High cheekbones, small chin ... oh and yes, there's a beauty spot on her left cheek. She's a very calm and reliable sort of person, very sociable and always very, very polite.

Robert

Robert's a wonderful person really. He's elderly but not old ... still very lively and amusing. He's probably in his early seventies. He's got white hair, receding a bit, and a small white beard. He's medium build, a little overweight perhaps. He's got very nice, large, brown eyes and he always seems to be smiling ... lots of wrinkles round the eyes, laughter lines I think you call them. He's got a very high, lined forehead which makes him look very intelligent, which he is, of course.

Unit 65

Mr Williams Good morning, doctor.

Doctor Hello, Mr Williams. Take a seat. What seems to be the trouble?

Mr Williams I'm not sure, doctor. But I haven't been feeling too well. I think I must have a touch of flu.

Doctor Mm. There's a lot of it going round at the moment. What are the symptoms?

Mr Williams I'm feeling very tired, and I'm aching all over. I've been sneezing a lot, and feeling pretty feverish, hot and cold all the time. Oh, and I've got a sore throat.

Doctor Any vomiting?

Mr Williams No, but I don't feel very hungry. I've got no appetite at all.

Doctor Well, let's have a look at you. Open your mouth. 'Aah.' Yes, your throat's a bit inflamed, and the glands in your neck are swollen. Can you just unbutton your shirt? I want to listen to your chest. Breathe deeply. Right. I'll just take your temperature. Don't say anything for a minute, just keep the thermometer under your tongue. I'll write out a prescription for you, but you know the best thing is just to go home, go to bed, and take plenty of fluids.

Unit 72

Estate Agent I'm afraid it's been rather neglected. The present owner is in his eighties. He's just gone into an old people's home.

Robin Yes. It looks as though a lot needs doing to it.

Estate Agent That's true, but the price is very reasonable. It would be ideal for a do-it-yourself man.

Robin Mm. I'm not very good with my hands, I'm afraid. We'd have to get most things done for us, wouldn't we, Jean?

Jean Oh, I don't know. Could we see inside?

Estate Agent Of course. I'll show you the kitchen first.

Jean Oh dear! Just look at that sink. It must have been there since the house was built.

Robin It's a nice large room, though, and there's plenty of light. We'd have to have kitchen units put in, and we'd need to get it tiled.

Jean But you could do the ceiling yourself, couldn't you? And the painting.

Robin Is that the only power-point there?

Estate Agent I'm afraid so.

Robin It looks pretty old. I'm sure the whole place would need rewiring. We certainly couldn't do that ourselves and we'd need to have more points put in at the same time.

Estate Agent Would you like to see the lounge? It's through here.

Jean Oh my God! It'd certainly need redecorating. I suppose we could do the painting and wallpapering. What's it like upstairs?

Estate Agent Pretty bad, really. It obviously hasn't been decorated for years, and as I told you on the phone, it hasn't got a bathroom. But you could have the small bedroom converted into a bathroom and get a grant towards the cost. All the other houses in the street have had that done.

Robin What about the toilet?

Estate Agent I'm afraid that's outside, but you could get one put in the new bathroom. And of course, you'd get a grant for that as well.

Jean Is there anything else that needs doing?

Estate Agent Well, you'd probably have to get the roof repaired pretty soon.

Robin The sooner the better if you ask me. It looks as though water's been coming in over there. And, of course, we'd want to have central heating put in, and the windows double glazed, it's a very noisy street. I couldn't do any of that myself.

Estate Agent Of course not.

Robin Anyway, thank you for showing us around. But really I think the best thing would be to knock it down and start all over again!

Unit 75

9.00

Amanda Mr Dawson's office.

Jenny Oh, it's Jenny. Can you give Mr Dawson a message? I won't be in till Friday, I've got flu. I saw the doctor this morning.

Amanda OK, Jenny. I'll pass the message on. I hope you feel better soon.

9.40

Amanda Mr Dawson's office. Can I help you?

Mr Watkins May I speak to Mr Dawson, please?

Amanda I'm afraid he's away on business. He'll be back tomorrow. Can I take a message?

Mr Watkins Please. It's Tom Watkins here. Look, I can't make the meeting on Tuesday afternoon. Something important's come up. I'll ring Peter on Wednesday.

11.30

Amanda Hello, Godfrey. What can I do for you?

Godfrey Mr Dawson isn't here, is he?

Amanda No, not till tomorrow.

Godfrey Ah ... it's just that I want Friday off. You see, my grandmother died yesterday. I'll have to go to the funeral.

Amanda Oh, I am sorry. How old was she?

Godfrey 92.

12.15

Amanda Mr Dawson's office.

Salesman Can you put me through to Mr Dawson?

Amanda I'm afraid he isn't here today. Would you like to leave a message?

Salesman Oh, right. Wadley's Garage here. It's about his new car. It isn't ready yet. There's a strike at the factory today.

2.10

Amanda Good afternoon. Mr Dawson's office.

Miss Dobson Good afternoon. This is Juliet Dobson from Western Video Systems. Mr Dawson's at the trade fair in Lyon, isn't he?

Amanda Yes, that's right. He should be here tomorrow.

Miss Dobson Well, can you give him this message first thing in the morning? I'm afraid we must cancel our last order. The customers have changed their minds, again!

3.20

Amanda Good afternoon. Mr Dawson's office.

Mr Gonzalez Hello, this is Miguel Gonzalez speaking. Is Peter there?

Amanda No, I'm afraid he's away on business today. Can I pass on a message, Señor Gonzalez?

Mr Gonzalez Yes. I may be in London from the 21st to the 25th. I want to see Peter then, if possible. It's about the agency in Mexico.

4.35

Amanda Mr Dawson's office.

Mrs Ellis My name's Samantha Ellis. Can you get Mr Dawson to phone me as soon as he gets back from Lyon? It really is very urgent.

4.55

Amanda Mr Dawson's office.

Mr Berry Ah, Miss Hayward. This is Charles Berry.

Amanda Oh, good afternoon, sir.

Mr Berry I've got an important message for Mr Dawson. Give it to him the minute he comes in. Just say, 'Don't supply Mason and Company until further notice'. I'll explain later.

Unit 78

A church wedding

Adrian and Caroline were married recently.

'Our wedding was a pretty typical one, really. Caroline and I met about three years ago, and we got engaged last summer. We both wanted a traditional wedding. I suppose it's expensive, and some people say it's a waste of money, but it is a day to remember all your life. Anyway, we wanted to please our parents, and we both wanted to get married in church. Caroline's father hired a white Rolls-Royce to bring her to the church, we wanted the whole works! You know, top hat, tails, champagne – the full treatment. The men rented their morning suits for the day. Caroline had three bridesmaids – her sister and two of her cousins, and a page. The page was her nephew. He's only three and he made a lot of noise during the ceremony. I didn't feel my best that day because my stag party went on until five o'clock in the morning. I do remember the photographs, though. We seemed to be waiting around for ages. Although it was a very sunny Saturday – it was in May – there was a pretty cold wind. The reception was at the Carlton Hotel, it must have cost Caroline's dad a packet. The speeches went on a bit too long, I think ... and of course some of them were a bit vulgar, but I suppose that's a tradition. It took twenty minutes just to read out all the telegrams. I'd been very careful, and I'd parked my car round the corner, but of course they somehow managed to find out where it was. You should have seen what they'd done to it! It was covered with lipstick, and they'd tied cans to the bumper. But anyway, they didn't find out where we were having our honeymoon. We went to Scotland.'

A registry office wedding

Stuart and Ann were married in a registry office.

'Stuart and I met last year. We were both working in Birmingham, although Stuart comes from Leeds and I'm from London. We didn't want an elaborate wedding and neither of us are particularly religious, so we got married in the registry office. Another thing is that neither of our families are very well off, and it seemed silly to go to all the expense, when you need the money to set up a new home. We just invited our parents and a couple of friends, who were the witnesses. It was all very simple. We didn't have a reception or anything. We just had a few drinks round at our place. We didn't even bother with a cake. We didn't have a honeymoon, because Stuart's just started his own business and we couldn't afford the time.'